Win, Tie, or Wrangle

PAUL KITCHEN

WIN, TIE, OR WRANGLE

The Inside Story of the Old Ottawa Senators · 1883–1935

Penumbra Press · Manotick, ON · 2008
Archives of Canadian Arts, Culture & Heritage

PENUMBRA PRESS, *publishers*
Box 940 · Manotick, ON · Canada
K4M 1A8 · penumbrapress.ca

Penumbra Press gratefully acknowledges
the financial support of the Government
of Ontario through the Ontario Media
Development Corporation's Ontario
Book Initiative.

Printed & bound in Canada on forest-
friendly, acid-free paper.

ISBN 978-1-897323-46-5 (Hardcover)

*A catalogue record for this book is available
from Library and Archives Canada*

For Anne, Christine, Kevin, Marianne, and Peter

Contents

Foreword · *Eugene Melnyk*   IX

Preface · *Brian McFarlane*   XI

Acknowledgments   xv

1   Saws, Laws, and Sewers   1

2   A New Winter Sport for the Capital   11

3   The Game Takes Hold   28

4   Building a Winning Tradition   46

5   A City and Its Team   69

6   Stars Along the Way   90

7   Quest for Supremacy   108

8   The Shillington Seven, Part I   118

9   The Shillington Seven, Part II   136

10   Professionalism and the Salary War   151

11   Real War and the Crisis of Conscience   173

12   The Tangled Web of Ownership   200

13   The Super Six, Part I   224

14   The Super Six, Part II   257

15   The Collapse of the Ahearn Dream   289

16   St. Louis   321

Afterword   333

Appendices   340

Notes   362

Bibliography   383

Index   388

Foreword

PAUL KITCHEN'S HISTORY of the old Ottawa Senators proves that writing history can be as meaningful as making history, and that few sports franchises in North America can boast a history as rich as ours.

To read Kitchen's book is to encounter a hockey tradition that spans three centuries. The nineteenth century gave teams to Ottawa that mirrored the city's rough-and-tough roots. The Senators of the early twentieth century delivered eleven Stanley Cups only to later abandon the city and its fans in 1934. Almost six decades later, in 1992, the modern Senators finally returned to bridge the twentieth and twenty-first centuries with the team's winning ways.

I know that our players understand the long tradition of Ottawa hockey every time they wear their Senators uniforms. With this long-awaited volume, now we fans can understand it, too.

EUGENE MELNYK
Ottawa · October 2008

Preface

OF ALL THE FORAYS of researchers into hockey's long and fascinating history, *Win, Tie, or Wrangle* is one of the most thorough, most revealing, and most captivating. Ahead you'll find nuggets of information about the gaslight game and what followed, as well as fascinating facts about the boardroom pioneers who nourished the game and the players and teams who helped make it our most talked-about sport — our national passion.

This romp into yesteryear provides a grand opportunity to get to know the early-day hockey heroes you may have heard about and wondered about.

Organized hockey's cradle days can be traced to Montreal and Ottawa. I say "organized hockey" because these two centres established the rules and the rivalries that quickly brought the game national attention.

Paul Kitchen, a former president of the Society for International Hockey Research, takes us back to an era that has always piqued the curiosity of hockey fans: an era when competing teams changed ends after every goal; when an early-day outdoor rink on the river might stretch for 400 feet; when dressing rooms were heated by coal-burning, pot-belly stoves, the coal supplied by the players themselves; when a player's spring skate might fly off his foot in the middle of a rush, sending him cart-wheeling to the ice; when he might be forced to stickhandle around an ice statue located in the middle of the rink.

An ice statue? At mid-ice? Really?

One can imagine a dinner-table conversation afterward. A curious father asks, "How'd you get that huge bump on your head, son?"

"Sir, I skated headfirst into an ice statue."

How embarrassing is that?

It was a time when an outbreak of smallpox might cancel a season's play, when a joyful skate along the Ottawa or Rideau rivers might end in tragedy — if the ice gave way and the skaters were pulled below by the frigid current, gone in an instant.

We all know the role Governor General Lord Stanley played in hockey. Simply by donating a small football-sized trophy — the Stanley Cup — to the "amateur" champions of the game, he became an icon of the sport, and in time an honourable member of the Hockey Hall of Fame, the only member never to have played, coached, managed, or even witnessed a trophy-winning game.

Kitchen reveals some little-known facts about Lord Stanley. Shortly after his arrival in Canada, he became a shareholder in a proposed new arena for Ottawa — owner of twenty shares in the enterprise. Alas, on a cold November night, the half-completed structure came crashing down, collapsing with such force it woke half the slumbering residents of the capital city.

And while Lord Stanley has been universally applauded for his modest $50 donation to the game, his sons and even his hockey-playing daughter, Lady Isobel, were admonished — at least once — for playing shinny on the rink at Rideau Hall — on the Sabbath. Clergymen rebuked the naughty Stanleys for violating "God's holy day."

Seems those enthusiastic Stanley kids simply couldn't stay off the ice, even for a day.

Did you ever wonder about the uniforms those gaslight-era players wore? Kitchen reveals that many of the snug woolen jerseys were not purchased but hand-knitted by the players' girlfriends.

"Here's your fresh-knit, woollen jersey, Chauncey. Now don't be spilling blood all over it."

One has to wonder, did it shrink when washed?

Kitchen writes about the incredible career of One-Eyed Frank McGee, about a less-revered player with the intriguing moniker Hozomer Godin, about the record-setting shutout exploits of Alex Connell, and about the signing of rookie Eddie Gerard to a Senators contract. The manager placed $400 in crisp new bills on the table and told Gerard, "Pick it up and you'll be a Senator." Gerard, who'd never received so much as a penny for playing hockey, picked it up.

He wasn't alone. Professionalism enabled players to flaunt $1,000-per-season contracts and drive around in flashy Russell-Knight roadsters costing $3,200.

You'll be amused to learn how Ottawa Senators player Harold Starr suffered a number of embarrassing red-hot poker burns on his backside.

Many of the old-time greats are revealed "up close and personal," as they say — nicknames included.

Frank "King" Clancy, Frank "The Pembroke Peach" Nighbor, Harry "Rat" Westwick (so named after a Quebec journalist called him a "miserable, insignificant rat"), and, of course, dynamic Fred "Cyclone" Taylor.

Win, Tie, or Wrangle is a gem — a fascinating, significant, and edifying addition to any hockey fan's library.

Guaranteed!

BRIAN MCFARLANE
Honorary President,
Society for International Hockey Research

Acknowledgments

I WROTE EVERY WORD of this book, and did the vast amount of research for it, on the premises of what is now Library and Archives Canada. This was over a seven-year period. I therefore wish to thank the management and staff of that treasured cultural institution for overseeing marvellous collections of printed and archival documents, and for ensuring their ready accessibility. Without these resources and the people who look after them, I don't know how I could have undertaken the project.

Of great assistance, too, were the Bytown Museum of Ottawa, the Ottawa Public Library, the City of Ottawa Archives, and the International Hockey Museum in Kingston.

I am grateful to Randall Ware, now retired from Library and Archives Canada, for first putting me in touch with my publisher, Penumbra Press, and its president, John Flood. A finer supporter of writers and their aspirations you would never hope to find. John in turn attracted the services of marketing executive Mark Jodoin, who helped immeasurably in getting the project off the ground and who was a constant source of encouragement throughout the post-writing period. It was a pleasure working with editor Dennis Choquette. Dennis brought a fine sense of rhythm and logic to his task, thus making the book a better one than it otherwise would have been. Thanks, also, to indexer Mary Jane Starr for producing that all-important access system.

Jim McAuley, Ottawa's premier sports historian, was most generous in giving me access to his rich collection of hockey photographs. David

Gorman was generous with his time, providing insights on his grandfather T.P. Gorman. Margaret Gerard, daughter of Eddie Gerard, and Aileen Wills, daughter of Jack Darragh, both received me in their homes. Their recollections of growing up with famous fathers were fascinating.

Several individuals whose judgement and hockey knowledge I trust read portions, or all, of the manuscript and made helpful comments that I incorporated: Frank Cosentino, Doug Fischer, Bill Fitsell, Anne Kitchen, Kevin Kitchen, Peter Kitchen, Len Kotylo, David Lee, Don McKenzie, Morris Mott, Don O'Hanley, Don Reddick, and Jim Vantour. As a member of the Society for International Hockey Research, I revelled in the hockey history atmosphere that pervades the meetings of this extraordinary organization.

Most important, had it not been for the overall active interest, guidance, and support of my family over several years, this project would not have been possible.

To all, I say thank you.

1 · Saws, Laws, and Sewers
Ottawa Before Hockey

Ottawa city is at present
in the condition of an unfinished house.
Stone, bricks, and wood lie about in piles.
JOHN B. ROWAN
British visitor, 1876

EARLY MARCH OF 1875 was like any other late winter in the capital. Cold winds blew through the streets. Snow piled up everywhere. People didn't know what to do with it. Loggers, sent up the Ottawa River to harvest the great pine forests for the Booth, Gilmour, and MacLaren lumber mills back in town, found it hard to reach the shanties because of the snow's depth. For most of the city's residents, too, life was difficult. Factory hands, carters, shop clerks, and mill workers put in long hours for low pay. Many in this largely Irish and French labour force faced seasonal unemployment. Women in charge of burgeoning families and confined to the cramped tenements of Lowertown and LeBreton Flats near the Chaudière Falls worked even longer days at the dreary and never ending tasks of cooking; cleaning; mending; and nursing myriad fevers, cuts, and scrapes. Some brought in a little extra money doing piecework sewing for the clothing trade. Before and after school, children had their assigned chores. What sport they enjoyed was of their own making, for playgrounds and organized games were non-existent. Typical was the plight of one young lad who was heard to mutter as he trudged up Griswald Street: "If I was a horse, I'd be stabled, rubbed down, and fed; but I'm a boy, and I've got to go home, clean off snow, tote for water, and rock the dumned old baby for an hour or two."

Life was better for the small but growing privileged classes of Upper Town and Sandy Hill. There with their families lived officials brought to the capital to design and run the machinery of a new Dominion government. There too were mill owners, successful merchants, physicians, and lawyers.

Ottawa was a rough-and-ready lumber town in the 1870s. Lord Dufferin, upon arriving in 1872, described Rideau Hall as 'nothing but a small villa such as would suit the needs of a country banker.' Above, a view of Parliament and Entrance Bay from Nepean Point. D. ESDALE COLLECTION/CITY OF OTTAWA ARCHIVES

The homes were imposing structures of many rooms, including quarters for domestic staff. Public servants enjoyed comfortable salaries, secure positions, short working hours, and time for leisure, which they pursued at curling and skating clubs and at meetings of literary and scientific societies.

On its front page, March 3, the *Daily Citizen* said the House of Commons would be moving into committee of the whole that day to consider a resolution providing a salary of $7,000 for the chief justice of the Supreme Court and $6,000 for the Puisne judges. Their superannuation was to be two-thirds of regular salary after fifteen years. These amounts could only be looked upon in awe by the ordinary working man getting by on nine dollars a week.

An event planned for Montreal that same day received no mention in the Ottawa press, nor did its outcome in subsequent editions. The occasion, announced beforehand and reported the following day by the *Montreal Gazette*, was "a game of Hockey," described as a "novel contest on the ice" played by two nine-man teams from the Victoria Skating Club. The article explained that the object was to knock a flat block of wood through flags placed about eight feet apart, much like the old country game of shinty. Afterward, the spectators "adjourned well satisfied with the evening's entertainment." In what is recognized as the first organized game of indoor hockey, it was left to the rival *Montreal Daily Witness* to tell readers the match actually ended in a brawl. Skating-club members, impatient at the length of the contest, took to the ice prematurely. A little boy was struck across the head, the perpetrator was called to account, and a melee followed in which a bench was broken and "other damage caused." Thus was the inauspicious debut of a sport that in Ottawa would take hold eight years later and would become immensely popular within another ten.

Ottawa in the 1870s was a curious contradiction. It was the new capital of a new nation, chosen for that distinction by Queen Victoria herself. But it was also an old lumber town: undistinguished, to say the least, and remote. The "civil Gothic" Parliament buildings resting on a bluff overlooking the Ottawa River were magnificent jewels set, alas, in a rough landscape of saw mills, small factories, warehouses, blacksmith shops, stables, tanneries, squat general stores, and grubby inns and taverns. Most office and commercial buildings were small and ordinary. To be sure, a few structures besides the parliamentary edifices did befit the status of a national capital. One was the twin-spired Notre Dame Cathedral in Lowertown, the most majestic of the city's churches. Another was Rideau Hall, the official residence of the governor general and the former estate of wealthy businessman Thomas McKay. Even so, Lord Dufferin, upon arriving as vice-regal in 1872, complained that the place was "nothing but a small villa such as would suit the needs of a country banker." Politicians and lobbyists frequented the five-storey Russell House hotel. A fine city hall opened in Upper Town in 1877, as did an impressive post office. The two- and three-storey homes of brick or stone clustering in the better areas contrasted sharply with the humble and far more numerous wood-construction dwellings of the working class.

When not covered in snow and ice, the streets were muddy and rutted. Thankfully, the accumulated refuse, for which the city was notorious, was considerably hidden in winter; but this esthetic improvement was offset by dangerous walking conditions. Cause for concern, too, were the squads of small boys on skates who darted about the icy stretches of thoroughfares such as Sparks Street. And newspapers chastised the habitually fast-driving teamsters for not equipping their horses with bells to warn unsuspecting pedestrians of the swift but silent approach of the rigs through the snow.

The Ottawa City Passenger Railroad carried residents along a three-mile route between the Chaudière Falls on the city's western fringe and the New Edinburgh extremity in the east. With its stable of thirty-seven horses, the company deployed eight cars along its tracks in the summer and five sleighs in the winter when snow and ice covered the rails. A one-horse cab accepted more affluent passengers at the municipally set rate of twenty-five cents for a fifteen-minute ride. Some might have been dropped off at Fred Fooks's London Restaurant for fresh shell oysters at twenty-five cents a dozen. Others might have been hurrying to the shop of chemist William Hearn at the east end of the Dufferin Bridge to pick up some "Parliamentary Pills," which he claimed were an antidote for "wind and indigestion." On blustery nights after a lengthy sitting, weary members of Parliament would have hailed cabs for the short trip to their temporary homes at the Russell House. Omnibuses connected the major hotels with the train depot, and stages ran regular routes to Billings Bridge, Aylmer, Gatineau, Richmond, and other outlying communities.

As John H. Taylor points out in his book *Ottawa*, it was the "age of urban infrastructure." Private enterprise provided transportation services and supplied the gas lines fuelling the street lamps. Until the mid-1870s, water supply was a responsibility shared by the city and private enterprise. Many residents filled buckets at the two municipal wells, while others relied on commercial carriers who brought water from the river and delivered it by the barrel. A hesitant city acted slower than other large communities in installing public water mains and it wasn't until late 1874 that residents could turn on a tap in their own homes. But the water was unfiltered and of suspect quality, and many households delayed hooking up to the system. A sure and convenient supply through hydrants immeasurably aided firefighting, now the task of a professional brigade. Telegraphic fire-alarm boxes connected with the fire stations. The chief, however, was unhappy at having to pay his own cab fare to the numerous conflagrations and asked the city council to defray the twenty-five-dollar annual expense. A new drainage and sanitary sewer system promised drier streets and basements along with reduced levels of disease. The newly established police force spent most of its time attending to drunken fights and petty thievery. Public schools were opening around the city and the Roman Catholic Separate School Board operated the Christian Brothers School on Sussex Street. The University of Ottawa taught philosophy, moral and dogmatical theology, languages, zoology, and mathematics. Benevolent institutions included two hospitals, three orphan homes, an asylum for the aged, and the Society of St. Vincent de Paul for the relief of the poor.

Such were the surroundings in which the city's 25,000 souls lived in the late 1870s.

Sports of All Sorts: Betting Men and Gentlemen Amateurs

THOUGH HOCKEY AS PLAYED in that seminal match in Montreal had not registered on the collective consciousness, other winter sports and amusements were in abundance. High-stakes ice trotting on the canal and at suburban Mutchmor Park was the spectator sport of choice. Prominent sporting men from the community, including the sheriff, entered their nags in the hopes of big payoffs. The *Daily Citizen* urged the sporting fraternity to "cash up" and make liberal subscriptions to ensure interesting purses. In a more sober moral tone, however, the same paper warned that since the racing crowd had come to the city, gamblers were operating a faro bank "in full blast at one of the Lower Town hotels," a running card game the paper thought the authorities should look into. Sparring matches featuring American pugilists at the Rink Music Hall drew rough-and-ready crowds. One such entertainment ended abruptly when the fighters knocked over an oil lamp, causing a fire, which, through the fighters' quick action, they smothered with the coats of some unhappy spectators.

But there were more reputable sporting diversions to occupy the spare time of those comfortable in the milieu of the upper civil service, the parliamentary domain, and the vice-regal entourage. Teams from the Ottawa Curling Club gained press attention competing against clubs from Quebec, Kingston, and Renfrew, and by hobnobbing at Rideau Hall where the Earl of Dufferin skipped his own rink. Tobogganing became all the rage after the Dufferins invited the society set to Saturday-afternoon outings on the grounds where guests hurtled down a huge wooden slide. A gullible *New York Herald* reporter who had come north to observe the glamour of the vice-regal's frosty sporting galas bought the tale that the locals practised tobogganing in summer by gliding down flights of stairs on tea trays. Snowshoe clubs organized evening tramps to the outlying areas, often covering ten or more miles, broken only by a stop for sustenance at a country inn. One club named itself the Dufferins. Rideau Hall was soon synonymous with winter sports. It was the curiosity and enthusiasm of successive governors general experiencing the exotic and exhilarating novelty of northern Januarys far from the moderate climes of England that did much to bring vigorous outdoor amusements into public favour. A Professor Burch, inventor of a combination ice boat, snowshoes, and toboggan, lugged his Rube Goldberg-like contraption to Rideau Hall seeking approval from Dufferin's successor, the Marquis of Lorne. Burch claimed that by putting a pair of oars on the iceboat, he could beat the time of famed rower Ned Hanlan. Lorne politely declined Burch's suggestion that the vice-regal try it out on the toboggan slide. The professor was then off to give a demonstration on the canal and was never heard from again.

Of all winter sports, skating was by far the favourite of Ottawans of every stripe. The canal and rivers were black with boys in the first days of December when, after a good freeze and before snow's blanketing effect, the ice, if sometimes rough, was at least skateable. Occasionally, foolhardy youths went on too soon with fatal results. Skating seemed to come naturally to Canadians. They simply went out and did it. By contrast, a Northampton, England, newspaper in December 1822 thought its readers would benefit from written, numbered instructions, seven in all. The *Mercury* advised "those wishing to be proficient to begin early in life" and "endeavour to throw off the fear which always attends the commencement of an apparent hazardous amusement." The article was at pains to describe the technique for turning on the inside and outside edges, suggesting that placing a bag of lead shot in the pocket next to the foot employed in making the outside stroke would assist in maintaining the skater's balance. In Canada, men, women and children outfitted themselves with Acme spring skates, invented by Nova Scotian John Forbes, who had patented his first version in 1865. Before then, the typical skate was an iron blade embedded in a wooden frame, which skaters attached to their walking boots with leather straps and a screw that came up from the frame into the heel. The all-metal Acme required no screws or straps. A single lever on the skate adjusted its size so that the sole clamp and the heel grip fitted snugly to any boot. A flick of the lever and the skate was detached. The Acme blade was also shorter, allowing better maneuverability on small surfaces. But Englishman John Rowan, describing his Canadian sporting adventures, said the Acme was useless for lengthy journeys. He preferred the longer blade of the earlier skate, claiming that with a breeze in his favour he could cover straight reaches of the Saint John River in New Brunswick at twenty miles an hour. The greater convenience of the new design, however, inspired a skating explosion, leading to the construction of covered rinks in eastern Canada and contributing to the development of modern hockey. In 1877 alone John Forbes's Starr Manufacturing Company sold 100,000 pairs of the Acme. In ceremonies at its Dartmouth factory, the firm presented pairs of gold-plated skates in walnut cases to Lord and Lady Dufferin and to the Marquis and Marchioness of Lorne. It was in the Dufferin years that Rideau Hall staff began the annual winter practice of laying down an outdoor rink — a tradition that continues today.

Fred Fooks, the small-time entrepreneur who ran the London Restaurant in Centretown, seemed always to be looking for a moneymaking angle. By 1875 he was operating an outdoor rink on the canal, charging admission, bringing in bands, and offering prizes to the best skaters. Somehow he was even able to secure the patronage of the governor general for the masquerade skating parties he arranged. In 1876 he brought skating indoors when he took over management of the Rink Music Hall on Maria Street near the corner of Elgin. The music hall was known for the many kinds of events it hosted, from curling to boxing, to walking races (known as "pedestrianism"), and various shows that came through town. Again Fooks succeeded in having the governor general show up and made sure these appearances were well publicized. The *Citizen* noted one such occasion when it said His Excellency and the Countess of Dufferin "with a number of friends went through several sets of quadrilles." At the same time, Antoine Ratte, who owned a large boathouse on the Ottawa River just downstream from the canal locks, offered competition by converting the structure to a rink in the winter. He installed dressing rooms, decorated the place with flags, brought in musicians, and served coffee in an anteroom. Enthusiasts could buy season passes or pay by the night. The two rinks vying for the favour of Ottawans illustrated the fact that the sport had passed from being merely a casual outdoor amusement to a viable business venture. This realization was soon to have a profound influence on the development of hockey, as rink owners ceaselessly looked for ways to put on revenue-producing events.

In the meantime skating held sway and became so fashionable that the city's most prominent residents accepted appointments to committees organizing the grand masquerade balls held every winter and which local newspapers reported in copious detail. Sandford Fleming, chief engineer for the construction of the Canadian Pacific Railway and soon to become famous as the inventor of standard time, was one such appointee for the

1881 event. Fleming was an excellent choice for a reason beyond his standing: he was an avid skater who, on his twenty-fifth wedding anniversary, thought no better way could be found to celebrate the occasion than to hold a skating party. The site was likely the rink he kept — thanks to the city's new water service — on the side lawn of Winterholme, his stately Sandy Hill residence. The famous Montreal photographer William Notman came down to the 1881 carnival with his understudy Henry Sandham to make composite photographs depicting the grand event. This he did by taking studio portraits of the costumed skaters and mounting them on an illustration of the rink. The studio was that of his Ottawa office, which was managed by William Topley, a photographer who would soon gain recognition of his own.

As for hockey, the structured indoor form introduced in Montreal in 1875 had not by the beginning of the 1880s reached Ottawa. In Montreal, members of the Victoria Skating Club and students at the University of McGill College, among others, played a somewhat-organized version under a simple set of rules adapted from rugby. For years before, soldiers, youngsters, and other sporting types had been playing versions of a stick-and-ball game on the ponds and lakes around Halifax, Dartmouth, and Windsor in Nova Scotia, along the Saint John River in New Brunswick, on a rink in Montreal, and on the harbour ice at Kingston. These games were known variously in different times and at different places as hurley, hurley-on-ice, ricket, bandy, shinty, shinny, and hockey. Since accounts in diaries and memoirs are sparse, hockey historians remain uncertain about such details as the use of skates, the make-up of sides, and the rules pertaining, if any, though it is known that a code called the Halifax Rules was in use in Nova Scotia before indoor hockey was played in Montreal.

It is hard to imagine that Ottawans did not also strap on "the irons," take bent stick in hand, and bat a knot of wood or pig's knuckle around long before the arrival of formal hockey. With the city situated on the Ottawa River and with the Rideau River and Rideau Canal cutting right through town, how could they not have? But recorded history is dim on this point. It is established that two teams did play a game of "shintie" in Ottawa on Christmas Day 1852. Exactly where and whether skates were worn is not clear. In his 1904 book of Ottawa sketches titled *The Hub and the Spokes*, journalist Anson Gard writes that he interviewed one of the participants in that match, Hugh Masson. Masson recalled that he played on the New Edinburgh team that day and that they wore "Scotch costume." He remembered six teammates: his brother Donald, John Lumsden, D.M. Grant, Allen Cameron, Peter Fraser, and William McDonald. The only player on the Ottawa team who came to mind was James Peacock, "the hatter." The Ottawa team were "plain clothes men." He said the game was refereed by the Hon. Thomas McKay's son-in-law John McKinnon and that the New Edinburgh team won 2-1. In 1959 Hugh Masson's daughter donated a silver medallion from that event to Ottawa's Bytown Museum. The medallion is illustrated in Gard's book and described on the museum's acquisition card. According to the card, the medallion was 1¾ inches in diameter and was presented by Thomas McKay to the winning team. On one side are engraved the words "Bytown and New Edinburgh Shintie Club Dec. 25ᵗʰ 1852." The reverse side shows two men in regular winter attire trying to hit a ball with what look like shepherds' crooks. Skates are not discernible and the playing surface appears to be a field. The museum caption refers to the game being played on "Rideau Hall grounds," which at the time were still on McKay's estate.

By 1880 the age of sporting infrastructure was well under way. Sports clubs had been established; athletic grounds cleared, leveled, and groomed; grandstands built; covered rinks erected; and inter-city competitions in such sports as curling and lacrosse begun. The impetus for sport's structural development came from middle-class businessmen, professionals, the universities, and the military. These elite and privileged groups not only possessed the administrative talents required to shape and organize individual sports, they enjoyed the affluence and free time necessary to pursue such interests. The upper strata of society shared a belief in the inherent value of athletic activity — a belief nurtured by the aristocratic leisure class of Britain. Sporting competition promoted discipline, co-operation, fair play, resolve, gentlemanly conduct, respect for teammates and opponents, and overall proper behaviour. In a nutshell, healthy body, healthy mind. Organized sport also provided a forum for convivial social contact, not to mention an opportunity for personal gain through the establishment of promising business and professional connections.

Imported and homegrown sports flourished. Military personnel from the British garrisons had done much to promote track-and-field sports at pioneer country gatherings and at more formal competitions in the urban centres of Montreal and Toronto. Scottish settlers had brought curling here as early as 1807, and by 1875 competitors enjoyed the patronage bestowed on the sport by Lord Dufferin through his donation of the Governor

General's prize. Rowing was popular in the Maritimes in 1867, when a four-oared crew from Saint John won a competition at the Paris International Exposition. Rowing also produced one of Canada's earliest sports heroes in the person of Ned Hanlan, who won numerous Canadian and international competitions in the 1870s and 1880s. Cricket was popular among the more affluent members of society, as was cycling, especially with Montreal's young leisure class. The ancient aboriginal game that came to be known as lacrosse was the first popular indigenous sport in Canada. The National Lacrosse Association came into being in 1867, and by the 1870s matches between Montreal and Toronto teams were drawing crowds of 8,000. Baseball was firmly established in southern Ontario by 1868 and openly employed professionals, most of whom were from the United States. Though British settlers and soldiers had introduced rugby to Canada many years before, it was in 1874 that a Canadian version came into play when the McGill varsity football team, in the second of back-to-back games in Cambridge, Massachusetts, met Harvard University in a scoreless draw, after the Americans had won the first game under their own rules.

Throughout this period, those who played sports for the love of the game, "gentleman amateurs," were confronted by the reality of others who engaged purely from a motive of pecuniary gain. To the amateur sportsman, sport should be valued for its own sake and should not be sullied by material considerations, considerations that led to unsportsmanlike conduct, rigged contests, and under-the-table payments. Lacrosse exemplified the conflict between idealism and materialism. Played in its early years by the upper levels of society, the sport attracted large crowds, allowing the clubs to prosper. Henry Roxborough in his history of nineteenth-century Canadian sport explains that as competition intensified, good players from all classes were recruited. Soon some were asking the clubs to supply their equipment, then associated expenses; finally players were demanding outright, but clandestine, payment for services. There was a stigma attached to professionalism, and its incursion into the sports clubs of gentlemen led to varying attempts to define "amateur" and to bar those who were not simon pure.

This, then, was the Canadian sporting environment as formalized hockey continued its evolutionary development from folk game to rule-based, structured competition.

*The Ottawa Hockey Club had its first contest
on the ice at the Royal Rink last night.
There was good play made on both sides.*
OTTAWA CITIZEN
March 6, 1883

Smart Sashes and Blunt Blades: Early Hockey in Montreal

FOR SEVERAL YEARS AFTER its first public demonstration in 1875, hockey remained a curiosity, rating cursory and puzzled attention in Montreal newspapers and none whatsoever in Ottawa's. If anyone in the capital had even heard of the new sport, it was through word of mouth from observers who had happened upon the sporadic contests "got up" at the Crystal and Victoria covered skating rinks and on the St. Lawrence River. In these early Montreal years the sport was the preserve of gentleman amateurs — those upwardly mobile members of the business, professional, and educated classes who were attracted to the exclusive sporting and men's clubs of the day or were attached to McGill College. Teams from the Victoria Skating Club (which counted among its honorary members Prince Arthur and Grand Duke Alexis of Russia) engaged in exhibition contests among themselves in 1875 and 1876; and a team from that club played a series of matches against McGill in 1877.

Early matches were played under the "Hockey Association Rules," which were, in fact, the rules of the English game of field hockey. Only in 1877 were the first-known ice-hockey rules printed, and these were applied in a match between "eight gentlemen" from the St. James Club and seven from the Metropolitan Club. The codes were virtually identical, the only difference being the substitution of the word "ice" for "boundary line" in the fifth of the seven rules. It was an on-side game. "When a player hits the ball, anyone of the same side who at such moment of hitting is nearer

A hockey game at the outdoor rink on the McGill campus, circa 1884. It was early Montreal matches such as this one that caught the attention of Ottawans Jack Kerr and Halder Kirby, who in 1883 decided the capital ought to have a team of its own. LIBRARY AND ARCHIVES CANADA C17831

to the opponents' goal line is out of play, and may not touch the ball himself." Players changed ends after each goal, called a "game." Play was started and renewed after each game with a "Bully in the centre of the ground." In the bully, the opposing centres banged their sticks together before trying to gain possession of the "ball," or puck, positioned between them. The penalty for an infringement of the rules, such as charging, tripping, collaring, or kicking, was simply a cessation of play and a new bully. These early rules said nothing of the number of players on a side. The players used spring skates but wore no protective equipment. They sported colourful jerseys or white shirts with smart sashes. Their sticks, short and blunt-bladed, were imported from Halifax. The object of their attention progressed from a ball to a flat block of wood to a square puck cut from a rubber ball, and finally to the conventional vulcanized-rubber disk of today. The evolution of the puck from ball to disk is explained by the fact that the ice surface in the first covered rinks was not enclosed by boards. Spectators stood on concourses raised a few inches above the rink and ran the risk of being hit by a flying ball. It was reasoned that if the puck were flat it would not soar out of play. Rink owners were also mindful of the replacement costs of the numerous lighting globes that fell victim to errant projectiles.

In what is believed to be the first photograph ever taken of a hockey team, members of the 1881 McGill varsity squad are shown poised for action on the Crystal Rink. If Ottawans had not yet heard of the McGill team, they would within three years become keenly aware of the young man on the left of the Notman photograph, Albert Peter Low. Ottawa, however, had neither a team nor on-ice celebrities of its own; but a pair of intrepid sportsmen were about to change that.

It was agreed. Jack Kerr and Halder Kirby would start a hockey club in Ottawa, one good enough, they were certain, to challenge anything Montreal could put up. As their homeward-bound train pulled away from the Bonaventure Station on the last weekend of January 1883, the Ottawa sportsmen settled back to reflect on what they had witnessed the previous few days. They had gone down to the first and much-heralded Montreal Winter Carnival, and among the array of spectacles and sporting events, they took special interest in the hockey matches. They were intrigued by the organized game and they admired the skills of the participants, experienced as they were at competing within a formal code of play. But Kerr and Kirby were also convinced that, though unlearned in the finer technical points and knowing nothing of hockey's rules, their friends back home could skate and handle a stick with the best of them. They had developed these skills quite naturally in the spontaneous matches that seemed to spring out of nowhere on the Rideau Canal and along the Ottawa and Rideau rivers.

Though the hockey matches were minor events at the carnival, the grand week-long celebration of winter's glory did give the new game a public platform of North American dimensions. The idea of a winter festival originated with prominent citizens within the English-speaking community, among them members of the recently formed Montreal Amateur Athletic Association. They saw such an event as a means of recognizing the city's cultural heritage and as a way of stimulating the economy through tourism. Organizers promoted the festival heavily in newspapers across Canada and in the northern United States weeks ahead, and distributed the printed program well in advance. The promotional centrepiece of the carnival was an immense ice palace rising 130 feet in

Dominion Square and constructed of 500-pound blocks cut from the Lachine Canal. The program included a curling bonspiel, grand sleigh parade, snowshoe steeplechase, trotting on the St. Lawrence River, skating races, a fancy-dress carnival at the Victoria Rink, a grand ball at the elegant Windsor Hotel, and, of course, the hockey matches. Thousands of visitors poured into the city, filling the hotels and boarding houses. Throughout the week, newspapers devoted page after page to every detail. Getting into the spirit, the *Gazette* intoned: "From the hour when Jacques Cartier and his brave companions were hospitably received at Hochelaga to this memorable day, when the first Winter Carnival is to be opened, recreation, in many forms, has played no slight or useless part in the history of Canadian progress."

It was on the St. Lawrence River where Kerr and Kirby took in the first matches of the hockey tournament. The huge rink, 400 feet long and 200 feet wide, had been prepared by the fire department using a steam-powered pumper engine. Here they saw the Quebec Hockey Club and the local Victorias play to a scoreless draw on the Friday morning. That afternoon the pair saw McGill defeat the Victorias. McGill won the Carnival Cup with a 2-2 draw against Quebec. In the McGill lineup were two graduates who only months before had moved to Ottawa, Albert Peter Low and Thomas D. Green. Whether they were known to Kerr and Kirby is a mystery; but if not, they were soon to become acquainted.

The Men From McGill and Ottawa's Own:
The Capital's First Hockey Club

KERR AND KIRBY WERE true to their word. On March 6 both of Ottawa's dailies, the *Citizen* and the *Free Press*, reported that the recently organized Ottawa Hockey Club had held its first practice the previous night at Fred Fooks's skating rink, recently renamed the Royal. For what was left of the season, the club practised on Friday evenings by playing matches among themselves. But the members anticipated "some good fun with their rivals next year." It was a felicitous convergence of like interests, for the club was made up almost equally of recent arrivals from Montreal and of Ottawa's own. The newcomers were fresh McGill graduates lured to the capital in 1882 by the Dominion government: Richard McConnell, Philip Foster, Low, Green, and Henry Ami. McConnell, Ami, and Low joined the Geological Survey of Canada. It had been founded in Montreal in 1842 as

Ottawa's first hockey team, the Ottawa Hockey Club, 1884. Back row, from left: T.D. Green, T.L. Gallagher, N.D. Porter. Middle row: Dr. H.S. Kirby, J. Kerr, F.M.S. Jenkins. Bottom row: G. Young, A.P. Low, E.L. Taylor. THE OTTAWA CITIZEN

a Crown corporation but was transferred to Ottawa and placed under direct government control in 1881. Its daunting task was to map the geology of the Canadian subcontinent, including the exploration and charting of Canada's northern rivers. Having earned a reputation for high scientific standards and technical skills, the survey needed qualified men. The three new recruits were considered prize catches since they were among only twenty-seven McGill graduates that year in arts, sciences, and engineering.

Of the Montreal contingent, only Low and Green would go on to represent the Ottawas in matches against outside clubs. Though there were similarities in their backgrounds, having been teammates on the McGill hockey club and classmates in the university's professional engineering program, their career paths in Ottawa immediately diverged. One rose steadily through the ranks to become a renowned explorer, geologist, and senior civil servant, only to come to a tragic end. The other struggled to find suitable employment and was eventually lost to obscurity.

Low's career was nothing short of brilliant. Born in Montreal in 1861, he attended Montreal High School before enrolling at McGill, where he studied mining and assaying. In the summer of 1881, before entering his final year, he gained his first experience with the Geological Survey earning thirty dollars per month. Upon graduating in 1882 with a bachelor of applied sciences, he moved to Ottawa to take a permanent position with the same agency as Surveyor and Explorer. As one of the new professionals on staff, his starting salary was $700 per year. By 1885 he had completed the survey and exploration of Lake Mistassini in northern Quebec and had caught the eye of senior management. In a letter to the minister recommending that Low be promoted, the deputy minister of the interior described him as "an active and energetic officer." He noted that in the examination required by the Civil Service Act, Low had scored 679 marks, where the passing grade was 400. The minister accepted the recommendation and Low's salary rose to $1,100.

As an explorer, Low spent a great deal of time away from Ottawa. Though retaining a strong interest in sports, he found it difficult to fit them into his schedule after his initial season with the Ottawa Hockey Club. Thereafter, when in town, he managed to play hockey occasionally, and in 1887 he captained the Ottawa Football Club. In a 387-page scientific report on explorations in the Labrador Peninsula, which he produced with the assistance of several colleagues in 1896, Low once more demonstrated his superior abilities. The sweeping document gives a chronological summary of previous explorations of the area, starting with Biarne the Norseman in 990. Not only does the report present a detailed physical description of the terrain, it includes observations on animal and plant life and what amounts to a sociological study of the natives and their way or life. He covered thousands of miles by canoe, on vessel, by dog team, and on foot in those explorations.

But Low's greatest achievement was in 1903–04 as commander of a government expedition to assert Canada's authority in the Arctic islands and waters. On board the chartered steamer *Neptune*, the exploration party was locked in the winter ice, allowing Low the time to study and photograph the Inuit of the region. He published these observations in his book *The Cruise of the Neptune*. Low was appointed deputy head and director of the Geological Survey in 1906 and became the first deputy minister of the new Department of Mines in 1907. In his history of the Geological Survey, Morris Zaslow recounts the tragedy of Low's declining years. Around the time of his 1906 appointment, Low had contracted what was diagnosed as cerebral meningitis, officially attributed to overwork. There was talk, however, that the illness was caused by a venereal disease. Whatever the reason, the illness finally forced his formal retirement in 1913, after a period of incapacitation. "Tragically," Zaslow writes, "he lived on and on, the mind of a child inhabiting his once powerful frame." Low died in 1942 at the age of eighty-one.

If Thomas D. Green came to Ottawa with high expectations, they would have been justified, for he and Low were two of only eight students in McGill's 1882 graduating class of engineers. But the dreams of the young and ambitious Six Nations man went unrealized. Unlike Low, Green was able to secure only temporary employment, with the Dominion Lands Branch of the Department of the Interior, and at half the salary of his classmate. He was paid $1.50 per day, 50 cents less than others similarly engaged at the branch, and it was only after he had, in a letter to the deputy minister, "the honour to humbly request" an increase to $2 that he achieved equity.

As an "extra clerk," Green found work in the Northwest Territories on temporary assignments, though he managed to keep his ties with the Ottawa Hockey Club for several years as a player and official. Relentlessly seeking permanent employment and staying in a succession of lodgings when in Ottawa, Green seemed to be in a precarious financial situation. Hockey diverted his attention from the troubles revealed in his correspondence with government officials. Acting on his behalf in 1885, the deputy minister of Indian Affairs wrote to the prime minister, Sir John A. Macdonald, to see if a permanent job might be found for "the Six Nations Indian surveyor and engineer." Macdonald forwarded the letter to the deputy head of the Department of the Interior with the marginal note "This Indian surveyor should I think be encouraged." It was all to no avail — there was no vacancy; there were other "deserving extra clerks" ahead of him; Green was "neither a good draughtsman nor a clever surveyor"; and why shouldn't Indian Affairs be asked to hire him instead of Interior? Finally, a year later the Interior Department did take him on "for the next two or three months" as he was, the deputy minister noted, "the only Indian on our list." So proceeded Green's uncertain career. He eventually found secure work as an assistant surveyor with the government and lived on and off in Ottawa until 1901 when he disappeared from the local scene.

The experience that Low and Green brought from McGill to Ottawa's original team must have been welcomed by the local boys who knew only the helter-skelter game they had grown up with in the capital. Though they were not wanting in competitive spirit, they were young and inexperienced. Tom Gallagher and George Young were 18, Ernest Taylor, 19, Jack Kerr and Halder Kirby, 20, and Nelson Porter, 21. Frank Jenkins was the oldest at 24, and it was he who would soon assume the role of team leader. As the neophyte players organized themselves for future competition, they also prepared for the world of business that lay ahead, a task that for many was eased by the strong community ties they enjoyed.

Tom Gallagher, a clerk, boarded for several years with the prosperous hardware merchant Thomas Birkett before becoming an agent for the Hamilton Powder Company and eventually relocated to Toronto. George Young was the son of Ottawa's first fire chief, William Young. The junior Young was soon to start a watch-making and jeweller's firm with his brothers, an interest no doubt passed on from their father who for many years had been in the same business. Some time later, George settled in Los Angeles. His brother Weldon would make his own mark with the Ottawa Hockey Club in the 1890s. Ernest Taylor was the son of Carleton County Justice of the Peace J.P. Taylor and was about to embark on a civil-service career with the Post Office Department. Jack Kerr was an all-round sportsman who wore Ottawa colours in rugby and lacrosse as well as hockey. After completing high school, he entered his father's hardware business, Blyth and Kerr, and eventually became manager of the successor firm, McKinley and Northwood. The fact that the business provided plumbing, gasfitting, and steamfitting services lends plausibility to the story circulating years later that the young player manufactured what was thought to be the first rubber hockey puck used in Ottawa. He married the sister of his Ottawa Hockey Club teammate Nelson Porter. Kerr spent the last eighteen years of his working life with the Customs Department of the Dominion government. He died in 1933. Halder Kirby, the son of Ottawa City Treasurer Thomas H. Kirby, was a young drug clerk when he joined the original club before going on to study medicine at McGill College. Upon returning to the capital to take up professional practice, he rejoined the Ottawas, becoming a fixture and star player, along with his brother Chauncey. Kirby later practised medicine in Vancouver, again in Ottawa for a short period, and in Winnipeg, where he died in 1924. Nelson Porter was born in Montreal and came to Ottawa with his family at age eight. Though active in several sports including speed skating, where he won a ten-mile event, he was never able to crack the regular lineup of the Ottawa Hockey Club and was relegated to a reserve role. But Porter enjoyed a long and successful business career in insurance and real estate, and was elected mayor of Ottawa in 1915. Porter died in 1961.

Of all the original players, Frank Maurice Stinson Jenkins had the longest and strongest connection with the Ottawa club. Though his participation as a player was frequently interrupted by injury or non-hockey responsibilities, Jenkins served as captain in 1884 and 1890; as club president in 1891; and as the club's representative to the Amateur Hockey Association of Canada in 1893, when he was also the elected president of that league. Jenkins' life away from the rink was one of accomplishment, too, but in endeavours so vastly different from the life of a sportsman that he might as well have been two different men so far as chroniclers of the age are concerned. They have never made the connection.

As a young boy, Jenkins came to Ottawa with his family from Kingston, where his grandfather, John Counter, had been mayor. Jenkins grew up loving and playing many sports. He finished school and entered the Post Office Department, where his father worked. There he became acquainted with a young dreamer who was indifferent to a civil-service career but completely absorbed in literary expression: Archibald Lampman, the budding nature and social poet. Though he must surely have enjoyed the intellectual company Lampman afforded, Jenkins had his eye firmly fixed on the poet's sister, Annie. Both were musically inclined, he as a church organist, she as a classically trained pianist and music teacher. At one of his earliest public appearances, before an audience of 300 at Christ Church on December 30, 1885, Jenkins performed Mendelsohn's *First Sonata*, a rendition the *Free Press* described the next day as "meritorious and well-conceived." In a musical career spanning more than twenty years, he inaugurated the organ at Knox Presbyterian Church, continued at Dominion Church, and for twelve years was organist at St. Andrews. He and Annie Lampman were married in 1892 and their names were frequently seen together in concert programs. Frank and Annie Jenkins also shared a love of camping and canoeing, which they pursued with their four children along the Ottawa River and through the Gatineau lakes on trips they meticulously detailed in notes and diaries preserved at Library and Archives Canada. Jenkins was the first musical director of the Ottawa Amateur Orchestral Society, founded in 1894, and he conducted the Schubert Club's choral group when it gave its first recital in 1895. Jenkins remained with the postal department throughout his working life and stayed active in sports, primarily as a curler. He died in Ottawa in 1930.

Thus was formed the nucleus of the original Ottawa Hockey Club, a group that assembled to play the game among themselves just for the fun of it, but one that also aspired through a representative team to challenge outside clubs. Founding member Henry Ami, who went on to a distinguished career as a paleontologist with the Geological Survey, recalled its purpose years later. He told the *Ottawa Journal* they met for the sake of good exercise, good sport, lively games played in the amateur spirit, and to win — for the sake of the club and the city it represented.

To the Carnival: A 'Grand Hockey Tournament'

ANOTHER OF OTTAWA's long, hot summers had finally ended, and none too soon for the budding hockey players. The stench from uncollected garbage in the streets and back alleys had subsided somewhat, and the steamy nights that made sleep almost impossible were over. Summer, though, had not been completely unbearable for active and athletic young men. Some, like Frank Jenkins, would find time for canoeing along the Rideau and Ottawa rivers and on the Gatineau lakes. Others, like Thomas Green, were on the rough and uneven sportsfields for lacrosse and baseball. Still, with the shortening days and bracing air of late fall in the capital, Ottawa Hockey Club members were turning their thoughts to what Ami had foreseen and what Kerr and Kirby had promised — the rush of competition on the ice.

By mid-December the ice bed at the Royal Rink was smooth and hard. The team was practising and its executive committee was in touch with organizers of the Montreal Winter Carnival. It was confirmed; there would be a hockey tournament at the second annual event and Ottawa's application had been accepted. The intensity of practices at the Royal signalled the club members' sense of anticipation as they vied with one another for selection to the team that would venture to the metropolis. Their commitment was not only to the expenditure of time and effort at the regular workouts, but also to meeting the costs of everything from skates, sticks, and uniforms to train tickets, hotel rooms, and even the coal to heat their dressing room.

As carnival publicity mounted with each passing day, it soon became apparent to the Ottawa players that the "good fun" they had looked forward to was taking on a slightly more ominous and stressful meaning. As a team, they had never played an outside club. Only two members had ever been in an organized game. And their matches against experienced opponents, it could now be seen, were going to be exposed on the front pages of major dailies in Montreal and Ottawa and likely elsewhere. In early January, a full month before the great spectacle, Ottawa papers were carrying reports on preparations. The ice palace was under construction. The toboggan slide was in order. Hotel reservations were coming in from New York, Boston, Chicago, and New Orleans. Then came the release and blanket distribution of the carnival program. It announced the range of events, including a "Grand Hockey Tournament on out-door Skating Rink." By the end of January, excitement was at fever pitch. Even the House of Commons took note. Montreal West Conservative Matthew Gault asked if it was the intention "to adjourn for two or three days to enable us to attend the carnival in Montreal?" Since the House in England adjourns for the Derby, he noted, there was no reason why the Canadian Parliament should not do similarly for the carnival. Occupied as the government was with a bill granting a loan to the Canadian Pacific Railway, Prime Minister Macdonald would have none of it. Nevertheless, and perhaps not coincidentally, the CPR did arrange for a parliamentary excursion the following week. Gault's interest in promoting the carnival was not merely a matter of hometown pride. The businessman, financier, and banker was also a director of the Windsor Hotel, one of the prime beneficiaries of the tourist influx the event would attract. Indeed, according to one newspaper account, the Windsor alone put up 1,300 guests each night through carnival week. The hotel would report afterward that guests consumed daily one ton of beef, half a ton of poultry and game, five barrels of flour, 200 dozen eggs, and 200 gallons of milk. All the hotels were filled and thousands of boarding-house rooms taken. In a dispatch from New York on the carnival's opening day, Monday, February 4, the *Montreal Gazette* told its readers that "so many prominent persons will leave here as to materially affect the gay world, and the entertainments announced for this week are in consequence few in number." By week's end, Bonaventure Station officials reported, some 869 passenger cars (excluding local trains) had arrived at the railway terminal from points east, west, and south.

In Ottawa, anxiously waiting to leave later in the week, Jenkins, Kirby, Kerr, and their teammates would read "by telegraph to the *Citizen*" staccato-like, present-tense descriptions of the opening ceremonies. "The weather is fine. The city is gaily decorated with flags, etc. Immense numbers of visitors are here chiefly from the United States." They would see that the

On the morning of Wednesday, February 6, 1884, the Ottawas left for Montreal on their first road trip on the 'mile-a-minute' Canada Atlantic Railway steamer shown at left. LIBRARY AND ARCHIVES CANADA C6317

After a three-and-a-half-hour trip, the Ottawa squad reached Montreal's Bonaventure Station, left, just in time for lunch. LIBRARY AND ARCHIVES CANADA PA164696

Marquis and Marchionesse of Lansdowne had arrived and had been accompanied to the Windsor by a 100-man guard of honour from the third battalion of the Victoria Rifles.

Departure time for the Ottawa Hockey Club was Wednesday at 8:00 a.m.; but passengers were warned that trains run by standard time, "which is 5 minutes faster than Ottawa time." The Canada Atlantic Railway passenger depot at the corner of Elgin and Catherine streets was reached quickly by one-horse hack or even without difficulty by foot from residences in the city's core. A lightly falling snow and a temperature of eighteen degrees Fahrenheit greeted the players as they stepped out of their homes. Once on board the "mile-a-minute train," as it was known because it reached nearly that speed at its fastest, they looked forward to the three-and-a-half-hour journey. Lumber tycoon J.R. Booth's line would take them east to Alexandria, where it would stop to drop off and pick up mail, then to Coteau Junction, where it would join the Grand Trunk Line into Bonaventure Station, arriving at 11:35 a.m. Sitting in the coach for the Ottawas were Low, Kerr, Kirby, Gallagher, Green, Young, and team captain Jenkins, all members of the starting lineup, and reserves Porter, Taylor, and Jack McMartin. Though Porter would see action in only one tournament game, his performance would prove decisive.

Railways always made sure there were plenty of newspapers on board, and the Ottawas, as they settled back to read, would have been stirred to take up the debate then raging in the *Citizen*'s letters pages — a debate touching on the carnival and on the summer interests of Green, Low, and Jenkins. The back cover of the tournament program featured an illustration of voyageurs carrying a canoe over a portage. What troubled some *Citizen* letter-writers on the subject, but not others, was the depiction of the canoe being carried gunwails up. "The correct position of a bark canoe when being carried," letter-writer Algonquin wrote, "is bottom up, and the number of men is regulated by its size and weight." But the canoeists among the Ottawa Hockey Club contingent would have known that right-side-up was indeed the practical way when there were supplies to be transported. What better way to relieve the building tension as the train rocked and rumbled its way to the team's rendezvous with destiny.

The air was electric as Jenkins led his team to their hotel through streets crowded with visitors. A skating promenade at the Victoria Rink behind the Windsor Hotel had just concluded, as had high-stakes trotting races on a track near the main hotels. A curling bonspiel was under way, and the first games of the hockey tournament had been played. A grand sleighing parade being marshalled on Dominion Square was about to begin. Everyone was looking forward to that evening's torchlight procession of snowshoe clubs, and to the carnival's spectacular highlight on Dorchester Street: the staged attack and defence of the ice palace, complete with fireworks.

McGill College authorities had given permission to the carnival's Outdoor Sports Committee to put down a skating rink on their grounds situated on Sherbrooke Street in the city's centre. The result was a surface measuring 250 by 140 feet. On the street side of the rink, organizers piled a huge mound of snow around and on top of two furnished waiting rooms and a refreshment stand they had constructed. The *Herald* judged the arrangements to be "very complete and satisfactory." The schedule called for the Ottawas to play their first game there on Thursday morning against McGill. On the first day, the Victorias were declared winners over McGill when the university men quit in protest over a disallowed goal. The Crystals defeated the Wanderers the next day. On the third day, McGill won by default over the Crystals, as did Victorias over Wanderers. Disputes, defaults, and scheduling confusion were not at all uncommon in hockey's early days, and there would be more trouble before this tournament ended.

Spectators gather round the snow-packed edges of the hockey rink at McGill College in Montreal, mid-1880s. It was at this rink, in front of a cheering and no doubt curious throng, that the Ottawas faced off against the McGill club for the first time as a rep team in 1884. LIBRARY AND ARCHIVES CANADA C81683

Pride and Petulance: Two Wins, Two Losses

ON A BRISK MORNING under a blue sky, the Ottawas, for the first time as a rep team, took to the hard, clear ice of the university grounds. Wearing red-and-black-striped jerseys and caps and dark knickerbockers (breeches gathered in at the knee), they felt a surge of pride in their team identity. Low was in goal, Kerr at point, Jenkins at centre; Kirby, Gallagher, Young, and Green played forward positions; Taylor, Porter, and McMartin watched from the sidelines. Opposite were the more experienced McGill men in red-and-white-striped jerseys, stockings, and caps, set off against white flannel knickerbockers.

The grounds were crowded and most gathered round the rink's perimeter to watch the contest. Immediately on the start of play, Jenkins rushed the McGill goal only to be thwarted by Budden and Brown. Retrieving the puck, McGill sent it sailing down the length of the ice where Green trapped it and lofted it back to centre. A scrimmage ensued with Green in the middle. Sent flying into a snow bank, Green wrenched his back, and though he continued to play, he did so with noticeable difficulty. Substitution of players was then not a part of the game. The teams appeared evenly matched and the first half-hour ended with neither scoring. By this time the governor general, who was supposed to have put in an appearance, had still not arrived. Though the teams waited twenty minutes before starting the second half, he was not to be seen, to the keen disappointment of players and spectators alike. Play resumed with both sides making dangerous forays. Ottawa's Low saved a goal by knocking a swift shot behind him and out of play. When the puck was brought back and faced, McGill's Ogilvie gained control and put it through at the ten-minute mark. As was the custom whenever a goal was scored, the teams changed ends and resumed play. Presently, Low's skate came away from his boot and skittered down the ice, stopping the action. After retrieving the errant blade, positioning his boot into the sole clamp and heel grip, and securing the fit with the locking lever, Low was ready and play began again. Gallagher, Green, and Kirby made long runs for the Ottawas in valiant attempts to tie the score, but the play of Hutchinson in the McGill goal was too much; the match ended with a McGill victory, 1-0. Low's play between the Ottawa flags was said to be excellent. For the Ottawas, it was an exhilarating experience. They had now worn their colours, played together as a team, and had acquitted themselves well against seasoned opponents. They had done so in the mecca of the game and under public scrutiny. Better days were surely ahead.

The first of those was the next day. Against the Victorias, the Ottawas knew they would be in for a tough time. In the tournament's first game, the Vics had defeated McGill. Steadily falling snow delayed the start of the game until late morning, but the enthusiasm of the spectators was in no way diminished. A large crowd of McGill students on one side of the rink had somehow decided that the Ottawas were going to be their favourites this day. Perhaps it was because they recognized former McGill players Low and Green in the lineup from the capital. The Ottawas made only one change from the day before: Porter replaced Young on the forward line. "Go it Ottawa, rush it through!" the students cheered. Green continued his previous day's robust play, becoming involved in "an indescribable struggle ... between a half dozen men, which lasted for fully a minute." Taking little notice of the popularity of their opponents, the Vics put up a stout defence against the determined Ottawas until, after fifteen minutes of play, Porter put the puck through. The reserve who was good enough to make the team but not sufficiently skilled to be a regular had scored the first goal ever registered by the Ottawa Hockey Club. The first half ended with no further scoring. By this time several inches of snow covered the ice. As the Ottawas anxiously waited for the second half to begin, officials, with the help of a gang of small boys they had conscripted, swept the surface. Play resumed, but the Ottawa men held on and there was no more scoring. They had won a hockey game.

On what was to have been the last day of the tournament, Saturday, February 9, Ottawa defeated McGill 3 to 0, while the Victorias prevailed over the Crystals. If the Victorias had lost that game, their total wins would have been two, the same as Ottawa. But Ottawa, because they had already beaten the Victorias, would have been declared tournament champions. The Victorias' win gave them more than any other team, but organizers decided a playoff would be required because of Ottawa's earlier win over the Victorias. The Ottawas had been handed a second chance, but they did not appreciate it. They reasoned that because they had already beaten the team that was first among all the Montreal clubs entered, they, from the capital city, should be given the title. Furthermore, Ottawa resented having to stay over until Monday to decide matters. Not so much so, however, that Gallagher, Kerr, McMartin, and Jenkins would not find themselves on the front page of Monday's *Montreal Herald* as having been among the smart set attending the carnival's grand finale, a fancy-dress masquerade at the Victoria Rink on Saturday night. Jenkins went as a bicyclist, his mates as hockey players.

The showdown was set for Monday morning at the McGill rink under ideal conditions. The Victorias dominated from the beginning, determined to keep the cup in the metropolis. Shot after shot rained in on Low, but he was equal to the task. After two thirty-minute halves, neither team had scored. The Ottawas had it in their heads that only a win for the Vics would give them the championship. With regulation time complete, the Ottawas figured they were entitled to the honours. Organizers thought otherwise and declared a third thirty minutes would have to be played. After fourteen minutes, Myers sent a "splendidly directed shot" through for the Victorias. That was enough as the home team held on for the win. The teams heartily cheered one another, but Ottawa's display of sportsmanship masked an underlying bitterness. The next day the *Ottawa Citizen* reported that the "team returned home last evening and to say they are disgusted with the way with which things were treated in that place would be drawing it mild." But the facts spoke for themselves. The Victorias had won four games, the Ottawas two. Upon reflection, a level-headed player like Frank Jenkins would have had to conclude that though the representatives from the capital had proven themselves a team to be reckoned with, they still had something to learn about Ami's ideal of good sport played in the amateur spirit.

MONTREAL WINTER CARNIVAL 1884

*All matches at McGill College Park outdoor rink**

February 4
Victorias 1 – McGill 0 [McGill quits in disgust before end of match]

February 5
Crystals 1 – Wanderers 0

February 6
McGill by default over Crystals [Several Crystals players could not get away from jobs]
Victorias by default over Wanderers

February 7
McGill 1 – Ottawa 0

February 8
Ottawa 1 – Victorias 0
McGill by default over Wanderers

February 9
Ottawa 3 – McGill 0
Victorias 2 – Crystals 0

February 11
Victorias 1 – Ottawa 0 [overtime]

Final Standings (wins-losses)
Victorias (4-1)
McGill (3-2)
Ottawa (2-2)
Crystals (1-2)
Wanderers (0-3)

* A non-tournament demonstration game between two sides of the Victoria Skating Club was played at the Victoria Rink on Monday, February 4, notwithstanding the existence of an ice grotto and snowshoe statue in the middle of the rink.

3 · The Game Takes Hold
1885–1890

Messrs. Dey's skating rink has been much improved since last season.
Three hundred flags of all nations are suspended from the roof and sides,
and three electric lights are being introduced to shed their effulgence on the scene.

FREE PRESS
December 15, 1885

Another Carnival and a Lost Season: 1885, 1886

BUOYED BY THE PROFILE it had established at Montreal, the Ottawa Hockey Club entered its second season with renewed enthusiasm. Treasurer Jack Kerr informed members at their November 1884 organizational meeting that the club was financially healthy. There were twenty-seven members — and that figure, the meeting learned, was expected to rise to nearly fifty. Members appointed a committee to arrange terms for the use of the new Dey's Rink, which was to open shortly at the canal basin in the heart of the city. That meant there would now be two good rinks suitable for hockey. Negotiations were soon completed and the club secured ice time at a splendid facility "beautifully lighted by the electric light as well as gas." The agreement included access to a nicely furnished dressing room. By mid-December the Ottawas were practising in their new colours of gold and blue under the leadership of Jenkins, the captain. Their immediate goal was to win the Montreal Ice Carnival tournament.

They would be without the services of their stellar goalkeeper, Albert Low, who was away on a survey expedition to northern Quebec; but his replacement, William O'Dell, was thought to be fully up to the task. Just as before, a happy excitement filled the Montreal air. The *Gazette* ran a celebratory five-stanza poem, which included the lines "In roystering fun, with billet and with stave / The Hockeis scamper o'er the frozen wave."

But the carnival fun wasn't without some frightening drama after Ottawa's first match. Two days earlier, tremendous dynamite explosions, thought to be the work of Irish nationalists, had rocked the British Houses of Parliament and nearby government offices. The evolving story was receiving blanket press coverage in Montreal, relegating carnival activities to secondary status. One bulletin reported a Canadian had been arrested running from the scene. Across the pond, meanwhile, someone discovered a mysterious package stashed in a dark corner of the Montreal post office. Fearing a catastrophe linked to the troubles overseas, police kept a close watch through the night. In the morning, they moved in to unwrap the object, only to find it was the cover of a water closet. No one, after all, had tried to sabotage the winter festivities.

Ottawa won its match 2-1 over the Victorias at the Crystal Rink and prepared for its next, against the Montreal Amateur Athletic Association (MAAA), a team that had been formed only two months earlier. The score was tied 2-2 at the end of the two halves and remained so after a third half-hour. At this point the Montrealers left the ice, leading the Ottawas to conclude they would be declared winners by default. To their displeasure, officials ordered a deciding match for the morning of the tournament's final day, Saturday, January 31. Again, three half-hours were needed before the MAAA came out victorious, 1-0. That afternoon, the MAAA won the tournament, once more taking three halves to earn a 1-0 victory over the McGill squad. This would be the beginning of a remarkable period of success for the new entrant in the hockey wars. It would also mark the beginning of an unexpected period of inactivity for the Ottawa club.

MONTREAL WINTER CARNIVAL 1885

All matches at Crystal Rink

January 27
Ottawa 2 – Victorias 1

January 28
MAAA 6 – Montreal Football Club 1

January 29
McGill 2 – Crystal 0

January 30
MAAA 2 – Ottawa 2 [decided Jan. 31]

January 31
MAAA 1 – Ottawa 0 [overtime]
MAAA 1 – McGill 0 [overtime]

Final Standings (wins-losses-ties)
MAAA (3-0-1)
Ottawa (1-1-1)
McGill (1-1-0)
Crystal (0-1-0)
Montreal Football Club (0-1-0)
Victorias 0-1-0

Back home, the Ottawas tried to arrange a follow-up friendly match with the MAAA; but this fell through, leaving them, because there were still no other teams in the city, with only intra-club games for the remainder of the season. An occurrence in Montreal that winter, completely unrelated to hockey, would pose further problems for the Ottawas in scheduling matches the following season. Pullman-car conductor George Longley, returning home from Chicago on the regular run of the Grand Trunk Railway, was too sick to proceed to his lodgings once the train reached Bonaventure Station. He was admitted to the crowded Hotel Dieu Hospital where, too late for quarantine measures to be taken, doctors discovered him to be the victim of the highly contagious disease, smallpox. The failure to diagnose his illness properly at the outset triggered an epidemic that wreaked havoc throughout the city for the next ten months. With Montreal in a state of emergency, authorities cancelled most large public functions, including the 1886 winter carnival. The only event at which the Ottawa team could meet organized opposition would not be held. Ottawa Mayor Francis McDougal contemplated arranging a replacement carnival but concluded it would be "a dangerous experiment."

Possibly realizing there was little chance for action that winter, Jenkins relinquished his captaincy. In any event, his career as a church organist was now taking up much of his free time away from the post office. Percy Myles of Montreal, where he had played with the Victorias, succeeded Jenkins. But this change in leadership came to nothing. The club made half-hearted arrangements to enter a tournament in Burlington, Vermont, that winter, buying a supply of sticks from the Caughnawaga Reserve; but they never followed through and ended the season without playing a single match.

Montreal remained the undisputed centre of hockey energy and innovation. Events there bore watching in the capital. In place of the cancelled carnival tournament, local teams organized their own series to decide a city champion. Montreal also sent two teams, the MAAA and the Crystals, to the week of winter sports in Burlington, an event seen as an unofficial substitute for the gala of the northern metropolis. And Montreal's leading hockey men set about revising and expanding the rules of play. Hockey would still be an onside game; there would be seven players on a team, with no substitution allowed for an injured player; the tops of the goals would be six feet above the ice and six feet apart; matches would consist of two half-hours, followed by sudden-death overtime in the case of a tie; the goalkeeper would have to maintain a standing position; and hockey sticks could be of any length, but no wider than three inches. But for the first time the object of pursuit was codified: "The puck must be one inch thick and three inches in diameter, and of vulcanized rubber."

Montreal newspapers, especially the *Gazette*, reflected the public's growing interest in the sport. It was not at all unusual for that paper to offer up editorial comment on how the game should be administered and governed. It advocated a city championship to be followed by a Dominion championship. It chastised teams for unnecessarily rough play. And the paper waged a campaign of sorts against the offside rule. Its hockey writer's position was that the rule slowed the game down and could not be consistently applied, because the referee was not always in a position to make a judgement. "Do away with the offside rule," the *Gazette* asserted, "and play hockey as lacrosse and there will be a better game."

Tom Green and the AHAC: Draughtsman? No — Hockey Man? Yes

WHERE IN ONE LIFE GREEN was struggling for recognition and respect, in another he was greatly admired for his ability and leadership. The Six Nations man was still getting the run-around from the Dominion government as the winter of 1886–87 approached. Though an engineering graduate of the University of McGill College, renamed McGill University in 1885, and certified by the Ontario Board of Governors as a Provincial Land Surveyor, Green was having great trouble securing a permanent posting with the government. Living at Ottawa's Windsor Hotel between temporary placements in the field, he had written to the minister of the interior, Thomas White, to "beg for employment in the Technical Branch." In private correspondence with Deputy Interior Minister A.M. Burgess, Deputy Minister of Indian Affairs Lawrence Vankoughnet, who was championing Green's cause, allowed that Green had admitted he was not a good draughtsman. But Vankoughnet noted "he is apparently possessed of great energy as well as ambition." Vankoughnet added that he would be glad to see Green succeed, "as his course affords a remarkable instance for an Indian of pluck and steadiness." Burgess, who had steadfastly opposed Green's employment, finally relented and wrote to the minister saying temporary work could be found. He referred to Green's application as one for "temporary employment" (and that is what he was grudgingly given), though what Green was expressly looking for, as stated in an earlier letter, was a "permanent situation" (Green's emphasis).

There was no such backhanded treatment of Green in the hockey ranks, which he must have found gratifying and a welcome relief from his professional humiliation. Green had played admirably for the Ottawa Hockey Club in both the 1884 and 1885 Montreal tournaments; and just as the latest round of deputy-ministerial correspondence was flying about, he was elected captain of the Ottawa team. His club also appointed him their representative to the founding meeting of the Amateur Hockey Association of Canada. This crucial and high-profile gathering on December 8, 1886, drew delegates to the Victoria Skating Rink in Montreal from hockey's best-established clubs for the purpose of organizing a formal league. Along with Green, representatives of the Victoria Hockey Club, the Crystal Hockey Club, McGill University, and the Montreal Amateur Athletic Association attended. Though invited, the Quebec Hockey Club did not send a spokesman. J.G. Monk of the Victoria club, saying he was expressing the sentiments of those present, praised the Ottawa club for the courteous manner in which it had responded to the idea of an association. The group then proceeded to elect Green as the first president of hockey's first association, the body to which the National Hockey League can trace its origin.

The meeting agreed the season should be from January 1 to March 15. But the most significant decision, and one that would provoke continuing controversy over the next several years, was to adopt a "challenge system" of play. The club holding the "championship trophy" was required to accept all challenges from member clubs in the order of their reception and to play challenges with an intermission of no more than seven days between matches. A champion team, on being defeated, was required to hand over the trophy to their victors within a week of defeat. Challenges had to be sent by registered post to the secretary of the team being challenged, and all unsatisfied matches on file at the time of the defeat of a champion team were to be honoured, in the original order of receipt, by the successor champion.

Rules of the Amateur Hockey Association of Canada
adopted at the founding meeting, December 8, 1886

> The captains of contesting teams shall agree upon two umpires (one to be stationed at each goal) and a referee.

All questions as to games shall be settled by the referee, and his decisions shall be final.

All disputes on the ice shall be settled by the referee, and his decisions shall be final.

The game shall be commenced and renewed by a bully in the centre of the rink. Goals, six feet wide and four feet high, which shall be changed after each game, unless otherwise agreed.

When a player hits the puck, anyone of the same side who at such moment of hitting is nearer the opponent's goal line is out of play, and may not touch the puck himself, or in any way whatever prevent any other player from doing so until the puck has been played. A player must always be on his side of the ball.

The puck may be stopped, but not carried or knocked on, by any part of the body. No player shall raise his stick above his shoulder. Charging from behind, tripping, collaring, kicking or shinning, shall not be allowed, and any player after having been twice warned by the referee, it shall become his duty to rule the player off the ice for the match.

When the puck gets off the ice behind the goals it shall be taken by the referee at five yards at right angles from the goal line and there faced.

The goal keeper must not, during the play, lie, kneel or sit upon the ice, but must maintain a standing position.

Hockey sticks shall not be more than three inches wide at any part.

Goal shall be scored when the puck shall have passed between the goal posts and below the top and passed from in front below an imaginary line across the top of the posts.
The puck must be made of vulcanized rubber, one inch thick all through, and three inches in diameter.

A team shall be composed of seven players, who shall be bona fide members of the club they represent. No player shall be allowed to play on more than one team during a season except in a case of bona fide change of residence.

Two half hours with an intermission of ten minutes between will be time allowed for the matches. A match will be decided by the team winning the greatest number of games during that time. In case of a tie after playing the specified two half hours, play will continue until one side secures a game, unless otherwise agreed upon between the captains before the match.

No change of players must be made after a match has commenced except for reason of accidents or injury during the game.

Should any player be injured during a match and compelled to leave the field his side shall have the option of putting on a spare man from the reserve to equalize the teams; in the event of any dispute between the captains as to the injured player's fitness to continue the game the matter shall at once be decided by the referee.

Should a game be temporarily stopped by the infringement of any of the rules the puck shall be brought back and a bully shall take place.

The challenge system, therefore, meant there was no fixed schedule of matches, and the championship designation could change from week to week. Teams that chose not to challenge, or were waiting for their turn, were free to engage in "friendly" matches with member or other clubs. The adoption of the challenge system was intended to accommodate teams at a distance from Montreal, such as Quebec and Ottawa. Since most of the clubs were from Montreal, a regular schedule, or "series system," would put the outside teams to a financial disadvantage in having to incur heavy travel expenses for the majority of their games. The Ottawa club favoured the challenge system, but the day would come when it would rue the position it had taken.

Within a few days, the AHAC executive produced a booklet containing the constitution, bylaws, and rules of the new league. The object of the association was to "improve, foster and perpetuate the game of hockey in Canada; protect it from professionalism, and to promote the cultivation of kindly feeling among the members of the hockey clubs." With few alterations, the rules of the previous season were retained, the most notable change being the reduction of the height of the goal posts from six to four feet.

To start the season, the Crystals, deemed to be the champions on the basis of their previous year's city-tournament record, defeated McGill but lost to Victorias the following week. Meanwhile, the Ottawas, who had sent in their challenge by registered post in December, sat in frustration waiting for the match to be scheduled. They had hoped for an early contest, reasoning that if they won there would be sufficient time remaining in the season to play one or more matches at their home rink, which would bring them gate revenues without travel expenses.

Ottawa's challenge was finally scheduled for January 27 at the Victoria Rink against the Victorias, the current champions. Stalwarts from Ottawa's original team included Green, Kirby, Kerr, and goalkeeper Low, whose survey work had kept him away from the club for two years. Before a large turnout, Ottawa scored first, but it was downhill from there as the Vics came back with five goals to win the match and dash any hopes of Ottawa playing an official game in front of its own supporters. Adding to the humiliation, the Ottawa players broke several sticks during the course of the struggle and had to borrow some from their opponents. In keeping with the association's aim of promoting "kindly feeling" among the teams, the Victorias entertained the visitors after the game.

The Ottawa Hockey Club would not play another official AHAC match for four years. Nor, for that matter, would the club, with the exception of a couple of friendlies, play any matches against outside teams. The club's descent was surprising but explainable. Ottawa was without Jenkins, whose leadership had propelled the club in the first place. Temporary survey assignments took his promising successor, Green, away from the city for extended periods. With the Royal converted to a roller rink, ice time was in short supply, an economic point not lost on the Dey brothers, who exploited their monopoly and became difficult to negotiate with for the use of their rink. On top of this, there were no other local teams against whom the Ottawas could hone their skills and keep interest alive. Under these circumstances, it was impossible to keep playing in the Montreal-centred AHAC. Something had to change.

Philip Ross, shown in his later years as publisher of the *Ottawa Journal*, brought his intuitive business sense and impressive connections to the Ottawa Hockey Club, helping to set the team's management in order and build the team's reputation in the press. LIBRARY AND ARCHIVES CANADA PA123539

P.D. Ross: Cultivator of Connections

PHIL ROSS WAS JUST the man to shake some life into the moribund hockey scene. He had a passion for the game; he had boundless energy; and he was comfortably connected with the sporting elite of hockey's mecca, Montreal. He had been so well trained in the art of cultivating influential friendships that the day he arrived in town to take up permanent residence, on January 3, 1887, he was smoothly able to pay a courtesy call on the mayor-elect. Soon he would be a central figure in local hockey circles and within two years would be a key member of the Ottawa Hockey Club's management committee.

Philip Dansken Ross was born in Montreal January 1, 1858, the eldest of the five sons and three daughters of Philip Simpson (P.S.) Ross and Christina (Dansken) Ross. Old P.S. was an astute businessman and founder of the accounting firm, P.S. Ross and Sons. His first offspring, known as Philip, Phil, and P.D., did not enter his father's firm. At McGill he studied engineering and played on the football and hockey teams. An all-round sportsman, Ross was a champion rower in his youthful days and participated in many other sports, including lacrosse, fencing, and boxing. Upon graduation he worked for a short while with the Montreal Harbour Commission, but his real interests, outside of sports, were literature and writing. Before long, he cajoled his way into a job as reporter at the *Montreal Star*, a move that gave him a sharp decrease in pay.

Ross's diaries, in several boxes at Library and Archives Canada, reveal the man's passion for — perhaps obsession with — hockey and skating. Athletic of build (six feet tall, 165 pounds, and by his own estimate in good condition on his twenty-first birthday), Ross meticulously recorded seemingly every morning, afternoon, and evening skate he took, every game he played or watched from the sidelines. "Best game I know of, hockey," his entry for Thursday, January 23, 1879, concludes, following the notation "went over to the rink and got my skates, p.m. down to the river to play hockey on the ice, hard work all afternoon, and came home pretty stiff."

His interest in journalism and sports soon led Ross to Toronto to take a position as sports and pastimes editor with the *Mail* newspaper. It was while on the staff of the *Mail* in 1883 that his interest in hockey first converged with that of Kirby and Kerr's. They were spectators at the first Montreal carnival tournament on the St. Lawrence ice; he was a reporter covering the matches. Conveying his bias in a January 26 dispatch, Ross wrote, "The game is one of the finest and fastest in the world."

P.S. Ross always kept in close touch with his first son, offering sage advice in long, didactic, yet heartfelt, letters. One of these while the twenty-six-year-old Ross was still in Toronto expressed the father's philosophy on getting ahead in life: "As you are becoming more awake to your position allow me my dear boy to say that next to money is the possession of friends and the more influential the better. Your present chums will be of use to you in future years so far as they succeed themselves but you must aim to cultivate the acquaintance and friendship of those who are already established in positions of influence." Admitting his maxims were "a little Machiavellian perhaps," P.S., underlining the key words, wrote: "Whenever you can get an introduction to and a friendly reception from one moving in an influential sphere cultivate it." That's exactly what Ross did, and the results would soon be seen in his business and social endeavours. So too would they be evident in the fortunes of the Ottawa Hockey Club.

Ross left Toronto in 1885 to rejoin the *Montreal Star,* where he was successively editor, correspondent in the Parliamentary Press Gallery, and managing editor. This broad and quickly acquired experience, together with a loan of $4,000 from his mother's insurance policy, allowed him to buy a half-interest in the *Ottawa Journal* and become its joint publisher in January 1887. Ross set about putting his floundering newspaper in order, reacquainting himself with press contacts from his previous days as a political correspondent, and, of course, establishing himself with the Government House and Parliament Hill crowds.

After a promising start, helping to inaugurate the AHAC, the Ottawa Hockey Club fell inactive. Ross, who would most certainly have become involved had there been anything to the club at the time, contented himself with skating on the Rideau waterway and engaging in impromptu games "got up" along its length. Witness these diary entries closing out 1888:

> *Wednesday, November 21*: Rideau canal frozen over. Had a gorgeous skate and game of hockey in evening, with Brigham, Cunningham, the Wrights, etc.
>
> *Thursday, November 22*: a.m. skating.
>
> *Friday, November 23*: Had skate in evening with Archie and A.F. May.
>
> *Sunday, November 25*: Skated up the Rideau to about two miles above Hog's back — a beautiful day.
>
> *Wednesday, December 12*: p.m. to Rideau for skate.
>
> *Thursday, December 13*: Up 7- a.m. to Rideau for skate.
>
> *Friday, December 14*: Up 7- a.m. to Rideau for skate.
>
> *Saturday, December 15*: Up 7- a.m. to Hurdman's Bridge, three hours splendid skating. In evening stayed home.
>
> *Sunday, December 16*: Up 8:15; a.m. skate.
>
> *Wednesday, December 19*: Ottawa, p.m. To Dey's rink at 4 p.m. for skate with Oxley.
>
> *Friday, December 21*: In evening to Reynolds with Hurdman — then to skating.
>
> *Saturday, December 29*: Up 7:30; at 8 a.m. for skate — Playing hockey at Rideau canal — shinny stick 0.25.

At the time Ross was entering these happy diversions in his diary, several area investors were watching work progress on their new venture, a combined skating and curling rink being erected on Theodore Street (now

Laurier Avenue East), adjacent Ottawa College. One of the investors was the new governor general, Lord Stanley of Preston, who bought twenty shares and was named patron of the enterprise, called the Rideau Skating and Curling Club. The project suffered a setback in the early hours of November 16, when the partially completed structure collapsed with a tremendous roar. Alarmed residents along Theodore Street ran out of their dwellings to discover that all eighteen of the forty-two-foot-high arches were lying in a heap, along with the wooden walls that had once stood about fourteen feet. There would be an unfortunate delay in the opening of what was to become the home of the Ottawa Hockey Club, but the rink's directors were determined to rebuild immediately. The rink had its formal opening on February 1, 1889, when Lord Stanley presided over a fancy-dress carnival gussied up by the three hundred Chinese lanterns he had lent the organizers. Four of Stanley's sons also graced the event, two dressed in Government House tobogganing costume and two in Lord Derby's colours. The elbow-shaped building, with its curved roof and elegant cupola over the front entrance, housed separate skating and curling surfaces. It quickly became a gathering place for the city's elite. Among them was the thirty-one-year-old Ross, by now circulating effortlessly among influential political figures and the social trendsetters from Rideau Hall.

Ross was a man to be reckoned with. Blessed with a keen intellect, an extraordinary curiosity, a refined social grace, and a prowess in sports, he found it quite easy and natural to fit in everywhere he chose to appear. Likewise, his position as a newspaper publisher and editorialist on the issues of the day meant he was sought out by others aiming to extend their own influence. Though Ross was a knatty dresser, he seemed to have little interest in materialistic display, choosing to live in a room at the Grand Union Hotel for his first five years in the capital.

The Rideau Rink breathed new life into the Ottawa hockey scene. The Ottawa Hockey Club quickly re-organized, with Ross now on its management committee. Familiar names included Jenkins, making a comeback as captain; Kirby; Kerr; Porter; Young, who brought along his brother Weldy; Green; William O'Dell; Gallagher; Low; and Ami. The club secured one-hour periods on Mondays at supper time and at mid-evening on Wednesdays and Fridays to practise and play intra-squad matches. (Another club attempting to get established had to be satisfied with a midnight start time.) Ross arranged through his brother "Billy," who was a member of the Montreal Amateur Athletic Association, to bring the MAAA second team to

The Rideau Rink — the building with the curved roof, on the right — was the home ice of the Ottawa Hockey Club from 1890 to 1896. The rink, on Laurier Avenue at Waller Street, was opened by Lord Stanley on February 1, 1889, and quickly became a hub for the capital's elite. LIBRARY AND ARCHIVES CANADA PA42366

the Rideau Rink for a friendly match, which would give the Ottawas some badly needed external competition. Ross refereed the game and afterward, in what was rapidly becoming a gentlemanly sporting tradition, entertained the two teams at the Grand Union Hotel. Billy, the MAAA captain, responded to a toast, saying the Montreal boys were glad to do what they could to encourage manly sport, and he promised they would reciprocate the kind treatment when the Ottawas next visited them.

There had been some public opposition to hockey being allowed at the new rink, on the grounds that the furious pace of the game destroyed the ice and deprived pleasure skaters of its use. Asserting his editorial prerogative, however, Ross made sure a letter of rebuttal signed by "A Humble Votary of the Game" appeared near the top-centre of the *Journal*'s front page.

Ross's top-drawer friends, undoubtedly attracted by the modern rink, were now ready to try the game. Just two weeks after the Rideau's opening, teams representing the city's exclusive men's clubs — the Rideau (not to be confused with the Rideau Skating and Curling Club) and the Ottawa (not to be confused with the Ottawa Hockey Club) — lined up. James (J.G.A.) Creighton, Senate law clerk and participant in hockey's first organized indoor match in Montreal fourteen years earlier, was the captain of the Rideau team. Other prominent members included Lieutenant A.H. McMahon, an aide-de-camp to Governor General C.J. Jones, and MP John Augustus Barron, chief clerk at Government House. Ross captained the Ottawa team. The circle expanded the next day when a civilian and a military team met on the same rink. McMahon was again on the ice, this time for the military team; Ross was referee; and Creighton an umpire. Also in the military lineup were three of Lord Stanley's sons: Fred, Victor and Edward, the latter having arrived from England only five days earlier. Here on February 14 and 15, 1889, then, was the genesis of what would become the famous Rideau Rebels, a loose aggregation of prominent citizens who would catapult the team into public prominence and promote the sport in and west of Ottawa over the next few years.

As a member of the Rideau Rebels circle and of the Ottawa Hockey Club, Phil Ross was at the centre of the city's hockey activity and in a strategic position to give the game the leadership it needed in the capital.

The Ottawa Amateur Athletic Club: Elitist or Egalitarian?

OTTAWA WAS STILL a small city; but it was growing and its political, social, and business influence was being felt. The Parliamentary Press Gallery fed copy about the day's happenings in the House of Commons to papers across the country. Government services, housed in new structures such as the stately Langevin Building, were expanding. Lumber baron John Rudolphus Booth was pushing his Canada Atlantic Railway across the St. Lawrence River. Local entrepreneurs Thomas Ahearn and Warren Soper were making their mark installing electric street lighting throughout the city. Telephone installations, which only a few years earlier were so novel that each new connection was reported in the papers, were now commonplace. And Rideau Hall had its own cachet as a glamorous trendsetter on the social scene.

The growing numbers of government officials, businessmen, and professionals created a sizable middle-class community, one of at least moderate affluence and with increased leisure time to enjoy. The Ottawa Amateur Athletic Association, whose purpose was to afford young gentlemen an outlet for respectable sporting and recreational activities, operated in rental quarters in a downtown building. Directors decided the time was right to build their own headquarters. They formed a separate corporate body, the Ottawa Amateur Athletic Club, to create and operate the facility. Here again Ross came to the forefront. Directors of the new entity elected him their first president, and one of his early official duties was to preside over the opening of a fine new three-storey structure in November 1889 at the northwest intersection of Elgin Street and Maria (now Laurier Avenue West). Modelled after the successful Montreal Amateur Athletic Association, the OAAC was to support itself through membership fees and fundraising events. It would provide gymnastic activities, billiards, and other games, and would serve as an umbrella body for the city's major sports teams. The Ottawa Hockey Club would be the first of these "connected clubs."

The opening ceremony was instructive, for it said a lot about Ross, his connections, Ottawa society, and the club's view of its own position and role. Ross had been well acquainted with Prime Minister Macdonald for several years and, in fact, considered him a friend. It was a relatively straight-forward matter, then, for Ross to have Macdonald on hand to declare the new club officially open. Following some pleasant remarks by the prime minister to the large and fashionable gathering in the gymnasium, Ross thanked him in familiar, even cheeky, terms. Personally aware of Maconald's fondness for strong drink, Ross assured him he would always be welcome at the club to "practice on the horizontal bar," or "to have a few rounds, Marquis of Queensbury rules." Anyone who could get away with comments like that, and Ross certainly did, was not to be taken lightly. Ross had a few more things to say, which, when held up to scrutiny, raise questions about his sincerity regarding membership eligibility in the club. Here is how the *Ottawa Citizen* reported his remarks:

> The qualification for membership was not that a man have a fashionable tailor, but any man of good moral standing and prepared to respect the rules of the association was welcome, whether he was a baronet or a mechanic.

> "Hear, hear," applauded the Premier, and taking their cue from him the audience heartily applauded this declaration of the liberal platform of the association.

But what were the rules of the club and how did one actually become a member? A neatly printed little booklet containing the club's constitu-

The Ottawa Amateur Athletic Club, at the intersection of Maria and Elgin streets, was the Ottawa Hockey Club's first institutional home. Visitors to Ottawa today will find neither the club nor Maria Street. The former is now the Lord Elgin Hotel, the latter Laurier Avenue. LIBRARY AND ARCHIVES CANADA PA 27272

tion and bylaws gives the answer. First of all, a prospective member had to be an amateur; he must never have competed for a money prize or staked bet, or competed with or against a professional for any prize, or have earned any portion of a livelihood from teaching or assisting with the practice of athletic exercises. The candidate had to fill out an application form stating, among other things, his occupation. His application was scrutinized by a special committee and then voted on by the board of directors who had "blackball" powers, one vote in five being sufficient to bar the candidate. A candidate successful to that point would then have to come up with the substantial membership fee of ten dollars for the year. Ross's seemingly magnanimous statement of membership openness was really code for something like the following: *You must meet our rigid definition of simon-pure amateurism, which we have adopted from the Amateur Athletic Association of Canada. We would appreciate your being fashionably tailored; you do not have to be a baronet as long as you act like one; and, if you are a mechanic, we want to know about it. If you wish to join you will have to find two members to recommend you; your suitabil-*

ity will be examined by a committee and judged by the board. And by the way, please understand that any one of our board members can blackball you. Finally, we trust you can afford our rather hefty membership fee. Ross's own newspaper got it right when it observed, "The new members are of the best class, including many well known city business and professional men."

There was no getting around it, the club smacked of elitism. But players on the Ottawa Hockey Club had no need for concern because, as a constituent club of the organization, its current members were exempt from scrutiny and granted automatic entry upon payment of fees. In fact, in a further concession, players who chose not to become OAAC members were allowed to play anyway on what was now an OAAC club team.

Red, Black and White: Ottawa's Official Colours

THE OTTAWAS HAD WORN the red, black, and white combination for their first matches in 1884, before switching to the old gold and blue; but it was their affiliation with the OAAC that officially returned them to their original colours. The *Constitution and By-laws of the Ottawa Amateur Athletic Club* states:

Article III. Colors, Uniform and Badge

Sec. 1. The colors of the Association shall be red, black and white.

Sec. 2. The uniform of the Association shall consist of a white jersey, trimmed with black with the winged-legs worked in on the brest, white knee breeches and black stockings.

Sec. 3. The badge of the Association shall be three winged legs — red and black on a white ground.

The Ottawa Hockey Club did not re-join the AHAC for the 1890 season, but it was getting back on track. Ross was now the president, Jenkins the captain. Old reliables Kerr and Kirby, along with Weldy Young, made up the management committee. The hockey club limited its membership to twenty-five, because, the annual report said, "a greater number would prevent satisfactory practices." Before each game, the management committee chose players from among the whole membership to represent the club on the first and second teams. The first team played only one match, an exhibition against the AHAC's Victorias at the Rideau Rink in conjunction with the Canadian skating championships. The second team, with Ross in the lineup, played five contests, four of those against the new Ottawa College team. Ross also kept up his connection with the parliamentary and Government House team, now becoming known as the Rebels. He joined the group for matches in Lindsay, Toronto, and Kingston, trips that would establish a solid relationship with hockey interests in those centres and would ease the way for the creation of an Ontario league, of which the Ottawa Hockey Club would be a member.

Sometimes on the Sabbath:
'They joined in the game and gloried in its shame'

MEANWHILE, LOCALLY, TROUBLE was brewing. So taken with the game were the Stanley boys that they began inviting friends and enthusiasts to partake of matches on the rink at Rideau Hall, sometimes on Sundays. Hockey on the Sabbath provoked a public controversy, leading one irate citizen, in a letter to the *Free Press*, to opine: "If it is seen fit to permit the residents of Rideau Hall to spend the day in this fashion, let them do so, but protest I must as a Sunday school teacher against inviting our young men to be present." The clergy soon entered the fray, denouncing the practice from the pulpit. Congregational Church pastor John Wood condemned those who had "joined in the game and gloried in its shame." He was joined by Reverend John Wilson at the Dominion Church, who told his congregation it mattered not "whether it was at the Governor General's place or the worst place in the city," Sunday sport was "a violation of God's holy day." It so happens that team captain Jenkins was the organist at Reverend Wilson's church, as well as being closely associated with the Rideau Hall hockey crowd. It may never be known whether he was one of the offenders, but, as if anticipating the pastor's further wrath, was absent from church the following Sunday. A substitute organist had to be found. The *Journal* said Jenkins had not yet recovered from his "recent illness." He rebounded sufficiently quickly, however, to referee a match at the site of the Sunday sinning six days later and a few days after that to take part in the Ottawa Hockey Club's important exhibition game against the Victorias of Montreal.

4 · Building a Winning Tradition

No game is stronger in fixing the attention of the onlookers.
BEVERLY BOGERT
Writer, 1893

Natural Ice or None at All: Praying for Cold Weather

OTTAWA'S WINTER SPORTSMEN sought warmth but prayed for cold. Without the former they would be too numb to compete; without the latter there could be no competition. The hockey fraternity wore roll-collar sweaters of thick wool, knitted for some teams by their female supporters. The dressing rooms, in otherwise-frigid natural-ice rinks, had to be heated, even if it meant teams bringing their own burlap sacks of coal for the stove. Body heat could be preserved by insulating apparel. And heat could be generated by combustive devices. But the requisite cold temperature to produce and preserve the playing surface was left to the whim of a mercurial Mother Nature — at least in Canada.

By the early 1890s covered rinks of natural ice had sprung up everywhere. Rink operators and hockey teams depended on consistently below-freezing temperatures for revenues and the completion of schedules. For the most part their needs were met, but rare was the winter when there was not a sudden thaw causing annoying postponements and cancellations. In warmer climes, mechanical refrigeration by means of vapour-compression heat transfer had been experimented with and successfully applied in the meat-packing and brewing industries. With varying degrees of success, artificial ice rinks began to appear in the polestar cities of New York and London in the 1870s, as well as in lesser British cities Manchester and Southport. Notable among these were the Southport rink, which saw ten years of service until 1889, and the 6,000-square-foot surface that opened in New York's Madison Square Garden in 1879.

46

Entrepreneurial Ottawa of the 1890s had certainly heard of mechanical refrigeration; but because the technology was expensive, largely experimental, and of limited application, area businessmen were in no hurry to embrace it. Refrigerators, such as the one patented by the Hanrahan brothers, who ran a butcher shop in the Wellington Ward market, used ice blocks as the cooling agent. Dairies, meat shops, brewers, hotels, and households relied on commercial ice dealers for the supply and delivery of blocks, which they cut from the rivers, insulated in sawdust packing, and stored in giant ice houses. As for the rinks, operators such as Edwin and William Dey simply accepted nature's rhythm, viewing hockey and skating as seasonal sports that inevitably followed football in the fall and preceded lacrosse and baseball in the spring. They saw no reason to prolong the ice sports artificially by expensive mechanical means and were prepared to accept the occasional mid-season mild spell.

The AHAC and Two New Leagues: Getting Ready for 1891

AS DECEMBER 1890 approached, Ottawa Hockey Club members had every reason to fall on their knees and pray for low temperatures, for the club was about to embark upon the most ambitious schedule in its short history. After an absence of three years, it would again compete in the premier association, the Montreal-based AHAC; it would take the lead in establishing Ottawa's first hockey league; and it would send a representative to Toronto to see about forming an Ontario league. The city, too, was readying itself for winter. Boats were being secured in preparation for the annual draining of the canal. The inside-folding double windows at Russell House were being positioned. And new information was being dispensed, advising citizens that to combat foul indoor air resulting from tightly sealed dwellings, they should cut openings through interior walls, thus allowing the bad air to be drawn into the chimney flue.

Bad air or not, just under twenty-five Hockey Club members filled the OAAC meeting room on November 19 to elect officers and arrange for a new season. Because captain Jenkins had seriously injured his leg during the summer and would not be able to play, the club simply agreed to reverse Jenkins' and Ross's duties. Jenkins would be president and Ross captain. It was a busy night. The club decided it was now well-enough established to re-enter the Amateur Hockey Association of Canada and seek a challenge match with the champion. It went farther, deciding to send a representative to a Toronto meeting called to organize an Ontario hockey association. Its delegate would be John Barron, member of Parliament for Lindsay and a hockey enthusiast who played alongside the Stanleys on vice-regal teams and was an active proselytizer of the game. Not content with a mere two associations, the meeting produced another resolution:

> That it is desirable a city league be formed, and that the Rideau Hockey Club, Ottawa College, Dey's Rink and the Rebel Club be invited to send two delegates each to meet two delegates from the Ottawa Hockey Club to discuss the proposed league; and that Messrs. Jenkins and Ross be the Ottawa delegates, and call the meeting as soon as convenient.

The club would continue to use the Rideau Rink as its home base, with practices on Mondays, Wednesdays, and Fridays between six and seven at night. The club would pay twenty dollars rent for the season, plus half of gross proceeds from matches, after advertising. Rink ticket-holders would be admitted free.

All that being settled, a feverish two weeks of activity lay ahead. In two meetings, proponents of the city league agreed on the entrants and on a tie-match system to determine a champion. Competing would be the Ottawa Hockey Club, the Rideaus, Ottawa College, Dey's Rink, and the Gladstones. The Rebels had second thoughts about the stiff competition they would face and decided against entering a team. Three elimination rounds would determine a champion, and that team would be subject to challenges from the other clubs. Each club was to pay three dollars to the league for the purchase of championship banners. In what was the first adoption by another league of the AHAC playing rules, the city league decided to apply the senior-circuit's code.

Meanwhile, Barron had gone to Toronto where he was to represent Ottawa Hockey Club interests at a meeting on November 27 to create an Ontario association. He was, in fact, one of the leading advocates of such a body, having experienced as a member of the vice-regal team the positive reaction to its visits the previous season to other centres in the province. The team had played in Kingston against a combined squad from Queen's University and Royal Military College, in Toronto against the prestigious Granite and St. George's clubs, and in his home town of Lindsay. The meeting at the Queen's Hotel brought together several of his friends and associates from those forays, and they promptly elected him chairman of the session. Two of these were vice-regal teammates, fellow member of Parliament Henry Ward of Port Hope and Arthur Stanley, both of whom were attending on behalf what was now becoming known as the Rebels. Also present were representatives of Royal Military College, Queen's University, St. George's Club, the Granite Club, the Athletic Lacrosse Club of Toronto, Osgoode Hall, the Victorias of Toronto, "C" Company School of Infantry, and the towns of Bowmanville and Lindsay. On the motion of Stanley and Ward, the meeting resolved that an Ontario hockey association should be organized. The assembly then elected Governor General Stanley of Preston, in absentia, as patron; A. Morgan Cosby, manager of the London and Ontario Investment Company and member of the Victoria Club, as president; and Barron and Ward as vice-presidents. Ross, who was not present but went to an OAAC dance that night, was nevertheless elected to the executive committee.

No sooner had Barron taken care of Ottawa Hockey Club business in Toronto on November 27 than the club dispatched Ed Grant to Montreal the next day for the annual meeting of the Amateur Hockey Association of Canada. It was patently clear to Ottawa that this was the top league and that the club's ultimate goal must be the AHAC championship. Achieving it would be no small feat. The powerful MAAA was the champion three years running, and there was no indication the winged wheels would not be just as strong in the coming season. The AHAC was Montreal-based, save for the occasional entry of teams from Quebec and Ottawa. The very name of the association caused some resentment elsewhere, but the objective of the founders had always been to welcome the participation of clubs from any part of the country where the game was competitively played. Indeed, one of the most discussed items on the agenda of its annual meetings was the scheduling of matches to accommodate outside teams. In years when Quebec and Ottawa did not enter, the AHAC asked why not; the same went for seasons in which Toronto showed no interest. Again at the 1890 meeting, in the rooms of the MAAA, the AHAC decided to apply the "challenge system," whereby there would be no regular schedule of games as in the "series system," but challenges issued by member clubs and accepted by the current champion in the order of receipt. Thus, a team from Ottawa or Quebec, or for that matter Toronto or Halifax if they joined, would be free to challenge the current champion in that club's home rink. A signal advantage of this system was that it relieved clubs of the costly travel obligation that a regular schedule of home-and-away games would entail. Ottawa still favoured the challenge system. Ed Grant came away from the Montreal meeting as the AHAC's first vice-president and reported to the Ottawas that in addition to themselves, the member clubs for the 1891 season would be the MAAA, the Victorias, the Crescents, and McGill, all from Montreal, and Quebec. A subsequent meeting of the AHAC council admitted the Shamrocks of Montreal.

Thus, in a matter of weeks, the Ottawa Hockey Club had gone from a forlorn group of enthusiasts seeking scratch matches wherever they could find them to a bona fide entrant in three leagues. If, indeed, the players had prayed for cold, their invocations were heard. In his report for the season, the club's honorary secretary-treasurer D'Arcy Scott wrote that from December 8 to March 20, "Practice was almost uninterrupted between these dates, showing an excellent season of three months and a half."

Albert Morel, the agile young goalkeeper for the Ottawa College team, certainly caught the eye of the Ottawas in the first elimination round of the city league. There is no record of Morel being in goal two weeks earlier in a practice match when the Ottawas trounced College 11-1. But on this evening he was very much in evidence, stopping, the *Journal* said, "dozens of hot shots" in his team's 3-1 loss. From that point on, Morel would be Ottawa's goalkeeper, too, in all matches played outside the city league.

With Morel between the posts, the Ottawas turned their attention to the AHAC, engaging in friendly matches against McGill and the Victorias at the Rideau Rink in preparation for a championship challenge they had issued and expected to play in February. They also had their first match in the Ontario elimination round, defeating the local Rideaus 5-0.

Ottawa City Championship: Downing the Deys

TWO DAYS LATER, Ottawa faced the Dey's Rink Pirates for the city championship. The winner of that match could then expect challenges from other city teams. Before a crowded rink, graced with the presence of the governor general, Lady Stanley, and a "large proportion of the fair sex," the two teams made for a striking visual contrast. The Ottawas took to the ice in their familiar white jerseys and knee breeches; the Pirates appeared in jet-black uniforms with white skull and crossbones on the breast of their shirts. Since this was a city match and Albert Morel was still a member of the College team in that league, he was ineligible to play for the Ottawas and was replaced by George Young. Frank, Ted, and Billy Dey, after whom the Dey brothers' rink was named, suited up for the Pirates. Indicative of the importance attached to this match, a Montreal referee, Fred Larmonth, was brought in to ensure unbiased rulings. The contest started out in rough fashion, but Larmonth was soon able to bring matters under control. The Ottawas held a wide margin of play, winning 3-0 and having three goals called back because of two fouls and an offside. The Ottawas could now, for the first time, call themselves champions. Make no mistake, they took this achievement seriously. But they also knew that as the most experienced team in the city they were fully expected to win. And, frankly, they had set their sights higher than that before the season ever started.

The AHAC Challenge: Good Sportsmanship All Round

AS EXPECTED, THE MAAAS were running rampant in the AHAC, the premier league in the country. The winged wheels had been champions for the three previous years and again this season had withstood all challenges, defeating the Victorias twice as well as the Shamrocks and the Crescents once. But Ottawa had also defeated the Victorias in a friendly match, giving the team from the capital reason for optimism. Ottawa had also defeated McGill in a friendly test, but that meant little because the college team, though a member of the association, was weak and wisely refrained from issuing challenges to the champions.

Hockey enthusiasts around the city knew very well the significance of their team's challenge to the MAAA, the most famous and successful club in all of hockey. The match was to be held on Saturday night, February 21, at the Crystal Rink in Montreal. Ottawa newspapers ran stories days ahead and the team's supporters could be assured of accounts of the outcome in the Monday editions, if, indeed, word did not spread before then. The Canadian Pacific Railway advertised a special excursion at $2.50 return. This was immediately matched by the Canada Atlantic Railway. The team would be traveling by CPR and advised friends and supporters to do likewise.

In the lineup for Ottawa were Morel in goal, Kerr at point, Weldy Young at coverpoint, and Kirby, his kid brother Chauncey, Ross, and C. Smith at the forward positions. The Montreal lineup was formidable: Tom Paton in goal, James Stewart at point, Allan Cameron at coverpoint, and "Bunny" Low, A. McNaughton, Alex Kingan, and J. Findlay playing forward. Paton was an exceptional goalkeeper of considerable experience, Stewart a defensive stalwart of many years standing. Up front, Kingan, Low, and McNaughton were noted scorers. Ottawa got off to a shaky start, giving up a goal after only thirty seconds. Once the Ottawas got their bearings, however, Paton was called upon to make many difficult saves for the Montrealers. In the second half, with the score still 1-0, the MAAAS began to demonstrate what had made them champions: brilliant combination play, with the whole forward line advancing down the ice as a unit. They scored twice more to put the game away and remain champions.

There was good sportsmanship all round, the teams having high praise for one another's work. "The Montreal passing was a revelation to the Ottawas," the *Ottawa Journal* reported, adding that Montreal thought "the Ottawas played the fastest forward game they had met this season." Five days earlier, as a goodwill gesture, the MAAA board had granted fifteen dollars to their team so that it might entertain the visitors with a dinner after the game in the Fencing Room at the MAAA headquarters. "A very enjoyable time was had," the *Journal* reported.

The Ontario Championship: Silver Cup, Red Ink

DISAPPOINTED THOUGH THEY WERE at having failed their ultimate test for the season, the players had little time to brood as they returned home on Sunday. There would be practice on Monday at 6 p.m., practice on Wednesday at 6 p.m., a city championship challenge on Thursday at 8 p.m., practice on Friday at 6 p.m., and a trip to Kingston on Saturday for an elimination-round match in the Ontario association.

The city championship challenge came from a gritty Ottawa College team. And Morel, who had played so capably for the Ottawas in Montreal, would be in the College goal. College's play was progressing noticeably well as the season unfolded, but they still could not match the power and experience of the Ottawa Hockey Club and succumbed by a nevertheless respectable score of 3-2.

Next up for the Ottawas was the Queen's University team in the Ontario series. With their victory over the Rideaus earlier and the default of the other team in the Ottawa grouping, the Rebels, Ottawa was advancing to the Ontario semi-final. Queen's had already beaten Kingston Athletics, Royal Military College, and the Kingston Hockey Club in the Kingston grouping, and had just defeated Lindsay. Ross and his teammates boarded the 11:35 a.m. train to Kingston, arrived just before five, freshened up, and had dinner at the British American Hotel. They hit the ice at 8 p.m. The plucky Queen's men fought hard, but like Ottawa College two nights earlier, the Kingston club could not withstand the speed of their opponents and lost the match 4-0. A tired Ottawa brigade, facing yet another practice on Monday evening, boarded the train to Ottawa after the game, and, as Ross ruefully notes in his diary, "engaged in changing cars most of night."

The Ottawas knew that on the following Saturday at the Rideau Rink they would be meeting the winners of the Toronto elimination round for the Ontario championship. But by Wednesday evening after practice, they still had not learned the identity of their adversary. Granite and the St. George's had advanced to the Toronto final and were to play the deciding match that same night. Unhappy that the association executive had selected the Victoria Rink for the contest instead of their own, Granite refused to play, thus defaulting the game. Call it resolute principle or just plain obstinacy, the decision to give up a chance at a championship simply because the club did not like the rink was puzzling. Hard though it may be to comprehend this stance, it was an all-too-common one in hockey's early days, not only in Toronto, but also in the hotbeds of Montreal and Ottawa.

So St. George's it would be. Ever the gracious host, and man about town that he was, Ross met the St. George's men on Saturday morning, took them down to the rink to see what it was like, and then escorted them to Rideau Hall for an at-home with the governor general. But the afternoon's warm hospitality soon gave way to the evening's cold reality of confrontation at the Rideau. The red cross of St. George emblazoned on the visitors' navy-blue jerseys elicited no mercy from the home team. Right from the bully, the Ottawas relentlessly attacked the St. George's end, and only Hurst's fine work in net prevented a goal. Near the close of the first half, though, Hurst mishandled Ross's flip shot from behind the goal, allowing the puck to dribble through the posts. Ottawa quickly scored two more goals, but the second was disallowed when officials discovered the puck had been put through more than a minute after halftime should have been called. In the second half, Hurst ran into more bad luck when the puck, being cleared with tremendous force by his point man, ricocheted off Ross's skate and shot back through the St. George's goal. Two more goals followed, giving the Ottawas a 5-0 victory and the first championship of the Ontario association. Satisfied with their work, Ross and his men were only too happy to revert to the role of gracious hosts by entertaining their felled opponents at dinner. The Ottawa Hockey Club did indeed exhibit great goodwill to their visitors. Not only did the club attend to the Toronto team before and after the game, it also guaranteed St. George's sixty dollars in travel expenses. Though, as reported in the Ottawa Hockey Club's annual report, the visitors "professed themselves very much pleased by their treatment here," they were not, as the Ottawas were soon to find out, about to reciprocate.

With the Ontario championship behind them, the Ottawas knew they would face one more challenge before a fast-approaching season's end. That would be from the Gladstones in the city league. But the date of the match was uncertain because Ottawa had already committed, weather permitting, to two friendly games in Toronto. By mid-week, however, it appeared the Toronto trip would be called off because the temperature there had turned too mild for ice to be maintained. Ross was therefore surprised to receive a telegram from the Ontario association secretary early on Friday afternoon advising him of a cold snap and saying his team was expected the next day for two matches, against St. George's in the afternoon and Osgoode Hall in the evening. Ross was never one to let work stand in the way of a good hockey game, but even for him the challenge of dropping everything, rescuing his team from their jobs, and leaving for Toronto in a matter of hours was daunting. Once again he put his influence and connections to the test. Here is how his own diary says he reacted: "Got hack and hustled round seeing men — got leave for Kirby from Piddington, leave from Burland for Young, and leave for Kerr from Northwood." Samuel Piddington was an accountant at the Quebec Bank and boss of clerk Chauncey Kirby. Samuel Burland was the president and general manager of the British American Bank Note Company, where Weldy Young was employed. And William Northwood was co-owner of hardware merchants McKinley and Northwood, who employed Kerr. The Toronto train pulled out at 10:45 p.m. with all men on board.

With one exception, the Toronto trip went well. The long-since eliminated "C" School of Infantry gave a luncheon for the Ottawas. The team had little difficulty defeating St. George's 4-0 at the Mutual Street Rink on Saturday afternoon, and Osgoode Hall 6-2 in the evening at the Victoria Rink. The Victoria Club, sponsors of the Victorias in the Ontario association, generously put on a supper after the game. Cosby, president of the Ontario Hockey Association, presented the Ontario Challenge Cup, won by the Ottawas the previous week, to club president Jenkins. Mounted on a tripod of hockey sticks, the silver cup bore an engraved representation of a hockey game on one side and on the other side the inscription "Championship of the Ontario Hockey Association, Challenge Cup, Won by the Ottawa H.C. 1891."

Especially in view of the cordial treatment the Ottawas received from several of the Queen City hockey clubs, it must have been grating for Ross and Jenkins to hit the one sour note they did in their Toronto excursion. St. George's, having received sixty dollars from Ottawa for their trip to the capital, reneged on their promise of twenty-five dollars to Ottawa for the return visit. St. George's later acknowledged the liability, but, according to the Ottawa Hockey Club annual report, "correspondence failed to produce any other result." A result of a much different sort, however, was to follow at the beginning of the next season.

Meanwhile, the Ottawas had one final chore. They attended to that the following week by disposing of the local Gladstones, who had been waiting in the wings with their city challenge. The city-championship banner and Ontario cup in their midst, the uniformed Ottawas and their dark-coated president present an image of supreme confidence in the Topley portrait taken at noon on Friday, March 21. The next day, in summing up the season, Ross's *Ottawa Journal* reported, "Matches won: thirteen, matches lost, one. Goals won, 56; goals lost, 11."

The on-ice numbers were impressive; the off-ice financial figures were not, showing a deficit of $70 on receipts of $51 and expenditures of $121. The difficulty was the rental agreement with the Rideau. The rink called for the club to pay, in addition to a flat twenty dollars for the season, half of the gross proceeds from games. But the club's expenses in putting the games on, principally guarantees to visiting teams, resulted in a net loss on matches. Added to the problem was the common practice at that time for rink operators to sell season tickets entitling holders to free entry for skating, hockey, and other events held in the premises. This meant lost gate potential for the hockey club, because it received no share from the rink's season-ticket revenues. Through their own personal contributions, however, captain Ross and president Jenkins covered the operating loss, thus allowing the club to enter the next season with no financial obligations.

Anatomy of a Season: Ottawa Hockey Club, 1890–91

THE 1890–91 SEASON WAS by far the most ambitious in the short history of the Ottawa Hockey Club, which a year earlier had come under the wing of the new Ottawa Amateur Athletic Club. With this solid organizational base, the club inspired the formation of the first Ottawa city league, joined in the move to create an Ontario league, and returned to competition in the challenge series of the AHAC. The players, all amateurs, had jobs or were students; but they found time to commit themselves to a demanding hockey regimen. Here is a day-by-day reconstruction of the team's 1890–91 activities beginning with the organizational meeting and concluding with a sitting for the team portrait at season's end.

Wed. Nov. 19
    annual meeting at OAAC
Tues. Nov. 25
    club convenes meeting at OAAC
    to form city league
Thurs. Nov. 27
    Barron represents club at
    founding meeting of Ontario
    Hockey Association (OHA) at
    Queen's Hotel, Toronto
Fri. Nov. 28
    Grant represents club at fourth
    annual AHAC meeting
    at MAAA
Wed. Dec. 3
    Ross represents club at OAAC
    meeting to draw up city-league
    schedule
Mon. Dec. 8
    first practice, 6 p.m. (all practices
    at Rideau Rink)
Wed. Dec. 10
    practice, 6 p.m.; club meeting
    follows
Fri. Dec. 12
    practice, 6 p.m.
Mon. Dec. 15
    practice, 6 p.m.

Wed. Dec. 17
    practice, 6 p.m.
Thurs. Dec. 18
    friendly match, second team (but
    with first-team prospects in lineup)
    vs. Ottawa College on College
    outdoor rink (**OHC 4**, College 1)
Fri. Dec. 19
    practice, 6 p.m.
Mon. Dec. 22
    practice, 6 p.m.
Wed. Dec. 24
    practice cancelled
Thurs. Dec. 26
    practice, 6 p.m.
Mon. Dec. 29
    practice, 6 p.m.
Tues. Dec. 30
    friendly match vs. Ottawa College
    at Rideau Rink (**OHC 11**, College 1)
Wed. Dec. 31
    practice, 6 p.m.
Fri. Jan. 2
    practice, 6 p.m.
Mon. Jan. 5
    practice, 6 p.m.
Wed. Jan. 7
    practice, 6 p.m.

Fri. Jan. 9
> practice, 6 p.m.

Mon. Jan. 12
> practice, 6 p.m.

Wed. Jan. 14
> first official match in city series vs.
> Ottawa College,
> 6 p.m. at Rideau Rink
> (**OHC 3**, College 2)

Thurs. Jan. 15
> Ross is club representative to
> city-league meeting at OAAC

Fri. Jan. 16
> practice, 6 p.m.

Sat. Jan. 17
> Ross to CPR station to meet
> McGill team; friendly match vs.
> McGill (AHAC), 8 p.m. at Rideau
> Rink (**OHC 2**, McGill 2)

Sun. Jan. 18
> Ross to CPR station to see McGill
> team off

Mon. Jan. 19
> practice, 6 p.m.

Wed. Jan. 21
> practice, 6 p.m.

Fri. Jan. 23
> practice, 6 p.m.

Mon. Jan. 26
> practice, 6 p.m.

Wed. Jan. 28
> practice, 6 p.m.

Fri. Jan. 30
> practice, 6 p.m.; later Ross and
> Kerr pick team for next match

Sat. Jan. 31
> friendly match vs. Victorias
> (AHAC), 8 p.m. at Rideau Rink
> (**OHC 1**, Victorias 0)

Mon. Feb. 2
> practice, 6 p.m.

Wed. Feb. 4
> practice, 6 p.m.

Thurs. Feb. 5
> first match in OHA series,
> 6 p.m. at Rideau Rink vs. Rideaus
> (**OHC 5**, Rideaus 0)

Fri. Feb. 6
> practice, 6 p.m.

Mon. Feb. 9
> friendly match, 6 p.m. at Rideau
> Rink vs. Rideaus (**OHC 4**, Rideaus 0)

Wed. Feb. 11
> city-championship match, 8 p.m.
> at Rideau Rink vs. Dey's Rink
> (**OHC 3**, Dey's 0)

Fri. Feb. 13
> practice, 6 p.m.

Mon. Feb. 16
> practice, 6 p.m.

Wed. Feb. 18
> practice, 6 p.m.

Fri. Feb. 20
> no practice, players prepare
> equipment for next match

Sat. Feb. 21
> leave by rail for Montreal, 11:40
> a.m.; AHAC championship challenge
> match vs. MAAA, 6:30 p.m. at
> Crystal Rink. (**MAAA 3**, OHC 0]

Sun. Feb. 22
> return to Ottawa by rail

Mon. Feb. 23
> practice, 6 p.m.

Wed. Feb. 25
> practice, 6 p.m.

Thurs. Feb. 26
> city-championship challenge from

Ottawa College, 8 p.m. at
Rideau Rink (**OHC 3**, College 2)

Fri. Feb. 27

practice, 6 p.m.

Sat. Feb. 28

leave by rail for Kingston,
11:35 a.m.; OHA tie match vs.
Queen's, 8 p.m. at Kingston Rink
(**OHC 4**, Queen's 0); leave by rail for
Ottawa, 11:30 p.m.

Mon. Mar. 2

practice, 6 p.m.

Wed. Mar. 4

practice, 6 p.m.

Fri. Mar. 6

practice, 6 p.m.

Sat. Mar. 7

Ross escorts Toronto St. George's
team to Rideau Hall for at-home
with governor general; OHA
championship final vs. St.
George's, 8 p.m. at Rideau Rink
(**OHC 5**, St. George's 0]

Mon. Mar. 9

friendly match, second team vs.
Gladstones at Dey's Rink
(**OHC 2nds 3**, Gladstones 1)

Tues. Mar. 10

practice, 10 p.m.

Wed. Mar. 11

friendly match, second team vs.
Ottawa College seconds, 6 p.m. at
Rideau Rink (**OHC 2nds 2**, College
2nds 1)

Fri. Mar. 13

leave by rail for Toronto, 10:45
p.m.

Sat. Mar. 14

arrive Toronto, 9 a.m.; guests at C

School of Infantry luncheon;
friendly match vs. St. George's, 4
p.m. at Mutual Street Rink (**OHC 4**,
St. George's 0); friendly match vs.
Osgoode Hall,
8 p.m. at Victoria Rink
(**OHC 6**, Osgoode Hall 0);
entertained at dinner by Victoria
Club and presented with Ontario
Challenge Cup

Sun. Mar. 15

leave for Ottawa by rail, 10:30
p.m.

Mon. Mar. 16

practice, 6 p.m.

Wed. Mar. 18

practice, 6 p.m.

Thurs. Mar. 19

practice, 1 p.m.

Fri. Mar. 20

final city-championship challenge
from Gladstones, 8 p.m. at Rideau
Rink
(**OHC 4**, Gladstones 0)

Fri. Mar. 27

to Topley photographers for team
portrait, noon

Sources: Ottawa Hockey Club annual
report, P.D. Ross diaries, and
newspaper accounts

OTTAWA HOCKEY CLUB FINANCIAL STATEMENT 1890–91

Receipts

Grant from OAAC	$30.00	
Member subscriptions	$21.00	
		$51.00

Expenditures

Net loss on matches	$58.86	
AHAC subscription	$10.00	
OHA subscription	$5.00	
Subscription to city league	$6.00*	
Rideau Rink, rent	$20.00	
Special rink tickets	$11.00	
Broken globes	$3.00	
Hockey pucks	$3.50	
Miscellaneous		
Secretary-treausurer's		
and captain's expenses	$4.25	
		$121.11
		$-51.00
Net deficit		$70.11

Audited, vouchers examined, and found correct.
H.S. Kirby & F.M.S. Jenkins.

*The acting treasurer notes in his report that the city league fee was three dollars but that the club paid also for the Gladstones, who refused to honour their commitment because of a difference with another team. The fees were for the purchase of a championship banner.

While travelling by tram in the dead of winter was undoubtedly more comfortable than its predecessor, horse-drawn carriage, winter service proved a challenge for the Ottawa Electric Railway. Hockey fans nonetheless piled into the cars, headed for the Rideau Rink. LIBRARY AND ARCHIVES CANADA PA8420

Ottawa Electric Railway: Getting There Was Half the Fun

THOMAS AHEARN AND WARREN SOPER, who had brought electric lighting to Ottawa and to the skating rinks seven years before, were now ready to bring spectators to hockey games. They had entered the mass-transit business and not a minute too soon for rink and hockey-club operators who saw the revenue potential of attracting large crowds to the games. But in January 1892 Ahearn and Soper's wondrous new Ottawa Electric Railway was having problems coping with its first winter. Ice on the rails disrupted service until work crews could be dispatched to clear it away. Soon, though, managers realized that if sweeper cars were sent out in inclement weather before snow and ice had a chance to accumulate, service could pretty much be maintained.

The two entrepreneurs had introduced electric street rail the previous summer in a splashy inaugural run out to the exhibition grounds. Four shiny new cars painted in orange and lemon yellow swayed along the track carrying a host of dignitaries: the mayor, cabinet ministers, the American consul general (who said the president of the United States himself wished he could be there), and, of course, the ubiquitous Ross. The cars were clean and comfortable: the seats were upholstered in English Wilton, the woodwork was of polished oak, the fittings of burnished brass. The cars had electric lighting and there was provision for heaters to be inserted between the seats on one side when winter came. The electric cars were a far cry from the now-outmoded horse-drawn service, especially in winter when the Ottawa City Passenger Railway trams had to be replaced by slow, cumbersome, and dirty sleighs. In fact, Ahearn and Soper bought that firm when they laid down their own tracks and immediately commenced phasing it out.

The railway did not bring passengers right to the Rideau Rink's door, but conveniently close. And the success of the Ottawa Hockey Club meant that more people than ever before wanted to go through that door. Not everyone could or was inclined to. The sport still appealed largely to the English middle and upper classes, those who could afford rink season tickets or game tickets and who felt at ease in the sort of milieu that regularly attracted the vice-regal set. Take, for example, the main-line car leaving its terminus at the CPR depot at LeBreton Flats. Few from that community of largely French and Irish millhands and labourers would be jumping aboard and heading for the rink. Coming off Broad Street, the car would swing east along Queen Street West and onto Albert. Reaching the upper town, it would stop at Bay Street, where hockey enthusiasts from the commercial, professional, and civil-service ranks would board. After heading to Metcalfe, north to Wellington, and down onto Rideau Street, the car would stop at Waller where passengers would get off, pull up their coat collars, and hike five minutes south to the rink.

More spectators would come in on the car from New Edinburgh. Their neighbour, Lord Kilcoursie, would not be among the civil-service clerks, topographical-survey draftsmen, insurance agents, and tradesmen trundling west on St. Patrick, south on Dalhousie, and west again on Rideau. The governor general's aide-de-camp would instead be well-bundled in a Government House sleigh leaving Rideau Hall with just enough time to reach the rink as the puck was about to be faced.

Florist Charles Scrim and his neighbours in the fast-developing Catherine-Bank area in the southern reaches of town were fortunate. They had a choice of the Bank car to Wellington via Albert and Metcalfe, or the car going north on Elgin to Wellington. If taking the latter line, passengers had the further choice of disembarking at Maria and walking east to Theodore, about six minutes, or continuing to Wellington and transferring to any car going east. Ahearn and Soper did not yet reach into the wealthy enclave of Sandy Hill. But not to worry, senior civil servants and professional people, such as Sandford Fleming, thought nothing of hiring a cab or having the stableman hitch up the horse and cutter.

Boatbuilder Joseph Dey and his sons, who operated the Rideau Rink's most serious competition, Dey's Skating Rink, lived right across the street from the Rideau. So did Reynolds Wrightson, city editor of the *Free Press*. Under-Secretary of State Ludger Catellier was around the corner.

Champions of Canada, For a Few Weeks

ENTERING THE 1892 SEASON, the Ottawas had only one thing on their mind: the AHAC championship. The club took no serious interest in local competition, so, unlike the previous year, made no attempt to organize a city league. The OHA, they knew, would give them reasonable competition, keep them sharp for AHAC contests. But there would only be a couple of games in that series because the OHA executive had decided to stick with the regional elimination, or tie, system. Ottawa had asked for the challenge system. The reason was easy to see. As champions, the Ottawas would have played lucrative challenge matches in their home rink. Several could have been expected, because they were sure no team was strong enough to take the title from them. Under either format, one thing was certain: the Ottawas would not have to worry about St. George's again reneging on their travel-expenses commitment. The OHA executive expelled them from the association after Ottawa's complaint at the November 30 annual meeting in Toronto.

Two days later in Montreal, Ottawa's Jenkins successfully pressed the AHAC at its annual meeting to retain the challenge system, in place since 1889 but lately undergoing a challenge of its own by clubs that wanted a regular schedule of games. Ottawa was annoyed the previous year when its challenge, sent in quite early, was not acted on until late in the season. This time the challenge was accepted with such promptness that the Ottawa players were taken off guard. They had had only two practices when they received word on January 4 that they were to present themselves at the Crystal Rink four days later to meet the reigning champions, the MAAA.

Frank Jenkins, wearing a dark coat and surrounded by his team, was president of the Ottawa Hockey Club when it won the Ontario championship in 1891. This team portrait was taken at the close of that successful, ambitious season.
LIBRARY AND ARCHIVES CANADA PA79289

"Champions of Canada," proclaimed the *Ottawa Journal* headline January 9, "Ottawa's Hockey Team Defeat Montreal 4 to 3." Hockey reporting, always colourful, was by the 1890s becoming crisper. Unlike the early days when readers were forced to plow through a long sequential account to find out the winner and score, a pyramid style of reporting was emerging that conveyed the essentials at the top and filled in the details later. Here is the *Journal's* lead paragraph in the story covering that seminal match:

> For the first time in four years the famous MAAA hockey team met a reverse last night, when the Ottawas defeated it by four goals to three and won the championship of Canada. The match was desperately contested. The score was three each at the call of time and the teams were then called on by the referee to play until one or other won another game, which the Ottawas did after a fierce ten minutes contest.

The writer was likely the *Journal's* owner and a former sports and pastimes reporter, Ross. No longer a player on the Ottawas, he had, we know from his diary, gone down for the game and had met Montreal family members at the rink. The match was indeed "desperately contested," with the MAAA taking the lead, then Ottawa, then the MAAA tying it with but ninety seconds remaining in regulation time. Twice the Montrealers demanded replacement of the goal umpire when rulings went against them, and twice the referee acceded. Kerr, in his ninth season with the Ottawas, ended it in extra time with his second goal of the match. Champions they were. "The Ottawas and their friends whooped and shrieked and embraced each other," the *Journal* reported cheerfully. The *Montreal Gazette,* fair in its coverage, was more subdued: "From a hockey point of view it was not a good game, not anything like the style of game that will be played a month from now." Perhaps, but not in Montreal, for the Crystal contest would prove to be the only championship match held in the metropolis that season.

It was now up to the Ottawas to defend their new title, which they would be obliged to do at approximately weekly intervals. But at their own rink. Large crowds could be expected, a fact surely not lost on railway men Ahearn and Soper. Financially, the hockey club and the rink stood to gain the most. The rink guaranteed the club forty-five dollars per match, about 15 per cent of the average gross. This left enough for the operator to look after expenses, including guarantees to visiting clubs, and to pocket a profit. For the money to keep coming in, though, the Ottawas would have to keep winning. A single defeat would mean the immediate loss of the title and the forfeit of further home dates until such time as the club might regain the championship in the rink of a subsequent title-holder. To the immense satisfaction of all concerned, the Ottawas did keep winning; hockey crowds in greater numbers than ever before seen in the city swarmed to the Rideau to witness the prowess of the local senior club. In one match, the crush of people was so great that some were squeezed right off the concourse and onto the unfenced ice while play was still on. Officials stopped the match for several minutes "to give the immigrants," the *Journal* said, "a chance to repatriate themselves on the promenade."

From mid-January to mid-February, the Ottawas withstood five challenges, one from the Shamrocks of Montreal and two each from the MAAA and Quebec. Surprisingly it was the inexperienced Quebec team that gave Ottawa the most trouble. Even the Ottawa audience, usually hostile toward visiting clubs, seemed appreciative of Quebec's pluck in its 4-3 loss, after ninety minutes of extra time, and in its 2-0 defeat two weeks later. Especially popular among the visitors was Herb Scott, who flew about the rink with a pink handkerchief around his head. The MAAAS were an entirely different story. They showed little resistance in the first match and the crowd showed them no mercy. It was expected the Montrealers would put up a tough fight. They weren't used to losing and they liked it not one bit. In the first contest, a rink packed with hooting and jeering partisans howled with delight at every MAAA misfortune. And there were plenty. Ottawa trounced the ex-champions 10-3. It mattered not to Ottawa supporters that the visitors were without several of their key players. One of those was goalkeeper Tom Paton, prevented by a business appointment from accompanying the team. His place was taken by Harry Shaw, the club's secretary-treasurer. The hapless substitute's only previous experience was as a last-minute replacement for the other team in an MAAA friendly. In their second challenge a few weeks later, the winged wheels showed better form but lost again, 3-1. The Ottawas had now won six consecutive AHAC championship matches and were rightfully seen as hockey's new powerhouse.

Ontario Champions Again: Pausing for the Cosby Cup

A final AHAC challenge awaited Ottawa. First, though, was the small matter of defending the OHA championship and the Cosby Cup. Queen's University had won its tie matches in the Kingston series and was ready to face Ottawa for the right to meet the survivor of the Toronto series for the title. Sensing the OHA to be a secondary league, only a few hundred spectators showed up at the Rideau. Ottawa easily disposed of the university men, 5-0. Then word came that Ottawa's opponent in the final match would be Osgoode Hall. Fearing bad ice for the March 2 date, Ottawa offered to pay the Toronto team $125 to come to the capital instead. The offer was refused, so after a warm-up against the Rebels, the Ottawas headed for Toronto, annoyed that no decision had been conveyed to them on who the referee would be. The Ontario champions had little difficulty in handing Osgoode Hall, dubbed the "legality rushers" by a peppy Toronto press, a 10-4 drubbing. After a pause for refreshments with their hosts, the Ottawa seven went straight to the North Toronto station to catch the CPR overnight train for home. They would be meeting the MAAAS in five days.

Canadian Champions No More: The MAAA settles accounts

KIRBY AND KERR HAD EVERY REASON to reflect on how far they and their hockey club had come since the day nine years earlier when, on the St. Lawrence River, they stood in fascination as Montreal's first hockey tournament unfolded before them. They had never before seen the game played in any sort of organized fashion. They vowed then and there they would start a club in Ottawa. Now their club was the champion of Canada. If they could win this last match, the title would be theirs for the year. What better way to end the season? With a touch of nostalgia, they might have reflected, too, on their being the only remaining members of the city's first rep team. But reverie would have to be set aside. With their teammates, they would have to focus on the challenge ahead, not on satisfactions of the past.

Around town, anticipation was building. Newspapers carried advertisements for the "Grand Championship Match." Seats downstairs at the south end of the rink and in the gallery could be reserved for fifty cents at Nordheimer's piano shop, Orme's pianos and organs, and Durie's booksellers, all on Sparks Street, or at the rink. General admission was twenty-five cents. A special excursion train would be coming in from Montreal and on board would be a goodly number of "sporting men," a quaint euphemism for gamblers. They could be expected to gather at the Russell House, the city's traditional betting centre. Also on the train would be members of the MAAA board of directors. In an unprecedented move, the directors, always fastidious about the regular scheduling of meetings, had postponed the one coinciding with the date of the big game, Monday, March 7. They would ponder association management questions on the Tuesday instead. Millionaire lumber magnate J.R. Booth, a great hockey supporter, had earlier decided to present medals to team members for the successes they had already achieved that season. The ceremony, it was announced in Monday's papers, was to take place the next evening at the Lacrosse Club concert at the opera house. The citizenry, in anticipation of a final championship victory, expected the occasion to be doubly joyous. For the Ottawas, the pressure was on. Was this another example of the "good fun" the founding members had foreseen?

There was pressure of another kind. Unseasonably mild weather had set in several days before. Snow was melting and wheeled vehicles were beginning to replace sleighs on streets quickly becoming bare. That suited

Ahearn and Soper fine. Free of the possibility of ice-covered rails, they had arranged for three of their electric cars to meet the Montreal excursionists at the Canada Atlantic Railway depot and take them up to the Russell House. The same cars would be waiting to take them back to the station after the game. The balmy breezes coming in from the northwest did not, however, suit the Rideau rink fine. Monday's temperature had reached forty-one degrees Fahrenheit in the shade, not a good situation for ice-maintenance men who had no acquaintance with that distant marvel, mechanical refrigeration. By early afternoon, a layer of water covered the ice. The men opened the drain to run it off. They spread snow over what was left to soak it up and then ploughed the heavy mixture off. Knowing there would be a tremendous heat build-up from the big crowd, they tried to open the roof windows to vent the warm air, only to find they had been battened down for the winter. There was nothing more they could do. Though soft and wet, the ice could be skated on and the game would be played. But where were the MAAAS? The crowd filled the rink to capacity long before the appointed time of eight o'clock, but the challengers, delayed along the way, did not put in an appearance for another half-hour.

Finally the match got under way. For the Ottawas, Morel was in goal, Russell at point, Weldy Young at coverpoint, and Halder Kirby, Chauncey Kirby, Reg Bradley, and Kerr at the forward positions. The MAAAS' lineup was a familiar one: Paton in goal, Stewart at point, Allan Cameron at coverpoint, and McNaughton, Hodgson, Bunny Low, and Kingan playing forward. In their reports, the *Montreal Gazette* and the *Ottawa Journal* agreed that these were indeed the lineups. They also agreed that the ice was in bad shape and that the game was rough. Beyond those points, the two papers seemed to be covering two completely different contests. The only goal of the match, by MAAA's Hodgson, was, in the eyes of the *Journal*, a "lucky lift." To the *Gazette* it was a "well directed shot." To the *Journal*, the stoppages in play during the first half, when one Montrealer was shaken up and another had his skate lace broken, were too long and gave the visitors an unfair chance to rest. The *Gazette* took little note. The *Journal* continued its theme of too much breathing time for the MAAAS, saying the half-time break lasted sixteen minutes. It was the standard ten-minute break, the *Gazette* said. When Kingan broke his skate, the *Journal* timed the delay at fifteen minutes. To the *Gazette*, it was nothing more than "a delay of some minutes." In a later article, the *Gazette* added that beyond these mishaps, "there was not an extra moment lost." Was the officiating good or bad? The *Journal*: "A referee is needed who has the courage and knowledge of the game to stop tripping." The *Gazette*: "Jack Arnton made an excellent referee." The Ottawa paper talked about the Ottawa supporters, the Montreal paper about the Montreal supporters. "The big audience," the *Journal* observed, "dispersed in a depressed mood, not because their pets were beaten, but because they knew they should have won." The *Gazette*'s attention was elsewhere: "The Montrealers went wild with excitement over the victory, and the members of the team had many compliments showered on them." The paper concluded: "They returned home at 11 o'clock, one of the jolliest excursion parties that ever left the Capital." The inter-city journalistic wrangling continued for a few days, but one fact remained: the MAAA had wrested the "championship of Canada" from a previously undefeated club. In a perfectly accurate summation, the *Gazette*, with some relish, observed: "The Ottawas now get back some of their own medicine. They did not want a series; they wanted a challenge system and they got it."

The Ottawas were nevertheless showered with attention: Booth's medals; monogrammed silk handkerchiefs from haberdasher M.M. Pyke; a promise of initialled jerseys from the ladies of the Rideau Skating Club; gold lockets bearing the club's monogram from the directors of the Rideau Rink; a dinner in their honour at the Russell House tendered by the Ottawa Amateur Athletic Club (to which Chauncey Kirby, in thanking the assembly, gave his oration while mounted on a table); and individual trophies from the Amateur Hockey Association of Canada for having won the greatest number of matches during the season. This last memento was bittersweet. They won the championship in their first game, as a challenge; they successfully defended the title five times; and they lost the championship in the last game, to the club they had defeated three times. It was six wins, one loss for the Ottawas; one win, three losses for the MAAAs. Something would have to be done.

5 · A City and Its Team

A handsome addition has been made
to the furniture of our Reading Room by our Hockey Club
presenting us with the magnificent clock
won by them at the Bazaar popularity voting contest.
OTTAWA AMATEUR ATHLETIC CLUB
Annual Report, 1894–95

A FEELING OF EXASPERATION lingered in the minds of the Ottawa players through the summer of 1892. They could not help but dwell on the injustice of a championship system that had denied them the title on the basis of one loss while allowing a team that had won only once to claim the prize. The Ottawas were determined to change things, and this they did at the next annual meeting of the AHAC.

Ottawa delegates Halder Kirby, Bert Russell, and Weldy Young even had the backing of league secretary J.A. Findlay when they went into the December 15 meeting in Montreal. Reading out the results of the previous season's contests, secretary Findlay said, "I would urge the adoption of the series system in place of the challenge, as a glance at the above will show the want of fairness, the Ottawa Hockey Club having won all but the last match, still they are not champions." By reverting to a regular schedule of games (home and home among all teams) that was last tried in 1888, the league was ensuring that truly the strongest team over the course of the season would emerge as champion.

The Capital at the End of an Era

IT WOULD BE ANOTHER eleven years before the Ottawas would capture hockey's ultimate title. The decade would witness the beginning of Wilfrid Laurier's political reign over country and the conclusion of Queen Victoria's reign over the British Empire. Victoria's death in January 1901 elicited a flood of public and state emotion. Thirty thousand yards of black cloth draped Parliament and government offices across the country. Many scheduled events, especially amusements, in the days leading up to the funeral were cancelled out of respect for the passing of a beloved monarch. In Ottawa on funeral day, department stores remained closed; the OHA postponed all matches on that Saturday; the Ottawa Hockey Club played its game against Montreal, but only because the two teams could not agree on a suitable substitute date. As if putting an end to the gloom of the past several days, the largest crowd of the season cheered the Ottawa victory lustily. In a small twist of irony, another hockey event that week took absolutely no notice of the grieving. It was a two-game series in Montreal to decide the holder of a Dominion championship cup donated eight years earlier by Victoria's personal representative in Canada, Lord Stanley of Preston. Press accounts of the games, detailed as they were, made no mention of any on- or off-ice gesture in recognition of the queen's death. The club wresting the cup from the Shamrocks of Montreal was the Winnipeg Victorias.

Ottawa at that time was, in the words of historian John H. Taylor, "the centre of government, but the periphery of nearly everything else." *Ottawa Journal* publisher P.D. Ross went further. Canada, he observed in 1899, was "the suburbs of civilization." Taylor's comment is grounded in business reality, Ross's in the cultural landscape.

The lumber industry, which had been hit hard by competition from the western United States, was beginning to look up again in the early nineties. California red pine, it was found, tended to warp and fell out of favour in the big American market. Since Canadian white pine did not warp, Ottawa-area mills experienced a boom. But lumber production, which hit its peak in 1896, went into steep decline in the years following. The great fire of 1900, which levelled much of the western portion of the city, destroyed most of the mills and the vast lumber piles surrounding them. And dreams of Ottawa becoming a railway hub never materialized. Added to these factors, as Taylor points out, was the inability of hydro-electric power from the Chaudière Falls, where the city enjoyed a natural advantage, to meet its production potential because of a weak industrial base.

Throughout the period, the seasonal nature of the lumber industry created hardship for sawmill workers. By November each year, about four-fifths of that workforce were laid off. Some, the "shantymen," went up to the bush to cut the forests. Others stayed home and out of work, surviving on bare necessities purchased from meagre savings from their summer wages. By 1898, however, the shantymen were disappearing from the local scene.

Lamenting their passing, the *Ottawa Journal* offered a street-level view of this colourful group and the effect of their reduced numbers on the economy. "The shantyman is passing from Ottawa, and every year fewer and fewer of these picturesque French-Canadian people are seen in the capital." Hundreds used to come back every spring, wearing "the regulation wide-brimmed hat or else the habitant toque, bright color shirts, heavy knicker-bockers, thick, fancy-colored stockings, and spiked boots." Putting off this garb, they would spend liberally for neat black suits, furnishings, and footwear. The Lowertown hotels, which had done very well from the shantymen's patronage, felt the pinch. Some, the *Journal* predicted, would have to close up.

It was the death of poet Archibald Lampman that moved Ross to make his provocative but thoughtful editorial comment about Canada being the suburbs of civilization. Only through "ill fortune" could a man of Lampman's creative genius be born into a land "raw, rough and mainly unbroken." Hardly an environment for intellectual nourishment. Ross, the old hockey man, was a keen observer of his times: "It is the land of the engineer, the railway promoter, the contractor, the hard-headed practical man. There is no leisure, little culture." Literally and figuratively, Ross captured the cacophony of the day. "However sweet the voice of the singer, it is scarce heard amid the roar of steam whistles, the grunt of engines or clang of hammers, the clatter of business and buzz of politics." Among the mourners at the Confederation poet's funeral was Lampman's brother-in-law Frank Jenkins, founding captain of the Ottawa Hockey Club.

Lampman's Ottawa was not quite as culturally barren as Ross would have us believe. True, Ottawa was alone among major centres in not having a free public library. But there was a parliamentary library rich in resources. And Stanley Cup trustees Ross and John Sweetland were behind a movement to have city council create a free library. The Ottawa Amateur Orchestral Society, founded by Jenkins, was in full swing, as was the Schubert Club choral group, also organized by the former hockey player. Harmony Hall and the opera house were favoured venues for cultural performances prior to the opening of the grand Russell Theatre in 1897.

The social whirl of the privileged classes may have been every bit as colourful as the spontaneous shindigs of Lowertown's shantymen; but these woodcutters, sequestered in the bush all winter, would have had no idea of the season's festivities in the city. Much of the gaiety surrounded hockey. Vice-regal parties frequently attended Ottawa Hockey Club matches, but so intertwined were high-flown social occasions with the fate of the hockeyists that Lord Stanley, concerned that an Ottawas match would conflict with a governor general's "drawing room" he was organizing, thought nothing of asking the club to reschedule the match. Guests, also upset about the conflict, sought merely to have the start of the game delayed so they could partake of both. Ottawa management tried to accommodate the socialites but were unsuccessful in rescheduling the January 1893 meeting with the Montreal Victorias. The club did, though, start the game an hour later than originally advertised.

The *Journal*'s cheeky society gossip column, variously penned by "Suzie," "Trix," and "Lillian," frequently alluded to hockey. Trix observed at the end of the 1893 season that there were "little spasmodic outbreaks of hockey during the week, with positively its last appearance at the Rideau rink last night, but the enthusiasm was snuffed out after the Montreal match and except as opportunities for informal adjournments to supper here and there, the games should have few spectators." Under the heading "Socialites as we Know Them," Lillian told her readers of a hockey party at the Victoria Chambers following an 1894 Ottawa-Quebec match. The young ladies attending, most named in the column, were chaperoned by Mrs. Thomas Bate. They, with the young gentlemen escorting them, had "occupied reserved seats en group at the rink." In her *Free Press* column, "Erminie" went on a bit about a visiting Winnipeg club, "a fine looking team" who commanded "many well wishers in the crowd of spectators." The clearly enchanted reporter noted that "there was a supper party of about twenty-five at the residence of Sandford Fleming afterwards, which made, for those who were at it, a charming ending of a very pleasant evening."

Winter was a season to be looked forward to. Outdoor activities abounded. In their enthusiasm to get an early start, however, Ottawans all too often skated on thin ice. Perhaps emulating the vaunted Ottawa Hockey Club, who were known to get in a few preliminary practices on Patterson's Creek in late November, hundreds of residents would take to the lightly frozen surfaces of the canal and the Rideau River well before the middle of December. In late November 1895, the *Journal* reported ominously "the first of the skating fatalities of the season." It was accepted that more would follow. A young Lowertown boy had gone through on the Rideau River at twilight. Detailing the gruesome search, the paper, by press deadline, could report only that the river was dragged with grappling hooks until nine o'clock without result. The *Journal*, astonishingly cavalier in its attitude toward the potential dangers of early-season skating, blissfully informed readers the next day that, "The skating in many places of the Rideau River is excellent and the fine moonlight last evening led a number of skaters of both sexes to stay out rather late."

Ross's diary entry for Friday, December 6, 1901, casually notes, "at 3 p.m. out on Ottawa (river) for an hour or two. Down to Kettle Island. Nicholson fell through ice." No mention that Ross, by hauling him out, had saved the boy from drowning. At about the same hour, in an unrelated incident, real-estate agent J.M. Cromwell also went through, and also survived. Bessie Blair and Henry Harper were not so fortunate. Remarkably, they were on the same ice that afternoon, as part of a skating party that included Alex Creelman and Jeannie Snowball. Bessie Blair was the daughter of the minister of railways and canals, Andrew Blair. Harper was the associate editor of the government's *Labour Gazette*, under Deputy Minister Mackenzie King. Jeannie was the daughter of New Brunswick senator Jabez Snowball. Creelman, an accountant in the Imperial Bank, was vice-president of the local Bankers Hockey Association, and two years earlier had been president of the OHA. Late in the darkened afternoon, skating together near Kettle Island, Blair and Creelman suddenly plunged into a stretch of open water. Ignoring Creelman's cry, "For god's sake, Harper, don't you come in too!" Harper jumped in, in a futile rescue attempt. Creelman managed to get out, but the swift current swept Harper and Blair under the ice. Coincidentally, Lord and Lady Minto and a sizable viceregal party had also been on the ice at nearly the same time, and two of their party had broken through, but into shallow water. So close were the two groups that Blair's sister May and another skater, who were lagging behind the Mintos, arrived at the scene of the tragedy in the midst of the frantic rescue attempt.

The drownings were a sensation. Prime Minister Laurier and the city's elite attended Blair's elaborate funeral. The funeral for Harper was more subdued; but at the regular Sunday service at St. Andrews Church, all stood in silent reverence as organist Jenkins rendered Chopin's *Prelude in B Minor*. A bronze statue, *Sir Galahad*, commemorates Harper's valour and can be seen today on Wellington Street in front of Parliament. An interesting footnote illustrates Ross's ubiquitous presence. Though Mackenzie King is credited with conceiving the idea of having a monument to his associate and dear friend, it was the former hockey player who chaired the committee to raise the necessary funds.

The Hockey Associations: 'Win, tie or wrangle'

IN EVER-INCREASING NUMBERS through the 1890s, citizens of the capital thrilled to the spectacle of Canada's royal winter game. Between 1891 and 1894, the Ottawa Hockey Club was in the unique position of competing in the senior divisions of both dominant hockey bodies in Canada. These were the Montreal-based AHAC, founded in 1886, and the Toronto-centred OHA, established in 1890. The associations were run in a strictly voluntary capacity by men who belonged to prominent athletic clubs and were well established in business. They had the know-how to create structured organizations with printed constitutions and playing rules, executive committees, annual meetings, and secretarial and financial records. (A fire that swept through the offices of the AHAC secretary's employer in 1896 claimed all of the association's files, forcing the secretary to construct his report to the annual meeting, one week later, completely from memory.) AHAC and OHA executives, in the time available to them away from their jobs and businesses, faced increasing complexities in managing their leagues' affairs. There was a constant need to refine hockey's rules because of the progressively sophisticated level of play. There was the issue of expanding the number of member clubs, brought on by the exploding popularity of the game. Schedules were drawn up at gruelling late-night sessions, often held right after the adjournment of the annual meeting. And there were other administrative chores, such as allocating travel expenses and scheduling Stanley Cup matches. Added to these were the not-so-routine and highly charged meetings to decide game protests submitted by disgruntled losers.

Executive bodies were made up of representatives of member clubs, which composition would occasionally see a delegate faced with a conflict of interest between his commitment to his own club and the best interests of the association. On the whole, though, and in keeping with the ideals of amateur sportsmanship, fairness and principled judgement prevailed. This did not mean the associations were free of management disputes. One such rift in the OHA, involving the Ottawas, came to a head in February 1894. It had started a year earlier when the league executive abruptly informed Queen's University and the Ottawas that they would have to play their semi-final elimination-round game in Toronto rather than in the home town of either of the participating teams. The two clubs thought the decision had no other purpose than to ensure a lucrative gate in Toronto at their expense. When they flatly refused, the association executive relented and allowed the match to take place in Kingston, with Ottawa's travel expenses paid. Ottawa won the elimination game but were a little put out when the Toronto semi-finalists, the Granites, defaulted the championship match, which was to be played in Ottawa at the Rideau Rink.

Ottawa's wariness of the Toronto power structure was borne out at the following season's organizational meeting when an all-Toronto group of officers was elected, and, with the exception of an ex-Toronto player who had moved to Hamilton, no one from outside the Queen City was put on the executive committee. Newspapers fuelled the issue. The *Hamilton Times*, as reported by the *Ottawa Journal*, noted how the "Toronto Hoggy Association" had "gobbled up all the officers at the recent annual meeting."

As in the previous season, Ottawa was to play Queen's in the 1894 elimination round, but this time it was to be a two-game, total-goal, home-and-home series. After the first game in Ottawa, which Ottawa won, the association notified the two teams that the winner would be required to play the Toronto winner in Toronto on Saturday, February 24. Based on their previous successes against Queen's, the Ottawas anticipated advancing to the final. They also expected to play that match at home because they were the reigning champions. For Ottawa, the order from Toronto was the last straw: the executive and players wanted nothing more to do with the OHA and resigned immediately. To Ottawa, it was a case of the Toronto contingent wanting everything their own way. The OHA executive had a different perspective. They sensed that the Ottawa club did not really care very much about the provincial association, that the Ottawas were more interested in national AHAC competition. This perception was accurate. Their local profile in the AHAC was sky high, and crowds for those matches were always their biggest. Moreover, the Ottawas, like most knowledgeable hockey observers, regarded the AHAC as Canada's premier league. The view of the OHA executive that Ottawa was finding it difficult to maintain commitments to two leagues may have had some truth to it. At the same time, Toronto clubs did not like coming to Ottawa and were tired of Ottawa being the perennial champions. But the OHA forced Ottawa's hand. Since the AHAC schedule had been published more than two months earlier, the OHA executive knew very well that Ottawa was scheduled to play Montreal on February 24, the date the Ontario executive chose for their league's championship match. Ottawa had no alternative but to resign, and this resolution of the conflict was to everyone's satisfaction. The Ottawa Hockey Club had outgrown the OHA and had shaken itself loose; the Toronto clubs had rid themselves of their formidable opponent from the distant capital.

A small incident concluded the affair. The Ontario championship Cosby Cup had been in Ottawa's possession for three years. In keeping with a general practice at the time whereby clubs winning a trophy three years in succession were given permanent possession of it, the Ottawas made no effort to send the cup back after quitting the association. Only when the OHA executive specifically requested its return did they do so. The club's annual report reveals that the cup's donor, A. Morgan Cosby, offered a substitute trophy in recognition of the team's victories; but the club committee, while grateful of the offer, "thought best not to accept."

Four years later, in 1898, the Ottawas figured in another dispute, and of even greater consequence, this time involving their preferred league, the AHAC. Two seasons earlier, the newly formed Capital Athletic Association, a rival of the Ottawa Amateur Athletic Club, had decided to form a hockey team, the Capitals, and to apply for entry into the AHAC senior series. The Ottawas didn't like the idea, believing that the existence of two senior teams would dilute the talent available and leave the city with two weak entries. The AHAC, however, turned down the Capitals' application, pointing to a clause in the constitution requiring any new entrant in the senior series to win the intermediate title first.

The AHAC's annual meeting in December 1898 considered a new application from the Capitals, who by then had entered the intermediate series and had won the title. This time they were at least qualified to apply but had another hurdle: the unanimous approval of existing clubs, as required by the constitution. The delegates to the meeting consisted of the association executive, plus representatives from all the clubs in both the senior and intermediate divisions. The intermediate delegates outnumbered the senior. The Shamrocks, who had a team in the senior series and who favoured the Capitals' application, moved a motion to amend the constitution so that only a majority of votes would be required to allow entry of a new team. Following some complaining about voting procedures, the motion was carried. The next step was a motion to admit the new team. Ottawa delegate J. P. Dickson, while acknowledging the "brilliancy" of the Capitals' play in the intermediate series, spoke against their inclusion in the senior circuit on the grounds that there would be too many games. "We have eight matches to play now, and that would make ten in nine weeks." Quebec, the MAAA, and the Victorias spoke similarly, complaining the schedule would require mid-week travel to Ottawa and it would be impossible to find enough players able to get away. Four of the five senior clubs were thus lined up against the inclusion of the Capitals, but the motion nevertheless carried because the intermediate clubs were in favour. The tail was wagging the dog, the newspapers declared, arguing that it did not seem right that the senior clubs should be overruled on who should compete in their own division. The rationale voiced for admitting the Capitals seemed honourable enough — giving encouragement to intermediate teams, in line with the Association's stated objective of furthering the interests of hockey. But there was a suspicion that, below the surface, the real reason why the intermediates favoured the Capitals was to get rid of them. The Capitals were too powerful, and the expenses of travelling to Ottawa were too great for intermediate teams to bear.

Immediately after the vote, Quebec, Victoria, and Ottawa spokesmen stood in turn and announced their clubs' resignation from the association. The meeting chairman, from the MAAA, asked the secessionists if they would reconsider and, hearing their refusal, promptly announced his own club's withdrawal. The delegates of the four clubs then gathered their papers, left the room, proceeded to the Windsor Hotel, and formed a new association. Remaining at the AHAC meeting, stunned, were six intermediate clubs and the two remaining seniors: the Shamrocks and the newly elected Capitals. If the motives of the intermediate clubs were questioned in some quarters, there was also a feeling abroad that the seceding organizations had engineered the whole crisis as an excuse to get out of the AHAC and free themselves from the intermediate bloc's voting power. In fact, the senior clubs had held a secret strategy session earlier in the afternoon. If they had signalled to all the delegates how strongly they felt about the issue, the vote for the Capitals might not have gone through. There would then have been no apparent reason for the senior clubs to abandon the association, but even if the intermediates had deferred on this occasion, their voting superiority would have hung over the seniors' heads on all future issues. Moving with celerity, the secessionists met again four days later, named their new league the Canadian Amateur Hockey League, drew up schedules, and adopted a constitution. It was identical to that of the AHAC but for one addition. Section 4 said that the admittance of an intermediate champion to the senior series must be by the "unanimous vote of all the clubs then comprising the series." In another speedy bit of business, the new league took in the Shamrocks, who admitted no shame in coming over after realizing they were in an untenable position alone with the Capitals in a disintegrating AHAC senior series.

By dealing with contentious issues such as the scheduling of matches and the admittance of new teams, hockey associations were rationalizing the structure of the sport as its popularity grew. But far more commonplace were the day-to-day arguments and protests that plagued individual matches. So numerous had these become, because of incomplete and vague rules coupled with the zealousness of players and team operators, that one newspaper labelled the situation "win, tie or wrangle." Winning the game had become far more important than early enthusiasts could ever have envisioned. The prestige of athletic clubs that sponsored teams was now at stake. The general public were demanding victories by their favourites, and the gates from matches (crucial to a club's continuance) often reflected a team's performance on the ice.

A match played on Saturday, January 26, 1895, at the Rideau Rink illustrates many of the incidents that vexed the presentation of contests, and gives an impression of the attention the citizenry accorded the sport. The Ottawas defeated Quebec 1-0. Both were considered strong teams. In the hometown lineup that night were popular returning players Harvey Pulford, Weldy Young, Bert Russell, Chauncey Kirby, and Joe McDougal. Goalkeeper Fred Chittick and forward Alf Smith had moved up from junior ranks. At least two thousand admirers crowded into the rink. Even at the stiff price of one dollar, all the reserved seats were taken. Spectators jammed the promenades at the side of the rink; the shareholders' gallery was filled. "Rickety, rickety, rickety rec; what's the matter with old Quebec?" taunted the Ottawa supporters as a Quebec contingent, who had come in on a special train to cheer their team, looked on. For a while there was nothing to cheer about. As the game progressed, spectators had every reason to stamp their feet in impatience. Here are the reasons for their frustration.

Late start: Advertised for 8 p.m., the match did not begin until 10 p.m. because the referee, stuck on a train from Montreal, failed to appear. The train's scheduled arrival of 7:30 p.m. would in any event have left little margin for the unexpected. Some of the Quebec players, on another train, did not reach the rink until nearly 9 p.m.. Late starts were infuriatingly common, whether from slow trains, the casual lounging of visiting teams in their hotels before pleasing themselves to leave for the game, or from arguments at the rink over who would officiate.

Failure to agree on referee: Unable to agree on a substitute referee, the teams made up their own lists of who would be acceptable and telegraphed these direct from the rink to the association president in Montreal for a decision. After waiting some time without reply, the captains approached a spectator from Quebec, with whom they were both acquainted and knew to be of honourable character. At first he refused the job, but he eventually relented and disappeared into a dressing room to put on skates.

Uncertain goal judging: Midway through the first half, Chauncey Kirby took a shot that the Ottawas and many spectators thought had gone through the Quebec goal. The goal umpire did not raise his hand, maintaining that the puck's path was outside the posts. As they were entitled to do, the Ottawas demanded the replacement of the umpire. The referee acceded and the game resumed with his brother occupying the position. Whether or not in this instance the umpire was right, there is no doubt his job was made more challenging by the absence of any device that, by entrapping a puck sent between the posts, would show conclusively that a goal had been scored.

Hockey observers in Ottawa, as elsewhere, voiced their concerns about league administration and game presentation, but changes were slow to come. One significant improvement at the beginning of the 1900 CAHL season was the introduction of the goal net, which dramatically reduced time-wasting disputes over goal judging. But other problems remained. Following an Ottawa-Victoria contest in 1901, in which numerous delays ruined the flow of the game and kept a large crowd in a very cold rink until after 11:30 p.m., the *Ottawa Journal* attacked the system. The article exhibited a perceptive feeling for the integrity of the sport. We know from Ross's diary that he was at the game, and it's possible he was the preternaturally astute *Journal* scribe who penned the prescriptive piece. "A radical change is most certainly necessary in the matter of the delays and stops which characterize so many hockey games and somewhat mar the enjoyment of a most pleasurable sport," the article said. Recounting the many long waits during the game in question while injured players recuperated and other players had broken skates fixed, the article blamed "the system under which hockey matches are conducted." The rules severely limited player substitution. In the first half of a match an injured player unable to return could be replaced. An injury in the second half meant the captain of the opposing team had the choice of dropping a man to equalize the sides or allowing the other team to bring in a replacement. In any event, the rules permitted stoppages of up to fifteen minutes to allow a player to regain his bearings or have his skates fixed. The *Journal's* remedy was to disallow substitution altogether and eliminate the fifteen-minute-delay rule. When a player is injured, the article recommended, the opposing side should be required to take one of its own players off the ice and the game should be restarted without delay. The newspaper's reason for not allowing a substitution was that most teams, when travelling, were reluctant to bring an extra man with them for economic reasons and would therefore not be able to replace an injured player. The *Journal* also took exception to delays in starting games caused by teams "taking their time to come around to the rink." The paper called on the league to fine teams "failing to be on hand after a short period of grace" or forfeit the game. With the passage of time, the *Journal's* complaints would be rectified; but, as far as injury delays were concerned, not in the manner recommended.

As for the broader issue of new teams being kept out of leagues, the Capital Hockey Club was still smarting two years after it was denied entry to the CAHL senior division. James Davidson, the club's founding president and a prominent municipal politician, expounded his views in an interview he granted to the *Journal* in November 1900. He objected to the attitude of league administrators in making it nearly impossible for a new team to gain entry. By putting up unnecessary barriers, he contended, they were preventing young clubs from showing how good they could be. He also thought the public had little interest in going to games where a club that was out of contention was merely playing out its final games in a lackadaisical fashion. His solution to these problems was an overhaul of the system. He thought a league should be formed consisting of senior, intermediate, and junior divisions. The way would be made clear for a junior series winner to move up to intermediate. An intermediate champion would play off against the lowest team in the senior series to see which of the two would be allowed in the senior circuit the following season. The losing team would play in the intermediate. In this way, teams would have the incentive to go all out in every game and the public's interest in late-season matches would be sustained. The system would also encourage promising clubs to reach for a higher level of play.

Davidson's vision went unrealized; but in spite of the frustrations encountered by ambitious clubs and faithful spectators, hockey's growth continued unabated.

Hockey in the Capital

ON A MIDWINTER Saturday in 1899, four Ottawa hockey teams and their supporters boarded Canada Atlantic trains for Montreal. The Ottawa Hockey Club senior and intermediate teams, a team of bakers, and Ashbury school all had matches scheduled later that day in the "Mountain City." This "great exodus of hockeyists," as the *Ottawa Citizen* referred to the excursion, exemplified the extent to which Ottawa's hockey infrastructure had developed. A popularity contest sponsored by the *Ottawa Journal* a year earlier resulted in thirty city and area teams receiving votes. These included the senior Ottawa and Capitals clubs, teams from the city league, and various squads from numerous industrial, commercial, and school leagues. With no restriction on the number of ballots supporters were permitted to clip and send in over the month-long contest, the city's 60,000 residents cast more than 80,000 votes. Curiously, the Bryson Graham department-store team won the contest with 25,273 votes. For all their fame, the Ottawa Hockey Club seniors could muster only 3,339 and finished fifth. Nevertheless, the contest proved two things from which the Ottawas could take solace: that hockey had become enormously popular as a spectator sport, and that the city was producing a large pool of talent from which the club could draw. To illustrate the latter point, the Ashbury team on the Montreal excursion included three future Stanley Cup champions with the Ottawas: Dave Finnie, Hamilton "Billy" Gilmour, and his brother Sutherland.

After the Ottawas, three local clubs stood out in the last years of the nineteenth century: the Electrics, the Aberdeens, and the Capitals. The Electrics and the Aberdeens started out as junior teams in the city league, but both had higher aspirations. In a rule amendment soon followed by other bodies, the OHA in 1898 limited junior eligibility to players under twenty years of age. Before then, the term "junior" referred not to age but to calibre of play. Players in their twenties and even thirties, as with the famous Rideau Rebels in their brief city league forays, were found on junior teams.

The Electrics, so-named because they were sponsored by the owners of the Ottawa Electric Railway, were a local powerhouse, winning the city championship in 1893 and the Canadian junior championship the following year. They went undefeated in those two seasons. With their success came perquisites. They sported fine woolen jerseys with the lettering "OER" embroidered across the breast. And on one occasion their sponsors

Future Silver Seven star, Senators coach, and Hall of Famer Alf Smith, far right, crafted his game with the formidable Ottawa Electrics. In 1893, the year this photograph was taken, the Electrics won the city-league championship on a perfect record. LIBRARY AND ARCHIVES CANADA PA 117926

arranged for a private tram to pick them up at the railway station on their return from a victory in Montreal. In the fall of 1894 the club executive sounded out the AHAC for admittance to the senior series, Canada's top league. When it became apparent their lobbying was not working, they instead applied to the intermediate division, only to be denied. The Ottawas, by virtue of their AHAC membership, were entitled to enter an intermediate team and offered their spot in that series to the Electrics. Proud team that they were, the Electrics declined the gesture, knowing that if they accepted they would have to play under the Ottawa Hockey Club banner and would lose their own hard-won identity. The most famous Electrics graduate, Alf Smith, went on to be a star player and then coach with the Ottawas, and was later inducted to the Hockey Hall of Fame.

In their earliest years, the Aberdeens struggled in the Ottawa city league, but by 1894 had become strong enough to enter the AHAC junior series. They continued to improve, winning the Canadian junior championship in 1901. The Ottawa Hockey Club took note. Always on the lookout for promising new players to bolster their senior team, the Ottawas saw the Aberdeens as a prime source, so much so that they broached the idea of bringing the junior club, a rival of their own junior team, under their wing. The initial overture in 1898 failed; but in 1902, after the Aberdeens had moved up to the intermediate ranks and won the Canadian championship, the Ottawas again approached them. Finnie and the Gilmour brothers, all Ashbury graduates, were now with the Aberdeens, as was the prolific scorer Frank McGee. Flushed with success, the Aberdeens responded audaciously, allowing how they would contemplate an amalgamation with the Ottawas only if two conditions were met: that the Ottawa Hockey Club adopt the Aberdeen name, and that the Aberdeens have equal representation on a new executive. That being too much for a club of proven status in the senior ranks to bear, the Ottawas dropped the idea and simply recruited the Gilmours and McGee for their 1903 team.

The Capitals were an entirely different story. Created in the fall of 1896 by the Capital Athletic Association, which itself had come into being only one year earlier, the new hockey club immediately began testing the establishment — the Ottawas, that is. No sooner had the Capitals adjourned their founding meeting than word on the street was they intended to put a team on the ice that would take second place to no other organization in Eastern Canada. Provocatively, they boasted that Ottawa Hockey Club stalwarts Harry Westwick and Alf Smith would be joining the new club. Furthermore, the Capitals would forthwith seek entry in the AHAC senior series. The Capitals' bid failed; but, undeterred, the club went about setting up a league of its own, the Central Canada Hockey Association (CCHA), in which it competed with Cornwall and Brockville. Westwick and Smith stayed with the Ottawas. For three years, the Capitals regularly challenged the Ottawas to a showdown and were regularly rebuffed by a team that had nothing to prove and everything to lose in terms of local prestige. Winning the CCHA title in 1897, the Capitals challenged for the Stanley Cup. What was supposed to have been a best-of-three series ended in embarrassment for the challengers after only one game. The champion Victorias of Montreal so dominated the contest in a 15-2 rout that organizers promptly called off the series. In the meantime, the Capitals again applied for and were denied admittance to the AHAC senior series. This time, however, they were taken into the intermediate division, which they won. After their third failed attempt to get into the senior division, the Capitals, in December 1899, joined the eastern division of the OHA senior series, with Cornwall and

Iroquois. Alf Smith, whom they had coveted as a player, joined the Capitals as coach. As far as the Ottawa Hockey Club was concerned, though, the Capitals had been marginalized.

While the Ottawas certainly benefited from the presence of the Electrics, the Aberdeens, and other second-tier organizations around the city, the main source of supply for the senior team was from within the club's own ranks. The "second" Ottawas had come into existence in 1890, playing local friendly matches before joining the AHAC junior series in 1892. While continuing in that series, the seconds, or "juniors," also competed in 1893 in the Ottawa City League against the Electrics, the Aberdeens, the Rideaus, the Rebels, and Ottawa College.

The seconds moved up to the AHAC intermediate division in 1895 to take the place the Ottawa Hockey Club had originally reserved for the Electrics. Operating an intermediate team in that league was a costly proposition. The meagre gate receipts these matches generated did not come close to matching the expenses incurred in travelling to Montreal for engagements with the three clubs there. The Ottawa Hockey Club annual report for 1895 notes receipts of $60 and expenses of $230 for the intermediates. But the club's continuing commitment to the intermediate series paid off with an AHAC championship in 1899. Among the players perfecting their craft with the junior and intermediate Ottawas before graduating to the senior team were Fred Chittick, Harvey Pulford, Bouse Hutton, Charlie Spittal, Chauncey Kirby, Harry Westwick, Joe McDougal, Reg Bradley, and Bruce and Hod Stuart.

Managing the Ottawas

UNTIL THE EARLY 1890S, management of the Ottawa Hockey Club was a relatively straightforward matter, which could be attended to collegially by the hockey players themselves. Recently retired players such as Ross and Jenkins also lent a hand on the executive. The typical executive body consisted of a president, a secretary-treasurer, a captain, and a three-man committee. They looked after all the arrangements: league meetings, travel, rink accommodation, promotion, recruitment, player selection, balancing the books. By the middle of the decade, however, senior hockey had acquired such a high public profile and expectations had become so great that winning games, not just playing them, was paramount. This in turn meant the expenditure of far more time than before in ensuring advantageous scheduling, secur-

The vice-regal and parliamentary personnel who formed the Rebels in the 1890s evidently didn't restrict their spirited play to the rink.

ing the best equipment for the players, negotiating good terms for rink rentals, making deals with railways for team travel and group excursions, finding agents for the sale of game tickets, dealing with proposals for amalgamation with other local clubs, and attending to a host of minor details. Management could no longer be left to the players alone.

Expansion of the executive in 1895 to meet these growing demands was preceded two years earlier by the appointment of an honorary president. The purpose was to attract an important member of the community who would enhance the organization's prestige and provide valuable contacts within the city's business and professional ranks. The first to be appointed in that capacity was T. Mayne Daly, minister of the interior and superintendent general of Indian affairs. The club occasionally went a step farther by naming a patron — an even more exalted position. Among those so favoured were the governors general Lord Aberdeen and Lord Minto and Prime Minister Wilfrid Laurier. The 1895 expansion created a position of vice-president, divided secretary-treasurer into two positions, and enlarged the committee. The position of captain had disappeared from the executive body by 1898 and the role of current players was gradually reduced.

Ross, whose role as publisher of the *Ottawa Journal* had made him one of the city's most influential citizens, returned for a three-year stint as club president in 1892, after having served while still active as a player in 1889. Other prominent men acting on the executive between then and 1903 included insurance broker S. Maynard Rogers; John P. Dickson, secretary-treasurer of the Canadian Railway Accident Insurance Company; N. Charles Sparks, who had been secretary-treasurer of the Journal Printing Company before entering the real-estate business; Llewellyn N. Bate, a grocery, wine, and liquor merchant; and George P. Murphy, secretary-treasurer of the Ottawa Transportation Company.

These experienced businessmen had plenty to keep them occupied besides league wrangling and amalgamation proposals. Among the issues were the inevitable clashes of personality. One such row in December 1896 resulted in the resignation of vice-president Chauncey Kirby, secretary John Dickson, and treasurer George Murphy. Incredible as it may seem, the dispute was said to be over nothing more than the alleged failure of Kirby and Murphy to consult players on plans to recognize departing teammate Herbert Russell the previous summer. The offended players, one of whom was reported to be Harvey Pulford, said they would not play on the club as long as Kirby and Murphy held office. Under pressure, the two executives resigned, whereupon, to show his distaste for the way they had been treated, Dickson also quit. At a general meeting of the club a few days later, a letter from Ross, now the honorary president, was read out announcing his resignation. He believed, as quoted in his own newspaper, that Murphy and Kirby, who had always been "loyal and valuable" members, "had not been treated fairly." Dickson and Murphy eventually returned to the executive and Kirby came back in 1898 as team captain.

Rogers, who as president had contended with the Kirby et al. affair, was confronted the very next season with more dissension. In late December 1897, club members called a meeting to dispute captain Harvey Pulford's decision to pick Weldy Young for the team that was to play an important exhibition game against a touring Winnipeg club. The problem was not with Young's ability as a cover point. In fact, he had been dominant in that position with the Ottawas for many years. The trouble rested with what his teammates saw as Young's apparent duplicitous behaviour over the previous few weeks. In early November, Young had attended, as usual, the club's annual meeting and was put on the sub-committee to negotiate rink terms for the coming season. What members did not know at the time was that he had met the day before with the son of Waterloo distiller Joseph Seagram to see about going to Waterloo to play on the Seagrams team. Seagram Sr. wanted a championship and was actively recruiting the best players he could find. One inducement was a job during the season. Young and Harry Westwick abandoned the Ottawas for Waterloo in mid-December; but less than two weeks later they returned to the capital, dissatisfied that the jobs they were promised would not be permanent positions. In selecting the again-available Young for the Winnipeg game, Pulford, according to other players, was overlooking Young's disloyalty and depriving some other more deserving player from suiting up. The objective of the meeting called by the players was to have Pulford's decision overturned, but the executive supported the captain. Young was back on the team. President Rogers, who agreed with the protesting players, then resigned his office and abruptly left the room. Kirby, who had planned to rejoin the team, was true to his word when he said he would refuse to play for the Ottawas if Young were put in the lineup. Kirby sat out the entire season.

The Young affair was at the heart of a much broader issue: hockey-club executives were facing the advent of professionalism. Paying athletes to perform in certain sports was common. It had been so in rowing and baseball for years, and by the mid-1890s many lacrosse clubs included professionals. As for hockey, as early as 1896 there were newspaper reports of players in Montreal receiving letters from a Pittsburgh club to come south. Travel and living expenses were promised, along with good jobs during the season. An indignant newspaper report said, "Hockey in Canada has kept clear of any professionalism, but though it is a novelty across the border, the national emblem — $ — has already made for itself a prominent place in the short history of the game there." Hockey interests north of the border soon followed suit. In the middle of the 1898 season, the OHA suspended the Berlin and Guelph teams from the senior ranks for putting professionals on the ice, and then took the intermediate championship away from Waterloo for the same offence.

Meanwhile, a messy scandal that would have a bearing on the Ottawa Hockey Club was being played out in the courts. During the course of a conspiracy trial over charges that certain members of the Capital Lacrosse Club had thrown a game against Toronto, it was alleged that the club had paid $100 bonuses to the 1896 team at the end of the season. On the team were

Alf Smith and Harry Westwick, both players for the Ottawa Hockey Club. Smith eventually admitted to receiving the bonus, but Westwick claimed innocence, saying he was only a spare, did not receive any payment, and was unaware of the bonuses to the other players. Midway through the 1897–98 hockey season, the Amateur Athletic Association of Canada, or the AAAC, declared all eighteen members of the Capital Lacrosse Club professional and disqualified them. Smith, who that season had switched from the Ottawa Hockey Club to the Capitals, and Westwick, who was still with the Ottawas, were therefore ineligible in amateur hockey and were shunted off their respective teams. Westwick immediately applied for reinstatement as an amateur, submitting affidavits from the Capital Lacrosse Club secretary-treasurer and Alf Smith, himself, asserting that Westwick received no bonus. Though the Ottawa Hockey Club complained that the association was taking its time with the application, the reinstatement did come through and Westwick was back on the team by the middle of February. Smith, who knew he had no grounds for reinstatement, did not even seek to regain his amateur status until the following summer. Even so, he remained debarred for several years. The public scandal led the AAAC's successor body, the Canadian Amateur Athletic Union, to toughen up its already-stringent definition of amateur. At its 1899 annual meeting, the athletic union decreed there could be no payment to a player for time lost from his job in order to compete; and that he could receive no consideration for any services rendered as a player except actual travelling and hotel. Furthermore, where a player was accused of being a professional, the onus was now on the player to prove he was not. To soften the harsh concept of "guilty until proven innocent," the union said that to prevent frivolous charges, officials must be convinced there was good reason for such an accusation, and would have authority to require an affidavit, if necessary, to support a charge.

The Pittsburgh inducements continued. The city was home to a three-team association called the Western Pennsylvania Hockey League. To all intents and purposes, it had been a professional operation for several years before declaring itself so at the beginning of the 1902–03 season. Most of the players were Canadian. Alf Smith, already branded a professional, went to Pittsburgh in 1901. The Ottawa Hockey Club's Art Sixsmith joined him. The next season, Ottawa lost Bruce Stuart, Harold Henry, and Charlie Spittal. Spittal was reported to have been offered a job at the Westinghouse Air Brake Company, as well as a salary of fifteen dollars per week for his hockey services (about as much as an Ottawa teacher earned).

As long as Canadian hockey teams wished to remain under the amateur code, their executive committees would have to contend with the brawn drain by finding inducements, such as assistance in finding good jobs, to keep the players at home.

By 1903 the Ottawa Hockey Club had still not acquired its own independent legal identity. Several other sporting organizations around the city, such as the Ottawa Skating and Curling Club, the Ottawa Canoe Club, and the Ottawa Baseball Association, had been incorporated since the 1890s. Following the model of some other senior hockey clubs, which were under the wing of an incorporated athletic association, the Ottawas had re-organized as a constituent body of the Ottawa Amateur Athletic Club (OAAC) in 1889. The OAAC was itself a creature of the Ottawa Amateur Athletic Association, incorporated provincially in 1887. But sometime between 1899 and 1901, the hockey club appears to have loosened or severed its ties with the OAAC. A clue that this might happen came in 1897 when rumours circulated that the Ottawas were contemplating seceding from the parent club. Significantly, the hockey club's annual report, which had always been included with the annual report of the OAAC, appeared there for the last time in 1899. Hockey-club president J.W. Smith told the *Ottawa Journal* in November 1900: "The Ottawa Hockey Club is an organization that is supposed to represent the city of Ottawa and is not the representative of the Ottawa Amateur Athletic Association." He said the hockey club met in the association's building only as a "matter of convenience." Curiously, the directors make absolutely no mention of their hockey brethren after 1899. If there was a falling out, the official record reveals nothing of it.

"The brilliant record of our Hockey Team for 1892 will long live in the memory of the Ottawa public," the annual report of the Ottawa Amateur Athletic Club reads. "They have done much to increase the interest in this our glorious national winter game." The report casually mentions that "a complimentary dinner was tendered by our members to the team at the close of the season." The OAAC's published record says nothing about a speech delivered to the large audience by Lord Stanley of Preston's aide, Lord Kilcoursie, in which he announces the governor general's intention to donate a trophy that "should be held from year to year by the Champion hockey team in the Dominion." The proposed trophy had no name, and no one knew what it would look like, nor how a champion was to be decided. Within a year, the Ottawa players would have those answers; but it would be eleven years before they would have the trophy.

6 · Stars Along the Way
1893–1903

I have for some time past been thinking
that it would be a good thing if there were a challenge cup
which should be held from year to year
by the champion hockey team of the Dominion.
LORD STANLEY OF PRESTON
1892

THE FINE HAND OF ROSS is evident in the parlour-room discussions at Rideau Hall, and within the confines of the exclusive Rideau Club in downtown Ottawa, that led to Lord Stanley's announcement that he was willing to donate a trophy for the championship hockey team of Canada. A telling point was the governor general's assertion he was "not quite certain that the present regulations governing the arrangement of matches give entire satisfaction, and it would be worth considering whether they could not be arranged so that each team would play once at home and once at the place where their opponents hail from." In other words, a regular schedule of games. The absence of a series system was the very point that stuck in the craw of the Ottawa Hockey Club, a group from which Ross was never distant. And it was no coincidence that Ross, in the early spring of 1893, had invited Lord Stanley's aide-de-camp, Lord Kilcoursie, to lunch at the Rideau Club the day before drafting the rules governing the awarding of the trophy, which by then had been ordered from England. Stanley had appointed Ross and the sheriff of Ottawa, John Sweetland, as trustees of the trophy; but it was Ross who assumed the leadership role because of his vast experience with the game. Sweetland brought a large measure of public trust to the job, but his exposure to the sport was marginal, pretty much limited to being a shareholder in the Rideau Rink where the Ottawas played their games. It bothered no one that Ross, the architect of the trophy rules and the man in charge of approving challenges to the holders, was at the same time the president of the Ottawas. Ross, according to his diary entry, drafted the terms on Sunday, April 23, 1893. They were as follows:

Lord Stanley of Preston, whose sons played on the Rebels, donated hockey's famous trophy bearing his name in 1893. One of his stipulations was that all Canadian championship teams, irrespective of which league they belonged to, were eligible to compete for the trophy. LIBRARY AND ARCHIVES CANADA PA25686

His Excellency's Conditions for the Awarding of the Stanley Championship Trophy

1. The winner to give bond for the return of the cup in good order when required by the trustees for the purpose of being handed over to any other team who may in turn win.

2. Each winning team to have at their own charge engraved on a silver ring fitted on the cup for the purpose the name of the team and the year won. [In the first instance the MAAA will find the cup already engraved for them.]

3. The cup shall remain a challenge cup, and will not become the property of any team, even if won more than once.

4. In case of any doubt as to the title of any club to claim the position of champions, the cup shall be held or awarded by the trustees as they may think right, their decision being absolute.

5. Should either trustee resign or otherwise drop out, the remaining trustee shall nominate a substitute.

Ross and Sweetland also offered specific suggestions for meeting Stanley's wish that the champions of all hockey associations in Canada be eligible to compete for the trophy. They had already decided that the MAAA team should be the first holders of the cup for having won the AHAC title in 1893. They recommended that thereafter the two main senior associations, the AHAC and the OHA, arrange their schedules so that a final match could be played between the respective champions. As other representative provincial associations outside Quebec and Ontario came into being, their winning teams would also be given a chance. Although Ross and Sweetland's proposals were never formally ratified by the associations concerned, and although there were many arguments about when challenges should be played, the trustees' basic idea was carried through. In the first ten years in which the Stanley Cup was awarded (1893–1902), teams representing five associations in Quebec, Ontario, the Maritimes, and Manitoba competed for it at one time or another. Among them were the Winnipeg Victorias, who successfully challenged twice, successfully defended once, and lost five times. Other unsuccessful challengers from beyond the AHAC were Queen's University (twice) and the Toronto Wellingtons, both of the OHA; the Halifax Crescents; and the Ottawa Capitals of the short-lived and second-rate Central Canada Hockey Association. During that period, the Ottawas contested the cup only once, in 1894, the first year in which there was a competition following the unilateral awarding of the trophy to the MAAA the year before. And when that contest occurred, both the Ottawa and MAAA players were more conscious of the AHAC title being at stake than they were of the prospects of winning the new trophy. The Stanley Cup was a side benefit that merited little attention, and its being up for grabs was not even mentioned in the Ottawa Hockey Club's annual report for the season. But it would not be long before the trophy came to symbolize hockey supremacy. Between 1893 and 1903, when the Ottawas first claimed the prize, several of the club's players made valiant efforts toward that end and came to be recognized as among the finest players in the game.

In all, fifty-three men wore the Ottawa colours between 1893 and 1903. Some, such as Billy Dey and Jim McGee, were fringe players who got into only a few games. Jack Kerr, an original from 1884, completed his playing career in 1893; and Frank McGee was just beginning his with the Ottawas in 1903. The players were local products. They didn't go to Ottawa to play hockey; they were raised there and learned the game on the city's rinks. A few of the younger ones were still students when they joined the senior team, but most were employed locally in a variety of occupations. They were well known around town and enjoyed at least modest celebrity, their off-ice doings frequently being mentioned in newspapers and in hotel-lobby and cigar-store conversations, wherever sporting types met to trade stories about local teams. People understood that these young men represented the city and were therefore curious to know as much about the stalwarts as they could find out: their travels in the summer, new jobs and business opportunities, gossip about marriage plans.

Three Goalkeepers to Remember

GOALKEEPER ALBERT MOREL, the son of a cabinetmaker, was a seventeen-year-old student at Ottawa College when he joined the Ottawa Hockey Club in 1891. He distinguished himself as a senior player the following season when the Ottawas came within one game of winning the AHAC championship. Morel, still at school, played every game for his team in 1893 when they finished in second place in the AHAC and defeated Queen's in the elimination round of the OHA. His final season, 1894, ended in disappointment when, though he played like a "stone wall," the Ottawas lost to the MAAA in the championship game for the Stanley Cup. Off the ice, Morel was often absent from Ottawa as a member of a government survey party. Later, he was employed locally as a private secretary and then as a bookkeeper with a lumber company.

Morel's successor in goal, Fred Chittick, was an unpredictable Irish Canadian. Wherever he went, commotion was his companion. In five seasons with the Ottawas, 1895–99, Chittick played thirty-eight games. He added one more as an emergency substitute two years later. During the working day, Chittick appears to have been the very model of the staid civil servant, fulfilling his duties as an accountant in the Department of Agriculture at the quite-comfortable annual salary of $950. It was another matter after he left the office. Chittick loved sports and the outdoor life. In the fall he played with the Ottawa Football Club but also found time for hunting. (He and some hockey chums returned from one shooting expedition with forty-seven partridge and a good number of ducks.) It was likely of no surprise to those who knew Chittick that he turned up on the stage of the opera house playing the role of Sanballat in the spectacular pantomime *Ben Hur*, the cast of which included the wife of Ottawa Hockey Club president Maynard Rogers.

Most of Chittick's public exploits involved hockey. He broke in with the Ottawa juniors and advanced to the intermediates before joining the senior team at the relatively advanced age of twenty-seven. Always a goalkeeper, he loved to rush the puck. Once, while a junior, he charged down the ice at practice, crashed into the goal post, and knocked himself unconscious. Attended to by a doctor, he was carried senseless to his home for recovery. Chittick was temperamental; if things did not go his way, he reacted, regardless of the consequences to his teammates. Claiming he was not given the extra tickets he was promised for a match at the Rideau Rink against the Victorias in 1898, he refused to play, leaving the Ottawas stuck for a goalkeeper. The junior Aberdeens goaler was found and the game went on, with Ottawa losing 9-5.

Turbulence followed in 1899. In a remarkable string of events that winter, Chittick provoked two bitter confrontations over his refereeing (a job he took on while still active as a player), threatened legal action over statements alleged to have been made about him, suffered the most humiliating defeat in hockey to that time, abandoned his team, and levelled serious charges of his own against the Ottawa Hockey Club.

Chittick's troubles began on Saturday, January 21. He had travelled to Quebec City to referee the match between Quebec and Montreal. This was possible because the Ottawas had no game scheduled that weekend. With twelve minutes remaining in an especially rough encounter, the Montrealers left the ice and refused to return. They were incensed at what they saw as the failure of Chittick to rein in an aggressive Quebec side. Several days later, Chittick heard that some of the Montreal players were said to have commented after the match that Chittick was intoxicated and unfit to referee. The accusations were thought to have been made by Herb Collins, Hugh Baird, and the McKerrow brothers, Clare and Andrew. Chittick responded quickly. He demanded an apology from the four, and through his lawyers, Code and Beament, threatened that if retractions were not forthcoming by the following Saturday, when the Montreal team was due in Ottawa for a game, he would serve them with writs for defamation. All of this was aired out in Ottawa newspapers, one of which tracked down a witness who said that Chittick had been perfectly sober and that when they went to the "club" together after the game, Chittick took only a ginger ale. Baird and Collins, in a letter from their lawyers, denied saying he was drunk but regretted any misunderstandings that might have arisen from their criticism of Chittick's handling of the game. There were no apologies from the McKerrows, only a denial from Andrew.

In the midst of this, Chittick was waging another public battle — with his own club. The Ottawas had lost two-straight games when they went into the Arena Rink in Montreal on February 11 to face the Victorias. The result was a complete disaster for Chittick. At the end of the first half, the

Ottawas were already behind 6-0. Into the second half, Chittick began showing his frustration and, taking matters into his own hands, launched himself into one of his rushes down the ice, only to shoot wide of the goal. Matters further deteriorated, and the game ended 16-0. It was the worst shellacking ever seen in senior hockey to that time. The following Saturday back in Ottawa, newspapers reported that Chittick would not be in goal that night at Dey's Rink against the MAAA. He was to be replaced by the intermediate team's goaltender, who had been playing well. No one from the club had bothered to tell Chittick. He read about it in the paper. He was incensed at the double slight of being laid off, and not being accorded the courtesy of hearing the decision direct from the club's executive. (President George Murphy later admitted Chittick had not been advised but said he assumed he would find out anyway by reading the *Citizen*.)

That night a *Citizen* reporter found Chittick in the Windsor Hotel with friends. He would not be going to the game. "I have returned my ticket to the Ottawa club and wash my hands of them forever." He said he was being made a scapegoat and that the general public would only conclude that the reason for his being benched was that the Ottawa executive really believed he was intoxicated when he refereed the Quebec-Montreal game. By this time, he had worked himself into a full lather. He was going to write to the Ottawa executive and tell them what he thought of them. "Perhaps, by the way, they will inform the public how the team has been run this season." Then came this: "I know one player on the Ottawa team who was offered $100 by a member of the executive this season for his services; but that's only a mole hill to other things that I will make public." Accusing the Ottawas, an amateur club, of offering an under-the-table payment to a player had explosive possibilities, especially in light of the recent Capital Lacrosse Club scandal resulting in the suspension of the entire team for taking year-end bonuses. Though drawing a denial from the Ottawas and a counter-charge that Chittick himself had once offered to contribute $25 toward paying members of the Ottawa hockey team, the issue was dropped. Chittick, it was concluded, had merely gotten carried away venting his anger. His days with the Ottawa Hockey Club, however, were all but over.

Were all of this not enough, Chittick was at the same time caught up in yet another public spat over his refereeing. After officiating a hotly contested Ottawa Valley League match and being verbally attacked by the league's secretary over his performance, Chittick, in what was becoming a normal pattern, wrote to the league president to tell him what he thought of the secretary. The acrimony reached the press, letters were exchanged through that medium, and legal action was threatened against Chittick. As with most sporting quarrels, nothing came of it. But Chittick's reputation as a combative personality was confirmed.

John Bower "Bouse" Hutton was the intermediate call-up who replaced Chittick in February 1899, following the veteran's disastrous performance against the Victorias. Had Chittick not quit the team in outrage, he might have returned to complete the season. But there was no doubt that Hutton would be the goaler of the future. Like Ottawa's first great goalkeeper, Morel, Hutton was still a student when he broke in with the seniors as a twenty-one-year-old. Unlike Chittick, there was nothing controversial about him. He simply played the game well, and other games, too, being an outstanding fullback with the Ottawa Rough Rider football club and a goalkeeper in lacrosse with the Ottawa Capitals. Hutton was the son of a cab owner and for a time was a driver before going to work for the Canada Atlantic Railway as a clerk. While there, and even as one of hockey's most prominent goalkeepers with the Ottawas, he managed to play for the Canada Atlantic Railway team in the very strong Canadian Railway League. Hutton went on to a civil-service career, starting as a draughtsman with the topographical-surveys branch.

Including regular-season, playoff, and exhibition games, Hutton appeared forty-five times for the Ottawas between 1899 and the club's first Stanley Cup season, 1903. He added another twelve games the following year, his last, when the club successfully defended the cup in three series. Hutton was inducted into the Hockey Hall of Fame in 1962.

Three Defensive Pillars

BETWEEN 1893 AND 1903, when the Ottawas rose from also-rans to champions, three defensive players stood out at the positions of point and cover point: Harvey "the Slugger" Pulford, Weldy "Chalk" Young, and William Duval. These were not glamorous positions; they did not afford much opportunity for creativity. The point and cover point defended against oncoming rushes, bowled over opponents at any opportunity, and retrieved the puck. Occasionally one or the other would take off on a solo dash, but mostly these defenders were content to find a forward to pass the puck to, always laterally, of course, since forward passes were not allowed. Other than through tough physical play, the best way for a

A plain 'O' on their white jerseys was enough to identify the championship-winning Ottawas of 1901. LIBRARY AND ARCHIVES CANADA C34882

defensive player to gain notice was by perfecting the art of lifting. Crowds loved it when a defender would flick his stick under the puck and hoist it high in the air and down the ice, both teams in pursuit. Occasionally the disk would disappear in the rafters and not return. Sometimes it would break a globe.

Chalk and the Bytown Slugger were quite the defensive pair. From 1894 to 1898 they were the dominant combination in the game, feared because of Chalk's spectacular rushes and the Slugger's punishing body checks. Chalk played cover point, the Slugger was at point.

Chalk lived at the fire station where his father was the chief superintendent. He worked as an engraver in the watchmaking and jewellers business he operated with brothers George and Robert. George had been a member of the original Ottawa Hockey Club. Chalk was best known for hockey, but he was also a good football player as a fullback with the Ottawa Football Club, where he was captain in 1895. His football teammates included Pulford, Chittick, Alf Smith, and Frank McGee. Chalk broke in with the Ottawas as a nineteen-year-old in 1890, and immediately became active on the organizational side. He was a member of the club's executive committee for four years, was team captain in 1893 and 1894, and was a vice-president of the AHAC from 1893 to 1897. Chalk was also a referee, and one so trusted for impartiality that he was chosen to officiate the MAAA-Victoria match in March 1894 to decide which team would play his own Ottawas for the league championship. He also had the distinction of refereeing the December 1896 Stanley Cup match in Winnipeg between the local Victorias and the Victorias of Montreal.

As a cover point, Chalk loved to take chances rushing the puck. His charges up ice were described as "ambitious," "splendid," and "beautiful" runs that usually resulted in a shot on goal or a sharp pass. Occasionally on these adventures he would lose control of the puck and not get back in time to defend. That's when Pulford, the Slugger, would come to his assistance by riding the attacker off to the side, punctuating his action with a shoulder to the chest. Chalk was also an excellent lifter who had a talent for lobbing a shot so that it would land a couple of feet in front of the goalkeeper and bounce crazily. For someone known as an even-handed referee, he could get into trouble as a player. He was not above taking a vicious slash at an opponent's ankle or going into the stands after a heckler. Once, at the Rideau Rink, he saw things differently from goal judge James Davidson, who happened to be the president of the rival Capital Athletic Association. Davidson raised his hand to signal a Quebec goal. Chalk disputed the call, and pointed to a path along the ice that he claimed the puck had taken. He prodded Davidson with the stock of his stick, whereupon Davidson bounded off the platform to get at his attacker. Spectators jumped on the ice and in the ensuing fracas, which police officers failed to quell, Davidson was knocked to the ice. It was left to the Bytown Slugger to restore order.

In their five seasons sharing defensive duties, Chalk and the Slugger played together in forty-three league, playoff, and exhibition games. Chalk's final season with the Ottawas was 1899. With the Slugger injured through the entire schedule, Chalk teamed with Bert Macdonald at point. Forgotten was the resentment he created in 1897 with his defection to Waterloo. After practice one night, the trainer brought Chalk before the team, and coach Bob Shillington, with the words "I christen thee Pa Young!" doused the unclothed ten-year veteran with a pail of cold water.

Weldy Young turned his eye west. He had worked in a mining operation in British Columbia through the summer and fall of 1896, and following the 1899 hockey season decided on Yukon. Settling in Dawson City, he secured a civil-service position and helped organize a hockey league. He also put his engraving experience to work, designing and inscribing an expensive trophy to be awarded to the winner of a contest to predict the winner of the 1900 United States presidential election. Young was closely associated with an idea first discussed in 1902 to assemble a Dawson City team that would challenge for the Stanley Cup.

Pulford joined the Ottawa Hockey Club senior team at the point position in 1894 after attracting attention with the juniors. At the time, he was supporting his widowed mother as a wholesale-dry-goods representative with the J.M. Garland Company. Though the job required some travel, the young man somehow found time to engage in a variety of summer and winter sports. An outstanding athlete, he excelled with the Ottawa Football Club as a wing and with the Ottawa Capitals lacrosse team. He was a champion paddler and rower, and also won the light-heavy and heavyweight boxing championships of Eastern Canada. Pulford played his entire hockey career with the Ottawas, retiring after the 1908 season. Highly respected by his teammates, he was chosen captain in 1898 and again in 1903, a title he held through the club's Stanley Cup glory years.

In the fall of 1898, Pulford broke his collarbone in football. The injury prevented him from playing hockey in 1899, except for a couple of games at season's end when he helped the second-string Ottawas win the intermediate championship. There seems to have been some confusion about his condition. In spite of the injury, Pulford accompanied the team to Montreal in late January for a match against the MAAA. Evidently, he was expected to play and when he declined to put on his uniform, captain Chauncey Kirby ordered first-year player Bert Macdonald to get dressed. Ottawa lost the match 5-1. Ottawa executives blamed Pulford because they felt his style of play would have made the difference. "We consider it a pretty mean throw-down," a member of the executive was quoted by the *Ottawa Citizen* as saying. Curiously, the paper said nothing of the unmended collarbone, reporting that Pulford stayed out because of a bad cold.

Pulford was a big player, not known for speed and finesse. He seldom carried the puck and did not score his first goal in senior company until his seventh year. He showed good judgment, took few offensive risks, and played a sound positional game. His style complemented perfectly the exuberant offensive tactics of Chalk at cover point. Newspapers used the words "cool," "steady," and "reliable" to describe his play. Pulford worked hard at keeping in good physical condition. "He was always the first man at the rink or on the football field," Alf Smith recalled years later, "and was always the last to leave."

When the Slugger lost Chalk as his cover point at the end of the 1899 campaign, William Duval stepped in and skated with the veteran for the next three seasons. Duval was a Lowertown boy who worked as a fitter for the Canada Atlantic Railway, CAR for short. He came to notice as a hockey player on the railway's powerful team in the Canadian Railway Hockey League. A controversial incident marked his first season with the Ottawas in 1900. After playing the first six games, he was left out of the lineup for the second-last match of the season. He was upset and so were teammates Hutton, Mac Roger, and Bruce Stuart. They too were CAR. employees and, like Duval, played on the company team even while members of the Ottawa Hockey Club. They demanded Duval be put back in the lineup for the final game in Montreal against the Shamrocks, but when the club executive said no, they refused to play and the game was forfeited. The club rejected the bold offer of the entire CAR team to go down to Montreal and replace the Ottawas for that match.

Duval was considered a good tactician and general on the ice, and one who freely offered pointers to his teammates. This quality was instrumental in his being made captain for the 1902 season. Duval was regarded highly enough to be invited to play professionally in Pittsburgh, where he joined several other Canadians for the 1902–03 season.

Seven Forwards Who Made a Difference

FORWARDS AS A RULE WERE NOT BIG MEN. What was needed up front were speed, agility, and a deft touch with the puck. There were four forward positions. At the start of play, the centre and two wingers lined up across the rink. The rover positioned himself slightly back of them. Then he was off, chasing the puck all over the ice and hounding after opponents when they got it. The other forwards tried to keep in their lanes. The best teams exhibited good combination play, advancing down the ice in unison. The puck-carrier looked for linemates in the clear and passed laterally to one of them when attacked. Occasionally a forward would hold onto the puck too long; but when the Ottawas were in good form, "the four white jerseys would go up the ice like snow birds, with the puck twittering between them."

Chauncey Kirby was the prototypical forward. Slight of build with a darting style, he had a quick and accurate shot. He was a scrappy performer who wasn't afraid to drop his gloves with a much larger opponent. Spectators laughed at such comical scenes. Once, when a youthful spectator at the edge of the rink grabbed at his stick while he was tussling in the corner, Kirby broke loose and let him have it with a butt end to the jaw — an action the *Citizen* judged "quite proper."

Kirby was the son of city treasurer Thomas H. Kirby and brother of Halder, who was a member of the original Ottawas. The brothers played together on the senior team from 1891 to 1894. Chauncey started out in hockey with the Rideau Colts in 1889 and moved to the Ottawa Hockey Club second team the next season. He graduated to the seniors in 1891 and starred with them until the end of the 1896 season, serving as captain in 1895. Following a personality clash with some of the other players, he left the team at the start of 1896–97 and stayed out for two years. When he returned for the 1898–99 season, he was again made team captain. His best year was 1893, when he scored ten goals in eight AHAC games.

Kirby was a clerk at the Quebec Bank, a position that prepared him well for his duties as Ottawa Hockey Club treasurer from 1891 to 1893. He was a member of the executive committee for the next two years and briefly served as vice-president at the end of 1896 before resigning that position when he quit the team as a player.

Herbert "Bert" Russell was no Chauncey Kirby. Described by a Quebec supporter as "a big rough brute," the Geological Survey draughtsman was more like a charging bull than a water bug when he got hold of the puck. He teamed with Kirby from 1892 to 1896, scoring twenty-nine goals in thirty-seven AHAC matches. His best effort came in January 1894, when he scored all Ottawa's goals in a 5-1 win over the Montreal Victorias at the Rideau Rink. His ten goals that season tied him for the scoring title with Quebec's Dolly Swift, one of the most prolific players of the time. Though Russell could mete out thundering bodychecks when he felt so inclined, he was sometimes reluctant to use his size and strength to full advantage. Surprisingly fast, he rushed the puck well and shot accurately. He was also unselfish, often preferring to pass to an open teammate rather than trying to score himself. And he followed back diligently.

After the 1896 season, Russell left the Ottawas and Canada to take an engineering position in Colorado.

Newspapers printed some pretty florid prose in describing Harry "Rat" Westwick's dashing play. "Time and time again he shot down the ice like a lightning flash athwart an inky black cloud," the *Ottawa Journal* exclaimed after one of his performances. He resembled Kirby: light (he played at 130 pounds), wiry, quick, and extremely competitive. Westwick was a bookbinder by trade, first with the Journal Printing Company, when he joined the Ottawas as an intermediate in 1894, then with Thorburn and Company, and later with the Government Printing Bureau. The eighteen-year-old showed so much promise with the intermediates that he was moved up to the seniors in only their fourth match of the 1895 season. This was an exhibition game against a touring American team that had defeated the Ottawas the previous night under American rules. For the follow-up using Canadian rules, Westwick was the goalkeeper, allowing only one shot to get by him in a game the Ottawas won handily. He then played two regular-season matches at the same position, but after that he was the rover. As a lacrosse player with the Ottawa Capitals, he was involved in the professionalism scandal of 1898. This meant he was ineligible to play hockey with the Ottawas. He was soon absolved of any wrongdoing and rejoined the team after missing only three games. Out of work as the next season approached, Westwick went to Waterloo for a job at Seagram distillers, where he also played for the company team in the Big Four League. Returning to Ottawa, he found a job with the printing bureau but did not immediately rejoin the Ottawas. Instead he went to the Ottawa Capitals in the OHA. He came back to the Ottawas in 1901 and remained with them for the duration of his career, retiring after the 1908 season.

After a game at Quebec in 1896, the *Quebec Chronicle* said Westwick was a "miserable, insignificant rat." A day or two later in a cigar store on Sparks Street where the players gathered, club treasurer George Murphy glanced through the news rack and spotted the issue carrying the insult. From that moment on, Westwick was "the Rat."

Another incident reveals the man's grit (and sense of priorities). In late February 1903, Westwick married former teammate William Duval's sister, Ruby. There was no immediate opportunity for a wedding trip, but Westwick seized the chance to combine one with the Ottawas' journey to Montreal for the first game of the Stanley Cup series against the Victorias. A slash from Bert Strachan's stick fractured Westwick's ankle. In the dressing room, with the game in progress, club doctor Halder Kirby set the bone, after which Westwick insisted on being carried to a seat in the arena to watch the remainder of the match with his bride. Fifty-four years later, at the time of his death, Westwick was getting around on a pair of crutches following the amputation of his leg years earlier as the result of nagging complications from the original broken ankle. They were the same crutches he steadied himself with in 1903.

The ladies called him Mac, the Aberdeens called him Duck, but his real name was John McLean Roger. A machinist with the CAR, he was one of a number of players who helped the Ottawas become a contending team but who received little recognition in later years. Roger joined the Ottawas in their second game of the 1899 season after starting with the intermediate Aberdeens. He made an auspicious debut, scoring two goals in a 3-1 win over the visiting Quebec team. The *Citizen* said he "glided down the ice with the speed of a cat getting around an ash barrel." He was known for his stick-handling ability and penchant for surprising goalkeepers with hard shots from difficult angles. Before leaving Ottawa for British Columbia, Roger helped the Ottawas win the 1901 CAHL championship.

Like Roger, Harold "Chic" Henry was effective but unheralded, playing in the shadow of stars Pulford and Westwick. Henry was an eighteen-year-old clerk at the Bank of Ottawa when he graduated to the senior team from the intermediates halfway through the 1899 season. His first game was as a second-half replacement for Roger who had aggravated a foot injury. Unfortunately for the rookie, the match was the 16-0 drubbing Quebec handed Ottawa. But Henry proved his worth, scoring four goals in the remaining three games. In his four seasons he scored twenty times in twenty-six games. Had Henry not left the club in November 1902 to play professionally in Pittsburgh, he would have been a member of the 1903 Stanley Cup champions.

The enduring reputation of Alf Smith is that of a dirty and aggressive competitor. In his later playing years he certainly was, but at the beginning he was quite the opposite. Though highly skilled, he tired easily, was shy of going into the corners, and was averse to back-checking, preferring to loaf in the middle of the rink. Even in his fourth year with the Ottawas, newspapers were still chiding his work habits. "Smith mostly played his old brilliant game, although hanging back from the corners as usual," the *Journal* said of his play in January 1897. Then, a week later, "Smith took it easy on the forward line and let the others do the lion's share of the work." These were typical comments.

Smith's sporting career, up to the Ottawas' 1903 Stanley Cup triumph, was a checkered one, to say the least. It included championships in football, lacrosse, and hockey; suspension from amateur sport; a season of professional play; and a coaching stint. The son of a bridgebuilder and contractor, Smith was born in 1873 and grew up with twelve brothers and sisters at Billings Bridge, just beyond the southern fringe of town. An all-round athlete, he was the quarterback of the 1896 Canadian champion Ottawa College football team. In lacrosse he was a member of the world-champion Ottawa Capitals in 1895 and 1896. Smith began his hockey career with the Electrics of the city league and moved up to the Ottawa Hockey Club seniors in 1895. In three years at forward, Smith did not miss a game and was a constant offensive threat, tying for the AHAC scoring title in 1897 with twelve goals in eight games.

Through lacrosse, Smith maintained close ties with the Capital Athletic Association and in the fall of 1897 decided to join the association's hockey team, the Capitals. It was a brief relationship, for no sooner had the season started than he and all other members of the 1896 Capital lacrosse team were, after a lengthy investigation, debarred from amateur play in any sport because the team had received cash bonuses at the end of that season. Smith was steadily employed as a woodworker and stairbuilder (he even tried his hand in the bicycle business with Charlie Spittal for a while) and was settling down to married life, but his suspension from amateur competition put his sporting life in disarray. He had nowhere to turn as a player. After a year of inactivity, he agreed in the fall of 1899 to coach the Ottawa Capitals, who were about to enter the OHA. The role suited him and the next season he switched to the Ottawas, where he gained recognition for his ability as a mentor. He was out on his skates at every practice giving tips and correcting faulty habits. His diligence paid off with the 1901 CAHL championship. But Smith could not resist the lure of play-for-pay south of the border and left the next season for Pittsburgh. His reasoning was straightforward: so long as he was prevented form engaging in amateur sport because he had accepted $100 in lacrosse money five years earlier, why shouldn't he benefit from his forced status as a professional? He joined the Pittsburgh Athletic Club hockey team, which promised Canadian imports cash for playing and jobs for the season.

Though he did well in Pittsburgh, tying with a teammate for the scoring title, Smith chose not to return the next season but to resume coaching the Ottawas. They had done quite well in his absence, finishing in second place with a record of five wins and three losses. But Smith was immediately confronted with a problem. Four members of that team

(Charlie Spittal, Bruce Stuart, Chic Henry, and Peg Duval) decided to do exactly what he had done the previous year and boarded trains for Pittsburgh. To everyone's surprise, the reconstructed team under Smith's guidance did even better, finishing in a tie for first place, with six wins and two losses, and a chance for the Stanley Cup.

Midway through the season and approaching his thirtieth birthday, Smith, even though he knew he was doing a good job as coach, still had the urge to be a player. So, after five years of debarment from amateur competition, he finally applied for reinstatement. That summer, the Canadian Amateur Athletic Union approved his application, clearing the way for one of Ottawa's best-known athletes to begin a second phase of his playing career.

As it turned out, coach Alf Smith had no need to be concerned about replacements for the four players who had gone to Pittsburgh. The three Gilmour brothers, Billy, Suddy, and Dave, filled the gap admirably. But another player exploding on the scene lifted the Ottawas to new heights. That was Frank McGee, who in his short career became the best-known hockey player of his time. His success in senior ranks came as no surprise to those who followed hockey in Ottawa. Their only puzzlement was why, at twenty-two years old, he delayed so long in joining a club he could have been with years earlier.

Frank came from one of Ottawa's most prominent families. He and his five brothers and two sisters grew up in a magnificent home in fashionable Sandy Hill. Frank's father, John J. McGee, was the clerk of the Privy Council, the highest-ranking civil-service office in Canada. The very name McGee had a dramatic aura about it, for everyone knew the family's connection to the late Thomas D'Arcy McGee. The journalist, poet, and politician was Frank's uncle. One of the "Fathers of Confederation" and a member of Parliament, he was the victim of an assassin's bullet as he entered his lodgings on Sparks Street upon returning from Parliament Hill one evening in the spring of 1868. The name McGee was legendary before Frank ever laced up a pair of skates.

Like brothers Charles and D'Arcy before him, Frank attended Ottawa College, where he was enrolled in the junior division. And like his brothers, he played on the varsity hockey team, which drew its players from both the junior and senior ranks. This is where Frank first came to public attention as a hockey player, suiting up as a seventeen-year-old forward against a touring Harvard University team in 1897. Newspaper reports say he acquitted himself well in his team's 6-3 victory. He also did well that year as a halfback with the Ottawa Football Club. From College, he joined the Aberdeens Hockey Club, playing on the junior team in 1898 and with the intermediates from 1899 to 1902. During this time, McGee worked as a timekeeper with the Canadian Pacific Railway. The situation suited him perfectly because the CPR had a team in the railway league. Playing for two teams simultaneously was not unheard of, and naturally Frank was welcomed on the company side. With the Aberdeens one night in 1899 against Buckingham, he took a puck over the eye. The gash required several stitches, and though he returned to complete the game, he was not himself. It was an ominous fore-shadowing. One year later McGee was playing for the CPR team in an exhibition game in Hawkesbury, Ontario, to support the Canadian Patriotic Fund, a charity that helped families of Canadian soldiers serving in the Boer War. Again he was struck over the eye, but this time the injury was severe enough to take him out of the game. Two months later the *Ottawa Citizen* reported he had "almost recovered, but it is doubtful if the sight in the injured eye will ever be perfect." Some suspected he would never play again.

McGee's debut with the Ottawas was anxiously awaited. Hockey followers were finally going to see what the gifted young man could do in senior company. The Ottawas had already played two games in the 1903 season, losing the first to the Montreal Victorias and winning the second against the Montreal Shamrocks. His supporters at Dey's Rink were not disappointed. McGee had three goals in a 7-1 rout of the MAAA. In six games McGee scored fourteen goals, second only to the legendary Russell Bowie of the Victorias, who had twenty-two in seven games. In two Stanley Cup series that season McGee scored four more goals, helping his team win the trophy for the first time and then successfully defend it.

Like many players of that era, McGee was not a big man; but he was of deceptively solid build. Billy Grant, the sporting editor of the *Calgary News Telegram*, gave his impressions of the Ottawa sensation after seeing him play for the first time: "I asked which was McGee and suddenly drew in my breath as my companion pointed to a fair-haired, blue-eyed, frail-looking stripling," Grant wrote. "His hair was as perfectly parted as though he had just stepped out of a tonsorial parlor; his spotless white pants were creased to a knife-like edge; his boots had been polished; his skates glistened under the glare of the arc lamps and his complexion — that was what magnetized my attention — seemed as pink as a child's." Other observers, too, commented on the fastidious attention he paid to his personal appearance; but he was far from a dandy on the ice. He was an aggressive competitor, in fact a little too much so. In consequence, the *Journal* quipped, "he generally decorates the side of the rink about half the time." The *Citizen's* version of a typical McGee gibe to an opponent after flattening him was, "Too bad old man, did you trip? Hope you are not badly hurt." As much as he was known for throwing his limited weight around, he was recognized as a superb stickhandler, graceful skater, and diligent back-checker. His teammates remembered him as "the grandest and gamest hockey player that ever pulled on a skate."

Ottawa's players were representative of the community in several respects. They came from different sections of the city and environs: Sandy Hill, Lowertown, Centretown, Billings Bridge. They were from working-, middle-, and upper-class families. And their employment covered a wide range of occupations, from white-collar government positions to banking, business, and the trades. But in another way they were not representative, for, from its beginning, the club was overwhelmingly English, in spite of the fact that fully one-third of the population was of French origin. Albert Morel was French Canadian, William Duval may have been, and a player by the name of Aumond, who made it into the lineup for two exhibition games in New York a month after the regular season ended in 1902, probably was. The executive committee was exclusively English. The only French Canadian associated with the club in a non-playing capacity was Prime Minister Laurier, appointed (possibly without his knowledge) to the figurehead position of patron in 1897. The makeup of the Ottawas reflected the composition of most teams, for hockey was still an English sport. Even in Montreal and Quebec, the senior clubs were virtually English only. The bilingual Ottawa College was a bastion of organized sport, and for the Oblate fathers who ran the institution, physical culture was an integral part of their educational philosophy. Students from both language groups engaged in several sports at the intramural and varsity levels, including baseball, lacrosse, football, and hockey. Hockey, or *"le gouret,"* was somewhat popular as a recreation among the French-speaking student body, but not as a sport to be pursued at the competitive level. The varsity team was far and away English. Within and beyond the confines of the college, lacrosse and baseball attracted many of the better French-speaking athletes, the powerful National Base Ball Club being an example of a French-dominated elite sports team. Albert Morel was therefore an exception to the trend when he joined the Ottawa Hockey Club as its first French-Canadian player in 1891.

7 · Quest for Supremacy
1893–1903

Hockey! Fast, furious, brilliant,
it is our popular winter sport.
ARTHUR FARRELL
Hockey player, 1899

ILL WILL ENDED the Ottawas' relationship with the Toronto-dominated OHA in 1894; but good will created and sustained a connection of a different kind with New York hockey interests at the beginning of the twentieth century. The Toronto clubs wanted little to do with the Ottawas because the team from the capital was too powerful and the Toronto teams did not relish the relatively long journeys to get there. The decision of the frustrated Ottawa executive to quit the OHA in mid-season, after being ordered to Toronto for a match that rightly should have been played in Ottawa, was understandable.

To New York: Post-Season Excursions

ILLUSTRATIVE OF AMERICAN competitive spirit, New York City's hockey teams were eager to test themselves against the best in the game's homeland. This resulted in invitations to top Canadian clubs to go down for "friendlies," and from 1900 to 1902, the Ottawas made such season-ending junkets for back-to-back weekend matches. The opening of the St. Nicholas Rink in 1896 gave new impetus to hockey in New York, and by 1900 several high-calibre teams were playing there. Situated a block from Central Park at 66th Street and Columbus Avenue, the rink was a high-class operation with a grillroom and lounges for members; but what really captured the attention of the Ottawas was the state-of-the-art artificial-ice plant. The surface it produced was flawlessly smooth and hard — too hard for the visitors, who were accustomed to the softer natural ice they had always skated on in Canada. Their blades slipped on the ice instead of cutting into it, and the Ottawas found themselves on the losing end of a 3-1 score against the strong New York Athletic Club in the inaugural match. Fortunately they were able to get their skates properly sharpened for the next night's game, which they won against an All-New York team 5-2. Matches such as these were important to the New York clubs. They wanted to promote themselves and the sport itself in a city and country where hockey did not enjoy a high profile. By showing they were competitive with the best in Canada, the New York teams hoped to gain new adherents to the game. These international matches helped the cause. St. Nicholas Rink was packed for every one, and newspapers gave the games more coverage than strictly local contests. For the Ottawa players, an excursion to the metropolis of 3.5 million people was breathtaking. Not only would they have a chance to show their skills abroad, they would get out on the streets to take in sights and sounds that only America's greatest city could offer. Getting out on the streets was one thing, finding their way back to the Continental Hotel was another. Bright and early on the Saturday morning of their first visit, four of the boys decided on a walk. After an hour or so, they realized they had no idea where they were. They approached a cabman, who allowed that for a sum of twenty-five cents each, a not-insubstantial fare, he would be happy to deliver them to their hotel. Agreeing to this arrangement, the visitors piled into the hack for what promised to be an interesting ride. One hundred feet later and around the corner, the horse and cab pulled up at the Continental's front door.

The Ups and Downs of League Play, 1893–1902

EXHIBITION GAMES were all well and good, and adventures to New York were easy to take; but winning hockey games in their own league was what the Ottawas really had in mind and what their supporters, turning out in ever greater numbers, expected of them. Over the eleven-year period from 1893 to 1903 the club did well, with a regular-season record in the AHAC and its successor league, the CAHL, of fifty-four wins, one tie, and thirty-three losses (a 60-per-cent success rate). That stretch included a first-place tie in 1894, an undefeated first-place finish in 1901, and another first-place tie in 1903. The club had only one losing season — their last-place finish of 1898.

The 1893 season was a milestone for the game. It saw a return to the series system of regular home-and-home matches among the five teams of the AHAC after five years of the challenge system when there was no set schedule. It also marked the debut of the Stanley Cup. Ottawa finished the season with a 6-2 record, second to the MAAA's 7-1 finish. Reg Bradley, who would leave Ottawa the next fall to pursue studies at the University of Toronto, led the team in scoring with eleven goals in eight games. Since trustees Ross and Sweetland had decided that initially the new trophy should go to the AHAC champions, the Montrealers became the first recipients.

Ottawa's first-place tie in 1894 was with three other teams: the MAAA, the Victorias, and Quebec. A championship roundrobin among three of the four contending teams (Quebec dropped out in protest over where the final should be played) resulted in the MAAA once again taking the trophy. The Ottawas finished second in each of the next three seasons. Then disaster struck. The 1898 season was an unsettling one from the beginning. In the previous year the Ottawas had moved from the outdated Rideau Rink on the perimeter of Sandy Hill to a brand-new building at Ann Street on the edge of town. The Dey brothers, Edwin, William, and Frank, had decided to build a new structure after the original Dey's Skating Rink, where the Ottawas got their start years earlier, was expropriated. The ice surface was bigger than the Rideau's and there were more seats, all with an unobstructed view. The club was quite pleased with its new surroundings. The Dey brothers, always hard bargainers, were quite pleased, too, but thought they could do even better by increasing the Ottawas' rent. Meanwhile the directors of the Rideau Rink were experiencing hard times. They had lost the Ottawas as their prime tenant and were in such dire straits that they appealed to city council for tax concessions because the rink was no longer paying a return on investment. After a lengthy and sometimes-heated discussion at the next Ottawa Hockey Club annual meeting, the executive committee voted to return to the antiquated Rideau. Added to the unhappiness among some of the players at this reversal was the dissension in the ranks over captain Pulford's decision to play Weldy Young (who had left and then returned to the team) instead of choosing from among other loyal recruits. And it didn't help the club's stability when president S.M. Rogers resigned over the issue and Chauncey Kirby, who was expected back after a year's absence, refused to return in protest. The signal problem, though, was not boardroom wrangling or where the games should be played, but player turnover. Veteran Alf Smith had left the team for the Capitals before being disqualified as a professional. Harry Westwick missed three games for the same reason before being reinstated. And Fred Chittick, who had been the league's top goal-keeper for the two previous years, quit the team mid-schedule. During the course of the season, five players who had had no previous senior experience were inserted into the lineup: Al Cope, Paddy Baskerville, Harry Rosenthal, Fred White, and fifteen-year-old Davie Glimour. Veteran Harvey Pulford seemed stoic about the situation. After yet another loss, he told the *Journal* that "almost an entirely new forward line cannot be developed in one season; the experience will be of great assistance to the team next year." The Ottawas finished with a 2-and-6 record.

Following two mediocre seasons back at Dey's Rink, when they lost as often as they won, the club returned to winning form in 1901, compiling an outstanding record of seven wins, one tie, and no losses under the tutelage of new coach Alf Smith. In his second full season, Bouse Hutton had come into his own as a bona fide senior-league goalkeeper; the heretofore cautious and conservative Pulford decided this was the year to begin rushing the puck; Art Sixsmith, new to the lineup but for one game the year before, surprised everyone with seven goals in seven games; veteran Chic Henry had eight goals in eight games; and Harry Westwick, who returned to the team after a two-year absence, scored six times in seven games.

Their two wins over the Shamrocks signalled the Ottawas' ascendancy, for the Irish club had been league champions and Stanley Cup winners in 1899 and 1900. The second of the victories, before an estimated 3,500 supporters at Dey's Rink, was the highlight of the season. Going into the game, the Ottawas had won five and tied one. The Shamrocks were in second place with three wins and two losses. If the Ottawas could win this game, no one would be able to catch them and they would finish as CAHL champions. At the end of the two halves, the score was tied at one goal apiece. Near midnight and after twenty minutes of overtime, Mac Roger secured the puck and passed it to Art Sixsmith, who beat the Quebec goalkeeper with a clean shot.

Earlier in the season, the Stanley Cup trustees had approved a challenge to the cup holders, the Shamrocks, from the Winnipeg Victorias. The westerners came east, won the series in two-straight games and went home with the trophy. As CAHL champions, the Ottawas were entitled to challenge Winnipeg but after some deliberation decided not to. They had just completed a tough schedule and the long journey to Manitoba, they reasoned, would put them at a big disadvantage.

In 1902 the MAAA finished with one more win than Ottawa to take first place. They then successfully challenged Winnipeg and completed the season as Stanley Cup holders. Ottawa's turn was finally about to come.

A Stanley Cup Season, 1903

THE OTTAWAS STARTED their next season in a brand-new Dey's Rink, and for a while it was touch and go whether they would be able to do so or would have to return yet another time to the old Rideau Rink. A violent summer storm had reduced the Dey brothers' structure to a pile of rubble. Meanwhile, private investors who had planned to erect a modern rink were forced to delay the project because they could not secure the necessary iron. But the evident shortage did not deter the Deys, who announced in September that they would build a new rink on the same site as the previous one and that the work would be rushed. Three months later, in the middle of December, it was up and ready. Though on a smaller scale, the design of the new rink was influenced by the Montreal Arena, which had opened four years earlier. Tiers of theatre-style seats completely surrounded the ice surface. The surface itself measured 200 by 80 feet and, like its Montreal counterpart, had semicircular ends — no corners. That feature, previously unique to the Montreal Arena, would be repeated and commented on for the next sixty-five years in two subsequent Ottawa hockey rinks. It was surprising that the Deys would choose this shape. Billy Dey had gone down to Montreal to see the new arena when it opened and told the *Citizen* that he was not at all taken with the "round corners." Neither were the Ottawa players. The circular ends made them think everything was spinning. "It seems like playing in a washtub," Mac Roger said. But when their own home rink adopted the egg shape, they changed their opinion, concluding that round corners would do away with the scrapping so prevalent in square-cornered rinks.

After a season playing in Pittsburgh, Smith came back to the Ottawas as coach for the 1903 campaign. He could count on veterans Hutton, Pulford, and Westwick returning; but three others, Bruce Stuart, William Duval, and Chic Henry would be lost to Pittsburgh. Charlie Spittal joined them in mid-season. Here is where the city's solid hockey infrastructure paid off, for four players from the Aberdeen intermediates came up to fill the breach: the three Gilmour brothers, Dave, Billy, and Suddy; and Frank McGee. Coach Smith used different combinations of the Gilmours,

Westwick, and McGee through the season. In the first game, a loss to the Victorias, the three brothers formed a line with Westwick. On the only other occasion during the schedule when all three played together, they teamed with McGee in another loss, this time to Quebec. The most frequent and successful combination had Billy and Suddy Gilmour on the wings, McGee at centre, and Westwick playing rover. Going into 1903 Westwick was the acknowledged star of the team. In six seasons he had scored thirty-three goals, including eleven in 1902. It must have been as much a surprise to him as to everyone else that all four of the new forwards would score more goals than the Rat in 1903: McGee, fourteen goals in six games; Billy Gilmour, ten goals in seven games; Suddy Gilmour, seven goals in seven games; Dave Gilmour, seven goals in four games; Westwick, six goals in six games.

If the Ottawas could win their last regular season game at the Montreal Arena against the MAAA, they would have six victories, enough to assure them of at least a tie for first place with the Victorias, who had four wins and two games remaining. Cover point Art Moore scored for Ottawa, as did McGee and Suddy Gilmour, in a 3-1 win. Mocking Ottawa's horizontally striped red, white, and black uniforms, Montreal supporters took to calling the players from the capital "barber poles." But Ottawa sportsmen loved to have pejorative titles bestowed on them. The Rat was proud of his handle. Indeed, the Ottawa Football Club was so enamoured of the "rough riders" label, intended as a slur by a Hamilton newspaper critical of the players' aggressive style, that it happily accepted the insult as the club's nickname. And so it was that "the Barber Poles" became an affectionate, if unofficial, sobriquet for Ottawa's beloved hockey team.

The Victorias won their final two games against the MAAA and Quebec to give them the six victories they needed to tie for first place with the Ottawas. A playoff would be required to decide a league champion, but that playoff would have even greater meaning because the Stanley Cup would be at stake. The MAAA, which held the trophy, had successfully fought off a challenge from Winnipeg; but because the MAAA failed to win the CAHL championship, the cup would pass to the team taking the league title.

Immediately after the Victorias' last game, league representatives met to decide dates for the playoff. Ottawa wanted a two-game, home-and-home, total-goal series on March 5 and 7. Quebec and the Shamrocks supported this proposal. Victorias' president Fred McRobie, who was also the league's secretary-treasurer, demanded the dates be March 7 and 10 so that his team could recuperate from a tough schedule. If this was not accepted, he said, his team would default. In taking this hard line, McRobie was mindful that his star player, Russell Bowie, was suffering from a foot injury and would need as much extra time as possible to recover. The wrangling continued. To meet Ottawa halfway, McRobie suggested a single, sudden-death match. Ottawa refused. League president Harry Trihey proposed flipping a coin. Ottawa president Percy Buttler agreed, McRobie did not. Finally, sensing an impasse, Buttler gave in to McRobie's insistence on the March 7 and 10 dates. They also agreed, despite McRobie's initial reluctance, that the winner would accept challenges already on the books from Rat Portage and the Toronto Wellingtons.

Tensions between the two clubs spilled over into the Ottawa dressing room when the teams met for the first game at the Montreal Arena. As the players were getting ready for the match, trainer Pete Green locked the door to keep the room from filling up with well-wishers and hangers-on. He did not notice that McRobie was inside. When the Vics president tried to leave and found the door locked, he raised a ruckus.

"Who let you in?" Green demanded.

"I walked in through the open door," McRobie replied.

"Well, we will let you out if you are civil," Green said.

"I want you to know that I am president of the Victorias and that I do not want any of your impertinence," McRobie replied.

"There you go now, with your back up like a camel," Green retorted.

"Who is the captain of the team, I want out."

"I am the captain of the team," Harvey Pulford asserted, "and you can get out as quick as you like. Pete, unlock the door and let the man out."

Feelings ran high on the ice, too. It was one of the dirtiest encounters seen in some time. Victorias' centre Bert Strachan, no doubt egged on by McRobie who was now up in the stands bellowing advice through a megaphone, punched, tripped, and slashed his way through the match and was ruled off four times. Rat Westwick fell victim to Strachan's stick-wielding near the end of the first half and left the ice with a broken bone protruding through the skin of his right leg. In the delay, McRobie tried to enter the closed Ottawa dressing room, identifying himself outside the door as the referee. Once inside he offered to call a physician. The Ottawa trainers, wanting nothing at all to do with the man, threw him out again.

Dave Gilmour replaced Westwick at rover and within three minutes scored to give the Ottawas a 1-0 lead at the half. The Vics' prolific scorer

Russell Bowie, who was doubtful for the game, made some dangerous rushes; but it was Strachan who tied the match midway through the second half. The game ended at a deadlock a few minutes before midnight.

Hobbling along on his crutches, Westwick somehow made his way through the crush of supporters and climbed up to the press stand in the rafters of Dey's Rink. Like three thousand other Ottawa partisans and a handful of Victoria devotees, he was determined to witness the playoff finale. Ruefully he looked down to see his nemesis, Bert Strachan, and the other Vics file out onto the ice. Then the Ottawas appeared: Hutton, Pulford, Moore, McGee, and the three Gilmours. Dave, the eldest brother, would again be Westwick's replacement, but coach Smith had the promising junior Percy Sims waiting in the wings in case of further injuries. Covered with a thin layer of water, the ice was treacherously slippery as Lord Minto, with a half-sliding step, navigated to the centre of the rink for the ceremonial faceoff. The game to decide the Stanley Cup was under way.

McGee scored after four and a half minutes. Presently Suddy Gilmour made it 2-0. Then brother Dave took over with three-straight goals in less than nine minutes. With the exception of a few well-directed whacks at McGee from Strachan's stick, the Victorias were unexpectedly docile. By halftime the Ottawas had a commanding 5-0 lead. The Vics showed some jump at the start of the second half but, unable to penetrate the defence put up by Pulford and Moore, soon became dispirited. Capitalizing on the scoreless Vics' lack of resolve, McGee scored twice more and Billy Gilmour wrapped things up with the Ottawas' eighth goal. Ten years after its inauguration, the Ottawa Hockey Club had won the Stanley Cup. Jubilant supporters swarmed the ice to mob their heroes and then spilled into the streets to continue the celebration.

The players would have precious little time to savour their success. They were fully aware that the Rat Portage Thistles had sat quietly observing the action at Dey's Rink from aisle chairs, having arrived in the city only an hour or so before the championship game. In approving the challenge of the western champions, the Stanley Cup trustees had scheduled a two-game, total-goal series for March 12 and 14. With spring mere days away, the matches had to be squeezed in before the ice melted. Thankfully, from an administrative point of view, the trustees had received word that the Toronto Wellingtons were withdrawing their challenge because of injuries to key players.

As for the Thistles, they were an unknown quantity. They represented a small mining, milling, and lumbering town on Lake of the Woods, thirty miles from the Manitoba border. As champions of the Manitoba and Northwestern Hockey League, though, they must have been pretty good, because the Winnipeg Victorias of that association had brought the cup home twice in the last seven years.

The series was anticlimactic, with Ottawa winning 6-2 and 4-2. Papers dismissed the visitors before the first game started. Evidently local hockey enthusiasts felt the same way, for fewer than half the number who had been on hand for the triumph over the Vics bothered to show up for the first game. Attendance for the second was no better, and the total gate receipts were a paltry $1,500. The Thistles left town wiser but poorer; their share of the proceeds came to $500, against estimated expenses of $1,300. By the midway point of the first game, the Senators, as the Ottawas were now frequently dubbed, had run up a 6-1 lead on the strength of Billy Gilmour's three goals, one by brother Dave, and two by McGee. Billy McGimsie, the Thistles' strongest player, scored in the first half and again in the second. McGimsie scored both Thistle goals in the second game. McGee, with two goals, and Billy and Dave Gilmour, with one each, gave Ottawa the win. Substitute Percy Sims finally got his chance when Suddy Gilmour's sore arm prevented the nineteen-year-old youngster from suiting up. From his unlikely perch in the press stand alongside the Rat, Smith, emulating the earlier antics of Victorias coach Fred McRobie, exhorted his players through a megaphone.

The season now ended, Ottawa would have a full spring, summer, and fall to relish its status as a Stanley Cup city before the challengers took aim. Ten years earlier, when the club tussled unsuccessfully with the MAAA for the championship, players and supporters alike were hardly aware of the strange new trophy at stake. Now the trophy was strange no more, and the current crop of Ottawa players had become familiar names across Canada.

Within days of their triumph, local sportsmen under the direction of former Ottawa Hockey Club president John Dickson mounted a campaign to honour the team. Press reports stated there would be a joint ceremony in which members of both the champion Ottawa Rough Riders football team and the hockey players would receive mementoes. The *Citizen* said the hockey team would be presented with engraved gold signet rings; the *Journal* said lockets. Whatever transpired was low key, for there appear to have been no printed accounts of the occasion. Equally low key, but far more significant, was another presentation by team manager Bob Shillington. Shillington thoroughly enjoyed his association with the hockey club and was extremely popular with the players. He had shared some laughs with them in New York and could be counted on to cheer the boys up with song when spirits were low — "The Stars Will Tell You Why" seems to have been a favourite. Shillington was a prominent Ottawa druggist whose business ventures led him to mining speculation, namely silver mining in the Cobalt area where he would eventually relocate. So elated was he over the Ottawas' Stanley Cup victory that he decided he should show his appreciation in a unique way. Westwick, weeks before he passed away in 1957, recalled the occasion in an *Ottawa Journal* interview: "Bob Shillington, our manager ... presented each of the players with a silver nugget. One of the fellows said, 'We ought to call ourselves the Silver Seven' and the name caught on right there."

8 · The Shillington Seven, Part I
The Game in the Boardroom, 1904–1906

The supporters of the victors are generally in a state of great excitement
while the supporters of the losers are in a state of despondency and gloom.
They nearly always have something unpleasant to say about their opponents.

GLADYS HUMPHRYS, 14
School essay, 1904

THE SILVER SEVEN might as well have been called the Shillington Seven. In fact the famous name that came to identify the team of the 1903-to-1906 glory years did not gain broad circulation until later. Newspaper reporters, looking back on that time, retroactively picked up on the name Rat Westwick's teammates thought would be a good one for the boys. Shillington had certainly never imagined the silver nuggets he gave the players would inspire the nickname. And rarely during their three-year run did local newspapers refer to the champions as the Silver Seven. Outside Ottawa the name was virtually unknown. In Ottawa the name Senators was occasionally seen or heard; but overwhelmingly they were the Ottawas.

Around town, too, the name Shillington was far better recognized than the name Silver Seven. R.T. "Bob" Shillington was an engaging personality, respected as a dynamic businessman and sports organizer, and adored by the players he rubbed shoulders with in football, lacrosse, and hockey. Shillington was born in 1866 at Merivale, a postal village on the city's outskirts. His parents sent him to Ottawa's Model School and then to the Collegiate Institute, and with that solid academic background he enrolled in the Ontario College of Pharmacy program at the University of Toronto. Returning to Ottawa, the young pharmacist set up his own business on Sparks Street, where he prospered and gained valuable experience in the world of commerce. Shillington loved sports, finding his niche at the executive level as a director at one time or another of the Capital Lacrosse Club, Ottawa Football Club, and Ottawa Hockey Club. What he relished most was being around the players, which made him accessible to the press. And with

Mining magnate and Senators manager Bob Shillington presented silver nuggets to the 1903 Stanley Cup-winning Ottawas, prompting the team's sobriquet, the Silver Seven. Shillington was an affable and outgoing character, which made his quotes regular fodder for the press. LIBRARY AND ARCHIVES CANADA C34882

his natural gregariousness he was always good for a quote. This was certainly true in his executive capacity with the hockey club, whose every move was scrutinized by reporters hard pressed to meet the voracious appetite of a hockey-mad city. By the end of the Ottawas' Stanley Cup reign in 1906, Shillington had been on the club executive in seven of eight years since 1898, missing only the 1901 season, and was more visible in his hockey capacity than some of the club's presidents. And he was hard-working. When the club was looking for a larger home rink after its 1903 Stanley Cup victory, Shillington served on the committee negotiating terms with the Central Canada Exhibition Association for the use of the cavernous Aberdeen Pavilion. He was the club's delegate to the Canadian Amateur Hockey League in 1903 and to the Federal Amateur Hockey League in 1906, and was team manager from 1903 to 1906. As manager, he was instrumental in re-affiliating the Ottawa Hockey Club with the Ottawa Amateur Athletic Club in 1904. The Ottawas had broken away years earlier, and the move to return to the OAAC fold assured them a firm institutional foundation. It was a dark day for Ottawa's sporting community in November 1905 when Shillington announced he had sold his druggist's business, for his decision signalled the restless entrepreneur's imminent departure from the local scene. The great Ottawas were the Shillington Seven in spirit, if not in name.

National Notice

OVER THEIR THREE-YEAR reign as Stanley Cup champions, the Ottawas attracted a large following among sports-page readers from Halifax to Vancouver. While they rolled to twenty wins against two losses in league play, it was their Stanley Cup prowess that took them from being a team of regional interest to one commanding attention across the country. In nine series against clubs from three provinces, the Ottawas won fifteen matches, lost three, and tied one. Even in Vancouver, where hockey meant the field version unless ice was specified, the Ottawas were becoming familiar names: Smith (forty games played in three years), Westwick (thirty-nine), Art Moore (thirty-eight), McGee (thirty-five), Pulford (thirty-five).

But that national acclaim was hard won, not because of any indifference on the part of sports followers but because of the nature of news distribution. Newspapers relied on the Canadian Pacific Telegraph wire service for non-local stories. The company had obtained the Canadian rights to the Associated Press news service, from which it selected and edited stories for distribution at a flat rate along the length of its telegraph line. AP gave short shrift to non-U.S. news, and Canadian Pacific's Canadian news-gathering, left to CP telegraph operators, was, in the words of the *Manitoba Free Press*, "so crude and the cost of transmitting it so heavy that no newspaper has sufficient resources to make even a partial success of the task." In *A History of Journalism in Canada*, Wilfred Kesterton observes that "the rate charged for American news was about a quarter of that charged for Canadian news." Upset by the almost-impossible task of offering an adequate interchange of information between the regions of Canada — information "so necessary to national development and consolidation," according to the *Free Press* — a group of western papers, led by the three Winnipeg dailies, established their own Western Associated Press in 1907. Its intention was to counteract the Canadian Pacific monopoly and increase Canadian content. But that was a year after the Ottawas' reign had ended. Under the circumstances, it was no small tribute to hockey's hold on the country that McGee and Pulford, and their illustrious opponents, found themselves on the front pages of big and small newspapers alike.

Such was the intensity of public interest in the fortunes of the home team that for an important game on the road some newspapers would go to extraordinary lengths to keep readers abreast of the action in the timeliest way technology permitted. Typical was the *Manitoba Free Press*'s setup for ensuring Winnipeggers were right up to the minute on how the Rowing Club team was doing in its January 1904 challenge to the Ottawas. The newspaper connected a direct wire from the Aberdeen Pavilion in Ottawa to its home office at the corner of McDermot and Albert streets. A correspondent in the press booth described the play as it unfolded to a telegraph operator seated beside him. He relayed the messages to the *Free Press,* where a receiving telegrapher decoded them. They were then converted into transparent slides, which were magnified through a stereopticon projector onto a large screen in the front window of the newspaper office. Not only did the hundreds of residents who gathered on the street through the cold evening enjoy a written description of the play as it went on, they chuckled at the humorous accompanying sketches hurriedly done up by staff illustrators. Here is a sample description:

Ottawa, Ont. Jan.1, 1904 — 8 p.m. — The Winnipeggers arrived at the rink about 7.30, had a good rub down, and are feeling fit for a hard game ...

8.29 p.m. — The Winnipegs have just trotted out and get a nice reception. It is noticed that to protect their heads they have all put on thick caps. They are taking their preliminary. Hamber makes a fine lift from one end to the other, and is a very likely looking substitute for Richards. The same officials will act to-night, namely: Trihey, referee and Messrs. Hanratty and Northey, umpires. The Ottawas have not got onto the ice yet.

8.40 p.m. — The Winnipegs are practising combination, and are making things lively for the crowd. The Ottawas have appeared on the ice, and as they do, the challengers go into the dressing room for the advice of "How to beat Ottawa."

8.41 p.m. — Referee Trihey has called both teams to the centre where he lectures them and says he will not stand for any rough play. Little Borland shakes the hand of Moore, and looks very small beside his antagonist.

8.43 p.m. — The Government House party have just taken their seats. Both Lord and Lady Minto are present, and are taking great interest in the players' movements.

8.45 p.m. — The game starts. McGee got the puck on the face. Hall trips McGee and gets ruled off for two minutes. Now Hamber relieves, but loses to Moore, Breen tries a shot but fails...

As Stanley Cup champions, the Ottawas had little time or inclination to engage in the exhibition matches they had quite readily accepted before. Their league schedule coupled with cup challenges that kept streaming in through trustees Ross and Sweetland were more than enough to keep them on the ice. At the start of the 1905–06 season, however, they did agree to a western tour that promised to be financially rewarding. It transpired through the efforts of Pulford, who was in Winnipeg on business. He negotiated a contract that would guarantee his team three thousand dollars for four games in Winnipeg, Kenora, and Fort William. In return, he promised to bring the full Stanley Cup team. As it turned out, the best-known star of all, McGee, was missing from the lineup, as were Dave Finnie and Billy Gilmour. The other big names, Pulford, Moore, Westwick, and Smith thrilled the capacity crowds and won the team throngs of new admirers who had never had the chance to see the champions in person, having only read about them in the newspaper.

The Game in the Boardroom

A PITTAWAY COMPOSITE photograph of the 1905 champions is revealing: twelve men in hockey suits, twelve men in business suits. Symbolically, the men with the jackets and ties are grouped at the top of the picture, the men in striped roll-collar sweaters at the bottom. Hockey was business, and a club that had achieved national fame needed all the executive support it could get. Making sure revenues met expenditures (with a little left over to be sure) was always a boardroom consideration, but the two main issues of the day were whom the club would play and who would get to play. The first had to do with league organization; the second was the headache of professionalism.

The key players in the boardroom during the Silver Seven years, besides Bob Shillington, were Dr. Halder Kirby, the statesmanlike president from 1903 to 1905; P.J. Baskerville, finance committee (1903–04), executive committee (1904–05), treasurer (1905–06); N.C. Sparks, finance committee (1903–04), executive committee (1904–06); L.N. Bate, finance committee (1903–04), vice-president (1904–06); and J.P. Dickson, advertising and rink committees (1904–05), executive committee (1904–06), Federal Amateur Hockey League delegate (1905–06).

All of the directors had an active hand in the affairs of the club, but Dickson and Shillington were the most visible. In temperament and outlook, however, they were two very different people. Equally at home in the boardroom and the dressing room, Shillington was the type to smooth things over when differences arose in league administration, and to cheer the boys up when they lost a tough game. Dickson was idealistic, resolute, and uncompromising. When he formed an opinion on what he thought was right, he was unbending. Rather than negotiate a settlement satisfactory to all concerned, he would resign from his duties as a matter of principle. In 1896 he quit as Ottawa Hockey Club secretary over internal dissension among board members and players. In 1904 he resigned from the board of the Canadian Amateur Athletic Union because he felt it was less punitive of Montreal athletes tainted by professionalism than of athletes elsewhere. Earlier that year he was the moving force behind Ottawa's withdrawal from the CAHL over a disputed game. In 1906 he resigned again from the Ottawa Hockey Club board over what appears to have been the trivial matter of the club's choice of the Grand Trunk Railway for the Stanley Cup excursion to Montreal. As secretary-treasurer of the Canadian Railway Accident Insurance Company at the time, he may have felt he had insights that were being ignored. (The decision to go with the Grand Trunk came one month after former Ottawa Hockey Club president and longtime executive Percy Buttler took over as the company's city passenger and ticket agent.)

Senior hockey was in turmoil during the Silver Seven years, so much so that the Ottawas, a team highly sought after by hockey organizers, wound up playing in three different leagues in three years. The CAHL was running, in effect, a "close corporation." Member clubs wanted a compact circuit of the best players. Additional clubs would dilute the talent, put a strain on schedules, and add expenses for trips to other cities. The premier senior teams had a history of thinking this way, and in fact this view led to the formation of the CAHL in the first place. Outvoted at the 1898 meeting of the AHAC by intermediate-club delegates who favoured the inclusion of the Ottawa Capitals, the senior clubs simply quit the league and created a new one of their liking, the CAHL. The Caps were left out in the cold. True to form, in 1902 the CAHL denied applications from Cornwall and the Aberdeens of Ottawa.

Through a convergence of forces, matters came to a head the following season. In a revolt that astounded many hockey observers, several prominent players of the Montreal Hockey Club, which was connected with the venerable MAAA, abandoned their team and vowed to establish an independent club. On the surface, the reasons were puzzling. Newspapers suggested the players felt their interests were not being looked after and that they resented having to take out MAAA membership in order to play on the team. Montreal Hockey Club president Harry Shaw remained tightlipped about the situation, but the club's minute book, though not referring to the defections, is revealing. Far from being hard done by, the players were treated like royalty. In recognition of their work in the season completed, the executive had given them diamond rings valued at $100 each (verified in the cash book), as well as team photographs. And if the players told the press they didn't like being forced into MAAA membership, they should also have revealed that in fact the hockey club paid all of their membership fees for them. There was something else behind the defections — a new league — and whenever there was a demand for rink dates, the Montreal Arena was always more than happy to oblige.

The timing of the Montreal defections was suspicious because just as these players, along with some from the Victorias, were organizing their own team, to be called the Wanderers, three other clubs announced their wish to enter senior ranks. Frustrated by previous rejections, the Ottawa Capitals, the Montreal Nationals, and a Cornwall team joined forces with the Wanderers to create the FAHL, the Federal Amateur Hockey League. There would now be two senior circuits. Shillington was sanguine about the prospects of two senior clubs operating in Ottawa and promised full co-operation with the new league and its Ottawa-based president, William Foran. The Ottawas would play at the Aberdeen Pavilion and the Capitals would take over Dey's Arena. There was some talk, however, that the CAHL would be greatly weakened by the departure of the key Montreal and Victoria players, and that as a consequence the Ottawas would dominate, leading to a collapse of the league and the shift of the Ottawas to the new loop.

Stanley Cup trustees Ross and Sweetland looked on with consternation. They were concerned that another senior league would add to the proliferation of cup challenges already coming in from senior champions; but they also felt that for the good of the game, promising new clubs should be given the opportunity to show their worth against the best. Ross, in particular, favoured the CAHL and FAHL uniting and adopting the divisional system common in British sports leagues and in OHA. The new league, he thought, should include an intermediate series. The intermediate champion would graduate to the senior series, while the lowest team in the senior would drop back to the intermediate. Years earlier, Ottawa Capitals president James Davidson had proposed just that arrangement.

Ross did not press the idea and by January 1904 the two parallel leagues were in full swing. It would not be long, however, before the Ottawa Hockey Club executive would have a crisis on its hands. The trouble began with Ottawa's third game in the CAHL season. They had gone to Montreal for a Saturday night game, January 30, against the Victorias. The Montreal Arena, the site of the contest, was actually in Westmount, where a midnight curfew was in effect. The Ottawas lost their baggage, causing a delay of one hour and fifteen minutes. With the curfew in mind, the teams agreed that if by midnight the game was still in progress but there were fewer than ten minutes remaining, the team leading the game would be declared the winner. If there were more than ten minutes, the match would be declared no game. To expedite matters and lessen the chances of running out of time, the referee suggested that in the case of player injuries, substitution be allowed and that the game resume immediately, rather than permit time for the player to recuperate. Ottawa agreed, but the Vics did not. As it turned out, some forty-three minutes were lost to Victoria injuries, and when the clock struck twelve there were still sixteen minutes on the clock. Leading 4-1, the Ottawas were convinced the Vics' injuries were no more than a stalling tactic.

Before the game, the league executive had agreed to meet at its conclusion to arrange the rescheduling of a Quebec-Ottawa match that Quebec could not make because of a severe snowstorm. Ottawa delegate John Dickson wanted the meeting to decide also what should be done about the aborted match they had just witnessed, but the executive refused to do so, saying that because the meeting had not been called for that purpose, notice would have to be given of another one. To Dickson's dismay, when the executive did meet the following week, president Harry Trihey demanded that Dickson explain why his team was late for the Victoria match. Unsatisfied with his response, the executive entertained a motion to invoke Section 3 of the "Laws of Hockey" — in other words, a ten-dollar fine for delay of game. Dickson then moved an amendment to the motion: "That in view of the lateness of other matches in the current season, that in this instance the rule be not carried out, but that all clubs be notified that in the event of any reoccurrence that the constitution will be carried out." It was a reasonable proposition. The Victorias had been tardy for games at both Ottawa and Quebec, and Quebec had failed to arrive in Ottawa at all. Moreover, in a twist of irony, on the same evening when Dickson was making his case at the Windsor Hotel in Montreal, the

Shamrocks were ninety minutes late for their date with the Ottawas at the Aberdeen Pavilion. Why should Ottawa be singled out? was Dickson's argument. That line of reasoning meant nothing to the body assembled. The amendment found no seconder, the main motion was passed, and the fine was levied.

The next item of business was the rescheduling of the Ottawa-Victoria match. Dickson objected to the idea that it be played later that month, proposing instead that it not be played at all unless the standings for the championship would be affected. He went farther. If the executive did not agree, he would take the Ottawas out of the league. Unimpressed with the ultimatum, the executive went ahead and rescheduled the match.

Returning to Ottawa on the Sunday, Dickson had a problem on his hands. His threat hadn't worked and he knew he lacked the authority to make good on it. He called a hurried meeting of the Ottawa Hockey Club executive the next morning and explained everything to them. Shillington favoured accepting the injustice and soldiering on, but to Dickson's relief the others were persuaded by his tough stance. There was a lingering worry, however. Would their resignation from the CAHL mean that Ottawa would forfeit the Stanley Cup? Before deciding to leave the league, they had better find out. It wouldn't take long; Ross, cup trustee, was in his *Ottawa Journal* office, just a few blocks over. Away went a deputation of Dickson, Shillington, and club president Halder Kirby. A most obliging Ross (co-trustee Sweetland seems not to have been around) assured his visitors that the cup would remain theirs to defend. After all, he reasoned, a precedent had been set in 1898 when the Stanley Cup-holding Victorias left the AHAC and were allowed to retain the trophy. But wait a minute. If the Ottawas dropped out of the CAHL, where would they play? Away the deputation went to the East Block offices of Parliament Hill. There sat the secretary of the Board of Civil Service Examiners, William Foran, who happened also to be the president of the FAHL. A most obliging Foran assured his visitors he would call a special meeting of the league forthwith to recommend the acceptance of the Stanley Cup champions. That was good enough for the executive, who gave CAHL delegate Dickson the green light to wire Ottawa's resignation to CAHL president Trihey.

Dickson was right to think Ottawa had been done an injustice. And Shillington was right to think the club, nevertheless, should have turned the other cheek and carried on for the good of the league. But Ross's judgement was suspect in letting the Ottawas keep the cup. If the Ottawas had stayed but not won the league title, the cup would have gone to the first-place team. Where is the fairness in allowing a team that quit the league at mid-season to take the trophy with it? The ostensible precedent set in 1898 was an entirely different matter. The Victorias did not leave the AHAC in mid-schedule. Rather, four of the five senior teams, including the Vics, abandoned the league before the season started and reconstructed themselves into a new one. With the collapse of the old league, had the trustees forced the Vics to give up the trophy, there would have been no other team or league to award it to.

Needless to say, Ross infuriated the CAHL and its member clubs with his decision. Rejecting his line of thinking, the league pointedly asked Ross when, and against whom, its champion might be expected to *defend* the cup. And the minute book of the Montreal Hockey Club shows that when the committee was advised by the CAHL of his decision, the secretary was "instructed to acknowledge receipt of letter and state that as far as our Club was concerned they would suggest Mr. Ross' retaining possession of the Cup, and that our Club would be willing to subscribe an amount towards a Championship Trophy to be competed for."

As expected, the FAHL executive council warmly welcomed the Ottawas, with play to commence the following season. The Stanley Cup champions would bring prestige to the league and would be a strong drawing card. As it stood, the Wanderers were the only bona fide senior-calibre team in the FAHL, going through the 1904 season undefeated. During the summer, Ottawa resisted entreaties from CAHL president Trihey to return to the league. Dickson later said that doing so would have been an admission that the Ottawas were wrong in the first place for quitting. But he was also adamant in his view that so long as the league was controlled by the men behind the Montreal, Shamrock, and Victoria clubs, Ottawa would be ganged up on in all league decisions.

As the new season approached, the Ottawa executive softened Dickson's position. At the CAHL's annual meeting in Montreal, Dickson hovered around the perimeter with a two-part plan. It hinged on the fate of the Wanderers. That club, after one year's experience, was not enamoured of the federal league it had helped to found and wanted into the CAHL, where a higher level of competition would be assured. If their application was accepted, Dickson would immediately submit one for the Ottawas, who, he anticipated, would merge with the Ottawa Capitals of the FAHL, thus spelling the end of that league. He would then try to convince the CAHL to reduce the number of Montreal clubs from seven to four through amalgamations, leaving a six-team league, with Quebec being the other club. He put his application in the hands of Bill Northey of the Montreal Arena, who was an observer at the CAHL meetings. The idea was that if the Wanderers were accepted, Northey would immediately place the Ottawa application on the table and call in Dickson, who was waiting in another room, to address it. Under pressure from the Montreal Hockey Club, which still harboured resentment toward the Wanderers for having stolen their players, the delegates denied their entry. Consequently the Ottawa application did not go ahead. The rationalization of senior hockey was not to be. The two leagues would continue their separate ways, with one thing in common — weak teams in each.

As far as league matters were concerned for the Ottawa executive, the 1905 FAHL season was uneventful. The Ottawa Capitals, who dropped out, and the Nationals of Montreal, who switched to the CAHL, were replaced by Brockville and the Montagnards of Montreal. Cornwall was still in. The Ottawas and the Wanderers had an easy time of it, finishing one, two in the standings.

The Ottawa executive professed loyalty to the FAHL but in reality, like the Wanderers, were less than enchanted with the calibre of play. They also took note of the public's lukewarm interest in contests against Cornwall and Brockville. Brockville posed another difficulty. There was no direct rail service there, meaning the Ottawas were forced to hire a special train at added expense. In compensation, they extracted fifty dollars from the Brockville club for the 1905 date and secured the same arrangement for the season ahead. As the 1906 season approached, though, the FAHL was in a shaky state: three mediocre clubs and two strong ones that wanted out.

On separate visits in November 1905, James Strachan of the Wanderers and Fred McRobie of the Victorias sounded out Ottawa Hockey Club officials on the possibility of forming a new league of the strongest senior clubs. Recently elected Ottawa president George Murphy was receptive and suggested that club representatives from the Wanderers, the Victorias, Montreal, Quebec, and Ottawa meet to discuss bringing one or two other clubs into a union. What McRobie did not tell him was that Montreal, the Victorias, the Shamrocks, Westmount, and Quebec, all currently of the CAHL, had formed an alliance and signed a document agreeing to stick together on all hockey business, no matter what league they were in. When the Ottawa directors found out, they, and especially Dickson, took exception to the ad hoc coalition because it seemed to confirm their suspicions that the Montreal-dominated group would give the short end of the stick to Ottawa in the management of the proposed new league.

Meanwhile, the Montreal Arena Company, never far from the scene, came front and centre. Arena president Ed Sheppard was unhappy about the co-existence of two senior leagues. Both contracted with his rink, but the weaker clubs in each proved to be poor drawing cards. A single league of only the strongest clubs would be financially more rewarding. In fact, he revealed in a *Montreal Gazette* interview that the arena had higher total net revenues in 1905 from FAHL Wanderers engagements than from the combined dates of the CAHL clubs. With this in mind, he wrote to the Montreal, Victorias, and Shamrocks clubs of the so-called "alliance" with a proposal for a new league, which would include also the Wanderers, Ottawa, and Quebec. In the letter he suggested that if such rationalization were not accepted, he would find it difficult in 1906 to accommodate all the senior teams in the arena. The alliance resented Sheppard's attempt to dictate league membership and his veiled threat to shut out the clubs from arena dates. As well, the Montreal Hockey Club still did not want anything to do with the Wanderers. When the alliance rejected the proposal in a letter to Sheppard, he called a meeting of the arena directors, at which they awarded most of the choice dates for the coming season to the Wanderers. The arena had forced the alliance's hand. The alliance would somehow have to accommodate the Wanderers in order to have a suitable rink.

Under pressure, the Montreal Hockey Club met the next day and on a split vote finally agreed to go in with the Wanderers in a new league. Four days later, Ottawa's Murphy, Shillington, and Dickson travelled to Montreal. In a secret afternoon meeting convened at the Montreal Arena by rink secretary-treasurer Bill Northey, Murphy and his counterparts from the Wanderers, Montreal, Shamrocks, Victorias, and Quebec clubs abandoned their former leagues and created the Eastern Canada Amateur Hockey Association. At the Savoy Hotel that evening, Shillington and Dickson joined Murphy for further discussions with delegates from the member clubs. They agreed that a disinterested person, not associated with any of their organizations, should be chosen president. Their man was F. Howard Wilson, who happened to be a director and large stockholder of the Montreal Arena Company. They also decided that the position of league administrator should be a paid one. Their choice was none other than Bill

The Central Canada Exhibition Association turned the Aberdeen Pavilion into a hockey arena for the 1904 Stanley Cup games. The Ottawas put $500 toward the retrofit, which included new dressing rooms, seating for 4,000, and a new entrance for the occasion. LIBRARY AND ARCHIVES CANADA PA8938

Northey. The Montreal Arena was now firmly in control of senior hockey. Its first move was to raise ticket prices.

Unlike the Montreal clubs, the Ottawas were not usually under the thumb of any single rink operator. When the Dey brothers got tough, the Ottawas could turn to the old Rideau Rink. By 1903, however, it was conceded that the Rideau had become obsolete — the ice surface and the seating capacity were both too small. As the 1904 season approached, the Ottawa directors were also concerned about the limited capacity of Dey's Rink. They anticipated that their club, as Stanley Cup champions, could expect an even greater demand for tickets. Ottawa president Percy Buttler approached the Central Canada Exhibition Association with the idea of converting its agricultural hall, the Aberdeen Pavilion, into a hockey rink. An arrangement was worked out whereby the Ottawas would pay $500 toward the fitting up of the building and the association would take 40 per cent of gross receipts. The association would provide dressing rooms, a new entrance, banks of seating to accommodate 4,000 spectators, lights, ushers, ticket sellers, and

Dey's Rink, the site of the Ottawas' first Stanley Cup victory, in 1903, was reduced to rubble in a 1920 fire. The rink at Bay Street and Gladstone Avenue, however, served the team well, and was the beginning of a long-lasting partnership with the Dey family. COURTESY NORMA KEW/SPRINGBROOK, ONTARIO

turnstile men. The agreement was subject only to the approval of Ottawa city council, owners of the fair grounds. It certainly didn't hurt the club's cause that two council members were hockey men. One was Phil Ross, who seemed to be everywhere. The other was Sam Rosenthal, who, with his brothers and father, ran a jewellers business on Sparks Street that supplied enamelled Ottawa Hockey Club pins and controlled the club's reserved-seat plan. Rosenthal moved and Ross seconded the motion to approve the agreement, which carried by a vote of sixteen to two.

The move to the Aberdeen Pavilion was not entirely a success. It quickly acquired a reputation as a damp and drafty building. People also complained about the long, dark walk down the unplowed road from the Bank Street cars to the pavilion's ticket wicket. Stung by the loss of their premier attraction, the Dey brothers added more seats to their Gladstone Avenue rink and offered better terms for the following season. It was to be the beginning of a long, unbroken relationship between the Deys and the hockey team.

The Roster Game: The Problem of the Pros

WHERE THE OTTAWAS would play (in what league, in what rink?) was thus a preoccupation of the club's executive throughout the Silver Seven years. Who could be persuaded, or would be allowed, to play was another. Professionalism, particularly south of the border, was robbing the Ottawas and other senior teams of many of their better players and prospects. By 1903 the Western Pennsylvania Hockey League had declared itself professional, though it had been relying on paid players from Canada before then. It was a curious league in that all four teams were based in Pittsburgh. They played their games in the city's Duquesne Gardens, which had artificial ice. Players were enticed by steady jobs for the fourteen-week season, plus hockey salaries in the twenty-dollars-per-week range. Among the Ottawa products lured to Pittsburgh were Hod and Bruce Stuart, Jack Roberts, Chic Henry, Charlie Spittal, Peg Duval, and, of course, Alf Smith, who subsequently returned to the Ottawas as coach and was eventually reinstated as an amateur. The situation became even more acute when Canadian dentist Jack Gibson went to Houghton, Michigan, in 1902 and formed a professional team, which engaged in exhibition matches in the northern part of the state. The advanced calibre of the American professional game became obvious in 1904, when the FAHL champion Montreal Wanderers lost four of five games against the pros in Michigan and Pennsylvania.

Despite the fact that in Canada one senior league after another included the word "amateur" in its name, newspapers were repeatedly making oblique references to teams paying their players. Though names and amounts were never mentioned, there was plenty of talk that the fledgling FAHL was "all but" professional. The sudden defection of Montreal Hockey Club players to the FAHL's Wanderers at the start of the league's inaugural season in 1904 certainly gave pause, as did the success of the Wanderers the next year in luring the great Charlie Liffiton from Pittsburgh, where he had played professionally. Officially he was allowed to suit up because the Canadian Amateur Athletic Union had reinstated him as an amateur. But was he? After only one game he quit the team and left for Houghton to resume his overt pro career and to benefit from a seasonal job there. He had been given a job in Montreal, too, but his employer, a jeweller who happened to be a member of the MAAA, was incensed when he found out Liffiton had played for the despised Wanderers in their opening match on the Saturday night. When Liffiton came to work on Monday morning, the owner fired him.

The hockey public were becoming alarmed at the loss of good players to the States, but they also resented the hypocrisy of players in the senior amateur leagues being paid under the table. Thus a cautious acceptance of outright professionalism began to emerge. One line of thinking was that while players who played purely for salaries should be condemned, those who were given jobs and also received pay for playing should be tolerated. "If they are good enough mechanics or clerks to hold positions in the United States, it seems they ought to be useful in Canada," the *Montreal Sunday Sun* said.

As might be expected, Ross expressed himself on the subject. What he said in a 1905 *Ottawa Journal* interview was in one sense surprising because he had always been dedicated to the philosophy of amateurism, but not so in another sense because he was a man of great practicality. "To tell the plain truth, I feel rather bewildered about the conditions in our athletic sports," he said. "I can't help feeling sympathy for the men at the heads of our various senior lacrosse, football and hockey leagues. They all would prefer simon pure amateur sport. And none of them know how to get it. Neither do I." He reflected on the situation of promising young athletes who make enormous sacrifices to perfect their abilities. "The better player he becomes the more we ask of his time and energy and pocket. We do all this in a country in which all of us have to work to earn our bread and butter, and while the most of us stick busily at earning our bread and butter, we expect the young athlete who has got into senior company to give up several hours a day to keep himself fit to give us the greatest possible amount of satisfaction and entertainment in athletic sports." Ross deplored the hypocrisy of secret payments to amateurs but acknowledged that "it is now done universally in the senior leagues without a doubt." His solution was to allow semi-professionalism. "Let athletes who prefer to play simply for the love of the game continue, but require the other class to openly list themselves in the field for compensation." He cautioned, however, that salaries within any league should be limited so that they would be within the reach of the weaker clubs. In other words, assure financial parity.

The solution Ross offered on the amateur-professional dilemma was not altogether original; but coming from a man of his stature, it signalled a green light for opening up senior sport, including hockey. Dickson had already resigned his position on the board of the Canadian Amateur Athletic Union over its treatment of the amateur-professional question. The CAAU was a federation of the governing bodies of various amateur sports. One of its main objectives was to keep amateur sport pure. The instrument it used to achieve this was its authority to declare athletes professional and debar them from competition in any of the associations under its jurisdiction. In other words, an athlete who was professionalized in any one sport was deemed to be a professional in all sports and was ruled ineligible for competition on any team in any sport in any association under the CAAU umbrella. Further, athletes would be labelled professional if they so much as played with or against professionals even if they themselves received no monetary rewards. It was a powerful sanction. But there was a widespread perception that the Montreal-dominated CAAU board was turning a blind eye to athletes of that city who received payment from their teams. This was one of Dickson's objections. The other was the union's failure to acknowledge the loss of so many good athletes to the United States and its refusal to work out some kind of accommodation whereby amateurs and professionals could compete together.

Shillington also took up the cause. Though his initiative was related specifically to lacrosse and its result was subsequently overturned, it helped to liberalize attitudes toward professionalism, and the effects would soon be seen in hockey. As representative-elect of the Ottawa Amateur Athletic Club (with which the Ottawa Hockey Club was affiliated), Shillington attended the CAAU board-of-governors meeting at Montreal's Windsor Hotel in June 1905. On the agenda was a request by the National Amateur Lacrosse Union (NALU) that the penalty under the CAAU constitution pertaining to amateurs competing against professionals not be enforced with respect to the national game of lacrosse. The NALU representative explained that for the good of the game it was important to have a national championship competition, but that under present rules, an East-West showdown was not possible because the western teams were professional. He argued that the lucrative gates from such attractions were needed to sustain his league, which incurred considerable expenses in the course of operation. He then moved a motion that the penalty for "amateurs competing against professionals" not be enforced in lacrosse. The motion sparked heated debate. Those opposing it felt approval would emasculate the treasured concept of simon-pure amateurism. Those favouring it pointed to the approval of mixed competition in association football in Britain. The CAAU president, who chaired the meeting, ruled the motion out of order because its acceptance would amount to an amendment to the constitution, which the board was not empowered to enact. The meeting, however, overturned his decision. This was a signal to Shillington that the board was receptive to the realities of the day, and he gambled on taking the issue a step farther. He moved an amendment, which, in addition to allowing amateurs to compete against professionals, would also permit the two classes to play together on the same team. It was the very solution Phil Ross would publicly advocate six months later. The board supported Shillington by a vote of five to four. Hockey executives caught in the amateur-professional dilemma, and at first under the impression the decision applied to all sports, hailed the more tolerant stance the CAAU had taken. The CAAU eventually reversed itself, but the Shillington concept lived on. As the Ottawas prepared for their second Eastern Canada Amateur Hockey Association season in the fall of 1906, league executives approved mixed competition.

9 · The Shillington Seven, Part II
The Game on the Ice, 1904–1906

We can't stand for these butchers who sneak up
behind us and cut us down without provocation.
DOUG MORRISON
Brandon Hockey Club,
after Ottawa match, 1904

THE GOVERNOR GENERAL was nowhere to be found among the small gathering in the spacious Aberdeen Pavilion as Bouse Hutton skated to the middle of the rink. The scene on this sub-zero evening in early January 1904 was a far cry from the electric atmosphere two nights earlier when the veteran Ottawa goaler took to his nets in the same building for the final game of the Winnipeg Stanley Cup series. With a day's rest in between, he was now ready to referee the opening game of the OHA senior series between Ottawa's Aberdeens and the pride of neighbouring Smiths Falls. There was nothing remarkable about the contest. The calibre was of intermediate level and the game was so bland that Hutton's job "was as pleasant as a ping pong party." One player caught people's eye, and most certainly Hutton's. That was Smiths Falls goalkeeper Percy LeSueur. He let nothing past him. LeSueur was destined to make his debut with the famed Ottawas two years later in the final game of their three-year reign as the Silver Seven. As for Hutton, the present season would be his last in an Ottawa uniform.

Playing careers, with few exceptions, were short and there was always an abundance of new talent eager to fill the breach. For Ottawa, two exceptions to the rule were Harvey Pulford and Alf Smith, both of whom had been in senior company since the mid-1890s. To the profound disappointment of Frank McGee's legions of admirers, the great star's playing days were all too brief. The 1904 season was only his second with the Ottawas and he would be through with the game on the night LeSueur started, March 17, 1906. Over his four years, McGee played in forty-five regular season and Stanley Cup games, and scored an amazing 131 goals. Art Moore and Pulford were the defensive backbone, and Harry Westwick and Smith contributed mightily on the attack; but it was the presence of McGee that elevated the team from solid to spectacular.

1904: The Aberdeen Defences

THE OTTAWAS WERE SCHEDULED to begin their sixth season in the CAHL in January 1904. But before it got under way, they were obliged to defend the Stanley Cup against the western champion Winnipeg Rowing Club. The best-of-three series started on December 30 at the newly fitted-up Aberdeen Pavilion. Bitterly cold temperatures caused a breakdown in car service, making it difficult for many of the spectators to reach the rink in the southern part of town. Nevertheless, about 2,500 hardy souls filed into the frigid building. Among them a host of press and telegraph people got ready to send bulletins of the game abroad.

The Winnipeggers were reported to have trained hard for the series, which is more than could be said of the Ottawas, several of whom had been skipping practice. Nevertheless, Ottawa routed the visitors 9-1 in one of the most brutish displays of hockey yet seen in the capital. The Winnipeggers were no angels, but it was clear even to Ottawa supporters, who booed and hissed their own team, that the Ottawas were looking for trouble. Smith, in particular, had fallen out of the wrong side of bed that morning and it did not take him long to go after Joe Hall, whose roughhouse reputation had evidently preceded him. Following behind the play, and the referee's back, Smith took his stick to Hall's head, laying him out cold and halting the game. Meeting again, they exchanged blows, leaving Hall with five stitches to his scalp and Smith four. Substituting for the injured Clint Bennest, the diminutive Claude Borland quickly got under Ottawa's skin. The only way the darting figure could be stopped was by tripping him, which McGee and Suddie Gilmour did and paid for with penalties. Having disposed of Hall, Smith set his sights on Nick Bawlf, who left the game nicely carved up. Smith sustained a cut foot but stayed in. Despite the time they lost in penalties, McGee and Smith led the Ottawas with three goals each. Winnipeg captain Billy Breen said afterward it was the dirtiest game he had ever played. An indignant *Manitoba Free Press* complained of the Winnipeg club's "hospital list.": "Just look at the casualties: P. Brown, lame; C. Richards, face swollen, leg hurt; C. Bennest, thumb broken, badly bruised; W. Breen, bruised and badly shaken up; J. Hall, cut on head; W. Bawlf, cut and bruised."

The Silver Seven, 1905 Stanley Cup champions. From left, D. Finnie,
H. Westwick, M. McGilton, H. Pulford, H. Gilmour, A. Smith, F. McGee, A. Moore.
LIBRARY AND ARCHIVES CANADA PA91046

Uncertain they could ice a full team for the second game, Winnipeg asked Ottawa for permission to dress an unlisted player, Tammy Hamber, who had once lived in Winnipeg but was now on the Toronto Argonaut roster. Bennest, Richards, and Bawlf would be out, club management said. Ottawa, seeing the possibility of a cancelled game and lost gate, reluctantly agreed. To Ottawa's surprise, both Hamber and Bawlf skated onto the ice. Chastened by their own supporters' condemnation of their disgraceful behaviour in the first game, Smith and company were a mildmannered lot, and to everyone's surprise, Winnipeg skated away with a 6-2 victory.

Some jaundiced viewers thought the Ottawas had let up in the second game to ensure a lucrative third gate, but any such suspicions were quickly dispelled in the deciding match. The Winnipegers showed right from the whistle they were a highly competitive team whose win two nights earlier was well earned. Hamber, the ringer, was again in the lineup, which prompted Pulford, Ottawa's captain, to hand referee Harry Trihey a written protest as the game was about to begin. The objection was little more than a formality, however, because Ottawa had allowed Hamber to play in the previous game. Ottawa's only change was Billy Gilmour, who replaced the injured Smith. The visitors set a torrid pace on the attack, while Art Brown was a stone wall in goal and Hamber rock solid at cover point. The first half ended scoreless. In the second half, one-hundred-pound Claude Borland, as irritating a little devil as the Ottawas had ever encountered, was here, there, and everywhere, leaping over players, stealing the puck, and even getting into a fight with Suddie Gilmour. In short, Borland was a royal pain. As distracting as Borland was (except for penalties he was on the ice the whole time), the Ottawas slowly took control. Finally McGee, following up on a Suddie Gilmour rush, got the puck and fired it past Brown. Then, with seven minutes remaining and Winnipeg's point Percy Browne at the timer's bench serving a penalty, Suddie Gilmour took a pass from brother Billy and put the game away.

The Ottawas had gotten the season off to a good start. Without the benefit of even one exhibition game to prepare for the regular schedule, they had successfully defended the treasured Stanley Cup against a western team that Pulford judged to be the equal of any in the East. While the Rowing Club was going down to defeat out at Lansdowne Park, the Ottawa Post Office was going up in flames in Centretown. The great edifice, one of the government's finest, was beside the Russell House hotel, where the Winnipeggers were staying. Returning after the match, the players found proprietor St. Jacques hosing down his property as flames and sparks shot out of the neighbouring inferno. Besides firefighting, St. Jacques was known for his fine cuisine. The next night, with the Russell saved, the Ottawas treated the Winnipeggers to a sumptuous banquet and "post-prandial proceedings" in what had become a time-honoured tradition of good sportsmanship.

When management yanked the Ottawas out of the CAHL in early February in a dispute over the rescheduling of a Victorias match, there was little for the team to do except defend the Stanley Cup against further challenges. To keep sharp, they played one exhibition game in which they demolished the FAHL's Ottawa Capitals 18-1. The first cup defence following the Winnipeg series was against the OHA champion Toronto Marlboros. Though the general opinion around town was that "nothing good in the way of a hockey team could come out of Toronto," the visitors jumped to a 2-0 lead before the first game was five minutes old. At that point in the best-of-three series, the Ottawas took command, winning 6-3 and 11-2. McGee had five goals in the two games, but much of the talk was about Pulford. In the first game, the big point man, known for his conservative play, treated onlookers to only his second goal in a ten-year span with the Ottawas.

Next up were the Wanderers, champions of the FAHL's inaugural season. The first match, of what was to have been a two-game, total-goal series, ended in a 5-5 draw in Montreal. The Wanderers insisted that the match be declared no game, and that the series be started over as a best of three. They were also unhappy with the refereeing and demanded that an official of their liking be selected. The trustees would have none of it and declared there would be one game only, in Ottawa, to decide the championship. The Wanderers refused and abandoned the challenge.

Ottawa finished the 1904 season with a series against Brandon, new champions of the Manitoba and Northwestern Association. The games marked the first appearances on Ottawa ice of Brandon point Lester Patrick, who would go on to fame in an outstanding twenty-two-year career in hockey's highest echelons. Clint Bennest and Joe Hall, however, did not make it onto the ice because of a trustees' ruling prohibiting a player from competing for more than one team in a Stanley Cup series in the same year. The two had been stalwarts with Winnipeg when the Rowing Club challenged Ottawa at the start of the season. For the champions, Jim McGee substituted for the injured Moore at cover point. They were the last two games of hockey he would ever play. The older brother of Frank, Jim was never more than a fringe player with the Ottawas. His favourite sport was football, at which he excelled as captain of the Ottawa Rough Riders. For most of his hockey career, Jim played at the intermediate level with the Aberdeens. But he was always willing to help out with the seniors whenever his presence was required. Loyal to the team, he faithfully attended practice, a habit not all of the regulars were known for. In fact, a few days before the Wanderers series, he was the only one to show up for a key training session. That earned him a place in the lineup for the aborted challenge. In the Brandon series, Jim acquitted himself well, as Ottawa retained the cup with relatively easy 6-3 and 9-3 wins. Two months later, while riding with the son of the minister of justice, Jim was thrown from his horse. Landing head first, he sustained a severe concussion and died five days later, forty-eight hours short of his twenty-sixth birthday.

Jim's death unsettled the McGee family. Having lost one athlete, they were all too aware of Frank's precarious situation as a hockey player. Here he was, with the sight of only one eye, playing aggressively in the most violent of sports. Living in the patriarchal home and coming in at night with ghastly cuts and bruises to the face and head, sometimes unnervingly close to his good eye, he was proof positive of hockey's inherent dangers. His family did not want him to continue. Declining their advice, Frank suited up for another season – Ottawa's first in the Federal Amateur Hockey League. The mood was somber when the players gathered for practice. The loss of Jim McGee saddened them. There was also the heartbreak of veteran Pulford. Adjoining notices in the December 7, 1904, edition of the *Ottawa Journal* gave the stark facts. "Died. Pulford — At no. 479 Besserer st., Ottawa, this Wednesday morning. Annis Mae Field, aged 29 years, beloved wife of Mr. Harvey Pulford and only daughter of the late Henry A. Field, Esq. of Brockville." Then: "Births. Pulford — to Mr. and Mrs. Harvey Pulford, this Wednesday morning, a son."

1905: The Dawson Debacle and the Thistle Threat

ON AND OFF FOR ABOUT FIVE YEARS, the Ottawas had been hearing about hockey in the Yukon. In large part this was thanks to letters home from former Ottawa Hockey Club star Weldy Young, who had left for the northwest after the 1899 season. In one letter, which his father shared with the press in December 1900, Weldy told of a seven-team league in Dawson and the aspirations of hockey people there to one day challenge for the Stanley Cup. By late 1902, the vision had taken sufficient shape for potential team members to be named and publicized. Finally, in a letter dated August 24, 1904, the president and the secretary of the Klondike Hockey Club issued a challenge to the Ottawas. Just why trustees Ross and Sweetland should approve such a series is open to conjecture. The picked team had won no championship and did not belong to any recognized senior league. Except for Young, the names being bandied about as team members were pretty much unknown in hockey circles. Young sent a cloying personal letter to Ross in support of the application. He warmly recalled his old home town, praised Ottawa's sports teams, and spoke sincerely of the enthusiastic support for the eastern adventure being rendered by Dawson's business and professional community. Young's postscript was revealing: "I might just add that Mr. Jos. W. Boyle will represent our club with full authority to enter into and arrange our eastern dates." Joe Boyle was no stranger to official Ottawa and dropping his name would certainly get attention. The Yukon mining entrepreneur had been coming to the capital regularly since at least 1897 seeking concessions along the Klondike River. He had been to the office of

Interior Minister Clifford Sifton many times and was a well-known personality around the Russell House hotel, where most of the high-powered lobbying was conducted. The name Boyle would not go unnoticed by Ross. Connections counted and the Klondikers got their Stanley Cup dates.

The Dawson quest became a serialized adventure in newspaper columns. Stories flowed about how the underdogs from "the northern zone" walked the 350 miles to Whitehorse; took the train to Skagway; missed the boat to Vancouver but caught one to Seattle; doubled back to Vancouver by rail; caught the train east, meeting throngs of well-wishers along the way; and arrived rubber-legged in Ottawa on January 11, two days before their first game and twenty-five days after their odyssey began. The Ottawas were curious but not especially concerned about this strange brigade. If the Ottawas had misgivings at all they would have been about the visitors' ability to put up any kind of a game. In fact, worried that the Klondikers might be exposed as a second-rate aggregation before the series even commenced, the Ottawa executive stipulated in agreeing to accept the challenge that the northerners were to play no exhibition games before meeting the champions.

And so the stage was set at Dey's Rink, to which the Ottawas had returned after one season at the Aberdeen Pavilion. A sell-out for the first game was assured. Shillington proudly displayed the Stanley Cup in the window of his drug store. Boyle was in town again, arranging details and sending dispatches back to the *Dawson Daily News*. Resplendent in their new uniforms of gold-trimmed black jerseys, white pants, and black stockings, the Klondikers posed for a team photo outside the rink. Then the hockey began, and the sham was soon revealed to all. Four goals by Alf Smith, two by the unheralded Fred White, two by Rat Westwick, and one by Frank McGee. Dawson's two replies were by the handlebar-mustachioed Randy McLennan, a medical doctor originally from Glengarry, Ontario, and George Kennedy of West Selkirk, Manitoba.

Likely embarrassed by his decision to allow the series in the first place, Ross put on a brave face in his *Journal* commentary: "It was only when the Yukoners tired and showed the effect of their long journey that Ottawa began to pile on the score." And then: "Some go so far as to say that given equal conditions this is the best team that has come after the Stanley Cup for two or three years." In that case, with two full days of rest before the second game, the challengers would surely do better. Seemingly taking Ross at his word, the crowds came back. The game was an utter fiasco: 10-1 for

Ottawa at the half; 23-2 at the final whistle. Those who commented on McGee's mellow play in the first encounter were not disappointed by his performance in the second. In the first half, he pumped in four goals; in the second, ten, including eight consecutive scores in a span of eight minutes and twenty seconds.

Weldy Young, a prime mover in the Dawson project and designated captain of the team, never got to play in the Stanley Cup series. Election duties in Dawson delayed his departure and he did not arrive in Ottawa until five days after the second game. A whirlwind visit with his family attended to, he boarded a train east to meet his teammates in Amherst, Nova Scotia, where the Klondikers were continuing their eastern swing.

As expected, the Ottawas breezed through the FAHL schedule, winning seven of eight games and finishing first. Their single loss was not to the second-place Wanderers, the only other legitimate senior team in the loop, but to Brockville. Their title as Stanley Cup champions thus confirmed, the Ottawas faced one more task, defending the cup against the Rat Portage Thistles. Two years before, Rat Portage had been the first team to challenge the Ottawas after their succession as champions. The Thistles had four prominent holdovers from the earlier roster: Matt Brown, Tom Hooper, Si Griffis, and Billy McGimsie. Tom Phillips, who had played for the Marlboros in their 1904 series against Ottawa, was seen as a formidable addition. According to reports from Rat Portage, the team weighed "1,060 pounds" and had an average age of twenty-one and one-seventh years.

Advance sales for the first game took up all seats around the oval, and Rosenthal Jewellers, who controlled the seating plan, were accepting no telephone orders. To accommodate the unprecedented demand for tickets, Ted Dey had workmen construct a standing-room platform behind the reserved seats along the south side. Based on the experience of their opponents, the Ottawas knew they would be in for a tough match, especially since Frank McGee and Billy Gilmour would be out with injuries. Horace Gaul, up from the city-level Emmetts, would replace McGee at centre and Hamby Shore, in only his fourth game in senior company, would take Gilmour's spot at left wing. The game turned out to be even more challenging for the Ottawas than they had cautiously anticipated. Though Gaul and Shore acquitted themselves well, each scoring, the Thistles came away with a 9-3 victory, largely on the work of Tommy Phillips, who scored five times. A difference in tactics favoured the visitors. While the Ottawa point and cover point repeatedly lifted the puck down the ice, only to have the opposition retrieve it and advance, the Thistle defencemen hung onto the puck and looked for a play. This style led to many dangerous forays into the Ottawa zone. Following the game, Montreal-based referee Hartland McDougall candidly predicted a second win for the Thistles, although by a narrower margin. A minor tempest sprang up after the game. A film of water had covered much of the ice surface, slowing down play. Thistle players and some of their supporters considered the Rat Portage team to be fast-skating, meaning that the watery ice put them at a disadvantage. They accused rink management of deliberately causing the condition by flooding the ice a few hours before game time. Owner Dey denied the charge, contending that the arena's tin roof attracted heat and that the large crowd further raised temperatures.

Ice conditions were the same for game two, but there was a different system for refereeing. Hockey rules in the West stipulated two referees, the second a judge of play, whose main responsibility was to look for dirty work and mete out penalties. The western rule was in effect for game one and the eastern for the second. With the distinct possibility that more rough stuff would result with only one official, referee Mike Grant donned a hard hat, which, to the delight of the crowd, he almost lost on the bad ice. Grant's portent was accurate, for the game proceeded in ugly fashion. "Frank McGee was at the side for too long," the *Journal* said. "His cruel jabs to the face of opponents cost the team twenty minutes of his play." The paper continued the admonishment: "McGee is far too good a man to have to descend to this sort of thing." Billy Gilmour was also back in the lineup and scored the winning goal in a 4-2 Ottawa victory.

The Thistles' claim that they would fare better with good ice was put to the test in the deciding game, for the surface was in "racing condition." It was a hard-fought and closely contested match, with Rat Portage taking the lead three times and the teams never being more than one goal apart. For once the Ottawas, universally acknowledged as the most brutal club in hockey, came out of the game with fewer penalties than their opponents, twenty-nine minutes against the Thistles' thirty-nine. McGee entered the game with a broken right wrist and management were concerned the Thistles, who knew he had been injured, might try to hack at it. To fool them, the trainer encased it in a concealed steel band, but put a heavy, showy wrapping on his other wrist. With the Thistles' attention attracted to it, McGee sailed through the game free of any punishment to the vulnerable member. Tommy Phillips scored three times for the Thistles and

McGee three times for the champions, including the game-winner with less than five minutes left in regulation time. Ottawa goalkeeper Dave Finnie made several fine stops in what would be his last game for the red, white, and black. In thirteen scheduled and playoff matches that season, he recorded eleven wins and two losses.

Though good ice in late winter was an uncertainty, the Ottawas fully expected to face a challenge from the FAHL-champion Montreal Victorias. The trustees had decreed a best-of-three series and Shillington said his team was ready, "though our fellows are a little shaken up after the Rat Portage Thistle games." Vics manager Fred McRobie, who always seemed to be looking for an argument, demanded a sudden-death or two-game, total-goal series. He was adamant his team would not play a third game, citing the possibility of soft ice. The trustees remained firm, the series was called off, and the Ottawas, as Stanley Cup champions, hung up their skates for another season.

1906: A Final Faceoff

DELIGHTED WITH THE CONTINUING success of his main tenant, Ted Dey made plans for rink improvements. By November he had added 1,200 seats on the north side, 500 more in the west end and north-east corner, and had managed to construct a new standing room promenade in a building with very tight property lines. Total capacity was now thought to be 4,500 or better — only time would tell how efficient ushers would be in finding space for standees.

Coach Smith also had to make plans. In early December he received the news that McGee was retiring and that Finnie had no intention of returning. Not only would Smith have to find replacements, he would have to shuffle the positions of his players according to their individual strengths — a season-long game of chess that would bring dramatic results. He brought in his brother Harry from junior ranks on a tryout to replace McGee at centre, and he gave the promising young Billy Hague of the city-level Emmetts a chance in goal. Both performed well in an exhibition swing through Winnipeg, Kenora, and Fort William and earned spots on the team. When McGee changed his mind in mid-season and returned to his old position at centre, Harry Smith moved to left wing, bumping Dion, who thought he had earned a place on the team. Three games later, Jack Ebbs, up from the Emmetts, filled in for the injured Westwick at rover. Ebbs played well but was replaced after only one game by Harry Smith, who was making room on left wing for brother Tommy. It was an easy decision for Alf to insert Tommy into the lineup. He had just completed a full season with the Ottawa Victorias of the FAHL and in his final game, February 24, scored eight goals in a 14-8 win over Brockville. The next night, the three brothers played together. In a 9-3 trouncing of a weak Shamrock side, Tommy scored once, player-coach Alf three times, and their centre, McGee, five more. Harry, the most prolific player on the team, was held scoreless. With Westwick back for the next game, Tommy sat out, and thereafter alternated with Harry. Alf would make one more chess move, the most startling of his coaching career, in the last game of the season.

As expected, the Ottawas and the Wanderers, the two powerhouses of the new Eastern Canada Hockey Association, dominated the league, finishing in a first-place tie with nine wins and one loss each. Billy Hague was solid in goal for Ottawa, but the real surprise was Harry Smith, who won the scoring title with thirty-one goals. In two routine defences of the Stanley Cup in mid-season, Ottawa defeated intercollegiate champion Queen's two straight and did the same to Smiths Falls, the 1906 FAHL title-holder.

The stage was thus set for a final Stanley Cup showdown between the Ottawas and the Wanderers. The teams were evenly matched, having split their two regular-season encounters. The series was to be two games, total goals, beginning March 14 at the Montreal Arena. The big question for Ottawa supporters and the club executive was the condition of the players. The game in Montreal would be Ottawa's eighth (and third on the road) in nineteen days, a grueling pace for thirteen-year mainstays Pulford, Smith, and Westwick. It would be only the third match for the younger Wanderers in the same stretch, all at home. A month earlier, clairvoyant Eva Fay, appearing at the Russell Theatre, had predicted Ottawa's first-place tie with Wanderers. Since she obviously knew what she was talking about, the Ottawa public took comfort from her further vision that the local favourites would retain the cup by a one-goal margin.

All available seats for the Montreal match were snapped up within two hours and speculators were commanding prices of three to five times face value. In what was surely a tribute to the reliability of rail travel, the Ottawas, with a large excursion of supporters, chose the 4:15 p.m. train to get them to their destination for that evening's game. They made it on time, but their punishing schedule over the previous few weeks immediately took its toll. The champions could just not find their legs. Managing two shots on goal, they trailed the Wanderers 4-0 at the half. Matters did not improve in the second half. The Wanderers scored three more before Harry Smith countered for Ottawa. With two more to finish things off, the Wanderers won the opening game 9-1. Part of the blame was placed on Ottawa's peculiar tactic of bunching three forwards on one side of the rink and having the cover point try to feed the fourth forward, alone on the other side. This consistently resulted in either offside passes or Wanderers interceptions. The rest of the blame fell squarely and unfairly on goalkeeper Hague. Though his forwards repeatedly left him vulnerable by failing to back-check, the little rookie, who had given his team thirteen league and Stanley Cup wins that season, was deemed "a complete failure" by his hometown *Ottawa Journal.*

Behind the scenes, Ottawa management and coach Smith agreed with the *Journal's* brutal assessment. For some time they had been quietly observing the work of Smiths Falls goalkeeper Percy LeSueur. In fact, LeSueur was in the nets when the nearby railway town team challenged the Ottawas for the Stanley Cup, just a week before the Wanderers series. Ottawa management hastily signed LeSueur, and Smith put him in the lineup for the concluding Wanderers game. Ottawa supporters, shocked by the outcome of the first match, did not object to Hague's betrayal. Rather, they grasped onto the notion that the change of goalkeepers might be just enough to reverse their team's fortunes. The Wanderers did not challenge LeSueur's insertion, but they could have. Two years earlier, trustees Ross and Sweetland had ruled that two members of the Brandon team were ineligible to play in a series against Ottawa because they had already seen Stanley Cup action for another team in the same season. This time, the Ottawa-based guardians remained silent and LeSueur's eligibility never became an issue.

As with Ottawa's trip to Montreal, the Wanderers shaved it close with their rail connection to the capital on game day, Saturday, March 17. The team left the Bonaventure station at 4:15 p.m. To save time, the players changed into their uniforms along the way in their private coach and proceeded directly to the rink from the Ottawa depot. Chaos surrounded them as they worked their way to the entrance, which was crowded with enthusiasts hoping, almost beyond hope, to secure tickets. The seating plan had long been sold out and there was slim chance that an usher could be bribed for a standing-room spot. A lucky few, with extra cash in their pockets, were allowed to sit in the aisles. The Wanderers were heartened by the nearly one thousand supporters who had come from Montreal, but every time they sent up a chant they were drowned out by the raucous locals. And then the game began.

Midway through the first half, Ottawa partisans fell silent as rover Lester Patrick scored — the same Patrick, who in 1904, as the point for Brandon, thwarted numerous Ottawa rushes at the Aberdeen Pavilion. The Wanderers were now ahead by a combined count of 10-1. But the most remarkable reversal ever seen in hockey to that time was about to occur. It started when Frank McGee gained possession, passed to Harry Smith, took a return pass, and drove a bullet behind the helpless Wanderers goalkeeper. Within minutes, Harry Smith scored twice, and the half ended with Ottawa on the upswing. The vast crowd wondered aloud whether the Ottawas could keep up their hot tempo or cool down in the intermission. The answer came immediately at the start of play. Within ten seconds, Harry Smith had scored his third in a row. Forty-five seconds later, Westwick chipped in, and, amazingly, within another thirty seconds, playing coach Alf Smith added another. With more than twenty-eight minutes left on the timekeeper's watch, the champions had narrowed the margin to three goals. Defensively, LeSueur was doing his part, especially on shots from Patrick, who was all over the ice. The Ottawa barrage continued. Harry Smith, in undoubtedly the finest game he ever played, scored three more times — his fourth, fifth, and sixth goals of the game. The contest was now deadlocked at ten apiece. Incredibly the young Smith took a sharp pass, went in, and beat goalkeeper Menard again, but the jubilation was wasted as the judge of play declared the attacker offside. Undeterred, the Ottawas launched a furious assault on the Wanderers' net. In the process, they forgot their defensive responsibilities. Predictably fortunes changed. Patrick took the puck, rushed the length of the ice, and with only one minute and twenty-five seconds remaining fooled LeSueur. One minute later Patrick scored again and the Wanderers were the new Stanley Cup champions, 12-10 on the round.

The End of an Era

FIVE DAYS LATER the banquet room of the Russell House was the scene of one of the most poignant moments in Ottawa sport. As had happened many times in the past, the Ottawas were being fêted at season's end. On hand was the usual crowd of hockey executives, past and present, political dignitaries, the press, and various sporting types. The occasion was at the same time festive and sad, touched, too, with nostalgia. Yes, the Stanley Cup, as before, was there; but this time it was destined not for storefront display at Rosenthal jewellers or the Shillington pharmacy, but for packing and shipping to Montreal. Yes, as before, magnanimous toasts were raised to the opponents, but as the victors not the vanquished. Speeches were sportsmanlike. Honorary club president Denis Murphy was resolute: "The team will have to go to Montreal and win the cup back again." As usual Jack Clarke was there to convulse the gathering with his imitation of the habitant dialect, a fashionable style of recitation made popular by the "people's poet" William Henry Drummond. The players were heard from. Veterans Harvey Pulford and Alf Smith vowed to bring the "mug" back. Billy Hague, embarrassed by his benching, never let on. Many years later, his daughter recalled the humiliation. "I always felt sorry that my father did not have a chance to redeem himself in the return game with the Wanderers, but, of course, that is sport. I never heard my father say anything bitter about the fact that he was replaced by LeSueur." Hague never did play another game with the Ottawas.

Nor did Frank McGee. The most sensational athlete Ottawa had ever produced knew this was his last banquet. He had been under family pressure to retire and was just embarking on a new career direction that would demand his full attention. Just three weeks earlier he had secured a promising position in the Dominion lands branch of the Department of the Interior. The job's temporary status was a mere formality. Though McGee was surely confident of his own ability to pass scrutiny for a permanent appointment, personal connections would not hurt his chances. At the banquet that night was William Foran, president of the FAHL and longtime athletic confrere of McGee. Foran's day job was as secretary to the Board of Civil Service Examiners, the body that would determine McGee's final acceptability. Not to be underestimated, either, was the unspoken influence of Frank's father, John, clerk of the Privy Council and the Dominion's ranking civil servant. As such, he was the one to sign the official appointment papers for all personnel, and this he did for Frank in July, shortly before retiring.

The banquet was a nostalgic moment for the beloved Shillington. He had sold his pharmacy business months before and was preparing to leave for the Cobalt area as a mining entrepreneur. This was the night he would shake hands for the last time with his Shillington Seven and move on. Shillington settled in Haileybury, where he became the first member elected to the Ontario legislature from the District of Temiskaming. He died in 1934 at the height of a successful business career.

The banquet marked the end of a season, but it also marked the end of an era, for the Silver Seven and for hockey. It had been a glorious, magical time for this collection of players and their adoring supporters, supporters from all walks of life and all corners of a vast country. The likes of the Ottawas would never be seen again. And hockey would never be the same again. Of necessity, there had always been a business aspect to hockey; but now hockey was strictly business. Rink owners were demanding better deals from their tenant clubs, and vice versa. Leagues were configuring themselves to ensure only the most popular clubs would be admitted. Poorly drawing clubs were squeezed out. Travel and equipment costs were going up. And, for the public, so were ticket prices. Players who had skated purely for the love of the game were now realizing their economic worth and demanding compensation. To be sure, these payments were still under the table in Canadian senior hockey, but everyone knew the game was on the brink of overt, full-scale professionalism. For the players, the idea of loyalty to community was about to become a thing of the past. The Ottawas and other clubs had already suffered players going where the money was, to the American pro leagues. Only a paycheque would now keep them home, and they were going to get it.

10 · Professionalism and the Salary War

*Over $200 a week for hockey, that seems easy money, but I can tell you when a man
draws that amount he pretty nearly earns every cent of it. I've had all my front
teeth knocked out and it costs money to get new ones.*

MARTY WALSH
Ottawa Senators, 1909

Professionalism Unmasked

THE MEN RUNNING SENIOR HOCKEY realized they could not sustain the sham
of amateurism. It was an open secret that many of the better players were
receiving pay equal to that of those who had gone south to the pro teams
in Pennsylvania and Michigan. Newspapers ridiculed the deception.
"Hockey and football players in Ottawa," the *Toronto Telegram* quipped in
1906, "are to remain on the 'old amateur playing status,' which probably
means that the club will make no attempt to cut salaries this year." Looking
back, an Ottawa Hockey Club executive recalled in 1909: "Ten years ago
when the teams were supposed to be 'simon pure' it was considered good
going if the clubs were able to hand each of the players $100 'on the side'
at the close of each season." The annual stipend soon rose to $200, he said,
and by the time the Ottawas won the Stanley Cup in 1903, "the men
received something like $250 per season."

For owners and players alike, however, the transition from amateurism
to outright professionalism was a sticky issue. For one thing, the public was
divided. Some detested the very idea of men receiving emoluments for
engaging in sporting activities. Others were not against professionalism per
se, but abhorred the hypocrisy of players receiving secret payment for competing in so-called amateur company, company that actually did include
some true blues. For another thing, some hockey players, such as Pulford,
excelled in other sports, in which they competed as amateurs. If they were
uncovered as pros in hockey, they would be debarred from other amateur

sports. It was therefore necessary for owners to hide their payments for fear that these athletes would stay away from hockey if their amateur status were to be put in jeopardy.

Matters came to a head at the annual meeting of the CAAU in the early fall of 1906. The MAAA, the oldest and most influential amateur club in Canada, had earlier reconciled itself to the reality of top-level sporting competition. Its directors amended the association's constitution to permit mixed play. Professionals could now compete on MAAA teams without the amateurs on those teams losing their standing. The association would simply declare the professionals as such. Everything would be above board. The MAAA asked the CAAU to adopt a similar policy. Representing the Ottawa Hockey Club at the meeting, D'Arcy McGee backed the motion. He and other supporters argued that the move would not emasculate amateurism but would, by openly dividing professionals from amateurs, "do away with the hidden practices existent up till now." The majority of delegates, however, could not be convinced and the motion failed.

But even the defeat of the motion was not good enough for Frank Grierson, president of the Civil Service Amateur Athletic Association in Ottawa. The Halifax native and son of a well-known missionary was a dedicated amateur in practice and principle. He introduced a motion to suspend all the clubs in the FAHL and the Eastern Canada Amateur Hockey Association (ECAHA) for professionalism. He wanted to get rid of the "scum," and he named names. Reluctant to take such precipitous action, the CAAU appointed a committee to look into the matter. But the Grierson list was leaked to the press and a few days later the names of those Grierson accused of being professionals appeared. Nine players from the 1906 Ottawa team were on the list: Frank McGee; Harvey Pulford; Harry Westwick; Billy Hague; Alf, Tommy, and Harry Smith; Art Moore; and the little-known S. Dion, who had played a grand total of two games.

Meanwhile, the MAAA dropped out of the CAAU over the latter's rejection of mixed competition, and the *Ottawa Journal* chastised Grierson for his stance. "To all intents and purposes," Ross's newspaper said, "the day of the revival of purely amateur sport ... has passed."

Events were now moving rapidly. At the annual meeting of the ECAHA, delegates approved a motion by D'Arcy McGee to allow amateurs and professionals to play together. "The league," he said, "is strong enough to act on its own initiative and conduct its own business, while the CAAU has not shown a proper grasp of the problems before the hockey players of the country." The meeting decreed that all member clubs must submit to the league a list of all their players, showing who is pro and who is amateur. The resolutions effectively ended the league's affiliation with the CAAU. Now released from the amateur-only yoke, the delegates nevertheless vowed to keep the league as free of professionals as possible. Though the Wanderers came right out and said they would play "at least one professional," other clubs were noncommittal about the proportions. Shrewdly assessing these developments, Stanley Cup trustees Ross and Foran (replacing Sweetland, who had recently died) let it be known that in the trophy's deed of gift there was no stipulation as to amateur standing. They were not about to let the vaunted symbol of hockey supremacy be relegated to the second-class status that would surely follow with such a restriction.

It wasn't until the middle of the 1907 season that the ECAHA clubs, with the exception of Ottawa, submitted the player lists they were to have sent in within two weeks of the start of league play. And there were suspicions about the declarations. The Victorias, Montreal, and Quebec all claimed they were entirely amateur. The Wanderers and the Shamrocks announced mixed rosters. While Ottawa stalled in disclosing its list, word was out that the CAAU, following its investigation of the Grierson allegations, was suspending a long list of players. Among them from the Ottawas were Percy Lesueur, Billy Baird, Harvey Pulford, Harry Westwick, Alf and Harry Smith, Hamby Shore, Charlie Spittal, Billy Hague, and Arthur Moore. The following week, the Ottawas released their list. Only one professional was declared: Billy Baird. To the hockey world and a public growing cynical, this was a stunning statement. Of all the clubs in Canadian hockey, the one most widely perceived to be out-and-out professional was Ottawa. The debarring of the players meant nothing so far as their hockey careers were concerned. They kept on playing, just as before. If, however, any had aspirations of competing in other sports as recognized amateurs during the off-season, these hopes would be dashed.

Driving home the point that Canadian senior teams were downright professional, the *Pittsburgh Sun* complained bitterly about the growing tendency of players to jump in mid-season from American pro teams to Canadian clubs offering higher pay. The paper specifically named the Wanderers and the Ottawas.

Though the ECAHA had withdrawn from the CAAU, the league's member clubs were not quite ready to abandon entirely their amateur identification. If, on principle, a good player wished to remain amateur, the clubs would not want to lose him. Also, getting him for free looked just fine on the treasurer's balance sheet. The Victorias did not take this hardheaded practical stance. For them amateur status was a matter of conviction. Fortunately the league was able to enjoy the best of both worlds, for a new organization, the Amateur Athletic Federation of Canada (AAFC), was coming into being. This body was a rival to the CAAU and the rationale for its creation was the acceptance of amateurs competing with and against professionals without losing their amateur standing. The league affiliated with the AAFC in mid-season 1907. But the relationship did not last. The Montreal and Victorias clubs quit the league just before the start of the 1909 season, leaving four, now entirely professional, clubs: Ottawa, the Wanderers, Quebec, and the Shamrocks. The conversion of Canada's premier league to full professionalism was now complete. The league dropped the word "amateur" from its title.

If the public had harboured any uncertainties about the true status of Alf Smith, these would have been swept away by a viewing of a document now held by Kingston's International Hockey Museum. Smith had played professional hockey in Pittsburgh, had been debarred from amateur competition and subsequently reinstated, and, as late as February 1907, was listed by the Ottawa Hockey Club as an amateur. It is difficult to imagine that a man whose life was sports, especially hockey, and who was renowned for his prowess, would suit up for the Ottawas without receiving financial consideration. In 1907, teammate Billy Baird, a lesser player, was declared pro. Was the public expected to believe that Smith was in it purely for the love of the game? The museum document is Smith's contract with the Ottawa Hockey Club, dated December 4, 1907. He was to receive $500 for the coming season, paid in equal instalments between January 15 and March 15, 1908. If sidelined temporarily by injury, he would receive his full pay during that period. If the injury were season-ending, he would get half-pay. That campaign would prove to be Smith's final full season as a professional hockey player. He appeared in nine of the club's scheduled games.

Cyclone Taylor and the Transition Years

IF THERE HAD BEEN any question about Smith's status, there was none whatsoever about Fred Taylor's. The man was a professional hockey player and the team most prepared to pay him top dollar would be the recipient of his services. Taylor's arrival in the capital completed the metamorphosis of the

Ottawa Hockey Club from concealed to overt professionalism. If Taylor had not yet been dubbed "The Cyclone" when he blew into town in the fall of 1907, he would certainly create a storm well before stepping onto the ice. Taylor's two-year stint with the Senators was a period of transition. At the time of his acquisition, the team was set to move into a spacious new rink, the largest in Canada. And his arrival marked the last year in hockey for four Ottawa greats, all Stanley Cup champions: Smith, Westwick, Moore, and Pulford. Taylor's tenure also saw the arrival of emerging stars Dubbie Kerr, Freddie Lake, and Marty Walsh. Thrown into the mix for the 1908 season was the sensational Tommy Phillips.

Born in Tara, Ontario, in 1884, Frederick Wellington Taylor learned hockey in Listowel, where his family moved when he was six. He was a natural athlete, whose prowess in lacrosse equalled that of hockey. But it was his talent in the winter sport that in 1903 drew the attention of William Hewitt, secretary of the OHA. In his biography *Cyclone Taylor: a Hockey Legend*, Eric Whitehead writes that Hewitt wanted the nineteen-year-old to come to Toronto to play for the Marlboros. When Taylor declined, saying he liked living in Listowel, the annoyed Hewitt told the young prospect that in that case he would block him from playing anywhere. True to his word, Hewitt imposed an OHA ban on Taylor when he agreed to play for the Thessalon club. Later Taylor went to Portage la Prairie of the Manitoba senior league and then to the Portage Lake team of Houghton, Michigan, where he turned pro. In his second season there, 1906–07, his team won the International League championship.

Meanwhile in Ottawa, local entrepreneur Edwin "Ted" Dey had secured a twenty-year lease on a parcel of land on Laurier Avenue beside the Rideau Canal, where he was having a huge new rink constructed. Dey's Arena was to be the Senators' new home. The up-to-date structure in a central location, in contrast to the cramped and obsolete Dey's Rink on Gladstone Avenue, was sure to bring in the crowds. With them would come the revenues to support a budget for professional players. But the team owners also knew that to keep the crowds coming back, and to pay the increased rent for the big rink, they would have to have a star attraction. Hence negotiations in the summer of 1907 to secure the services of Fred Taylor. Whitehead recounts that the Senators dispatched Malcolm Brice of the *Ottawa Free Press* to Listowel as their emissary. From there negotiations continued, and on November 7 the *Ottawa Journal* reported that Taylor was coming. Knowing their way around official circles, Ottawa club directors

A rare interior view of the newly built Dey's Arena on February 10, 1908, a month after the Senators' home opener against the Montreal Wanderers. With seating for 7,500, the spacious arena was a testament to hockey's stature in the capital. LIBRARY AND ARCHIVES CANADA PA203558

arranged for the new recruit to be taken on strength as a clerk in the railway and swamp lands branch at the Department of the Interior. On December 4, the Senators' executive announced what they took to be the official signing and Taylor was soon on the practice ice.

Then followed one of the most curious episodes in the history of player negotiations. Some say that Taylor was a shrewd operator, who, fully conscious of his value, played off one bidder against another, in what was about to ensue, until, steely-nerved, he landed the best possible deal. Whether Taylor's interpretation of his talks with the Senators agrees with theirs is not known. What is known is that there were going to be more talks. With the prized young player apparently under contract to the Senators, the Ottawa Victorias of the FAHL nevertheless invited him in late December to play for them in a two-game series against Renfrew, champions of the Upper Ottawa Valley Hockey League. The winners would meet the Montreal Wanderers in a Stanley Cup challenge. Renfrew protested on the grounds that Taylor had signed with Ottawa and should not be allowed to

This view is of the rear of Dey's Arena, photographed from the then existing Rideau Canal turning basin. True to form, the Deys proved themselves savvy marketers, exploiting the view to promote another one of their businesses.

play for the Vics, unless for the full season. The cup trustees agreed, whereupon Renfrew immediately tried to secure him for the same series for fifty dollars. To get around the obvious duplicity, Renfrew management additionally offered Taylor a contract for the full season, but not payable until April 1. In this way Renfrew management could justify having him for the Vics series yet not be liable for the full season's salary should Taylor return, as they anticipated he might, to the Senators. On December 30 Taylor took the train to Renfrew with the intention of signing for the $50 (plus the $1,500 to be paid later) and suiting up for the second game against the Vics. Finding out that he had left for the Valley town, Ottawa manager J.P. Dickson raced there on the next train to intercept him before he could fall into the clutches of the Renfrew executive. Dickson succeeded and immediately brought the bedazzled athlete back to the capital.

Two versions of the Taylor equivocation have emerged. Renfrew said they tried to get him only after he told them he had no contract with Ottawa, but only an unsigned document (a personal agreement with the club's vice-president, L.N. Bate), which he carried around in his pocket for a couple of weeks; and that he had heard that the Senators did not really want him after all. When Renfrew officials then went to Ottawa to sign him, they said, Taylor agreed to go if captain Alf Smith approved. According to Renfrew, Smith referred them to Bate, who did not object but told them to confirm with Smith. Advised of Bate's willingness, Smith said that in that case he had no objection either and gave the Renfrew agents permission to retrieve Taylor's skates from the arena.

The Ottawa account says that when the Renfrew officials went to see Bate, they told him they only wanted Taylor for the Vics series, not the whole season. Bate had no problem with this request, but the Renfrew people, going back to Smith, told him that Bate had released Taylor outright. Taylor himself said he accepted the fifty dollars for the Vics game but offered to pay it back when advised that Ottawa had not, in fact, released him and that their supposed lack of interest in him was nothing more than a false rumour.

Was Taylor a crafty bargainer, or was he simply a young man who, having difficulty making commitments, was susceptible to the blandishments of the last person to speak with him? Whatever the case, Ottawa newspapers played up the whole mess for a good two weeks, leaving Senators supporters to wonder whether they would ever see the heralded newcomer in a home jersey.

Ottawans were also beginning to ask questions about the Renfrew club and its backers. How could a team in such a small town with such a tiny rink and competing in an obscure country circuit manage to bid up to $1,500 for the services of a hockey player? Who were the money men behind the audacious offer and what were they up to? They were a father and son team, well known throughout the Valley: Michael John O'Brien, a fabulously wealthy railway contractor and mine operator, and his son, J. Ambrose, who looked after much of his father's business affairs. The elder O'Brien was not known as a hockey fan, but he had a strong sense of community and felt that a champion team would attract favourable attention to his town. Ambrose had been a forward on the team for five years and was now a member of its management committee. Money was no object, hometown pride was what mattered, and though father and son did not land hockey's newest prospect this time, they were not about to give up.

Taylor was not the only player demanding the attention of Ottawa management. In fact, for a few weeks in the early autumn, the whole team was giving trouble. The players wanted better pay and more say in running the club. Management held firm and pointedly advised the aging aggregation that if they did not like their situation in Ottawa, the club could always find new players. Following a confrontation with the Ottawa executive at the Russell House, veterans Smith, Westwick, and Pulford, all coming to the end of the line as players, along with the younger Percy Lesueur, backed away from their tough stance. At the same time, the executive had their eye on two other rising players: centre Marty Walsh, a former Queen's University standout with pro experience in the International League; and Tom Phillips, a left winger with the Kenora Thistles Stanley Cup team of 1907. Management came to terms with Walsh quite routinely but had to chase Phillips. The Montreal Wanderers, who had lost the cup to the Thistles, badly wanted Phillips in their lineup and were offering big money — reportedly $1,500 to $1,800. With Phillips on the verge of signing, Ottawa secretary John Dickson went to Kenora to make one final pitch. Possibly with the financial assistance of some Ottawa sportsmen, who, it was rumoured, had kicked in around $1,000 toward the star's salary. Dickson got Phillips's signature. Phillips explained the bargaining in a wire story out of Kenora. He said he had agreed to sign with the Wanderers, but when the contract arrived it did not meet all the promised requirements. Moreover it was signed by two of the club's officers and bound no one personally. "I had in view a personal guarantee from individuals of sound standing, not a contract with a club that has no corporate existence."

With Taylor, Walsh, and Phillips added to the lineup, prospects looked good and the Ottawa club embarked on its season-ticket plan, the first of its kind for the big new rink. "Prompt attention is requested," the club advised, in reserving the $3.75 packages for five games at the Laurier Avenue arena. By season's start, 2,400 had been sold.

The much-anticipated home opener was set for Saturday, January 11, 1908, against the Montreal Wanderers. Though the Senators had lost the previous week in Quebec, the 7,500 fans in attendance were optimistic. Among them, and equally hopeful, were Governor General Earl Grey and a party from Government House. The Senators did not disappoint, overwhelming their opponents 12-2. By the end of the first half, Ottawa was ahead 6-0. In all Walsh had five goals and Phillips four. Playing cover, Taylor added two, the first on a sensational rush in which he stepped around the defence, drew the goaler out, and deposited the puck behind him. Fans were ecstatic about their new star and all three Ottawa dailies gave him rave reviews in their Monday editions. The origin of Taylor's nickname "Cyclone" is unclear. Reporting on the game, the *Ottawa Free Press* said: "Taylor came here with the appellation of 'the whirlwind of the International' tagged to him. On his performance Saturday he can well be styled the 'tornado of the E.C.H.L." Though Taylor biographer Eric Whitehead asserts that in the same report, the *Free Press* attributes the origin of "Cyclone" to Lord Grey, the paper, in fact, makes no such mention. The allusion of a meteorological disturbance did, however, catch on quickly and within weeks "the Listowel Cyclone" sobriquet began appearing in print.

The Senators finished the 1908 season with seven wins and three losses, good for second place behind the Wanderers, as in 1907. With twenty-eight goals, Marty Walsh tied the Victorias' Russell Bowie for the scoring title. Tommy Phillips was right behind them with twenty-six. Taylor, who remained at the defensive position of cover all season, had nine.

Taylor and Walsh remained with the Senators in 1909, as did LeSueur, but there were dramatic changes. The club failed to keep Tommy Phillips, even after an attractive salary offer, and the promising player left for Edmonton. As expected, Moore, Pulford, and Westwick announced their retirements. Smith, finishing out his playing career, went briefly to the Duquesne Athletic Club in Pittsburgh. But the rail line between Pittsburgh and Ottawa operated in both directions. Allen "Dubbie" Kerr and Fred Lake, both of whom had started the season with the Pittsburgh Athletic Club, abruptly quit and joined the Senators, as did Edgar Dey, who had been bouncing around in the same Western Pennsylvania Hockey League. Hasty departures such as these irritated the American clubs. At the time the supply of American hockey players was very limited, so when the imports jumped contract, the owners were left with big gaps that were hard to fill. In Ottawa, the players' committee, headed by L.N. Bate, did an effective job in replacing the old guard. Their biggest success was in persuading the great Bruce Stuart to give his old team one more turn. He had started his senior career with Ottawa years earlier and had enjoyed lucrative years in the International Hockey League. Rounding out the additions was Billy Gilmour, who had played on Ottawa's first Stanley Cup team in 1903. He later wore the McGill University colours and in 1908 played the full season with Montreal Victorias of the ECAHA.

Before the start of the season, the Victorias and the MAAA dropped out. With four fully professional clubs left (Ottawa, the Wanderers, the Shamrocks, and Quebec), the league struck the word "Amateur" from its title and became the Eastern Canada Hockey Association (ECHA). An odd and mildly distracting development followed. A resurrection, of sorts, of the FAHL was under way. Plans were made for four teams: Renfrew, Smiths Falls, Cornwall, and an outfit from Ottawa, to be called, surprisingly, the "Senators." Smith, back from Pittsburgh, was a guiding force as playing manager, and it was he and former Ottawa goalkeeper Bouse Hutton who decided to appropriate the nickname, by then well established informally as that of the Ottawa Hockey Club. Since the Ottawa Hockey Club was not yet an incorporated body and the name "Senators" had never been registered, there was nothing to stop the new organization from assuming the name. Joining the new-style Senators from supposed retirement were Moore and Westwick. The league never did amount to much, but it enjoyed a measure of credibility at the outset when the western champion Edmonton team, following an unsuccessful Stanley Cup challenge against the Wanderers, met and defeated the upstart Senators by a narrow margin in an exhibition game at Dey's Arena.

As for the time-honoured Senators, now dubbed the "Professionals" by the Ottawa press, it soon became clear that management had assembled a powerhouse. After losing their first game in overtime to the current Stanley Cup holders, the Wanderers, Ottawa went on a nine-game winning streak, in the course of which they overwhelmed Quebec and the Shamrocks in several matches. Marty Walsh and Bruce Stuart were scoring prodigiously. Behind them, Freddie Lake and Cyclone Taylor made a tough defensive pairing. Record crowds were turning out at Dey's, prompting the club to announce ticket price increases of up to 25 per cent at mid-season (from $1.00 to $1.25 for the first two rows). Only the denizens of the rush end were spared. Known as the "millionaires section," this vast and tiered standing-room area commanded the same 25-cent admission as before.

In two more encounters with the Wanderers, the Ottawas eked out narrow victories. The final game between the rivals on March 3 in Ottawa would be a crucial one. A win for the Ottawas would clinch the league championship and give them the Stanley Cup. In the three games to date, one goal separated the teams — Ottawa had scored twenty, the Wanderers nineteen. The huge crowd gave the Ottawas a warm reception as they stepped onto the ice. Taylor, the last man out, got the loudest ovation; but the crowd saw right away that he was shaky on his feet during the warm-up. A bad cut on his foot in the previous game had forced him to leave and some railbirds were sure he wouldn't finish this one. In fact, taking a lot of punishment, he played the whole game and made numerous spectacular rushes, one of which resulted in a goal. At halftime, the score was 3-3. The Wanderers were known as a team of strong finishers, but this time they had nothing left and the Ottawas added five unanswered goals in the second half to win 8-3. As expected, Marty Walsh and Dubbie Kerr had strong games, each scoring three times. To Ottawa supporters, the final whistle was a sweet moment, for many recalled that the last time the teams had met for the cup, in 1906 out at the Gladstone rink, it was the Wanderers who prevailed. In a meaningless game to complete the regular schedule, Quebec handed the Ottawas their second loss of the season. They were then off to New York for a two-game exhibition series against the Wanderers. It was Ottawa's first visit to the St. Nicholas Rink since 1902 and marked New York's introduction to the highly publicized Cyclone.

Reporting on the Ottawa Hockey Club's wrap-up banquet, the *Ottawa Citizen* said in its March 17, 1909, edition: "Fred Taylor made the unusual request that he be allowed to take the Stanley Cup home to Listowel with him at Easter time." He wanted people there to get a good look at it and promised to return the trophy in "perfect order."

Birth of the National Hockey Association

WHEN OTTAWA HOCKEY CLUB executives met on the evening of November 10, 1909, to firm up affairs for the approaching season, they had no idea that the league in which they were entered was about to collapse. Their main business was to appoint Dave Mulligan and Percy Buttler as the club's delegates to the annual meeting of the ECHA in Montreal. One big issue to be discussed at that meeting was the status of the Wanderers. The owners had transferred their interests to another member of their group, Fred Strachan. He promptly sold the club to Montreal entrepreneur P.J. Doran, but stayed on as his representative. Doran had just built a new rink, the Jubilee, in the East end and wanted a team. The other clubs were opposed to playing games at the Jubilee because its capacity was too small to generate the revenues they needed to survive. Meanwhile, William Jennings, one of the original Wanderers principals, objected to the sale. Nothing in its transfer to Strachan, he maintained, gave him the right to then sell the club. Days before the Montreal meeting, he went to the capital seeking support from the Ottawa executive for the continuation of the original Wanderers franchise, under the old regime, and rejection of Doran's Wanderers. In other words, he argued, his group had relinquished only the team and not the franchise itself. The Ottawa executives assured him that they would back his position. At the same time Ottawa was reluctant to see an additional Montreal team in the league because of extra travel expenses. Also, because they were Stanley Cup champions, the Ottawas favoured a light league schedule in order to accommodate the lucrative home-ice cup challenges they anticipated.

In addition to the Wanderers question, the other main item on the agenda of the league meeting at Montreal's Windsor Hotel was an application for admission from another club, the Nationals. The Nationals were unique in that they were a strictly French-Canadian team, the first such to aspire to senior status. Before these issues could be dealt with, however, there was the matter of electing officers for the new year. It happened that Doran's spokesman for the Jubilee Wanderers, Fred Strachan, was the league vice president. Under normal circumstances he would move up to president. This would mean that the meeting's chairmanship would succeed to a representative of a team whose place in the league was under question. Seizing the moment, Ottawa delegate Dave Mulligan immediately sought and won a recess. The tactical move gave everyone present an opportunity to discuss the situation informally in the corridors.

Over the years, the venerable old hotel had witnessed many scenes like the one unfolding: small circles of delegates in animated conversation, outside hockey men hovering in the background, and newspaper reporters trying to glean what they could. Two of the outsiders, at least as far as the formal meeting was concerned, were William Jennings and Tom Hodge of the old Wanderers organization. They were in the process of establishing a new team, with the hope of getting into the ECHA. They wanted to know what had being going on in the meeting and to press their interest. Seemingly out of nowhere, a document appeared that cast doubts on Jennings' assertions that Strachan had not been entitled to sell the Wanderers in the first place. Going from hand to hand, the piece of paper contained the agreement to transfer the club from the original owners to Strachan. There was nothing in it to stop Strachan from disposing of the club if he so wished. The agreement bore Jennings's signature, along with those of the other owners. With this now exposed, Jennings altered his original position. Forced to accept the legitimacy of the Jubilee Wanderers, he now suggested in the hotel corridor that the league have two divisions, one to include his new team and the other the Strachan/Doran club. Ottawa's Dave Mulligan could see that the meeting's informal pause, far from allowing matters to be sorted out, was complicating things even further. Upon reconvening, and following the election of officers (in which Strachan was relegated to executive member rather than being elevated to president), Mulligan moved adjournment for two weeks. With this accepted, both the Wanderers' and the Nationals' questions remained unresolved.

By the time the ECHA meeting reconvened on November 25, Ambrose O'Brien had already been around town for a few days lobbying informally for his Renfrew club to be admitted to the league. Dave Mulligan, again representing the Ottawas, was by now convinced that with Nationals and Renfrew wanting in and the Wanderer question still up in the air, professional hockey, and specifically the ECHA, needed reorganization. The best way to do this, he thought, was to start over. As a first step, he withdrew the Ottawas from the league. The other clubs followed suit and that was the end of it. The Ottawa, Shamrocks, and Quebec delegates then banded together in private and shortly threw their meeting open "to all interested in hockey." They had reconstituted themselves as the Canadian Hockey Association (CHA) and were ready to consider applications. Waiting in the corridor were the applicants: William Jennings on behalf of his new club, to be called All-Montreal; Fred Strachan of the Wanderers; Nap Dorval of the Nationals; Ambrose O'Brien on behalf of Renfrew; and, lately on the scene, Cornwall's J. Kervin. After two hours of interviews and deliberations an announcement came out of the meeting. All-Montreal and Nationals were accepted into a five-team Canadian Hockey Association.

Jimmy Gardner, one of the Wanderers representatives, was stunned by the rejection of his club. Spotting the equally unhappy O'Brien in the lobby, he approached him with the idea that they form their own rival league. He knew the O'Briens had a strong financial interest in the Cobalt and Haileybury clubs of northern Ontario and proposed that they be brought in. Meeting in Montreal on December 2, the four clubs established the National Hockey Association (NHA). The idea had also emerged that a second French team be created. It was to be bankrolled indirectly by O'Brien money and would be called the Canadiens. Meeting again on December 4 at the Windsor Hotel, the fledgling league elected its officers and formally admitted the Canadiens, who, along with the Wanderers, would play their matches at Doran's Jubilee Rink. Curiously, at exactly the same time, the CHA was meeting down the hall in what the *Montreal Gazette* was now aptly calling "the storm centre." There had been some anticipation of movement between the two rooms — that either the Ottawas, Shamrocks, and Nationals would step over to the NHA, or the Wanderers and Renfrew would be taken in, after all, by the CHA. Neither happened. There were now two professional leagues. Five of the ten teams were in Montreal, two were in the other traditional senior-hockey markets of Ottawa and Quebec, and three were in small towns. Observers doubted this arrangement would work. They questioned how even the proven hockey centre of Montreal would be able to support five pro clubs, and similarly how Haileybury, Cobalt, and Renfrew would manage at the gate in their tiny rinks.

The Salary War

THE INEVITABLE SALARY WAR was about to begin. Where there had been four teams in the previous premier professional league, there were now ten in two leagues. In addition the Ontario Professional Hockey League (OPHL) in southern Ontario had commenced in 1908. In its four-year existence it served as the starting point for some future greats, such as Newsy Lalonde, Goldie Prodgers, and Skene Ronan, and as a temporary stopping-off point for a few other prominent players, such as Joe Malone and Harry and Tommy Smith. Though the league never posed a serious financial threat to the Senators and other eastern clubs, their managers did take note. And no sooner had the OPHL folded after the 1911 season than a much more worrisome obstacle to the recruiting of players at affordable pay sprang up — the Pacific Coast Hockey Association. The initial impetus for salary escalation, however, was the coexistence of the CHA and the NHA, and once again, Cyclone Taylor was in the eye of the storm.

As early as November 1909 the Ottawa executive had spoken confidently of retaining Taylor for the coming season. But they had not taken account of Renfrew's determination to put a Stanley Cup-contending team on the ice. The O'Briens, along with another wealthy Renfrewite, Alexander Barnett, were prepared to put up whatever money it took to realize their dream. They launched an open raid on the Ottawa team, aggressively pursuing Taylor, Walsh, Lake, and Kerr. As if to give emphasis to the depth of the O'Brien wealth, newspapers reported M.J. as saying there was $5 million worth of ore blocked out in his silver mine at Cobalt, that his asking price was $7.5 million, and that "he would not take a cent less." The team he assembled came to be known as the Millionaires.

After Renfrew's first attempt to sign Taylor, Ottawa vice-president L.N. Bate assured reporters that the Cyclone would again wear the Ottawa colours. "We did not have to sign him," he said. "Taylor's word is as good to us as all the contracts that were ever made. Taylor will play with Ottawa. He would not go to Renfrew now if they offered him all the money up there." Taylor was equally buoyant. "I have just written to Renfrew telling them that I am going to stay with Ottawa. They offered me two thousand dollars and a position all right, but I'm going to continue with Ottawa." Two weeks later, Taylor's name was on an agreement with the Renfrew Hockey Club to play the 1909–1910 season for $1,500. But the evening after signing, Taylor was at a Senators practice. The *Ottawa Citizen* explained that there was a provision in the contract allowing him to opt out if a better arrangement could be made with Ottawa. That contract is held by the Renfrew Archives and is reproduced in Frank Cosentino's book *The Renfrew Millionaires.* It contains no such clause. Possibly, Taylor had an unwritten undertaking to that effect with James Barnett and George Martel of the Renfrew organization, who, respectively, signed and witnessed the document. By December 31 Taylor was back with Renfrew, this time for sure. Conjecture about his salary was rampant. One figure was $3,000 for the season. Eric Whitehead, in *Cyclone Taylor,* states that seventy years after the event, Taylor recalled signing for $5,250. Scott Young and Astrid Young, in their biography *O'Brien,* say that Ambrose O'Brien put the figure at $2,000. Fancy numbers were also tossed about for Kerr, Lake, and Walsh; but in the end all three settled for Ottawa, where jobs on the side were promised. The O'Briens, nevertheless, attracted a star-studded and high-priced cast for the 1910 season, including, in addition to Taylor, Newsy Lalonde, and Frank and Lester Patrick, the latter with a reported $3,000 price tag.

Other clubs in the newly formed CHA and NHA also experienced salary pressures. Further complicating bottom-line considerations, especially in the CHA, was fan apathy brought on by a combination of talent dilution and over exposure of hockey, given the five clubs in Montreal alone. With high player costs and low ticket revenues, the CHA gave up after only two weeks. All-Montreal, the Nationals, and Quebec ceased operations entirely, while the Senators and the Shamrocks were admitted to the rival league, where a new schedule was drawn up.

Before that happened, however, the Senators were obliged to honour two Stanley Cup challenges. The first was from Galt, the OPHL champions of 1909. Ottawa won both games handily in the total-goals series, 5-3 and 3-1. As it turned out, the gates were disappointingly small. The most notable feature of the otherwise-dreary series was the Senators' new uniforms. The familiar red, black, and white stripes were still present, but instead of being horizontal they were vertical. This provoked quite a stir in Montreal a few days later when French-speaking Nationals' fans took to calling the visitors "*les suisses*," a slang term referring to the chipmunk, whose black and white stripes run the length of his coat. In the second series, the Senators outclassed Edmonton, the Alberta champions, 8-4 and 13-7. The crowds were better at about 4,000 for each game, but fans did not appreciate the boost in ticket prices, necessary to defray Edmonton's travel costs. Ottawa finished that first NHA season with nine wins and three losses, second to the Wanderers at eleven and one.

The league contraction of 1910 continued in 1911 when the Shamrocks dropped out, and the Haileybury and Cobalt franchises were taken over by the Canadiens and a resuscitated Quebec operation. Ottawa, the Wanderers, and Renfrew remained intact, thus making for a compact five-club circuit and no rival league. The new structure also put owners in a more favourable bargaining position with the players, and the league immediately introduced a salary cap of $5,000 per club. Owners exceeding that limit faced a $1,000 fine.

Predictably the players objected. "I would rather quit the game than accept the sum which is allotted to me according to NHA rules," Ottawa's Dubbie Kerr said. And captain Bruce Stuart, who had just announced his retirement, did not deny going to Montreal, nevertheless, to see Art Ross about forming a players' union. Ross, who had jumped from the Wanderers to Haileybury for a big pay increase the previous year, went public. In a letter to the *Montreal Herald*, he noted that players run the risk of injury, which would mean the probable loss of time in other jobs they have. He pointed out that the players had entered professional hockey with the expectation of earning good money and now that the owners were cutting back the pay, the players were in a bind, for they would no longer be able to afford to play professionally yet had sacrificed their amateur status. Disingenuously, he added, "I would gladly give back all I have made as a professional player to regain my amateur standing." Offering the opinion that the clubs "have or should have made money" before there was a salary limit, he wrote: "All the players want is a fair deal." There was also talk of holdout players forming an outlaw league to play exhibition games. Two Senator dissidents even staged a visit to the tiny Rideau Rink to examine its suitability as a home for a new team. But these pleas and threats cut no ice; the owners held firm and the salaries worked out to a range of $375 for a lesser player to $900 for the best.

Like the other owners, the men behind the Senators now thought they had financial matters in check. They announced they had signed eight players for the coming season at an average salary of $625, compared with the previous year's $1,200. Assuming that attendance for games in a compact and competitive league would hold up, club president D'Arcy McGee and his executive committee could look forward to a tidy profit on the season's operations. As it turned out, the club did very well financially, and so did the players, notwithstanding the salary cap. Though management remained tight-lipped about the balance sheet, the *Ottawa Journal* did a little mid-season arithmetic of its own, based on ticket prices and announced attendance. If support for the remaining three league games remained strong, the Ottawas would take in at least $25,000 for the full season. Two of those games would be big draws for sure: Cyclone Taylor and the Renfrew Millionaires, followed by the Canadiens in what was shaping up as a championship showdown. Indeed, huge crowds attended all three. Moreover, and not taken into account in the *Journal*'s calculations, the Senators did win the championship, and with it the Stanley Cup, thus giving them what amounted to two bonus dates, cup defences against Galt and Port Arthur. Still champions, the Senators were then off to New York and Boston for four exhibition contests against the Wanderers. As bonuses to the players, management had promised them the net proceeds from the cup and exhibition games. The cheques worked out to about $300 each. At the conclusion of the regular season, in conformity with NHA regulations, the club had presented the league with the player contracts, showing a total salary expenditure of $4,987.60 ($12.40 under the $5,000 cap). The club did not regard proceeds from post-season play to be part of the league agreement, and with this interpretation were able to bring the total pay per player up to nearly $1,000. This gesture of generosity and good faith, management thought, would stand the club in good stead when it came time to sign the players for the next season. In adopting this line, McGee, Bate, Rosenthal, and the other power brokers making up Ottawa's management group might well have presaged another development on the horizon.

Long before any official announcements were made, word was on the street that the Patrick family were talking hockey out on the West Coast. Joseph Patrick had sold his lumbering empire in Nelson and sons Lester and Frank were thinking of ways to invest the family fortune. They were the same Patrick boys who had starred with Cyclone Taylor on the 1910 Renfrew club. Their intentions soon became clear. They were going to build artificial-ice arenas in Victoria and Vancouver and establish a new professional league. They would need experienced players and the place to get them was Eastern Canada. If the salary war had abated, it had not ended.

In the meantime Ottawa management were thinking expansively. Buoyed by the team's success in the past season, they envisioned building a state-of-the-art, artificial-ice arena on Preston Street in the west-central part of town, an area served by two car lines. With this in mind, and experiencing the annual rigours of salary negotiations, management realized the time had come to put professional hockey in Ottawa on a solid business footing through incorporation. The first thought was to capitalize at $150,000, but when plans for the new rink fell through, that amount was reduced to $50,000. November 29, 1911, was a historic day for hockey in Ottawa, for it was on that date that the secretary of state of Canada granted letters patent to the Ottawa Hockey Association, Limited. After twenty-eight years of existence, the Ottawas had become a legal entity. The incorporation document reveals that the company's capital stock was to be divided into five hundred shares of one hundred dollars each. The provisional directors were all familiar names in local hockey circles: Martin Rosenthal, Nicholas Sparks, Percy Buttler, Charles Irvin, Llewellyn Bate, Patrick Baskerville, and Thomas D'arcy McGee.

Other NHA clubs also incorporated in anticipation of the looming salary war with the Pacific Coast Hockey Association (PCHA). The Tommy Phillips decision in 1907 to eschew a contract with Wanderers because the club had no corporate existence, and to insist, rather, on an agreement with a responsible individual of sound financial standing, was a telling point as far as salary contract administration was concerned. With player budgets on the increase, owners were no longer interested in being personally responsible for salary obligations. Incorporation would also bring a more formal status to contracts and reduce the chances of players jumping from one team to another, especially to the PCHA, which had no agreement with the NHA whereby the two leagues would recognize each other's signed contracts.

Ottawa lost no players to the PCHA in that league's first season, but other eastern clubs were not so fortunate. Among those going west were the great Canadiens star Newsy Lalonde, Harry Hyland and Ernie Johnson of the Wanderers, Don Smith and Bobby Rowe from Renfrew, and Tommy

Dunderdale and Ken Mallen from Quebec. The PCHA was actually a syndicate owned by the Patricks. Players signed with the league, rather than with individual clubs, and were doled out to the three teams as the two brothers saw fit. One reason why the Ottawas escaped defections was the club's ability to find steady jobs, including in an expanding civil service. Cyclone Taylor, for example, remained in the position the Senators had secured for him at the Department of the Interior even through his Renfrew tenure, and when his rights were assigned to Wanderers after the Millionaires disbanded, he refused to report because he wanted to hold on to his Ottawa job. He sat out the full season.

Just as predicted, salaries rose. Canadiens manager George Kennedy, stunned by the loss of crowd-pleaser Lalonde, was openly admitting he had exceeded the $5,000 team limit and had topped the $8,000 mark. Most other NHA clubs likely forgot about the salary cap, too. And by the next season, the very idea was a thing of the past. It had to be. Lester Patrick had come east in the fall of 1912 with the intention of luring more players west. In Ottawa he systematically interviewed Senators players Skene Ronan, Jack Darragh, and Clint Benedict and made offers to all three. He was reportedly prepared to hand Ronan $1,500 for the season. The raid was reminiscent of the 1907 O'Brien sojourn to the capital. Again Ottawa management withstood the attack, for reasons revealed in the club's ledger for the 1913 season. One of the few financial records known of the Ottawa club for those early years, the ledger details player pay, right down to the bi-weekly cheques. So precise were the entries that even the amounts for player fines can be calculated. At that time, when a player received a penalty in a game, he was obliged to pay a fine to the league. The club's responsibility was to collect the money from the guilty parties and remit the total to the league secretary at the end of the season. Skene Ronan's eighth paycheque, on February 22, for example, was $26 short at $124, and his total pay for the season was $1,474, instead of $1,500 – the same amount, incidentally, promised by Patrick months earlier. Jack Darragh also earned $1,500 and Hamby Shore's pay came to a curious total of $1,500.05. Fred Lake earned $1,350 and Percy LeSueur $995.99. Young goalkeeper Clint Benedict, in his first pro season after playing with the local New Edinburgh club, received a respectable $772 as LeSueur's understudy. Harry Broadbent and Horace Merrill, two other rookies also up from "the Burgh," both earned $500. Eddie Lowrey pocketed $500 and Joe Dennison $490. Tommy Westwick, who appeared in twelve games and saw spot duty, was a bargain at $200. The profit-and-loss statement for 1913 records total salaries at $10,237.79, which includes pay to the coach and trainer. The total amount going to the players is not segregated there, but from the line entries per player, the sum comes to $9,808.04 before the deduction of fines. Thus, one year after the inception of the rival PCHA, player salaries for the Ottawas of the NHA had doubled. Payroll inflation had a devastating effect on the bottom line, for in spite of healthy ticket revenues of $16,344.25, the club's expenses (including $5,770.15 to Dey's Arena) totalled $20,214.91 — an operating loss of $3,870.66.

In a few short years, players' salaries had come a long way, a point surely not lost on Harry Westwick. After twelve seasons as a stellar performer with the Ottawa Hockey Club, the Rat retired in 1908. His hockey income in that final year would not have been more than $500. And by 1913, after several years service as a government printer, his annual pay had risen to only $950. Not only did Hamby Shore's $1,500 for three months of part-time work as a hockey player look handsome indeed, his additional $1,000 salary in the Department of the Interior's railway and swamp lands branch put the popular star in the capital's comfortable middle class. In fact his total income of $2,500 was greater than the salary of the branch director, a career civil servant. Other Ottawa players, too, held down day jobs. Clint Benedict worked for Mortimer printers, Percy LeSueur was a clerk in the engineering branch of the Transcontinental Railway, and Horace Merrill was a partner in the printing and advertising firm of Kuhn-Merrill Ltd.

The hockey players were affluent, and seen as such. The idea of athletes being paid to engage in their sport, as a job, was still somewhat new to the public. Ottawans were aware from their newspapers that champion prizefighters in distant places commanded fabulous purses, and that some American baseball players earned large sums. But this was Ottawa, and the realization that local athletes were making more for their winter exploits than many regular people were bringing in for a full year's labour gave pause. Especially so at this time, as the cost of living was going up and their pay, unlike that of the hockey players, was not keeping pace. In just three years, the rent for a typical workingman's dwelling had risen by more than 50 per cent to $22 per month. At $675, a Model T Ford was out of reach for most. The much admired Packard shoes that the old Senators player Bruce Stuart was retailing at his Bank Street store for $6 were a special purchase for the typical tradesman receiving $4 for a ten-hour day, but always subject to winter layoffs and other industry uncertainties. Little wonder that the rush-end, general-admission standing room at Dey's Arena was usually the first section to fill up. Fortunately for the players, there were other more affluent citizens who were prepared to purchase season tickets or reserved seats for individual games in the pricier sections. They were senior civil servants, businessmen, and professionals — the sorts who lived in $4,000-and-up four-bedroom brick homes in the Glebe or Sandy Hill (possibly brokered by real-estate agent Nelson Porter, an original Ottawa player in 1883); who sported $25 suits from Fishers and adorned their wives in fine $12 coats from A. Rea & Co. department store; and who might even have thought about acquiring a shiny black Russell-Knight "28" Roadster, listed at $3,200.

11 · Real War and the Crisis of Conscience

Far and near, high and clear,
Hark to the call of war!
ROBERT SERVICE
"The Call," 1914

AS POLITICIANS WARILY LOOKED cast to Europe in late summer 1913, the hockey moguls of central Canada peered nervously west to British Columbia. Regular Canadians, faced with ever-rising costs and high unemployment, were mainly occupied with getting by as best they could. They had little time for the looming world crisis brought on by the German military buildup and none whatsoever for the trivial matter of hockey's salary wars.

Conservative Prime Minister Robert Borden had warned Parliament of the ambitions of Kaiser Wilhelm to support his already-dominant army by assembling the world's most powerful navy. Britain's supremacy on the high seas, thought essential to the safety and security of the empire, was being challenged. The escalation of Germany's striking fleet was alarming. Projections showed a planned increase to 245 warships and torpedo boats by 1920 from the 153 of 1898. Among them would be 41 battleships and 20 large cruisers. Britain's response included a request to the dominions to assist with the financing of additional dreadnoughts, the most awesome battleships afloat. Borden's Naval Aid Bill to grant $35 million to the mother country for the construction of three of these behemoths went down to defeat, however, in a Liberal-dominated Senate in the summer of 1913. On the other hand some 60,000 militiamen, part-time volunteers, had received military training.

Hockey's Peace Accord

WHILE PREPARATIONS for a possible European conflict were under way, the small and inconsequential world of pro hockey was seeking peace between western and eastern operators. The Patrick syndicate on the Pacific Coast needed players that British Columbia could not supply. To get their league started, the Patricks had been willing to pay top dollar for experienced men from the East, but the time had now come to give priority to the bottom line. Their objective was to balance assurances of a talent pipeline with cost control. In the East NHA clubs were tired of watching the Ontario and Quebec pool being drained of many of its best players. Owners also resented the inflated salaries they were forced to hand over to counter the lure of the West. In Ottawa there was concern over the health of the feeder system. Partly because of a shortage of rinks and partly because of the number of junior and senior city league players moving up so quickly to pro ranks, the local hockey infrastructure was on a shaky footing. The Senators had long prided themselves on their ability to recruit locally. If hometown amateur prospects were going to be skimmed off prematurely, the leagues in which they were developing their skills would be hurt through the dilution of talent. The Senators were mindful of past contributions made by such teams as the Cliffsides, the Emmetts, the Aberdeens, and New Edinburgh, not only to their own organization but to other professional clubs. They wanted the flow to continue, of course, but in a measured way.

Against this backdrop Frank and Lester Patrick came east in early September to fix things. In a meeting presided over by NHA president Emmett Quinn, they hammered out an agreement with the eastern owners on territorial rights and inter-league player transactions. Pacific clubs would have first call on all players hailing from Port Arthur and west, and NHA clubs from points east of that dividing line. The western league would have the right each year to draft three players from the NHA for a purchase price of up to $500. In the first year one player from each of three teams could be selected. In the second year the choices would be made from the remaining three teams, and so forth. By the same token the eastern clubs would have the right to protect three players from the annual draft. Those refusing to report west were to be suspended by the NHA. The Pacific league would be prohibited from flipping back east any player it had acquired in the draft without the approval of the supplying club. All clubs in both leagues would be permitted to purchase or exchange players regardless of the East-West boundary. The accord had another point of agreement, a groundbreaking one in which the Senators would figure before long. There was to be an annual post-season series between the eastern and western champions. Implicit in this agreement was the logical assumption that the

Stanley Cup would be at stake, even though its trustees had not yet approved the competition.

With salary-inflating player raids now in check, Ottawa management could talk bluntly. "We are not worrying so much about paying the salaries as we are that the players give value for the money after they get it," one Senators executive said to the *Ottawa Journal*. "The players who fail to deliver the goods will be fined or suspended without pay until they live up to their obligations this winter." As for the initial PCHA draft, Ottawa lost no players. The Patricks took Art Throop from the Tecumsehs, Frank Nighbor from the Torontos, and Newsy Lalonde from the Canadiens. An Ottawa trade to the West Coast, however, ran into complications. In exchange for Skene Ronan, the Senators were to get another forward, Carroll Kendall. Wanderers owner Sammy Lichtenhein coveted Ronan and tried to block the deal, claiming a clause in the new PCHA-NHA agreement stipulated that before any inter-league trade could be effected, the players involved would have to be waived out of their respective leagues. He made it clear he was not prepared to see Ronan go west. No one seemed to know anything about this purported clause, and when NHA president Emmett Quinn checked the document, he found no such proviso. The ploy was simply a typical example of Lichtenhein's operating style. All the while Ronan was refusing to budge. After a stalemate Percy LeSueur, now Ottawa's playing manager, signed Ronan for another season. Kendall ended up with Lichtenhein's team.

LeSueur and business manager Frank Shaughnessy felt personnel changes were necessary to shake off the mediocrity of the 1913 season when the team won nine games, lost eleven, and finished in third place. They saw Hamby Shore as an untouchable and resisted the entreaties of the Wanderers for emerging star Jack Darragh; but they deemed Fred Lake and Joe Dennison expendable, selling them to Toronto. Joining the team at the start of the season were the diminutive Leth Graham (five-foot-five, 125 pounds), and "the big Pembroke boy," Allen Wilson. Harry Smith was brought in for three games after a six-year absence. In the middle of January Angus Duford was called up from New Edinburgh, but it was another product of the same organization who caused the biggest stir when he signed ten days later.

Eddie Gerard was one of the city's most prominent athletes. In addition to his prowess in hockey, he excelled in paddling and in football as a halfback with the Ottawa Rough Riders. The Senators had been trying to entice him for some time, and only when they were finally able to assure him that a pro contract would not interfere with his civil-service job at the Geodetic Survey did he agree to join the club. The day he put his name to paper was a memorable one. Called into the Senators' business office on Bank Street, Gerard found himself face-to-face with secretary-treasurer Martin Rosenthal and manager Shaughnessy. The club had issued Shaughnessy a cheque for $400, which he cashed. The money sat openly in a pile on a table. Shaughnessy told Gerard that if he agreed to play for the Senators he could take the money away with him. Gerard wasted no time in signing. His father was a hard-working, God-fearing man of Scottish origin. He knew the value of a dollar. When the young man, who had never played hockey for anything but the fun of it, told his father about the money the Senators were handing him, the senior Gerard, suppressing his delight, exclaimed, "They must be a bunch of damn fools!" At Dey's Arena before his first game, a contingent from the New Edinburgh hockey and canoe clubs marched onto the ice and presented Gerard with a silver loving cup, after which the big crowd gave him a resounding cheer. Playing left wing on a line with Darragh and Ronan, Gerard put on a memorable show that night, scoring a goal against the famed Paddy Moran in his club's 4-3 victory over Quebec.

Though Darragh and Ronan were productive that season, scoring twenty-three and eighteen goals respectively, overall scoring was down by twenty-two; and while the Senators reversed their record of the previous season, winning eleven and losing nine, they finished fourth. If Ronan was unhappy with his situation in Ottawa, knowing that management had wanted to trade him — and if reports were true that he had wanted to go to the Wanderers — he nevertheless appeared to integrate well with his teammates and the community. In fact he seems to have been a colourful entrepreneur on the side. He had the agency in Ottawa for a novelty souvenir, which he sold at the arena. Dubbed by the press the "Carrie Nation rooter," after the American temperance crusader who used a hatchet to wreck saloons, the device was a miniature hockey stick with a split blade and red, white, and black streamers attached to the handle. Popular with fans, the gadget made a terrible clatter when banged against the seats, a practice their purchasers enthusiastically engaged in, either to demonstrate their pleasure or displeasure over what was happening on the ice. And there was a lot of whistling, on and off the ice. Winger Punch Broadbent's customary call for a pass was a piercing whistle that carried across the rink and into the stands. Fans in the "millionaires section" often brought whistles to games to create mischief trying to halt play whenever the visiting team threatened. Following one game, a Montreal newspaper accused Ottawa goalie LeSueur of skating to the other end and inciting the crowd to abuse his Wanderers counterpart, Billy Nicholson. LeSueur, a poised and elegant professional, was indignant and threatened to sue the paper. He said he had gone to the visitors' end simply to get the boisterous millionaires to stop blowing their tin whistles, because they were interfering as much with the Senators as the Wanderers. Ironically, the urbane student of the game had failed to heed his own counsel. Years earlier in an instruction book he wrote, he proffered the advice, "Do not listen to remarks from the spectators. It is a habit, particularly at the general admission end of the rinks, to call all kinds of things at the goalkeeper and he cannot listen to them and keep his mind on the game."

Peerless Percy

THE YEAR 1914 WOULD BE Percy LeSueur's last with the Senators. Following his single appearance with the club in the 1906 Stanley Cup final, he was the regular goalie for eight seasons. In all he played in 113 regular-season games (including one as an emergency replacement at defence in 1914), seven playoff games, and nineteen exhibition matches. He was a Stanley Cup champion twice, in 1909 and 1911.

Off the ice LeSueur was as powerful a presence as on. Clearly the man loved hockey and was one who promoted the sport relentlessly, both as a teacher and an innovator. His nifty little instructional book, *How to Play Hockey*, was exactly the sort of treatise that, found under the Christmas tree, would cause any budding young player to completely forget all else. Published in a timely fashion just before the start of the 1910 season, and following the Senators' Stanley Cup championship, it gave practical advice on the playing of each position and was laced with photos of the most popular players and teams of the period. The book carried ads for the Art Ross line of hockey supplies, the Lunn laminated hockey skate (which the author personally endorsed), and the Ketchum "Patent" Hockey Boot. He also plugged an invention of his own. "A small pad, which I invented in 1909 and which I think is on sale at most sporting goods stores, will possibly be found to help considerably, while interfering very little with the handling of the stick." It was a goalkeeper's hand pad, designed to be inserted under either glove. Clinching his sales pitch, LeSueur offered the helpful information that it "is sold at a comparatively low figure."

The innovation for which LeSueur was best known, however, was the hockey goal he patented in 1911, which the NHA immediately adopted. The standard goal at the time had an elbowed iron crossbar set back four to six inches from the tops of the posts and to which the netting was attached. This left a narrow gap between the imaginary line joining the tops of the goal posts and the recessed bar. A puck could thus drop through this open area and into the goal from behind the posts. LeSueur removed the crossbar, fixed a U-shaped upper frame to the tops of the posts, stretched a cord tightly between the tops, and added netting to form, in effect, a roof with no gap. Having a cord instead of a bar was seen as a safety feature. The new frame also made it possible to hang the netting more loosely to prevent pucks from rebounding out. Though the crossbar was eventually put back in to replace the cord, the basic structure of the LeSueur net remained official for many years. The LeSueur goal can still be seen on playground rinks.

In his last game wearing the red, white, and black, LeSueur shared netminding duties with his brilliant young understudy of the past two years, Clint Benedict, in a meaningless 7-3 exhibition loss to the touring Vancouver All-Stars. The season now over, the *Ottawa Journal* reported dissension within the ranks. Someone associated with the club had voiced the opinion that the reason for the team's poor performance that year was the bad feeling caused by a clique who preferred the backup to the veteran. True or not, the comment hardly seemed a fitting endnote for one who had contributed so much to the game, to the success of his team, and to the enjoyment of the fans. Billy Hague, who in 1906 had been summarily dismissed in favour of LeSueur, would have understood the slight. Before the start of the 1915 campaign "Peerless Percy" would be traded to Toronto, where he was to play for two more years.

Comfortable and Complacent

THE NORTH WINDOWS of Ottawa's Langevin Building on Wellington Street afford a perfect view of Parliament Hill. The massive, ochre-coloured sandstone edifice creates a feeling of serious and substantial business, befitting the work going on inside where civil servants attended to the affairs of a sprawling nation. Outside, on August 17, 1914, a steady downpour started the day, but the clearing skies later on did nothing to lift the sombre mood. Frank McGee and his co-workers in the lands branch would have gathered at these windows to witness with concern the stately procession that afternoon. Accompanied by an escort of the Princess Louise Dragoon Guards, the Duke of Connaught arrived in front of the Centre Block, where he was met by a one-hundred-man contingent from the Governor General's Foot Guards. His task was to deliver the Speech from the Throne, which would open an emergency session of Parliament. "Very grave events vitally affecting the interests of all His Majesty's Dominions have transpired since prorogation," he began. "The unfortunate outbreak of war made it immediately imperative for my Ministers to take extraordinary measures for the defence of Canada and for the maintenance of the honour and integrity of our Empire." Two weeks earlier, Germany had ignored Britain's ultimatum — get out of Belgium by midnight, August 4. Britain was at war and that meant her loyal dominions were, too. Within days some 25,000 Canadian militiamen were under arms, and even as the governor general spoke, troops were on their way to the Val-Cartier, Quebec, staging area.

Though there was a sense of foreboding around the parliamentary precinct, and families and friends of those suddenly in khaki were becoming apprehensive, the vast majority of Canadians did not share this gloom. The war was far away and would be over quickly. "Comfortable and complacent" is how historians Robert Craig Brown and Ramsay Cook describe the mood of the land. On the day of Connaught's speech, as war news dominated newspaper front pages everywhere, the Ottawa Hockey Club was worrying about finding opponents for its newly formed exhibition baseball team. Horace Merrill, Hamby Shore and Skene Ronan were in the outfield "garden," Clint Benedict was at first, Eddie Gerard at second, Angus Duford at shortstop, and Leth Graham at third. Only the battery came from outside the team. No such amusements would be in store for the club's former star. McGee was to enlist within two months. So too would Harry Smith. Charlie Spittal, a versatile member of the Ottawas in days gone by, was one of the first of the city's athletes to go overseas when he left as a major with the Army Services Corps in late 1914. Before war's end Angus Duford, Harry Broadbent, Horace Gaul, Leth Graham, Harry Westwick, and Percy LeSueur would be in uniform. These players were not comfortable and complacent, nor was the Ottawas' former captain and president, Phillip Ross. Two days after Canada was officially at war, he published a boldface notice at the top of the *Journal's* front page:

Any employee of The Journal who is attached to the Volunteer Force of Canada, or who wishes to join it, and who may be called from his position by Volunteer duty, will be given leave of absence for whatever term may be required. His position will be kept open for him. Full salary will be paid to his family during the first month of absence, and half salary thereafter until he resumes his position.

As military recruitment proceeded at a feverish pace, the Senators prepared for another season of professional hockey. The team was essentially home brew. Clint Benedict, Harry Broadbent, Jack Darragh, Angus Duford, Eddie Gerard, Leth Graham, Horace Merrill, and Hamby Shore had all learned their hockey in the various school, church, junior, and intermediate leagues that flourished in the city. Another local product, Eddie Lowrey, re-joined the team in mid-season after a year with Shamrocks and a short stint with the Canadiens. Of the few imports the most notable was Art Ross, a husky defenceman who had played several years for the Wanderers but who was as well known for his agitation on behalf of better hockey salaries. For his efforts in signing Wanderers and Canadiens players to contracts in an aborted alternative league he had tried to organize, the NHA had suspended him from organized hockey, only to reinstate him when officials realized that if he were not allowed to play, then, logically, neither should the popular stars (and gate attractions) he had signed.

As the season began, some newspaper reporters indeed appeared comfortable and complacent. Evidently failing to grasp the true horror of the conflict unfolding in Europe, one writer chose ill-advised battle imagery in his glib story on the Senators' first appearance in Montreal against the Wanderers, a lopsided 15-6 loss. "Admiral Alf Smith, and the good ship Ottawa, essayed a daring raid into the territory of the enemy last night with the destruction of the Wanderer Dreadnought as its object." The tasteless report continued: "Unfortunately, correspondents were regretfully obliged to report that the invading cruiser met with grief. Just whether it was struck by a torpedo from a hostile craft or whether it became the victim of a mine or a bomb, the war office is not yet in a position to explain." On the same day this unfortunate piece appeared came news that a German submarine had sunk the British battleship *Formidable*, with great loss of life. As sacrifices mounted in the desperate days of 1915, chastened sports reporters began softening their metaphors.

As the Great War raged in Europe, the Senators fought battles of their own, squaring off against the Vancouver Millionaires in the 1915 Stanley Cup championship on the West Coast. LIBRARY AND ARCHIVES CANADA R11922-0-4-E

Hockey Battles and the 1915 Cup Quest

BY MID-SEASON THE SENATORS had engaged in their own battles — hockey style. This would be the year in which the NHA-PCHA agreement for an East-West series would take effect, a series to determine the Stanley Cup champion. By the middle of February, the Senators were in first place, but the Wanderers were nipping at their heels. The current cup holders, the Torontos, were well back in the standings. Playing against the champions in the Toronto Arena, the Senators needed a win to stay ahead of the Wanderers. It was a vicious encounter. Toronto's rambunctious right-winger Cully Wilson lit into Senators goaltender Clint Benedict, who had tripped him as Wilson sailed past the net. Benedict warded off his attacker until referee Cooper Smeaton finally grabbed Wilson around the waist and dragged him away. Cooper ejected both players from the game, but as they were leaving, Wilson landed Benedict a nasty crack in the face, to which Benedict responded with a cool smile. After the game an irate fan got access to the referee's dressing room and challenged Smeaton to a fight for letting the players carry on too long before intervening. Smeaton, known as a combative official, happily obliged and pummeled his aggressor. Letting up, Smeaton said to him, "Well, if you have had enough, I will catch my train."

That confrontation did not attract the police, but another in the same game did. It had all started two weeks earlier in Ottawa when "Wild Man" Minnie McGiffin, charging around the ice with his team three goals behind, decided it was time to carve someone up. He chose Ottawa's toughest player, Art Ross, and walloped him over the head. Naturally Ross replied in kind. In the return match the two felt it necessary to resume hostilities. Smeaton, in his customary style, let them go at it for quite a while, with Ross quickly gaining the upper hand. With Smeaton doing nothing, the police jumped on the ice and arrested the combatants. "There were three hundred women in the audience," the arresting officer said. "It is time that players should learn that no rowdyism will be tolerated." It was left to arena manager Lol Solman to put up $100 bail for each of the players. Ross was not on board when the Senators pulled out of Union Station with a 3-1 win. He was to appear in court the next day with his adversary, the two now the best of friends, having shaken hands at the bout's conclusion. Acting on their behalf, T.C. Robinette entered an apologetic plea of guilty. "Don't the crowd want hot stuff?" he asked Magistrate Ellis. Eight dollars or fifteen days in jail, the judge ruled, commenting, "If I could fine the referee, I would." Ross and McGiffin flipped a coin to see who would pay the fine. McGiffin lost.

The regular schedule ended with the Wanderers and the Senators deadlocked in first place at fourteen wins and six losses apiece. The right to defend the Stanley Cup against the West would be decided in a two-game, total-goals series. In the first, played at Dey's Arena before a boisterous crowd of nearly seven thousand, the Senators came out strong. Ross, playing point on this occasion, scored early on. Duford added one in the second, and Merrill and Darragh finished things off in the third to give Ottawa a comfortable four-goal lead in the series. Back in the dressing room the high-spirited players had a cocky response to manager Frank Shaughnessy's announcement, "Remember, fellows, the train leaves at 3:15 for Montreal." In unison Broadbent, Duford, and Gerard hollered back, "What time does the train leave for the coast?"

For the Saturday-night return game in Montreal, rush-end spectators formed a line nearly half a mile long outside the Westmount Arena during the afternoon and were in their standing-room spots two hours before game time. Nearly one thousand Senators supporters came in from the capital. With the 15-6 and 8-1 drubbings the Wanderers had administered to the visitors in two earlier matches in Montreal, their boosters expected the hometown team to overcome the deficit and win the series. What they saw was a defensive wall thrown up by coach Alf Smith's boys. Smith's tactic was to play two forwards and three defencemen, and not to worry at all about scoring more goals. The Senators repelled attack after attack, allowing only one goal, by eleven-year senior hockey veteran Donald Smith.

The train, connecting in Montreal for the coast, left Ottawa on Monday afternoon, March 15, and the Senators were on it. It was a five-day journey by private coach through Toronto, Chicago, and Seattle, ending in Vancouver on Saturday, March 20. No Ottawa team had ever been west of Winnipeg before, and with only Sunday to rest before the first game, the players had little chance to adjust — either to the time change or, as Smith explained it, the "low altitude." No one had heard any excuses about *high altitude* when, ten years earlier, the Dawson City Klondikers came east from Vancouver and with one day's rest faced Smith and the Ottawas in a disastrous cup challenge.

Unlike the Senators, the Vancouver Millionaires were well rested, perhaps too much so, not having played since March 2. The only concern that some confident Terminal City supporters had was that their team might be too stale to put up a good show, at least in the first match. Nevertheless, there was every reason for optimism. The Millionaires had won the Pacific syndicate league handily, with thirteen victories and four losses. Their roster included a forward line of Cyclone Taylor, Frank Nighbor, and Mickey Mackay, who among them had scored 77 of their team's 115 goals that season. Frank Patrick ensured reliability in the defensive zone.

Because the PCHA still played seven-man hockey, it was agreed that a rover would be used in alternate games, all to be played in the spacious Denman Arena. In game one, Eddie Gerard filled the position for the Senators, Cyclone for the Millionaires. Following instructions from Smith, the Senators paid special attention to the Cyclone, but it was no use. The old Ottawa and Renfrew stalwart had little trouble eluding his checkers and scored two of his team's six goals. Darragh and Ross replied for the Senators.

It looked like the Senators had found their legs for the second game. At the end of the first period, they led 2-0 on goals by Punch Broadbent. But Ottawa could not sustain the pressure and, while Punch added a third, the momentum swung to the Millionaires. They won the contest 8-3, Cyclone accounting for three. The match was not without incident. The western practice was for the goal umpires to be stationed on the ice. Near the end of the second period, Frank Patrick scored on what Ottawa goalkeeper Clint Benedict maintained was a deflection off the umpire. Frustrated by this strange positioning and its unfortunate result, Benedict argued strenuously but to no avail. He did win one point. At the start of the third period, the umpires were off the ice — just as in the East.

Observers agreed that game three would be nothing more than a formality, and they were right. The Millionaires humiliated the eastern champions 12-3. The Senators concentrated so much on Cyclone, who scored five goals in the previous two games, that they forgot about everyone else, including Barney Stanley. Stanley, who had turned professional only a month earlier, scored four times. Not lost on the Senators, either, was the performance of Ottawa Valley product Frank Nighbor. His five goals in the series were to be the last he would ever register for a western team. In winning the Stanley Cup the Millionaires became the first club west of Winnipeg to do so. "I have got to hand it to the Vancouver team," Ottawa manager Frank Shaughnessy said. "They surely earned the championship."

Sell Your Garment and Buy a Sword

SHAUGHNESSY AND HIS DEJECTED band of hockey players headed for home, while half a world away their compatriots of the 1st Canadian Division were preparing for battle. Ypres was the last remaining Belgian soil under Allied control, and the Canadians were about to enter the trenches in front of the town. Soon after the awful events of April 22, and over the weeks following, the public would learn of the horror. From a stockpile of iron cylinders, the Germans had released billowing clouds of sickly green chlorine gas. A light wind carried the deadly fumes over the Algerian-French defenders, forcing them to retreat. The Canadians moved in to close the gap but were driven back. Later the Germans dispensed more gas, but the Canadians kept fighting and held the line. The cost of their success was appalling — more than 6,000 dead and wounded during the month-long engagement. The news horrified Canada. Though the war was far away, its effects were close to home.

Even so, recruitment, already flagging, was hurt by these ominous reports. If for many of those who had enlisted the war was expected to be a short adventure, for those still at home it was now seen for what was: untold carnage and horror with no end in sight. There was nothing glamorous about it. Clergymen, politicians, and platform speakers urged young men to sign up. They drew on the holy scriptures and appealed to patriotic sentiments. More pointedly, others resorted to shaming techniques. Judge John Barron, a former member of the Rideau Rebels and founding chairman of the Ontario Hockey Association, told a St. Mary's, Ontario, audience: "Because others do their duty is no justification for another neglecting his duty; because one brother goes to fight is no reason why another brother should abstain from fighting." Captain James T. Sutherland, president of the Canadian Amateur Hockey Association and quartermaster of the 146th Overseas Battalion, drummed the players' sense of duty. "Exchange the stick and puck for a 'Ross rifle and a bayonet,' and take your place in the great army that is being formed to sweep the 'oppressors of humanity' from the face of the earth." Speaking later as president of the OHA, Sutherland noted there were "some 750 players and club members in khaki." But that wasn't enough. "I am quite sure the members of our association who have not as yet offered themselves will at once see the urgent necessity of doing so and thus swelling the number of OHA men who are prepared to aid our common cause."

On a pleasant Sunday evening in June 1915, The Very Reverend Dr. William T. Herridge, attired in the uniform of an honorary lieutenant-colonel as a Canadian army chaplain, addressed his congregation at St. Andrew's Church in Ottawa. His sermon would draw more attention than even he might have anticipated. His choice of evening service for this particular message was shrewd, for that was the most popular time for young men (and young women) to attend. He took as his text Luke 22:36: "He that hath no sword, let him sell his garment and buy one." It was a call to war, a recruiting sermon. "Even Christ shows the fighting spirit sometimes, and will not accept peace at any price," the words rolled out from a pulpit draped in Union Jacks. "Why should we not have at least a quarter of a million men in training for such emergencies as the future may unfold?" Warming to his theme, the good reverend thundered, "Whether we buy a sword or not by selling our garment, it will be a poor boast that we have kept our garment, even if we are able to keep it, when it becomes the badge of degradation." Then, in words that would reverberate through hockey circles and the sports world for many months to come, he opined:

By all means let our young lads play their games and make their bodies strong and clean. But the professional sports, where a few are paid to take exercise, while the rest look on: the race-track courses, the moving picture shows and such like things attract too many of our full-grown men who might well ask themselves just now whether their time could not be spent in a more useful way. Perhaps we might even dispense for a while the elaborate sporting columns in our newspapers. They do not fit in very well with the cablegrams from across the sea. We have serious tasks confronting us as a people; and if we fail to discuss their importance, and to try, as best we can, to discharge them, any attempt at lighter fun is nothing but a hideous and disgraceful mockery.

Were the young men in the pews inspired to action? Did their sweethearts alongside nudge them to take up sword? Perhaps. The fact remained that by the end of the year 60 per cent of Canada's enlistees were British-born. Too many native-born remained unmoved. Regardless of the reverend's immediate impact, the Ministry of Militia and Defence was delighted with his exhortations, and his sermon soon became a widely distributed recruitment pamphlet.

Not everyone agreed with Herridge's views on professional sports. Not even the government. Around the time of the sermon, Frank and Lester Patrick had, according to biographer Eric Whitehead, received a letter from "Ottawa" responding to Frank's reported desire to join the Irish Fusiliers of Vancouver. "The two brothers were told to stay put." Keeping their professional hockey league going was seen by the authorities as essential to the maintenance of morale on the West Coast. But Herridge's message still resonated in 1917. "Does the clerical gentleman who deplores the playing of hockey, the carrying on of horse racing, speak with knowledge?" the *Ottawa Journal* asked. "Does he think that it will make things any better if everybody becomes a 'Gloomy Guse,' or does he think that cutting out amusements will boom enlisting?" The writer continued: "The people need something to divert their mind from the terrible European struggle just as the soldiers do in the trenches."

But there was a curious contradiction here, one that the Senators and other pro clubs faced almost daily. Ottawa's professional hockey team was needed, so the argument went, to keep spirits up during a dark period of history. At the same time thousands of able young men were refusing to enlist, even when the shortage of troops was such that conscription was being considered. These same young men were also the backbone of the Senators' fan support. Without them the viability of pro hockey would be doubtful. Without pro hockey home-front morale would sag. The resentment toward this segment of the fan base was palpable. The *Ottawa Journal* treated the issue as a scandal. On March 9, 1917, the paper ran a front-page photo of a long line of supporters waiting to buy tickets at the Senators' Sparks Street office for the season's championship match. Under the headline "HOW DOES THIS PICTURE STRIKE YOU?" the *Journal* sized up the gathering. "Nine out of ten were healthy, normal young men from 18 to 25 years." An observer of the scene vented his frustration in a call to the newspaper. Saying it was an insult to all mothers and fathers who have given sons to the cause, he lamented "a sight to make the angels weep." The *Journal's* position, then, was to support the continuation of pro hockey while scorning those who ignored military recruiters and attended Senators games.

If there was any criticism of the professionals themselves for continuing to ply their trade, it was muted. Certainly, as the war dragged on, attendance at Ottawa dates began a steady decline; but many people still did enjoy going to games and the important matches were sure to fill the arena. And such was the adulation for the Senators that at one game fans showed their appreciation by showering the ice with coins (many of them half-dollar pieces). It took the players ten minutes to gather up the largesse, an amount slightly diminished by small boys who scrambled over the boards to scoop up what they could. Ottawa management made the most of public-relations opportunities by organizing benefit games for patriotic initiatives and co-operating with the Ladies' Corps, who took up collections at the rink on behalf of the Returned Soldiers Associaton. Returned servicemen also had free admission to Senators games. As well, management made sure the press was aware the team was generating substantial revenues for patriotic purposes through the provincial war tax on home gates ($1,173 for the 1916–17 season, according to the club's ledger book). In a widely publicized decision at the start of the 1916–17 season, the NHA committed its member clubs to contributing 2.5 per cent of gate receipts to the Red Cross Association. For the Senators that should have amounted to $572 on the season, but the ledger shows no remittances for that purpose.

It was also in the interest of the Ottawa press to present the professional game in a positive light, since Senators news dominated the sports pages and sold papers. As well, there was revenue to be gained from the acceptance of Senators ads. Club management helped the process along in another way. The 1916–17 ledger reveals, under the advertising account, not only cheques to the *Citizen* and the *Journal* but also to their respective sporting editors personally, Tommy Gorman and Wilson Tackaberry. Gorman picked up two payments of $150 each, and Tackaberry received payments of $25, $50, and $25. In there too is Malcolm Brice. He had been the long-time sports editor of the *Free Press* until the paper ceased publication and merged with the *Journal* at the beginning of 1917. He collected $150 in January and the same amount in February. All told, the writers together garnered $700, the same amount that went to their corporate employers for advertising space. For anyone wanting the latest on the Senators, plenty of news was assured.

The press's daily listing of war dead and wounded brought home with painful regularity the magnitude of Canadian sacrifices at the front. Hardened though they had become to the scanning of these columns for familiar names, Ottawans were taken up short in September 1916 by one in particular. "Lieut. Frank McGee, son of Mr. and Mrs. John J. McGee, 185 Daly Avenue, has been killed in action in France," the *Ottawa Citizen* reported. After having been wounded in a previous skirmish, McGee was with the 21st Division as a motorcycle dispatch rider when the division joined the Battle of the Somme. At an undetermined moment on the afternoon of September 16, his life came to a sudden end. A stark note in a military file at Library and Archives Canada reads, "Body unrecovered for burial."

How McGee ever got into the army in the first place has been a puzzle for generations. His loss of sight in one eye following a hockey accident in 1900 is a familiar story. That handicap should have ruled out his enlistment in 1914. According to popular legend, he tricked the examining physician on the eyesight test. The story goes that he read the chart with his good eye while holding his hand over the bad one. Then, instead of covering his other eye, he merely switched hands and read the chart with the same eye. The results of his medical are found on an army form held by Library and Archives Canada. On the line for right-eye vision, the medical officer has written "good." Nothing is entered for left eye. If Captain Cooke had been fooled, he would have written the same evaluation as for the right. For whatever reason, perhaps the pressure to enlist anyone remotely capable of serving, Cooke ignored the handicap. McGee was deemed fit for active service.

By the time of McGee's death some seventy-five hockey players were among the three hundred Ottawa-area athletes in uniform. And despite Herridge's rebukes, professional hockey struggled on in a climate of fear and apprehension, where any pretext of normalcy was welcomed.

E.P. Dey, Ottawa's White Knight

WHETHER OR NOT HE SAW IT coming, events beginning with the 1915–16 season were unfolding in a way that would transform the nature of Ted Dey's business as a rink owner. Dey would soon be taking a far greater interest in professional hockey and the Senators franchise than being simply the collector of rent from the Ottawa team. For the better part of twenty years, "E.P." had been the Ottawa club's landlord, first at the Gladstone rink, which the Senators still occasionally used for practices, and then at his Laurier Avenue arena. The 1915–16 season would be the Senators' ninth in a structure where crowds of 7,000 were common. At 30 per cent of the gross gate, Dey stood to earn from $6,000 to $10,000 per season from the Senators alone. The cornerstone of his success was the hockey team. For Dey to make money, there had to be a stable team in a stable league.

The first sign of trouble came in the fall of 1915, when the Patricks decided to expand the PCHA by placing a team in Seattle. More players from the East were needed. At the same time, the Patricks were furious with the NHA for not living up to the agreement reached two years earlier to rationalize player distribution. In 1914 they had drafted Tommy Smith, whom they understood to be a member of the Quebec team. At just about the same time, however, Quebec had traded Smith to Toronto, whose owner, Eddie Livingstone, refused to release him. NHA president Emmett Quinn, to the dismay of the Patricks, did not intervene and force Toronto to send Smith west, not even after an independent arbitrator ruled in the Patricks' favour. Added to this irritation was the continuing refusal of Canadiens owner George Kennedy to pay the Patricks the $750 transfer fee he owed them for Newsy Lalonde, whom Kennedy had brought back to Montreal in 1913 after one season in Vancouver.

The Patricks demanded Quinn be fired and at the end of October issued an ultimatum that until that happened, the accord was off. The NHA rose to the challenge at a special meeting convened at Montreal's Windsor Hotel on November 9. Representing the Senators, secretary-treasurer Martin Rosenthal and business manager Frank Shaughnessy backed a resolution that squarely confronted the issue: "The Patricks having declared that the peace agreement with the National Hockey Association is at an end, the latter body decided to govern itself accordingly and from now on, all players not on the reserve lists of the National Hockey Association will be considered free agents." The war for players was back on and it couldn't have come at a worse time. Players were in shorter supply than ever and the fan base that would finance inevitably greater salary demands was showing signs of sagging. Nevertheless the Senators hung on and even improved their lot. Though the Torontos lost six players to the PCHA, the Senators remained unscathed. Living up to the letter of the NHA's November resolution, they viewed Vancouver's Frank Nighbor as a free agent and signed him to a $1,500 contract, making him the highest-paid player on the club, ahead, even, of Art Ross and Eddie Gerard.

By the end of the 1916 season, with attendance down throughout the league, owners openly worried about the effect of the war on the public's taste for hockey and the league's ability to keep players in the face of vigorous military recruitment. Ottawa's directors appeared to be losing their appetite for running a professional sports franchise during this period, and president Llewellyn Bate made it known that management wanted out of the league until the war was over. The NHA executive refused his request to suspend operations, but there was nothing the league could do if the Senators simply quit. This would have been disastrous for Ted Dey's rink operation. Club management entertained the possibility of turning the team over to the local 207th Battalion, to which Shaughnessy, now a lieutenant, was attached; but this did not materialize.

Faced with the possibility of losing the main tenant of his big rink, Dey had no choice but to take the team, which the directors were only too happy to unload, at least until the end of European hostilities and the return of normalcy at home. The directors were business and professional men whose main economic interests were away from the rink. Bate was the president of a successful grocery operation, the Chelsea Trading Company; Patrick Baskerville was the secretary-treasurer of Jones and Girouard general contractors; Percy Buttler was the Grand Trunk Railway's passenger agent; T. Frank Ahearn was vice-president of Rowatt-Ahearn insurance agency; T. D'Arcy McGee enjoyed a high profile as a partner in the Fripp & McGee law firm; and Martin Rosenthal, the most active of the directors with six years of service as the club's secretary-treasurer, was a leading optician. Experienced as they were in their business careers, and committed as they had been over the years to ensuring professional hockey in Ottawa, all but Rosenthal felt they could no longer give the time required to continue the team. Financially it had never been an especially lucrative association for them. From time to time they collected directors' fees and dividends, but these never amounted to much, perhaps two or three hundred dollars in a good year. With gate receipts going down and player salaries going up, a sharper focus on the day-to-day affairs of the team and the bottom line was needed.

Dey was just the man to take over the team, for he had a greater stake in its success than any of the directors. He and family members had long been associated in the boatbuilding business (motor boats, canoes, racing sculls), but the arena was a major enterprise. Members of the Dey family had also been directly involved with the game itself. Ted and his two brothers, William and Frank, had played briefly with the Dey's Rink Pirates team in 1901, and Frank's son, Edgar, had been a notable professional player (including with Ottawa's Stanley Cup team of 1909) before dying from a hockey-fight injury in Halifax in 1912. In business Ted Dey was a tough customer, who, as evidenced in team photos, often presented a dour visage. He had had run-ins with Ottawa Hockey Club management almost from the beginning of his rink business, usually holding out for the last dollar he could squeeze before finally settling on rental terms. Occasionally there was no settlement, as in 1903 after the Ottawas won their first Stanley Cup and could not secure a favourable lease for the next season at Dey's Gladstone barn. This had forced management to turn to the Aberdeen Pavilion for games in 1904 before returning to Dey's Rink. Now, under an agreement with the directors, Dey assumed total responsibility for the team's operations and financial obligations. The directors would be available for consultation but would not resume an active role, if ever, until some undetermined date.

The Ottawa Hockey Club''s books did not look encouraging. Gate receipts were down 17 per cent from the previous season to $27,600, and there was no reason to believe the slide would stop there. If fewer people were prepared to attend matches during the war years, there was nothing Dey could do about it. By ensuring the team's continuation, however, he would still be able to earn his 30-per-cent share of the gate, even if it was smaller than before. Better that than nothing at all. Dey did see another trend that he could do something about and was determined to reverse — the escalation of player salaries. Already at an all-time high in 1915, salaries had gone up a further 6 per cent to $11,400 in 1916. Immediately upon taking control, Dey spoke out about the situation. "I have received from [NHA] secretary Calder a list of the salaries paid by the different clubs last season," he told the *Ottawa Citizen*. "It shows that the Ottawas were handing over far more than any of the others." Through the newspaper he called on the players to co-operate in making the season a success, but he warned they could not expect "anything like the money they received last season." Dey took personal charge of player negotiations and, true to his word, lopped 30 per cent off their payroll to just over $8,000. In the case of Art Ross, who had the second-highest salary at $1,400, no action was necessary. Ross, wanting to stay in Montreal to look after his sporting-goods business, signed with his old team, the Wanderers. Angus Duford, who had a lacklustre season while taking in $1,000, quit hockey to enlist. New players brought in at various stages, notably Cy and Corbett Denneny, signed for lesser amounts. As for the returning players, some of whom threatened to quit after Dey's public pronouncement, all but George Boucher finally accepted reduced pay. Boucher got a $195 raise to $800. Frank Nighbor took the biggest hit, agreeing to play for $1,000 compared with his previous contract of $1,500. Jack Darragh and Hamby Shore both took a cut of $200, bringing their pay to $800.

As it turned out, the drastic payroll cut was absolutely necessary. Gate receipts continued to slide and Dey's Arena received only $6,700 in rent for eleven home dates, the lowest since 1913. Dey himself took no fee for running the team. Martin Rosenthal, the only director to keep an active role, earned a salary of $600. The relationship of *Ottawa Citizen* sports editor T.P. "Tommy" Gorman to the organization at that time is unclear, but again in the 1916–17 season he received personal payments for "advertising," a label that is given no explanation in the accounts and which was separate from the advertising fees paid to the newspaper direct. Though Dey's new business venture came precariously close to ending the season in the red (receipts of $22,905 against expenses of $22,781) the shrewd entrepreneur had to judge it a success. He had protected his arena investment by bringing in $6,700 more than if he had not accepted the challenge of running a professional team in a time of national uncertainty — a challenge that no one else was prepared to take on. To the hockey-loving public, the scowling figure with the bowler hat was Ottawa's white knight.

Player signings and arena revenues were a preoccupation for Ted Dey, but there was still the actual game on the ice to be played, and, of course, league politics to contend with. Taking over the team, Dey had a reasonable foundation to build on. The Senators had finished the 1915–16 season with a record of thirteen wins and eleven losses, second to the Canadiens, who went on to win the Stanley Cup. Benedict had allowed fewer goals than any other regular netminder, including the fabulous Georges Vezina, while Nighbor, Darragh, and Gerard all had productive goal-scoring seasons. In a move that might have been seen as a way of injecting new thinking into the team, Dey fired manager Alf Smith and replaced him with Gerard. But the bottom line was likely the real reason for the change, for Gerard stayed on as a player. Not only did Dey save on Smith's $750 salary, he also talked Gerard into accepting a $125 pay cut while doubling his responsibilities. Dey's take-it-or-leave-it approach to salary negotiations was working very well indeed.

A Split Season and a Fractured League

AT THE LEAGUE LEVEL, the new season saw two major developments, one of which was to be little more than a distraction for the Senators, while the other presented an extra, and fatal, hurdle in their pursuit of a Stanley Cup. At the end of September the 228th Battalion, which was stationed in Toronto and was not expected to leave for Europe until spring, sought admission to the NHA. The battalion had recruited several professional players, including Goldie Prodgers, Gordon Meeking, Amos Arbour, and George and Howard McNamara. The military felt that the formation of a top-level hockey team would highlight the good example being set by well-known athletes who chose to join the war effort, and that more young men would follow their lead and enlist. League owners too saw the public-relations value of accommodating the soldiers at a time when professional hockey was losing popularity. Their decision was unanimous and the battalion joined Eddie Livingstone's Blueshirts in the NHA

At its annual meeting in November, the NHA concocted a split schedule, with separate sets of standings for the two halves. The team finishing on top in the first half would meet the second-half winner for the league championship and the right to advance to the Stanley Cup final against the West. In the event of a tie for first in either half, a "percentage" system would come into play. The total goals scored by a team in all games during the half would be calculated as a percentage of total goals for and against that team over the half. The team having the higher percentage would be declared the winner. The players thought it was a ridiculous arrangement, but what could they do? They were paid not to perform mathematical feats, but to play hockey.

The first application of the newfangled system came on the last night of the first half, Saturday, January 27. The Senators, the Canadiens, and the 228th were tied for first place with six wins and three losses apiece. The 228th were at home to the Canadiens and the Senators were at home to Quebec. According to the percentage system, the Canadiens were theoretically in first place at that point, with a scoring record of .590 (49 goals for, 34 against), the Battalion was second at .579 (66, 48), and Ottawa third at .557 (49, 39). A win for the Canadiens would put the soldiers out of the running; but for Ottawa, a big win would be required to overcome the Canadiens' percentage advantage. How big a win, no one could know, because the arithmetic would have to wait for the final score of the contest at Toronto going on at the same time. The players were as confused as the fans, and league secretary Frank Calder knew he would have to be fast and accurate with his longhand addition and division.

Ottawa's one advantage was that Quebec had a weak team, having won only one game to that point. Ottawa would have to score a lot of goals, while also minding their defensive responsibility in order to widen the gap as much as possible between goals for and goals against. They looked to Benedict to keep the score down and to Nighbor to put the puck in the net. Nighbor had played in eight of his team's nine games and had already scored twenty-one times. At Dey's big rink that night he did not disappoint, scoring five goals in leading the Senators to a 7-2 victory. Their percentage now stood at .577 (56, 41). Meanwhile in Toronto, the Canadiens pounded the battalion squad 9-4, giving them a percentage of .604 (58, 38) and the first-half title.

Though the first-half outcome lacked the decisiveness that players and supporters would have preferred, at least the six clubs got through the schedule without disruption, something that was not going to be said about the second half. To start the so-called new season the 228th visited Ottawa on January 31, a key date as it turned out. The teams had split the first two games. On this night Cy Denneny made his long-awaited debut with Ottawa, following his last-minute acquisition from Toronto. Had he been inserted into the lineup any later, he would not have qualified for post-season Stanley Cup play, according to long-established rules. Ottawa won the game 8-0 and Denneny did not figure in the scoring. The 228th immediately protested, arguing that Denneny was ineligible. In fact league secretary Calder had so notified Ottawa management on the grounds that the trade had not yet been cleared by the league office. The exchange had been complicated by the protest of Wanderers owner Sammy Lichtenhein, who insisted he had secured the sought-after player's agreement to join his club, notwithstanding the fact that Livingstone held Denneny's rights. But that was just Lichtenhein and another of his extravagant and unfounded claims. His protest was dismissed and Denneny's trade to Ottawa was cleared; but the protest over the player's premature use was yet to be settled.

One week later came the news that the 228th Battalion was being ordered overseas and would not be able to complete the season. The NHA called a meeting on February 11 to deal with the crisis. The schedule would have to be revised and the standings adjusted to settle the status of the departing team's games, both played and unplayed. But in a sudden and stunning move the owners expelled the Toronto Blueshirts, reducing the league to a four-team circuit. There had been ongoing friction between Blueshirts owner Eddie Livingstone and some of the other owners, and there was the perception that Toronto was a declining market for professional hockey. With the Toronto-based battalion team now out, why not make a clean sweep of it? they thought. On the spot the owners dispersed the Blueshirts players to their own teams for the balance of the season and ordered Livingstone to sell his franchise before June 1. A new owner would then be able to reclaim these on-loan players for the following season.

For the Senators, who had supported the coup, a more contentious issue was the settling of the standings. The league upheld the 228th's protest and took Ottawa's January win away. To exacerbate Ottawa's position, the league then awarded Quebec a win for their unplayed Battalion game. That left the two teams tied for first place with three wins and one loss apiece. The players were furious and sent Eddie Gerard and Hamby Shore to see the club's titular president, Llewellyn Bate, about the situation. They demanded he get in touch with league president Frank Robinson to insist their victory over the Battalion be reinstated. Bate agreed and sent a telegram threatening to withdraw the Senators from the league if they did not get satisfaction. "We are not bluffing," he told the *Ottawa Citizen*. Robinson stood fast and Ottawa's blustering came to nothing.

The Senators' final game was a showdown with Quebec at Dey's Arena. The visitors had eight wins and one loss, while Ottawa stood at seven and two. The Senators, however, enjoyed a better goal-scoring percentage. A

Quebec win would give them the second-half championship, but an Ottawa victory, which would tie the teams in wins, would clinch the title for the Senators on the basis of the percentage calculation. For Eddie Gerard's men, the mathematical approach, which would obviate a risky sudden-death match, appeared quite sensible after all. Though the Senators needed only one more goal than their adversaries, they left no doubt in anybody's mind with a 16-1 thrashing. Nighbor's five goals tied the Ottawa favourite with Quebec's Joe Malone at forty-one for the scoring title.

Only a two-game, total-goals series stood in the way of the Senators heading west to Seattle to meet the PCHA champions for the Stanley Cup. Their chances against the first-half champion Canadiens looked good. Over the full season Ottawa compiled a 15-and-5 record, while their opponents were 10 and 10. Moreover, Ottawa had won all five encounters with Canadiens in convincing fashion, outscoring them nineteen goals to six. At the same time the Senators were wary. They had had to extend themselves right to the last game of the schedule just to make it to the final and worried that they might have lost their pep. The Canadiens, on the other hand, had coasted in the second half, knowing that they had already earned a berth. They were rested and ready. Where the Senators may have had an advantage in speed, the Canadiens would counter with brute force. Their average weight was 177 pounds to Ottawa's 163. And Montreal had two bruisers on defence, Harry Mummery at 210 pounds and Bert Corbeau at 195.

As expected, the first game at the Montreal Arena was a rough encounter from start to finish, with both Newsy Lalonde and Tommy Smith of the Canadiens receiving majors for clubbing their opponents. Early in the third period, with the game tied 2-2, Smith slashed Nighbor across the knees, forcing him to limp off the ice. There was no penalty on the play and Smith soon scored. The Canadiens added two more to win 5-2, but not before Lalonde set his sights on Nighbor and laid him out cold. The Pembroke boy was carried off the ice unconscious and remained so on the dressing room floor for several minutes.

For the second game back in Ottawa, Eddie Gerard set a clear objective for his players: two goals per period. Though badly cut and sore, Nighbor would be in the lineup. Lalonde, suspended for his attack on Nighbor, would be replaced by Tommy Smith. For a little while anyway, the war in Europe was forgotten as Ottawa partisans flocked to the Senators' Sparks Street ticket office. Speculators, at their usual place of trade in the lobby of the Russell House, were doing land-office business dispensing pairs of choice seats for up to twelve dollars. Unfortunately for the fleet-footed Senators, the weather had turned mild and the arena ice was soft, meaning their one natural advantage of speed on hard ice would be nullified.

In the first period the Senators lived up to Gerard's objective, with Nighbor and Darragh scoring. Their deficit was now a single goal. In the second, big Bert Corbeau scored for the Canadiens, but Boucher replied. Ottawa's tumultuous NHA season had come down to a final third period. They needed a goal to tie the series and another to advance against Seattle. The Canadiens withdrew into a defensive mode, time and again thwarting Ottawa rushes until Denneny — showing why Dey had been so determined to acquire him — took a pass from Nighbor and beat Georges Vezina to tie the series at six goals apiece. Canadiens were now forced to abandon their strictly defensive style and go on the attack. The pace was furious, as if the ice were in January form. With less than three minutes to go in regulation time, Tommy Smith, "loafing around in the right spot," trapped a puck that Benedict failed to clear and flipped it into the net. That was it; Gerard's men were finished. The Canadiens headed west, where the Seattle Metropolitans handled them easily to become the first American team to win the Stanley Cup. Had Sammy Lichtenhein's motion for a split schedule not been adopted, the Senators, on the basis of the actual outcome of games, would have won the NHA championship by a wide margin and would have been the East's representative in the cup final.

Dey's on-ice concerns for the season were over, but new ones were just starting — in the courtroom. While the Senators and the Canadiens were preparing for their playoff series, lawyers for Eddie Livingstone were putting the final touches on a lawsuit against the NHA and its member clubs. Livingstone sought reinstatement of his Toronto club in the NHA, the return of the players the league had dispersed, damages for lost revenues from cancelled games, and an injunction to stop the league from forming an independent association. Among his grievances were: that his club was effectively unrepresented at the meeting in which it was thrown out of the league (he could not attend and claimed that his proxy, league president Frank Robinson, failed to act on his behalf); and that Lichtenhein's club had tampered with players from his team, who were placed temporarily with the Wanderers, by offering them jobs as an inducement to stay on for the next season.

In *Deceptions and Doublecross*, Morey Holzman and Joseph Nieforth offer an almost comic sidebar to Livingstone's action. They recount how the feisty Toronto owner went to Ottawa for the Senators' final playoff game with the intention of serving writs on the NHA owners, who were sure to be there. He found Canadiens owner George Kennedy, who took the papers and shoved them in his pocket without even glancing at them. Wanderers' owner Lichtenhein, also at the game, refused to accept them, telling Livingstone he could see him in his office in Montreal. Senators secretary Martin Rosenthal was equally unimpressed. He took the documents but tossed them in a locker in the Ottawa dressing room, forgetting them until called by league secretary Frank Calder, who wanted to know if Rosenthal had received, by any chance, a notice of action. For Dey and the others, the whole affair would be a headache for many months to come.

Unhappy Times

A TURBULENT HOCKEY SEASON was over, but the shenanigans of eastern operators left the sporting public in a sour frame of mind. Seemingly well-intentioned NHA owners had admitted a military team, a move seen as an indirect contribution to the war cause, but one, also, that had direct economic benefits for the member clubs. Whatever good will the owners had created they squandered through an appalling attempt to claim for themselves the $3,000 bond the 228th Battalion team had posted as a guarantee to complete the season. The public was outraged that the league would go to the courts when the 228th, having thought it could see the schedule through, was ordered overseas to fight for king and country.

The case of Eddie Oatman hadn't helped the league's image either. The Patricks had released him from the Portland club of the Pacific Coast Association on the understanding that he had enlisted and would play for the 228th Battalion team until leaving for Europe. When the call came midway through the season, not only did Oatman stay behind, he claimed unpaid hockey wages of $700 for the remaining games the team was unable to play. If he was a soldier, why wasn't he with his comrades? If, in fact, he had never enlisted at all, but had merely been recruited for hockey, was that not an action that held the public in contempt? The controversy raged in the press for days, giving the NHA and hockey operators a black name at a stressful time when the game was supposed to be keeping morale up on the home front. As it turned out, Oatman had enlisted; but, as shown in military documents held by Library and Archives Canada, he was discharged two days after the 228th Battalion was ordered overseas on the grounds that he was "not likely to become an efficient soldier."

In Ottawa there remained a parochial bitterness over the team being euchred out of the right to play for the Stanley Cup as a result of the despised split-schedule arrangement. The public was also disgusted with the reckless behaviour of the owners in bringing the league to the verge of collapse. Ross's *Ottawa Journal* had this to say in an editorial: "The season for professional hockey in Eastern Canada this winter has ended in such a way as to ridicule arguments which have been urged to justify continuance of the sport during the war." Calling the league's performance an "undignified fiasco," the paper said, "Professional sport in Canada, even apart from patriotic considerations, has received this winter a blow from the effects of which it may not recover for years."

Short weeks after the end of an unfortunate hockey season, the nation received word that the Canadian Corps had launched a massive assault on Vimy Ridge, a strategic German stronghold on the Hindenburg Line in northern France. The battle was a source of pride and despair. For the first time the Corps' four divisions had attacked together, driving the Hun back after fierce and sustained fighting. It was a glorious victory for the courageous Canadians, but it came at a terrible price: 3,600 dead, 7,000 wounded. Across the country, families were opening the dreaded Defence Department letters and telegrams they hoped never to see. With losses mounting overseas and enlistment drying up at home, conscription was near at hand, bringing with it new schisms between English and French, urban and rural citizens.

Ottawa's hockey fraternity endured a sense of uneasiness. Many of the boys whom those in the city had competed with or paid money to be dazzled by were in France. The capital's beloved Frank McGee had been killed at Courcelette, Leth Graham wounded in action. Harry Broadbent had been at the Somme, but where was he now? Angus Duford was over there somewhere. Would either come home?

For hockey and for a nation, these were unhappy times.

12 · The Tangled Web of Ownership

Receipts 22,905.30
Expenses 22,781.53
Balance 123.67 [sic]
Profit and Loss Account,
Ottawa Hockey Club, 1916–17

WRITING TO A FRIEND in the fall of 1917, Harry "Punch" Broadbent, known to be somewhere in Europe, revealed exactly where he was: at "the firing line" in Flanders. A sergeant in the field battery, he had been at the front for two years. Mud was everywhere, so deep that horses and guns had to be watched every minute for fear they would sink out of sight. Whether Broadbent realized it or not, the Canadian Corps was about to engage the Hun at Passchendaele. Pressing the attack over terrain that looked like a quagmire, the Canadians seized the town, but at horrendous cost: 15,000 dead and wounded. The war was going poorly as German armies marched westward following the collapse of Russia. At home the consequences of the prolonged conflict were being felt. Farm-labour shortages made it difficult to harvest full crops. The government advised the people to eat less, as if they had any choice. The Food Control Board arranged for butchers to purchase seafood display counters at half price. The strategy worked, for by the end of the year the consumption of fish had tripled from prewar years. With the war industries devouring coal supplies, citizens were told to observe "fuelless Fridays." A new round of inflation further contributed to a depressed public mood.

This was not a good time to own a professional hockey club. Ottawa Senators directors openly worried about whether they would be able to operate a team in the coming season, and, indeed, whether the NHA itself would be in business. "In view of the turbulent conditions," an Ottawa director warned, "no salaries can be guaranteed." The players would have to come in on a co-operative basis. Hamby Shore averred that his teammates might be prepared to do just that and finance the enterprise for the season. Captain Eddie Gerard would have none of this foolishness, declaring in no uncertain terms that the players were not in a philanthropic frame of mind.

Hanging over NHA team owners was Eddie Livingstone's lawsuit against the league for the suspension of his club midway through the 1916–17 season. Though numerous documents from the plaintiff and defendants were on file with the Supreme Court of Ontario, the case was yet to be tried. Livingstone demanded reinstatement, damages for the non-completion of games, and, presciently, an injunction restraining the other clubs from releasing their own players so as to permit the clubs to form an independent league from which his own would be excluded. From NHA meetings through the fall, at which Livingstone was represented by his lawyer, John F. Boland, it was clear the Toronto owner was still intent on getting back into the league. It was equally clear that the other owners wanted nothing to do with him. Their concern was to confirm which other clubs would operate and to fix a schedule. The Wanderers and the Canadiens were certain, Quebec was undecided, and Ottawa was yet to be heard from. The owners preferred either a four- or six-club league. That way each team would play two games per week, one at home and one away. With five clubs, or any odd-numbered total, there would be weeks when two teams would have to play three games, an arrangement that would be difficult to guarantee because of the curtailment of passenger-rail services, and one that would cause problems for players who held down day jobs. As for Toronto, the owners were prepared to accept a Toronto Arena franchise to be managed by sportsman Charles Querrie, so long as the club had no connection with Livingstone, who still controlled the players who would be expected to make up the new club. It was little wonder, then, that through the early autumn, Llewellyn Bate and the other Ottawa directors viewed the pro game, at least for the coming season (if not the duration of the war), as a dubious proposition.

Why anyone would want to own the Ottawa Senators at this time was one question, but another was what "ownership" actually meant. When Bate, Martin Rosenthal, Thomas D'Arcy McGee, and others sought to incorporate the Ottawa Hockey Club in 1911, it was as just that, "The Ottawa Hockey Club, Ltd." Their primary purpose, as stated in the application, was "to conduct and carry on a hockey club." But the under-secretary of state, who was responsible for the issuance of letters patent, advised the applicants that as the club appeared to be a purely local affair, they should seek provincial incorporation. When informed that Bate and company wanted a Dominion charter because the business would be operating largely in Quebec, the under-secretary's unrelenting response was that he could not see how clubs, which "are purely local affairs, can carry on their affairs in two provinces." He suggested that the word "Club" be replaced by "Association." If a simple wording change was all it took to obtain government approval, the provisional directors were perfectly prepared to go along with it. Hence the legal entity that was formed to operate a hockey club in the NHA became the Ottawa Hockey Association Ltd. The word "club" is not to be found in the organization's charter. In fact there is no mention of the operation of any specific hockey team. Though the impetus for incorporation remained that of facilitating the management of the Senators, the directors also saw the future possibility of erecting an emporium that would serve not only their hockey team but other athletic attractions. The charter refers to the promotion of hockey and other matches and competitions, co-operation with like-minded organizations, and the acquisition and operation of rinks and other structures for carrying on hockey and other sports events. The association never did fulfil this latter ambition.

What came about, then, was an incorporated body that concentrated exclusively on the Senators, while keeping alive on paper the notion of a broader enterprise. In common parlance, the names "Ottawa Hockey Association" and "Ottawa Hockey Club" were frequently applied interchangeably. But a distinction, albeit a murky and little-understood one, soon emerged. The major assets of the association were its franchise in the NHA and player rights, but it operated the hockey club as a distinct unit. The association made the players available to the club and allowed it to compete in the NHA under the association's franchise. When Ted Dey took over the Ottawa Hockey Club for the 1916–17 season, he was effectively leasing the team. The agreement was that he would assume the team's financial obligations and retain any profits. He did not own the team; it was his for the season.

Lease to Own: the Dey-Gorman-Rosenthal Syndicate

WITH THE APPROACH OF A NEW SEASON, some arrangement for the operation of the team would have to be made. Association directors had no taste for running the club, but rink owner Dey had a vested interest in its being kept alive. Indeed he had had ambitions of owning his own team, which would be an assured tenant for his rink. A first step was to seek partners for the takeover of the Senators. These he found in Martin Rosenthal and Thomas Patrick "T.P." Gorman. Rosenthal was certainly a known quantity. He had been associated with the club for seventeen years and had been its secretary since 1908. He was a dedicated and experienced hockey man and, as a successful optician, had money to put up. Rosenthal's part ownership of the team was to be short-lived and his involvement with professional sport was soon to end. For thirty-one-year-old Gorman, his association with Dey was the beginning of a long and colourful career as a sports manager and impresario. Gorman was known to Dey as sports editor of the *Ottawa Citizen* and as a part-time publicist for the Senators.

Tommy Gorman was born in Ottawa in 1886 and from an early age seemed destined for a life in sports. His father's death when Tommy was only nine years old qualified the youngster for a coveted position as a parliamentary page. "Few people who see these nimble footed little fellows from the galleries imagine how well paid they are," reads a news clipping in the Gorman archival collection. The forty-five dollars per month he received was a handsome addition to his family's otherwise-meagre income. While running messages for members, including Prime Minister Laurier (who took a special liking to the affable child), Tommy also found time to have fun on the House of Commons page-boys baseball and hockey teams. His best sport, however, was lacrosse, and in 1908, while a parliamentary reporter for the *Citizen*, he played on Canada's gold-medal-winning team at the 1908 Olympic games. He was soon to become the paper's sports editor and while covering the Senators had no qualms about appearing on the club's payroll as a publicist.

So it was that in September 1917 Gorman, Rosenthal, and Dey got together as financial partners for the purpose of acquiring the franchise, players, and all other rights and assets of the Ottawa Hockey Association. They started by forming a new company called the Ottawa Hockey Club, installing Llewellyn Bate as president, Percy Buttler as vice-president, and themselves as directors. The actual financial terms of the business arrangement they negotiated with the association have never been made clear, and confusion dogged the transaction for another year. In later court testimony, not directly related to the acquisition, Dey was straightforward about his involvement. He said that in the 1917–18 season he, Gorman, and Rosenthal formed a syndicate that jointly owned the Ottawa Hockey Club: "I was an owner, I was one of the syndicate." This was consistent with Gorman's own recollection in a 1927 letter to his old paper, in which he attempted to clear up the ownership situation. "In the fall of 1917, the Ottawa Hockey Association's interests were *purchased* [original emphasis] by the Ottawa Hockey Club, then consisting of E.P. Dey, Martin Rosenthal and myself." In a 1957 series of memoirs Gorman added a new twist. He said that the purchase price was $5,000 and that Montreal Canadiens owner George Kendall (also known as Kennedy) called to urge him to buy the team. Kendall, Gorman recounted, lent him $2,500 to go in with Dey on the purchase. In this later recollection Gorman makes no mention of Rosenthal. While Gorman said he paid Kendall back out of the club's first-year profits at Dey's Arena, the Ottawa Hockey Club's first annual report, over the signature of Secretary T.P. Gorman, indicates there was virtually no profit. "Our receipts were approximately $18,500 and all of our surplus was applied to the liquidating of the indebtedness of the Ottawa Hockey Association. Hence, while on the season's operations we would show a good balance, the balance on hand is trifling." In an interview with the author, Gorman's grandson David observed that many of his grandfather's business dealings to this day remain a mystery.

Gorman, Rosenthal, and Dey's purchase of the Senators appears to have been, in today's terminology, a lease-to-own arrangement. While there is no reason to believe the partners were in any way attempting to mislead anyone by the use of the term "purchase," a fuller explanation of their transaction would have been to the effect that they were in the process of acquiring the players' contracts and the NHA franchise over a period of time, conditional on the fulfillment of certain terms, including eliminating the Ottawa Hockey Association's debt and, following a down payment, paying off the full purchase price, said to be between $5,000 and $7,000.

Through the early autumn period in which the control of the Senators was being negotiated, and the question of whether they would operate at all had yet to be answered, other NHA owners were in a quandary. A league schedule had to be set and, obviously, that could not be done until all teams were confirmed. Lichtenhein's Wanderers and Kennedy's Canadiens were anxious to settle matters. Mike Quinn was not certain about operating his Quebec club, thinking he might manage by amalgamating it with the amateur Sons of Ireland team. Regardless of what other clubs might be acceptable to the league, the three owners agreed they would not countenance any club with which Eddie Livingstone was associated. He had been a thorn in their side from day one, especially because of his habit of taking minor issues to the press before they could be resolved behind closed doors. Kennedy in particular could not stand the sight of the man, nor was Lichtenhein fond of him.

After missing the league meeting of September 29 and being told to hurry up and confirm their intentions for the season, Ottawa representatives Dey, Rosenthal, and Gorman appeared at the continuation of the session on October 20 and announced that the Senators were in for the season. Ottawa management was more mellow in its attitude toward Livingstone than the other owners. The Torontos were a better draw in Ottawa than Quebec and Ottawa's travel costs to the Ontario capital were lower than to Quebec. Nevertheless, if there were to be only four clubs in the league, the Senators were prepared to stand by their old loyalties and prefer Quinn's team from the ancient capital. Livingstone, however, was adamant about asserting his rights as a franchise holder. Aside from the question of his personal presence in the league, his team would be the fifth (assuming Quebec's continuation) and would create just the unbalanced schedule the other owners were determined to avoid. Finally at yet a third session, on November 10, the Ottawa, Quebec, Canadiens, and Wanderers owners did what had been rumoured they would do. With Livingstone, through his representative John Boland, still insisting on his place in the league, they voted to suspend NHA operations for the 1917–18 season. Hockey observers expected that the next announcement would be a new professional league, with no Eddie Livingstone.

With nowhere to turn Livingstone leased his players and equipment to the Arena Gardens Corporation of Toronto, a company controlled by the owners of the Montreal Arena. At the same time Quinn was about ready to throw in the towel, but he could not find a buyer for his club. Thus the expected happened on November 26 at Montreal's Windsor Hotel, a gathering place long accustomed to the intrigues and machinations of hockey's prime movers. Representatives of the Ottawa, Wanderers, Canadiens, Quebec, and Toronto hockey clubs created the National Hockey League. While holding a place on the board of directors, Quebec, as anticipated, decided not to operate its franchise in 1917–18, leaving four teams to make up an evenly balanced schedule. Fittingly long-standing Ottawa executive Martin Rosenthal assumed a seat on the new league's founding board. The owners took it upon themselves to disperse the Quebec players among

In 1909 Jack Darragh, shown in his youth, starred on the Stewarton Boys Athletic Association team. A year later, though, the young player was flying down the rinks as a professional with the Ottawas. It wasn't long before his name was a favourite among fans: during his first home-ice game with the Senators, Darragh electrified the Dey's Arena crowd with four goals. CITY OF OTTAWA ARCHIVES

their own teams, while leaving up in the air the manner, if any, in which Quinn would be compensated for the loss of his team. In the redistribution Ottawa acquired five-year veteran forward Rusty Crawford and later, by way of the Wanderers, defenceman Dave Ritchie.

A Shaky Start in a New League

IT WAS NOW TIME TO GET DOWN to the actual business of playing hockey. There would be a split schedule, with the first-place teams in each half playing off to decide a league championship and the right to contest the Stanley Cup against the Pacific Coast winners. First, though, Senators management, ever concerned about adverse reaction in some quarters to pro hockey in wartime, was once again put on the defensive. Writing to the *Citizen*, "Inquirer" noted that many amateur players had been drafted into the military. "How comes it that the pros are free?" he asked. "Can it be possible that they are all married — or is hockey regarded as of national importance? Or is their physical condition inferior to the amateur's?" The Senators responded the next day. An unnamed executive, likely Gorman, explained: "Every eligible member of the Ottawa Hockey Club's squad has responded to the call to color." He named the men who had signed up: Alan Wilson, Harry Broadbent, Leth Graham, Angus Duford, Frank Nighbor. "Benedict,

206

Shore, Gerard, Denneny, Darragh and Boucher are all married, so is Crawford, our new defence player." Recounting the various fundraising activities that professional hockey was participating in, the team spokesman said: "We have letters from several patriotic associations endorsing the good work of the Ottawa Club in helping worthy war charities."

Jack Darragh, for one, was expected to have a good season. He would be entering his eighth year of professional hockey. In 130 career games with the Senators he had scored 126 goals, including a best-ever 26 in the previous season. Facing him in the Canadiens' net on opening night would be the great Georges Vezina. They had broken into professional hockey against each other in December 1910. On that auspicious occasion at the Montreal Arena, Darragh scored the first goal ever recorded in a third period, the league having just embarked on a two-intermission division of playing time.

Admired for his athletic ability, Darragh was also popular because of his community identity. He had grown up and learned his hockey in the Arlington Avenue-Bank Street area of Centretown, where he played on church and school teams. So competitive was school hockey in Darragh's youth that in one notorious case a public-school principal turned a blind eye when someone from the school persuaded a star player from a Catholic institution to switch in mid-year without the boy's parents knowing anything about it. Only when Eddie McGrath came home with a different report card did they find out. The principal's excuse for not disallowing the transfer was that he was too busy "night and day" looking after the rink. Hockey was an intensive experience and young Darragh learned well in that environment. The budding player soon advanced to the Stewarton Hockey Club of the city league. He captained the team, which played its games at the old Dey's Rink on Gladstone Avenue, the Senators' former home. At the conclusion of the 1910 season, the Cliffsides of the higher-level interprovincial league called him up for three playoff games. This put in jeopardy his eligibility to return to the city league the next season, but by that time Senators management was convinced the nineteen-year-old was ready for pro ranks. In his first home game after his successful debut in Montreal, Darragh thrilled the overflow Dey's Arena crowd with a four-goal performance against the Wanderers. Cited in that first season for his accurate passing and conscientious back-checking, management awarded the rookie a fifty-dollar bonus as the team's most unselfish player.

But Darragh was not above criticism. After an overtime loss to the Canadiens, the *Journal* took him to task for missing a glorious opportunity to win the game when he directed the puck harmlessly into Vezina's pads. He hadn't been expecting a pass, he explained, and didn't look where he was shooting. "That was a fine excuse for a player who has been in the game as long as Jack has and is getting the money he is," the reporter railed. "He should have expected the pass, what was he there for, and players that are supposed to be good enough to play in the NHA, and draw money for doing so, should look where they are shooting the puck. The goal isn't the width of the rink and it isn't empty very often." Following a Wanderers match two weeks later, the reporter recanted. "After last night's game it is a pleasure to take back all we said. Darragh was the best man on the ice last night by a good margin. He never stopped going from the time he took to the ice until the finish and if he played any better hockey during the last three years we didn't hear of it."

Of all the Senators players, none would be certain to receive a more boisterous welcome on the opening night of the National Hockey League's inaugural season than Darragh, now a high-profile star. Thus, on the evening of December 19, a huge crowd in high expectation converged on Dey's Arena. After an unexplained delay of fifteen minutes, a dejected and depleted band of Senators appeared on the ice, neither Hamby Shore nor Jack Darragh among them. There had been trouble in the dressing room over contract disputes. Benedict, Gerard, Eddie Lowrey, Shore, and Darragh had all refused to go out for the warm-up. Shore was claiming back pay; Lowrey had yet to sign a contract. The others were protesting that the contracts they signed were for twenty games, while the schedule was calling for twenty-four. After some frantic negotiations, all but Shore and Darragh were appeased and the game started — minus the two veterans. Rusty Crawford, who had arrived in town that day from his Alberta ranch, was pressed into action on defence in Shore's place. He had not been on skates for ten months. Untested rookie Morley Bruce filled in for Lowrey, who was moved to Darragh's position on right wing. The Canadiens seized the moment and by the end of the first period were ahead 3-0. Meanwhile in the dressing room, management's haggling with Shore and Darragh continued. Finally, Shore came to terms and joined his teammates for the start of the second period. Darragh remained resolute. He was experienced at this tactic. As a holdout in 1914 he had practised on the Rideau Canal before finally signing. Midway through the second period the dollar issue was resolved and Darragh took his position on the ice. Though holding the Canadiens even through the rest of the game, the Senators were unable to overcome the three-goal margin and lost the encounter 7-4.

It was a shaky start to a mediocre season, for the Senators and the league. Two weeks later the Montreal Arena burned to the ground, leaving both Montreal teams with no home and no equipment. The Canadiens moved to the smaller Jubilee Rink, but the Wanderers folded. There were now only three teams in the fledgling NHL. But there was one bit of relief for the Ottawa syndicate and the Canadiens' owner, George Kennedy. In February the Supreme Court of Ontario dismissed the lawsuit Eddie Livingstone had launched against the NHA the previous spring for forcing his Torontos out of the league. The court said that, "acting honestly," the owners had the right to adopt a new schedule that excluded one of their members. Only by doing so, the judge ruled, could the owners avoid financial loss to themselves and the players.

From the defunct Wanderers, the Senators picked up defenceman Dave Ritchie and forward Harry Hyland. "Hibernian" Harry was a passionate player whose emotions sometimes got the better of him. But his enthusiasm for the game coupled with his prolific goal-scoring ability made him a colourful addition to the team. The Senators finished the first half in third place. To have any chance of competing for the Stanley Cup, they would have to win the second half and force a league playoff. Dey, Gorman, and Rosenthal had been contemplating the appointment of a paid coach, an idea that did not sit well with the players. They thought it would be a waste of money, and even Eddie Gerard, now the manager, frowned at the notion. Nevertheless, the three owners had their way and made Hyland the playing coach. He was also to assist Gerard. As mentor, Hyland did not forsake his spirited style. Chased for a hooking infraction in a game against Canadiens at the tiny Jubilee Rink, Hyland was the target of some choice words from fans jammed right up beside his seat in the penalty box. Harry had a few opinions of his own, which he punctuated with a swing of his stick. A mob ensued, with the Senators' inspirational leader standing his ground while police, officials, and players rushed to restore order. It was all to no avail. His charges remained unmotivated on this evening and fell 10-4. A week later Hyland was involved in another incident that left them laughing, not brawling. Just before the whistle blew to start a game at the Arena Gardens, Toronto's Ken Randall skated out to ante up a thirty-five dollar fine, payment of which would make him eligible for that night's contest. In his wisdom he thought it would be a good idea to hand the referee thirty-two dollars in bills and the remaining three dollars in pennies, which he carried in a paper bag. The referee took the paper money on account but refused to touch the bag. When Randall set it down at centre ice, Hyland decided to take an interest in the matter. Skating over he walloped the parcel with his stick, sending the three hundred coppers all over the place. Players on both teams spent the next few minutes picking up and pocketing the coins. For the Senators it was another of Hyland's antics and another loss, this time 9-3.

The Senators had allowed nineteen goals in their last two outings. At this rate, with only three games remaining, they would have to reverse their fortunes dramatically to overtake Toronto and win the second-half schedule. Clint Benedict was taking a lot of criticism for his inconsistent play. Until 1917 goaltenders were penalized for falling down to stop the puck. They had to remain upright. But to avoid an infraction Benedict had perfected the ruse of pretending he was knocked down. So well known did this trick become that other goaltenders copied "Praying Benny" to the point where the rules were finally amended in 1917 to permit the tactic. His flopping style, now legal, was no longer giving the Senators veteran any advantage.

But management was more concerned about the loose play of the entire defensive corps. Hamby Shore had been paired first with Eddie Gerard and then with Dave Ritchie. Neither combination was effective, even though Shore was given plaudits by the press on several occasions for his offensive and defensive play. To strengthen the back end, Gorman coaxed Horace Merrill out of retirement and, to make room for him, released Ritchie. Though Shore professed satisfaction with having his old partner rejoin him, that combination did not work well, either. Alarmed, management now reversed itself, brought Ritchie back, and stunned Ottawa fans by releasing Shore with only two games remaining. Just as Jack Darragh was reaching the pinnacle of his career, fellow Centretown native Hamby Shore had come to the end of the line after nine years with the Senators. In his final game Shore sat on the bench and watched as the Senators, with Merrill and Gerard on defence, trounced Canadiens 8-0. The Senators then won their final two games, but it wasn't enough. Toronto finished first and, after eliminating the Canadiens, defeated Vancouver for the Stanley Cup.

Just a Matter of Business

AS THE 1918–19 HOCKEY SEASON approached, Ted Dey was in a difficult position. He and his brother William, or "Billy," were the owners of one of the largest rinks in Canada, and to keep it profitable they needed a professional hockey team as a tenant. But prospects for having one were uncertain. The National Hockey League had finished its first season in a precarious state. The cavernous Montreal Arena had burned down, forcing the Canadiens into the smaller Jubilee Rink and the Wanderers out of business entirely. Quebec had dropped out of professional hockey. Since a replacement for the Montreal Arena had not yet materialized, the Canadiens, if they were to continue at all, would be forced to stay in the unprofitable Jubilee. There was even doubt that Montreal's sporting public was in a mood to support pro hockey in the dark days of 1918, with conscription on everyone's mind. The Canadiens, in fact, had had to transfer a late-season game the previous spring to Quebec because of poor attendance at home. Under these bleak conditions and with the league down to three teams, not to mention the player shortage caused by enlistment, Dey could not be sure the NHL would operate in 1918–19. Added to all this was a decision taken by the dormant NHA at the end of September. The owners, over the objection of Eddie Livingstone, voted to continue the previous year's suspension of league play for another season. There was a real possibility, then, that there would be no professional hockey in Eastern Canada and that Dey would have no major tenant for his rink. In spite of the negatives, Dey still harboured an ambition to be a team owner. Having a one-third interest in a syndicate with Gorman and Rosenthal that had leased the players and franchise of the Ottawa Hockey Association was not good enough. He did not want to rent a team; he wanted to own one — and he wanted to be the sole owner.

Immediately after the NHA meeting in Montreal, Eddie Livingstone approached Dey with an interesting proposal. Rebuffed by the NHA owners, Livingstone had a back-up plan to re-enter professional hockey. He was working with Toronto sportsman Percy Quinn on the formation of a new league. The idea was to have a team or two in Toronto, possibly another in Montreal, and two teams in Ottawa. Would Dey, Livingstone proposed, be interested in giving ice time at his rink? Twelve dates for each team at $500 per game would amount to $12,000 for the season. How could the Ottawa entrepreneur not be interested? It would mean calling off the verbal agreement he had already reached with his Ottawa Hockey Club partners Gorman and Rosenthal to rent ice to the Senators, who, quite possibly, might not have a league to play in anyway. Dey followed up the Livingstone proposition with a trip to Toronto, where he met Livingstone and Quinn to discuss the idea. After a couple of preliminary sessions with each, he got down to real business over a late dinner at the National Club on October 2. Nearing midnight, as the dinner party was breaking up, Quinn wrote out a hastily worded note on a menu card summarizing what he thought was the outcome of their talks. It was in the form of a memorandum of agreement:

> Toronto, Oct. 2/18.
> I hereby agree and undertake to grant an option for ice accommodation to Percy J. Quinn to play and operate two (2) hockey clubs in the rink known as Dey's Arena at Ottawa, Ontario, in consideration for which he is to pay the sum of at least $500.00 a night for each game. Details for same to be arranged later and option to read for a period of 30 days.

Dey read it, all three signed it, and they went home. As any good businessman should, Ted Dey was looking after his interests. If a few days earlier he had been entertaining the prospects of having no pro team in his rink, he now could look forward to the possibility of two teams in a new league. In the event of that league not coming off, his fall-back position would be to come to terms with the Senators, should the NHL indeed operate. All the while he had not lost sight of team ownership. If he were able to buy out his partners and take over sole control of the Senators, he would easily be awarded one of the two Ottawa franchises in the new league. For their part Quinn and Livingstone were anxious to have Dey as an owner, not simply as the lessor of a rink. In fact they had in mind Dey taking over the Senators and entering them in their league. The prestige brought to the new loop by the Senators would help to ensure its acceptance by the public. To facilitate this, they even eased the way for Dey to obtain the necessary financing from the Royal Bank.

Later, in court proceedings, Dey maintained that on returning home from his Toronto meeting he did not report to partner Tommy Gorman (nor presumably to Rosenthal) on his agreement with Quinn. It was not a partnership based on warm personal relations. Dey was frustrating his Ottawa Hockey Club associates by locking the club out of his building and adding insult to injury by giving an option on the rink to a Toronto operator. But to Dey, as he stated in court documents, it was "just a matter of business." In spite of Dey's non-communicative coolness, Gorman knew right away what had transpired, and, as sports editor of the *Citizen*, had the story in print within two days. From Montreal, Canadiens owner George Kennedy neatly summed up Dey's maneuverings. "Dey is working a colossal bluff to try to exhort more money out of his partners in the Ottawa Club. He went to Toronto and actually double-crossed the men who stepped in and helped him out last winter when his old rink would have lain idle."

Was Dey in a conflict of interest with his partners? Yes, with both sets of partners but not with his own interests. His position of part ownership of both the arena and the hockey club assured him of coming out on top, no matter what amount of wrangling was required. On the one hand it was in his interest, with Gorman and Rosenthal, to obtain a favourable rink lease for the Senators; on the other hand it was in his interest, in partnership with brother Billy, to extract the highest possible rent from the Senators for the arena. In essence Ted Dey was negotiating with himself. How could he lose? "It was just a matter of business."

Dey worked his pivotal position to another advantage. That was in his quest for total control of the Senators. By entering into an option agreement with Percy Quinn, he was leaving a message with Gorman and Rosenthal that he was prepared to abandon the interests of the Senators and lock them out of the arena. If this were to happen the franchise would be virtually worthless because the team would have nowhere to play. In that case surely Gorman and Rosenthal would be prepared to sell him their interests at a cheap price. Rosenthal, for one, was not prepared to give up the fight. He approached the Central Canada Exhibition Association to see if the Senators could have the Aberdeen Pavilion refitted for hockey as it had been in 1903–04, when Dey last locked out the team. The association president was agreeable, but permission would have to be granted by the Ottawa Board of Control because the city was the owner of Lansdowne Park and all of its buildings.

At the same time Eddie Livingstone and Percy Quinn seemed to be working at cross purposes. The day after drafting the sketchy memorandum of agreement with Dey, Quinn remembered he had not backed it up with a deposit and sent Dey a cheque for twenty-five dollars as proof of his intentions to follow through with a concrete proposal on details of the arrangement as provided in the document. He was also talking with the Royal Bank about securing a loan to Dey for the purchase of the Senators. Meanwhile Livingstone was going about the business of promoting the new league. He wanted rink operators and the public to see that it would have instant credibility through the signing of proven stars. In his enthusiasm he went so far as to approach Ottawa players Clint Benedict, Eddie Gerard, and Cy Denneny with enticements to join the new league, to be called the Canadian Hockey Association. It was to be a syndicate, much in the model of the Patricks' Pacific Coast Hockey Association. The *Journal* reported that the offer to Benedict of $1,500 had come by wire and that he was asked to have Gerard and Denneny relay their terms. Dey was thus receiving bad vibrations from his Toronto associates-to-be. One was encouraging him to buy the Senators and enter them in the new league. The other was attempting to raid the same team. It is little wonder that Dey played a wait-and-see game with Quinn. He did not respond to letters Quinn was sending, refused to regard them as the necessary "details" the agreement called for, and left the cheque uncashed.

Dey was now ready to make a bid for total control of the Senators. As part owner of the Ottawa Hockey Club, which leased the team, he could try to buy out his partners and complete the lease-to-own arrangement entered into the previous year with the Ottawa Hockey Association, which still controlled the franchise entitlement in the NHL and player rights, and would continue to do so until full payment was received. If Gorman and Rosenthal would not budge, Dey could try an end-run and acquire the stock of the Ottawa Hockey Association itself. He could then cancel its arrangement with the Hockey Club, and presto, the Senators would be his. To this end he approached Ottawa Hockey Association president Llewellyn Bate with an offer and was told to put it in writing. This he did; but at the same time his Ottawa Hockey Club partners, who together had controlling interest in the company, made an independent bid on its behalf to complete the original arrangement with the association.

The fine points of what transpired next are a mystery, but in the end Ted Dey got almost all of what he wanted. Ottawa Hockey Club documents held by Library and Archives Canada shed no light on the financial transaction and accounts in the *Journal* and the *Citizen* on October 19 are incomplete and confusing. Why this should be is a curiosity. Tommy Gorman, a central figure in the negotiations, and one who would surely understand what was taking place, was still responsible for the *Citizen*'s sports page, which carried the story. Strangely the rival *Journal* version is almost word-for-word identical. The papers, it appears, were working from the same prepared text, a text issued by one, or both, of the negotiating parties. Both papers said control of the team, together with the playing rights of the

Ottawa Hockey Association, would stay in the hands of the Ottawa Hockey Club. They referred to Dey's competing offer. The stories appeared to use the terms "team" and "Association" interchangeably, though there is a clear distinction between the two entities. The stories reported there was a third bidder but did not identify him. Evidently this bidder wanted to operate the team in the Aberdeen Pavilion, just as Rosenthal said the Ottawa Hockey Club wished to do. The *Citizen* said: "Mr. Dey was part owner of the club last winter, but *is understood to have severed* his connection after his spectacular jump to Toronto for the formation of the proposed Canadian Hockey Association." The *Journal* was more definite on this point: "Mr. Dey was a part owner of the club last winter, but *severed* his connections after his jump to Toronto, when the Canadian Hockey Association was formed." But Dey did not divest himself of his interest in the Ottawa Hockey Club, and even if it were thought that he had, the stories do not touch on why or under what conditions he would have.

The whole affair is made to look perfectly clear in the minutes of the club's annual meeting. Over the signature of secretary-treasurer T.P. Gorman, the document simply says, "Mr. Dey announced that he had acquired the stock of Mr. Martin Rosenthal in the Ottawa Hockey Association Limited; also his shares, amounting to one third of the total, in the Ottawa Hockey Club." In court testimony Dey said much the same thing. Whereas the hockey club had been a syndicate of three in 1917–18, Dey explained, he bought out Rosenthal's one-third interest, and under a new arrangement he and Gorman each controlled one-half. In neither account is there any mention of an intermediate step whereby the hockey club, as reported in the newspapers, first purchased the franchise and players from the association in a bidding competition with Dey himself, before Dey and Gorman took over Rosenthal's share. In his 1927 *Citizen* recollection of events, Gorman, if vague, is equally succinct. "In 1918, Mr. Rosenthal found it necessary to sever his connections with the Ottawa Hockey Club. He was then paid the nominal sum of $500 for his interests."

Martin Rosenthal did indeed sell out to Dey, in little more than a week following the club's reported purchase of the association's NHL franchise and player rights. The reason seems clear, for only four days after the Hockey Club took control, the City of Ottawa rejected Rosenthal's application on behalf of the club to move into the Aberdeen Pavilion. With Percy Quinn's thirty-day option on Dey's Arena still in effect, there was nowhere for Rosenthal and Gorman to put the team. With no rink the franchise would have no value. It was a good time to let go. At the same time Rosenthal was making a big change in his non-sporting business life. As an optician he had decided to leave private practice and continue his work in that field with the A.J. Freiman department store. He said he was too busy in his new job to stay in hockey and would confine his sporting activities to lawn bowling and curling. Clearly Dey had squeezed one associate out, but "it was just a matter of business." Gorman, however, could not be moved and so began a successful and lucrative, if uneasy, partnership.

Dey now had half interest in the outright ownership of the Senators, much better than the previous three-party partnership in a lease arrangement. Meanwhile Percy Quinn's thirty-day option on Dey's Arena was about to expire, an option that Dey was ignoring anyway. He could see the Canadian Hockey Association was going nowhere. For one thing the Montreal owners of the Toronto Arena were refusing to allow any team with which Eddie Livingstone was associated to have access to it. Quinn and Livingstone were also unable to secure the Jubilee in Montreal for the same reason. The whole operation was dubious. Even before the November 1 option deadline, Dey knew he was going to give his own club exclusive rights to his rink and exercise his franchise in the NHL. He returned Quinn's twenty-five dollar deposit cheque.

On November 4 Dey convened the annual meeting of the Ottawa Hockey Club and announced his acquisition of Rosenthal's interest. Secretary-treasurer Gorman recorded that a new five-year, exclusive agreement with the owners of Dey's Arena had been drawn up, significantly, "this day," giving exclusive professional hockey rights to the Senators. The meeting received and accepted Rosenthal's resignation and passed a resolution thanking him "for his good work in the past." The meeting also regretted his "unavoidable retirement." The minutes then state:

> It was decided, in view of the retirement of Mr. Rosenthal, to dissolve the Ottawa Hockey Club and to organize a new syndicate, to be known as the Ottawa Arena Club. The Ottawa Arena Club, it was moved, seconded and carried, should take over all the assets of the Ottawa Hockey Club, and the secretary was instructed to communicate the results of this meeting to the president of the National League, Mr. Frank Calder, and to have the rights and privileges in the National Hockey League turned over to the Ottawa Arena Club.

On November 14 Ted Dey presided over the first meeting of the Ottawa Arena Club, at which a letter was read from Mr. Frank Calder, president of the National Hockey League, "conveying the assurances that the Ottawa franchise in the National Hockey League was held by the Ottawa Arena Club, consisting of Messrs. E.P. Dey and T.P. Gorman." Present, in addition to Dey and Gorman, were Llewellyn Bate and T. Frank Ahearn. The little group then proceeded with elections. Dey formally assumed the presidency, Gorman was confirmed as secretary-treasurer, and Bate and Ahearn were each given the title honorary president. Gorman was authorized to sign players and secure a coach. In view of "unsettled conditions," his salary budget was set at $5,000.

None of this, of course, sat well with Percy Quinn back in Toronto. He believed that in unanswered letters and telegrams to Dey through the month of October, he had submitted the details of league operation called for in the October 2 memorandum of agreement, and that Dey had reneged on the deal by not honouring the thirty-day option. In fact he was convinced that Dey had actually agreed to a lease with the Senators before the thirty days were up. Quinn, likely inspired by the litigious tendencies of his associate, Eddie Livingstone, began legal proceedings. The day after the Ottawa Arena Club's first meeting, the Supreme Court of Ontario issued a writ of summons on Dey. Quinn was immediately seeking an injunction to prevent Dey from leasing his arena in violation of the October 2 agreement granting an option to Quinn to operate two professional hockey teams at that venue. It was the first item in a statement of claim that also sought an order requiring Dey to deliver the option and to pay $10,000 in damages for anticipated lost profits. In a subsequent affidavit, Quinn tabled follow-up letters to Dey and claimed that, though unstated in the October 2 memorandum, it was further arranged that not only was Quinn's right to the rink to be for five years, it was to be an exclusive one for professional hockey.

Meanwhile Dey had turned his attention to the forthcoming National Hockey League season. At a meeting in Montreal on November 9, he was officially installed as a board director, replacing Rosenthal. The meeting confirmed three teams for the season: the Canadiens, the Senators, and one to be operated by the Toronto Arena Company. The directors also offered a second Toronto franchise to Percy Quinn, provided he have no connection with Livingstone. The offer's deadline expired, however, without action from Quinn. At Dey's insistence the three clubs signed an agreement to continue together for a five-year period. Evidently, according to the *Citizen*,

Dey and Gorman "had heard stories to the effect that on the reconstruction of the Montreal Arena in Westmount next year, a 'Big Four' was to be formed, with the Capital excluded." It was a preposterous rumour. No league in its right mind would want to debar a club from one of hockey's strongest markets. Nevertheless Dey and Gorman were not about to take any chances with their investment.

With the National Hockey League season already under way, Dey presented himself for Ontario Supreme Court examination on December 23. He readily admitted signing the memorandum of agreement with Quinn and not delivering the option for Quinn to operate two teams at his rink. But he said he had not refused it, either. He denied the agreement was an exclusive one and said the details to be arranged later never were. Dey produced the November 4 rental agreement with the Senators and allowed that notwithstanding that team's sole right to the rink, he was nevertheless prepared to honour the Quinn document of October 2. It was not a magnanimous offer, for he revealed that in addition to the Senators' scheduled games, the team also had practice hours on Tuesdays, Thursdays, and Saturdays from 7 to 8 p.m. Presumably, then, Quinn would be free to book any other available (though mostly unsuitable) times he might choose, if indeed he could assemble a team or teams at such a late date and create a league in which to place them. (Dey formalized his offer in a December 30 letter through his lawyer.)

On December 26, after the Senators had already occupied the rink for numerous practices and one exhibition game, the court rejected Quinn's application for an injunction that would limit the leasing of Dey's Arena for professional hockey to his own team or teams. Ted Dey had cleared the first hurdle, but the remainder of Quinn's claim had still to be dealt with: delivery of the rental option and the $10,000 in damages. Quinn now pursued this action, arguing that if the October agreement did not reflect the true intent and meaning of his arrangement with Dey, then it should be revised to do so. He maintained he was always ready and willing to arrange the details that his adversary insisted were never forthcoming, but admitted that no such specifics were ever put in writing. When pressed by Dey's lawyer, in fact, Quinn admitted that "outside of discussing them with him in a general way," no details had ever been arranged, let alone in writing. As for damages, Quinn included the cost of purchasing the Quebec franchise, which he had intended to operate in his new league, and the projected earnings "of a good professional hockey team, managed properly."

Challenged on his certainty in calculating profits, Quinn observed, "Ottawa is known as a good hockey town, a money maker, always has been." In a judgment rendered January 29, 1919, Mr. Justice Clute dismissed Quinn's claim. He ruled that the evidence and exhibits presented did not disclose a contract binding on the defendant sufficient to satisfy the legal test of fraud.

Down with the Kaiser

In the months leading up to the start of the NHL's second season, the mood of the country was, in the words of historian Desmond Morton, "grim" and "repressive." With the tightening up of the Military Services Act, all exemptions to conscription were cancelled. In the battle at Amiens the Canadian Corps lost more than 1,000 dead and nearly 3,000 wounded. Draft-dodgers were rounded up. A nervous government, apprehensive about social unrest, ordered police spies to keep a close watch on labour and political meetings. Added to the misery was the onset of a worldwide epidemic. In September the influenza reached Canada and by the end of the year had killed more than 30,000 people. One of those, it could be said, was Hamby Shore. Caring for his wife, who had been stricken by the dreaded disease, the popular athlete contracted pneumonia and within a week was gone, at age thirty-two. Ottawans were shaken. Senators supporters, former teammates, fellow workers at the Department of the Interior, all were alarmed that the scourge had arrived at their door so quickly, and with such a direct and personal result.

By November the Germans were on the run. On the very day, November 9, that E.P. Dey and his hockey confrères were formalizing league play in Montreal, Canadians joyously flooded into the streets to celebrate the end of the war. How the rumour of the "false armistice" started, no one knew; but two days later they were in the streets again, this time for the real thing.

With the cloud of war lifted, citizens revelled in their sense of relief. People could be happy again. There were no more emotional barriers to enjoying life, seeking amusements, and stepping out unapologetically to entertainment events. There was even renewed talk of the longstanding dream to create a skating rink on Ottawa's Rideau Canal. Philip Ross's *Ottawa Journal*, of course, endorsed the idea. "Particularly is it desirable now, from the standpoint of health, when thousands of people are relaxing from the straits of war activity and other thousands are endeavouring to regain their strength after suffering in the recent influenza epidemic." Hopeful letters to Santa Claus filled the papers.

> Dear Santy,
> I am happy this year, and I would like you to bring me a pair of skates and boots that will be all, if you come down the chimney you will see a pudden there, and the cat is waiting for a rat to come out. If you see the rat tramp on it. My address is David Stewart, Laurentian View, Ont. Down with the Kaiser.

It didn't matter that it was only an exhibition contest, carefree Ottawans descended by the thousands on Dey's Arena to witness the Senators' first postwar game. Caught up in the euphoria around him, Ted Dey declared that his team would enjoy "phenomenal success." He expounded on the reasons for this well-received pronouncement: the termination of the European war, the new playing rule allowing forward passes in the centre zone, and management's assembling of "an all-star team as Ottawa's representation in the National Hockey League." Most of the previous year's players were back and all were signed. This time around, the mood in the dressing room was spirited. The players bantered happily. The newly acquired Sprague Cleghorn discovered that, like himself, Jack Darragh was a motorcycle enthusiast. As they piled on their hockey gear again and again through the season, nothing would do but to trade stories about their machines. Cleghorn felt it necessary at every opportunity to remind Darragh, and anyone else, of his racing success on Quebec tracks. The less flamboyant Darragh was not a racer. His machine had a sidecar, which served as a carrier on his weekly grocery shopping expeditions to the ByWard Market. Skene Ronan, coming out of retirement for one last whirl, lost no time in commanding the admiration of all the players for his prowess in checkers, which he regularly demonstrated in backroom games at Ketchum's sporting-goods store.

Despite Ted Dey's "all-star" predictions, the Senators were not doing especially well as the first half of the season drew to a close. They had won four and lost five, with one game remaining. This put them well behind Canadiens, who had a 7-and-3 record. It mattered not a jot to Ottawa fans. They kept coming to the rink in record numbers. For the last game in the first half, the Senators bolstered their lineup with two veteran players. Punch Broadbent had just returned from Europe and on the very night of his arrival, Tommy Gorman was at his door. Punch had been overseas for three years, had been wounded, and had put on a lot of weight. Needed on a call of duty of a different kind, however, the Military Medal-winner responded. Admitting his sea legs were better than his ice legs, Broadbent was in the lineup four nights later as the Senators defeated Toronto 3-2 in front of another large turnout at Dey's. Also in the lineup for the first time as a Senator was the outstanding defenceman Harry Cameron. A Stanley Cup champion, Cameron had fallen out of favour with the Toronto Arena Club and had been suspended for indifferent play. This led to a dispute over his salary, and when he went to the rink to get his skates before boarding the Ottawa train, he was refused. Fortunately there was another pair at his Pembroke home. They arrived in time for a practice the Senators had arranged for him with St. Brigid's of the City League.

As in the 1917–18 season, the pressure was on the Senators to win the second half. Only by doing so would they play the first-half winners, the Canadiens, for the championship. Responding to the challenge and the boisterous support of their fans, the Senators won seven of eight games to finish first. Over the full season Clint Benedict, who had experienced some rough patches the year before, again shone, allowing twenty fewer goals than the legendary Georges Vezina. Cleghorn was the defensive stalwart, teaming first with Eddie Gerard and then with Harry Cameron. But it was a new forward combination in 1918–19 that truly sparked the team. Though Jack Darragh, Cy Denneny, and Frank Nighbor had been teammates for the previous two years, they had not played regularly on the same line. They complemented one another perfectly in their first season together, throwing the puck back and forth, and mastering the newly deregulated centre zone. Nighbor was a natural centre who saw the whole ice, made clever passes, and released quick and accurate shots on net. He was conscientious defensively and became known for a deft poke-check that swiped the puck from an unsuspecting attacker's stick. Like Nighbor, right-winger Darragh was a clean player who, nevertheless, did not shy away from hard physical contact. He had that uncanny knack of scoring important goals, often from a backhand shot that surprised goalies. Cy Denneny, at left wing, was the rough one of the three. Of stocky build, he made sure opponents paid a painful price when they confronted his linemates. He was also an exceptional goal-scorer. Their offensive record spoke for itself: Denneny, eighteen goals in eighteen games; Nighbor, seventeen in eighteen games; and Darragh, twelve in fourteen.

Cy Denneny, left, was a bold wingman to the quick and careful centre Frank Nighbor, right. Along with J.P. Darragh, the trio were a lethal mix of speed, agility, and brute force. Denneny threw his weight around, Nighbor was nimble, and both of them could put the puck in the net. CITY OF OTTAWA ARCHIVES

The Senators entered the playoffs with high hopes. They had won their final three games in the league schedule, including a convincing 7-0 victory over the Canadiens, whom they would now meet in a best-of-seven series. Before the opening game in Montreal, Frank Nighbor was called to the telephone. It was long distance, he was told. "My sister is dead," he blurted out in front of his teammates before grasping the receiver. Frank's premonition was right; his sister had died suddenly in Detroit from blood poisoning. The Senators would have to play without him, but he was hopeful of being back in time for the next game. He wasn't, and his team lost three straight before he returned. For those games Darragh took Nighbor's place at centre, and Broadbent and Gerard alternated in Darragh's usual position at right wing. With the season on the line Nighbor joined his team in front of a home crowd. His presence sparked the Senators to a win; but back at Montreal's Jubilee Rink, the Canadiens finished them off. If Nighbor had not missed those games, might the Senators have won them? If so, it would have been they, and not the Canadiens, who made the long journey to Seattle for, as it turned out, the fateful 1919 Stanley Cup final.

As it was, the Senators did go west, for a four-game exhibition series in Victoria and Vancouver. At the same time the Canadiens were battling it out with the Seattle Metropolitans. Keeping an eye on proceedings south of the border, Dey made tentative arrangements for his team to continue its exhibition swing in Seattle. It all depended on the outcome of the fourth game in a best-of-five series the Mets were leading with two victories. If they could win that one, the cup would be theirs and the Senators' match-up could be scheduled. As fate would have it, the game ended in a score-less draw after one hundred minutes of overtime. With the series thus pro-longed, the Senators' appearance in Seattle was cancelled. After yet another exhausting overtime game, during which the Canadiens' Joe Hall took ill and was rushed to hospital, the influenza epidemic, now over with in Ottawa, interceded. Three more Canadiens players, along with manager George Kennedy, took to their beds. The Stanley Cup series was called off. Arriving back in Ottawa, the Senators were given the shocking news that on Sunday afternoon, April 6, at the Columbus Sanitarium in Seattle, Joe Hall had died of pneumonia following a severe attack of influenza. As politi-cians often do, athletes can also set aside bitter rivalries in times of defeat or tragedy. "Bad" Joe Hall was truly deserving of his nickname. He was the dirtiest and most feared player of his day. Nevertheless, on behalf of the Senators, Gerard commented, "I am really sorry. Joe was a great player and although rough at times was a real gentleman."

The hockey season now over, Ottawa's sporting types turned their attention to the games of spring and summer: cycling, rowing, baseball. Never far from their minds, though, were thoughts about the next season. There had to be reason for optimism. Club ownership was clearcut, the arena was consistently filled, and, above all, the Senators seemed to have the nucleus of a powerhouse team. The redoubtable Cleghorn had said he wanted to make his home in Ottawa. There was no reason to think Nighbor, Darragh, and Denneny would be released or would seek trades. Same for Benedict. Broadbent could be counted on to be in top form, and the versatile George Boucher had come into his own. Good times had surely returned.

13 · The Super Six, Part I
The Game in the Boardroom, 1920–1927

And the parties hereto further covenant and agree
to purchase, incorporate or otherwise acquire
a hockey club at the equal expense.

T.F. AHEARN & T.P. GORMAN

Memo of Agreement, 1922

ON THE ICE THEY WERE the Super Six, a brilliant collection the likes of which had never been seen. But the players who made up the Senators over the memorable period of 1920 to 1927, when they dominated professional hockey, did not simply materialize out of nowhere. The team, which won four cups in eight seasons and finished first six times, had to be assembled, there had to be a rink to play in and a league in which to compete. Most of all for the players, they had to be assured of a regular payday. All of this was the job of the team in the boardroom.

The Shifting Sands of Ownership

Contractually the Dey-Gorman partnership controlling the Senators was for a five-year period, starting in the 1918–19 season. It worked well, with Ted Dey as president of the Ottawa Arena Club and Tommy Gorman as secretary-treasurer. Dey looked after the business side of the arena's operation and Gorman oversaw everything else, including the team's publicity function (for which he had a particular bent) and overall hockey management. The Senators were not making the partners rich by any means, but there were profits, especially for Dey because he was certain every winter of a full season of lucrative pro-hockey bookings for his rink.

By 1922, however, Dey knew he was at a turning point in his entrepreneurial career. He had been in the rink business for thirty-eight years and he was now fifty-eight years old. His arena was on leasehold land and his agreement with owner Esther Sherwood would be expiring in five years.

Even if he had harboured any thoughts of renewing the lease, which is doubtful, it was no secret that the Dominion government was eyeing the valuable, centrally located property as part of a plan to improve the capital. Moreover, the era of the natural-ice arena in pro hockey was about to end. Post-season playoff games and the annual Stanley Cup championship series with the West demanded a longer skating season, one that could only be assured through costly ice-making installations. Dey could still look back ruefully on the 1920 cup series against Seattle, when mild weather forced the final two games, for which sellouts at the arena were assured, to be moved to Toronto. In a panic, Gorman once recalled, Dey had pleaded with NHL president Frank Calder to hold off cancelling the Ottawa games, insisting the cold weather would return. It did, the day after the two teams packed up and headed for Toronto. Now, in 1922, only one year remained on the Dey-Gorman arrangement. Ted's rink partner, brother Billy, had passed away, and other prominent business interests were talking of building a modern emporium, which would have artificial ice.

One of those interests was spearheaded by T. Franklin Ahearn. At age thirty-six, Frank Ahearn was already well established in business circles as president of Wallace Realty and as a director of numerous other firms, including Ottawa Car Manufacturing and the Ottawa Electric Railway. His father, Thomas, was a true business titan, who, along with Warren Soper, founded the streetcar line. As a five-year-old in 1891, Frank ceremoniously threw the switch that first sent the current racing through the overhead wires. Frank grew up loving sports, especially hockey, which he played as a schoolboy. While still a youth, he organized the Buena Vista team of the city league. The team played on an outdoor rink but lacked a dressing room. Frank's solution was to install an old streetcar on the site, a formidable accomplishment for anyone but the son of the line's owner. A veteran of the Great War, Frank returned from France with the rank of captain and served briefly as orderly officer to the minister of militia before entering the corporate world.

Through the spring and fall of 1921 Ahearn had been quietly following the overtures of a syndicate called Stadium of Ottawa Ltd. to build a rink on King Edward Avenue, a lush, tree-lined boulevard in the heart of the city. By December notices appeared in local newspapers seeking investors for the venture, the authorized capital of which was set at $310,000. Reports next said the syndicate had approached Dey about purchasing the Senators but that Dey was not biting. It was now time for Ahearn to make his first move. He knew that Gorman's partnership with Dey would be expiring after the 1922–23 season. He was also well aware of Gorman's talent for sports management and his thorough understanding of the world of pro hockey. Consequently, in April 1922, he entered into an agreement with Gorman whereby they would be equal partners in the owning and operating of a professional hockey club in Ottawa. The agreement was to take effect after the 1923 season. Ahearn would be assured of Gorman's "exclusive and unrestricted services" in return for an equal share in the club. The partners would share equally in associated expenses and would have equal representation on the board of directors. The agreement was to be for a ten-year period from the expiration of Gorman's contract with Dey. Ahearn also approached Dey with a similar proposition — that is, an equal, three-way split — but again Dey refused.

At the same time Ahearn was putting together his own syndicate of prominent businessmen to build a state-of-the-art arena. To that effect Canada's secretary of state issued letters patent on November 27, 1922, incorporating The Auditorium Ltd. Its fundamental purpose was to "construct, erect, lease or otherwise acquire, own, operate, equip, maintain, and manage, auditoriums, arenas, community halls, summer and winter garden buildings, or other buildings or erections necessary for the operation of the company." Among its objectives was to "carry on, conduct, hold, equip, lease, operate, and promote hockey matches, skating, roller skating, masquerades, and summer and winter sports and amusements...." The business's capital stock was set at $500,000, divided into 5,000 shares of $100 each. Ahearn would become the dominant shareholder, and in press interviews took pride in noting that all of the subscriptions would be taken by local interests and that no agent was being retained to sell shares. The rink, he assured the public, would be up and running in time for the start of the 1923–24 hockey season.

If a fine new place to stage professional hockey was now a sure thing, Ahearn still had to deal with the matter of acquiring players. Whatever team he and Gorman assembled would come under the umbrella of the Ottawa Hockey Association, of which Ahearn had long been a director. Ever since Gorman and Dey had originally purchased the Senators from the association in 1918, however, that organization had remained inactive, even to the point where the secretary of state had complained that it had failed to file annual returns. Joining Ahearn in reviving the Ottawa Hockey Association and investing in Auditorium were two of his close business associates: Frederick Burpee, manager of the Ottawa Electric Railway, and William McIntyre, general manager of the Ottawa Car Manufacturing Company. Ahearn became president of the Ottawa Hockey Association, and Burpee president of Auditorium.

The next move was to acquire players, which Ahearn and Gorman did by putting the squeeze on Dey. In forming a partnership to own and operate a professional hockey team in the first place, it was none other than the Ottawa Senators they had in mind. In the fall of 1922, before the last season of the Dey-Gorman regime was about to begin, Ahearn and Gorman reminded the players that the Ottawa Arena Club partnership would be expiring at season's end. If they signed standard contracts containing a reserve clause, they would be bound to an organization that was about to expire. In that case the NHL would take over their contracts and divide up the players among the other clubs. To stay together as a successful team and to remain in Ottawa, which they recognized as a highly desirable home base, the players should insist that the reserve clause be deleted from their 1922–23 contracts and at the same time sign with the Ottawa Hockey Association for the following season, a season in which the team would open at a splendid new arena. The reasoning was flawless and the players followed suit. Dey would soon be losing a partner, a team of hockey players, and a tenant for his rink. But he still held one card, half interest in the NHL franchise itself: that is, the right in Ottawa to operate a team in hockey's premier league.

Meanwhile the Auditorium project was taking shape. The syndicate had initially thought of locating the arena on the King Edward Avenue site of a former gasworks, the location previously favoured by the now-defunct Ottawa Stadium consortium, but changed its mind. Instead the directors chose a parcel of land at O'Connor and Argyle streets in Centretown, directly across from the majestic Victoria Museum. It was a leafy, mostly residential neighbourhood, well served by the Bank, Gladstone, and Elgin lines of the Ahearns' Ottawa Electric Railway. Some homeowners protested the intrusion, but the city planning commission eventually gave its approval and contracts were awarded in April 1923 for the construction of a 6,000-seat sports-and-entertainment emporium. The syndicate hired local refrigeration expert Percy Sims to advise on an ice-making plant. The whole enterprise was operating on a tight deadline. The Auditorium was expected to stage its opening event in eight months.

As construction progressed through the summer months, there was still the nagging question of franchise rights. The Ottawa Hockey Association had locked up the players for the coming season and would certainly have an arena in which to play, but Ted Dey could not be moved to hand over his half interest in the Senators franchise. By September it was becoming a critical issue, both for Ahearn and Gorman, and for the NHL. In several meetings NHL president Frank Calder tried to mediate a settlement that would allow the Ottawa Hockey Association to complete the takeover. But Ted Dey always operated that way. He was a steely-eyed bargainer who consistently used time, a valuable commodity in hockey scheduling, to maximize his return. Finally, in late September, the two sides came to terms. No money changed hands except, perhaps, for the same one-dollar amount that Ahearn had paid Gorman to cement their deal in April 1922. Rather, Dey accepted shares (said to be a one-quarter interest) in the association. In a separate transaction Dey did purchase shares in the Auditorium; but his financial involvement did not last long. To the astonishment of many in local sporting and business circles, he abruptly sold out to his partners and moved to New York. It was truly the end of an era. It seemed unimaginable that after all these years the hovering presence of the little man with the clipped moustache would no longer be felt in an Ottawa rink on hockey night.

Visiting the Auditorium construction site, Lester Patrick, Vancouver's pioneer rink builder, declared that the arena would be the finest in North America. When it opened at the beginning of December, Ottawans could see exactly what he meant. In keeping with the neighbourhood, the building had a red-brick façade. The stands were set on reinforced concrete. There were six exits at ice level and one in each corner of the upper concourse. Steel posts supporting the roof were set back six rows from ice level. The sixteen rows of hardwood seats on both sides and at one end were bench-style with backs. Following the Dey's Arena model, the south-end tiers were seatless. This was the standing-room gallery for those on a budget. The Auditorium followed the design of its predecessor in another, and peculiar, way. The ends of the rink were semicircular. For years afterward, visiting teams could not get over this egg shape. It took some time for them to catch on to the Ottawa trick of rifling the puck in along one side and sending a player over to the other to capture the disk when it whipped around behind the net and came out to him.

City zoning regulations thwarted Ahearn's intentions of setting up an ice-manufacturing business to maximize use of the rink's refrigeration plant. He would have to be content with the ice on the floor of the arena. That surface required special care. Between periods, attendants plowed the ice with iron scrapers. A team of three went around and around, blades angled inward toward the centre of the rink to keep the snow from spilling over onto the freshly scraped area. Then the three men teamed up, scrapers overlapping, to push the accumulation to the northeast corner, where a gate in the boards was opened. A fourth attendant lifted a trap door on the floor of the aisle and shovelled the snow through. Next, two teams of two men pulled the ice resurfacing wagons around the rink. The device was a steel, water-filled barrel set on its side on a frame that had two rubber-tired wheels. The warm water fed a trough having a porous canvass bottom that rested on the ice, producing a thin, even covering that filled in the gouges and quickly froze. Never again would a game have to be called off because of mild weather.

Ahearn and his partners had presented a wonderful gift to the people of Ottawa, a gift that served its sporting and non-sporting publics equally well. The Auditorium immediately fulfilled its purpose as a major entertainment venue and conference centre. It screened the latest Hollywood movies: *Dorothy Vernon of Haddon Hall*, starring Mary Pickford; Cecille B. de Mille's blockbuster *The Ten Commandments*. An audience of nearly 5,000 swayed to the strains of "What'll I do?" played by Paul Whiteman's twenty-five-piece orchestra. Religious leaders brought church conferences there. These non-hockey revenue streams flowing into the Auditorium accounts were important to the Ottawa Hockey Association as well because the success of the Senators depended on the viability of the rink in which they entertained their fans. It was a symbiotic relationship, and Ahearn's role as an owner of both enterprises was pivotal. At the first annual meeting of Auditorium Ltd., president Fred Burpee announced a profit of $20,300 and declared a dividend on preferred stock.

Ottawa fans were on top of the world as the Senators' first season under new ownership began. Their team held the Stanley Cup. The nicest rink in North America was sitting there on Argyle Street — six thousand seats and plenty of standing room. The owners ensured stability: Ahearn's deep pockets and Gorman's hockey savvy. But barely two months into the schedule — and the Senators comfortably in first place with twelve wins, four losses and one tie — a newspaper headline jolted team supporters: "Frank Ahearn May Sell Hockey Stock." Why on earth would he want to do that?

Ahearn had always loved hockey; he admired the skills of the players and the flow of the game. He was also devoted to good sportsmanship, something that was not always high on the agenda of the typical sports entrepreneur. The Senators, to the amazement of many, had in recent years come to embody their new owner's ideal. Gone were the days when the likes of Alf Smith and, yes, even Frank McGee, demonstrated their skill with the carving knife, also known as a hockey stick. Gone also was the belligerent Sprague Cleghorn, who saw the stick not as a knife but an axe. The team's leader was the gentlemanly Frank Nighbor, a player Ahearn greatly admired. Attending his first league meeting at the start of the season, Ahearn, with Gorman's assistance, fashioned a resolution to impose stiffer penalties for deliberate attempts to injure. It succeeded and sent an immediate message to the other owners on Ahearn's philosophical approach to the game. But in two matches in mid-January Cleghorn, now with the Canadiens, was at it again. Denneny left the first game bloodied, as did Broadbent in the second. In a letter to Calder, Ahearn demanded a league meeting to deal with the recalcitrant Cleghorn and to bring an end to the violence, which he believed was besmirching the sport. The NHL president agreed and summoned Cleghorn to appear. Ahearn was armed with his own affidavit and those of several players. Cleghorn denied all the charges against him, but the meeting refused to allow arrangements to hear the testimony of the Ottawa players.

Voting *en bloc* the other owners threw out Ahearn's complaints and added further insult by chastising the Ottawa club for bringing its charges before the public, which Gorman had done in typical florid style. In one final gesture Ahearn offered to meet with Canadiens owner Leo Dandurand to see if the two of them could at least come to some gentlemen's agreement on how best to abolish the dirty work, but Dandurand turned him down.

It was shortly after this that an apparently disheartened Frank Ahearn went to the press with his announcement that he had had enough. He was going to sell his holdings. He stated why he had protested to the league: "We wanted to put an end to Cleghorn's continued attacks on the Ottawa players. I thought that this would meet with the support of the league owners, who should, in my opinion, be glad to stop dirty play. I have every reason to believe that my opinion is shared by the vast majority of those who attend NHL matches." While there can be no doubt about Ahearn's sincerity concerning the particular issue of violence on the ice, that issue may well have been a mask concealing an entirely different reason for Ahearn wanting out. Months went by with no movement on Ahearn's wish to sell until the following December when the explosive news hit the public that not only did Ahearn now want to buy out Gorman, but that Gorman wanted to buy out Ahearn. They had reached an impasse over the management of the team and could no longer work together. Said Ahearn bluntly, "I am anxious to terminate our partnership."

There had been growing dissatisfaction inside the dressing room over the handling of the team. Pete Green was ostensibly the coach, but Gorman, as manager of the club, extended his involvement right down to ice level. Ahearn told the press he had met with the players and that on their behalf, and his own, he had advised Gorman to "give up the management of the team on the ice and hand it over to a coach." When Gorman took no note of this recommendation, Ahearn tried to get rid of his partner by offering him $20,000 for his shares in the club. Gorman rejected the buyout and on the same day, December 13,1924, made a counter-proposal of $50,000 for Ahearn's shares. He did not disclose the names of his financial backers. In a letter dated December 16 Ahearn formally accepted Gorman's proposal, but a hitch arose on the day in early January when the deal was finally to be closed. In exchange for two $25,000 cheques, Ahearn was to hand over 250 stock certificates. He produced endorsed certificates for 248 shares and assignments and powers of attorney for the remaining 2, held by Ottawa Hockey Association directors Major Thain McDowell and Fred Burpee. This was not good enough for Gorman. He had to have the actual certificates, and because Ahearn had failed to produce them and they could not be found (even though it would have been a routine matter to have duplicates issued), the deal was off. It was a mere quibble and left the impression that either Gorman's backers had not come through or that some even more interesting venture had suddenly presented itself to the ever-enterprising hockey executive. The whole affair had become, in the words of an *Ottawa Journal* editorial, "an unedifying public squabble." Said Phil Ross's newspaper, "The Journal suggests, as a curtain raiser for the next professional hockey match, a fistic bout between the 'owners' of the club, the winner to take the other's company stock at a reasonable figure fixed beforehand."

Two weeks later, following the intervention once again of league president Frank Calder, the matter was finally settled: Ahearn acquired Gorman's half of the club. Shortly after came the announcement that

Tommy Gorman had been appointed manager of an expansion team, slated to begin play the following season in New York. In his memoir Gorman wrote, "I sold out to Ahearn for $35,000 plus his shares in the Connaught Park Jockey Club." If this was indeed the price, it is easy to see how the figure was arrived at, for $35,000 splits the difference between Ahearn's offer of $20,000 to Gorman and Gorman's offer of $50,000 to Aheam. According to the *Journal* Gorman was to receive $20,000 in cash, half of the club's profits for the season, the remainder of his salary for the year, fifty per cent of the club's expected revenues from the league for the season, and a percentage of the club's share of expansion fees received from new franchise holders in Boston, New York, and Montreal. Legal correspondence in the Gorman collection at Library and Archives Canada confirms that Ahearn did indeed transfer $4,387 worth of stock in the Connaught Park Jockey Club in neighbouring Aylmer, Quebec, in March 1925. Perhaps this total package equates to the amount Gorman said he received. Whatever the details, Tommy Gorman's long association with the Ottawa Hockey Club had come to an abrupt end, and for the first time in its forty-two year history, the club had come under the control of a single owner.

Putting a Team Together

The most noticeable feature of the Senators' roster between 1919–20 and 1926–27 was team stability: in eight years only thirty players wore the Ottawa colours. Of those, twenty-two had graduated to pro hockey from Ottawa's amateur leagues, some playing elsewhere before joining the Senators. Of the thirteen rookies, twelve were graduates of the Ottawa amateur system. Seventy per cent of the players were products of local amateur ranks. The city was thus maintaining its reputation as a rich source of hockey talent. This was due to the existence of a strong local hockey program organized and operated by dedicated amateur-sports enthusiasts who oversaw the various sporting clubs. One of these men, David Gill, would himself eventually graduate to the Senators as manager.

A fast-paced city league, divided into two sections in 1920, drew sizable crowds. Group 1, playing at the Rideau Rink, comprised the Munitions, New Edinburgh, the Knights of Columbus, the Victorias, the Malettes, Cliffsides, St. Brigid's, and GWVA (Great War Veterans Association). Group 2, whose home base was Dey's Arena, had the Wanderers, the Gunners, the Royal

Canadiens, and the St. Patricks. Tommy Gorman encouraged this league, making sure that reasonable terms were in effect for the teams operating in his partner's building and ensuring they had suitable dressing rooms and storage space. It is easy to see the reason for his support. The existence of a healthy, high-calibre development league was a decided convenience for manager Gorman and coach Green, who were able to keep a close eye on prospects as they progressed near at hand. In 1920 alone fans of the city league saw four players who would later turn pro with the Senators: King Clancy, Alex Connell, Jack Duggan, and Ed Gorman. Fans also cheered two other future pros: Aurel Joliat, who went to the Canadiens, and Harold Darragh, who signed with the expansion Pittsburgh Pirates.

Whether joining the Senators direct from the city league or coming from other pro teams, players wanted to be in Ottawa. Salaries were among the highest in the league. The team travelled by private rail car and stopped at the best hotels where they enjoyed the finest in dining. Important, too, were job opportunities in the bustling city. It had been a longstanding practice for Ottawa Hockey Club management not only to help players find work during the summer but also to allow them to pursue their off-ice employment during the hockey season, a benefit that not all clubs extended.

Aside from the local connection, there were external factors that influenced team composition. One of these was the NHL's practice of direct intervention when the league perceived this to be in the best interest of competitive balance. Before the start of the 1920 21 season, for example, the league executive decided that each team should contribute to the strengthening of the new entrant, Hamilton. Ottawa objected and was the only team not to send a player. The St. Patricks gave up three. Initially the league did not force the issue and the season began. After the first week it was clear the Senators were again going to be a powerhouse. In three games they had outscored their opposition seventeen goals to five, including an 8-1 drubbing of the St. Patricks. At this point the league renewed its interest in parity. It decreed that Punch Broadbent, one of the NHL's all-time leading scorers, be sent to Hamilton, and that Sprague Cleghorn, the most feared defenceman of the time, be transferred to the St. Patricks (presumably in compensation for the Pats having given three players to Hamilton). The league returned Broadbent to Ottawa with five games remaining and then allowed Cleghorn back for the Stanley Cup finals in Vancouver. Cleghorn's departure from the Senators has been misunderstood. In view of the violent acts he perpetrated against Ottawa players after changing teams, chroniclers have assumed he was thrown off the Senators' roster because of bad blood in the dressing room. In fact he did not want to leave Ottawa, nor did Senators management and players want to lose him. "We do not believe in trafficking in hockey players," an Ottawa Hockey Club release said. The reason for Cleghorn's subsequent bitterness toward Ottawa was that after the league re-assigned him to the St. Patricks and he refused to report, Gorman stopped paying him. Cleghorn, for some reason, thought the paycheques should keep coming, while Gorman reasoned that because Cleghorn was no longer on the team, by league edict, there was no justification for keeping him on the payroll. Eventually, however, the Senators smoothed things over by awarding him a half-season's salary.

Also influencing team make-up was the league policy of giving the Canadiens the first call on French players. The French-English rule was played out in high comedic confusion in the case of Frank Boucher, younger brother of the Senators' George Boucher. Frank had been in Lethbridge in the spring of 1921 when Gorman placed him on the Senators' reserve list, identifying him as "the Boucher who is in the west." Presently Frank joined another brother, Billy, in Iroquois Falls. Meanwhile Canadiens manager Leo Dandurand had reserved "the Boucher of Iroquois Falls," (who in fact was Billy) in the mistaken belief he had taken Frank. Dandurand then claimed that notwithstanding the mix-up, he was entitled to reserve Frank because he was French-Canadian. But the Boucher family, Gorman tried to assure him, was Irish in spite of the French-sounding name. Dandurand scoffed at the notion, saying it was as sensible as claiming "Sullivan" was French. Gorman won the battle and Frank Boucher, who would go on to be one of hockey's all-time greats with the Vancouver Maroons and New York Rangers, suited up with the Senators for his first season as a pro.

At its annual meeting in the fall of 1921 the NHL amended its policy of reserving new players by shifting from racial origin to geographical territory as the determining factor. The Canadiens were given the province Quebec; the Senators, the city of Ottawa and the Ottawa Valley; St.Patricks held claim in Toronto; the Hamilton Tigers, western Ontario. The thinking was that this arrangement would eventually produce home-brewed teams with which fans would better identify. This had never been a problem for the Senators, but under the new rule the club would now be allowed to sign local French-Canadian amateurs. That management never took advantage of this opportunity puzzled many observers. The club remained almost entirely English, even though about one-third of the area population were French. One who was overlooked or ignored was Aurel Joliat. Born in Ottawa to a Roman Catholic, French-Canadian mother from Quebec, the French-speaking Aurel learned his hockey on local rinks and played on the prominent New Edinburgh team in the city league. Having gone west for the harvest and about to begin a pro career with the Saskatoon Sheiks in 1922, he was traded to the Canadiens for Newsy Lalonde. The Senators thus witnessed from afar the blossoming of a player who in a brilliant sixteen-year career with their Montreal nemesis would prove to be one of the game's most popular attractions. This blindspot in failing to recognize the gate appeal that a French-Canadian player would have in the local market remained through 1927 when attendance began dwindling and French-speaking fans, many from neighbouring Hull, Quebec, bought tickets only when Les Canadiens visited the Auditorium. On one such occasion, after a Canadiens victory over their English foes, the mayor of Hull himself appeared at the dressing room door of his beloved *bleu-blanc-rouge* with a cheque for $500 as a reward.

The "west" had always been a problem for eastern operators. Territorial agreements between the Patricks' Pacific Coast Hockey Association and the National Hockey League seemed to come and go over the years and were often skirted by clubs from both sides of the country. Again in 1922 the NHL's Frank Calder and the PCHA's Frank Patrick, along with (for the first time) Western Canada Hockey League representatives, hammered out yet another arrangement. The five-year pact said the two western leagues would have exclusive rights to entry players from the United States and Western Canada; the NHL would have Quebec and the Maritimes; and all three leagues would have equal rights in the fertile province of Ontario, with the exception that the Ottawa, Toronto, and Hamilton clubs would have first call on amateurs from their respective cities.

Thus professional hockey club managers, such as Ottawa's Tommy Gorman and, later, Dave Gill, needed to be shrewd in their judgement, both of the skills of individual players and of the labour market. Scouting around at the amateur rinks, they had to ask themselves whether a promising prospect really did have what it took to be a professional. In the league boardroom they had to make sure that territorial agreements being negotiated would not put their own club to a disadvantage. Gorman knew a hockey player when he saw one and was an acknowledged master of boardroom politics. His successor, Dave Gill, was thor-

Senators co-owners Ted Dey, third from left in this 1923 team photo, and Tommy Gorman, fourth from left, ended a five-year partnership with a Stanley Cup victory in 1923. LIBRARY AND ARCHIVES CANADA C33076

oughly knowledgeable of the local amateur scene when he replaced Gorman in 1925.

"Hunting big game in Africa is mild-mannered sport compared to hunting amateur hockey players," Gorman once observed. Among his prizes was the rambunctious teenager Frank Clancy, who had caught his eye while playing city league with St. Brigid's. Small in stature (five-foot-seven, 155 pounds), Clancy was nevertheless a defenceman. What impressed Gorman, beyond the youngster's skating and stickhandling ability, was his aggressive and energetic style of play. Gorman knew that though Clancy was not ready to step in as a starter, he would be a capable substitute who, after learning the ropes, was sure to be a team leader. In short, Clancy was a good investment and Gorman signed him.

The typical Ottawa Hockey Association contract was, in fact, the standard NHL player agreement, the boilerplate wording of which dated back to the days of the former National Hockey Association. It was heavily weighted in favour of the club and was usually presented as a take-it-or-leave-it offer. For many players, especially wide-eyed rookies, the numbers were all that seemed to matter. Once salary was agreed, more experienced players might occasionally win other concessions. The standard contract said a club could terminate a player's services on one-day's notice without further pay; was obliged to honour his salary for only the first fourteen days of an injury, after which it could terminate him with no additional pay; and could impose "reasonable fines" for the violation of team rules. The player was obliged to participate in pre-season practices and games and had to obtain the club's permission before taking part in other sports. The player was to receive a complete uniform but was required to pay a thirty-dollar deposit for it, refundable upon its surrender. The standard agreement's final clause stated that if the club were to trade or sell the player, it must inform him in writing on the conditions of the transfer.

Such was the document that Gorman and Ahearn presented to Clancy before the start of his third year. It was for one season at a salary of $1,400 plus an additional $100, which gave the club an option on his services for the following year. The twenty-year-old was satisfied with the pay but balked at the termination and transfer clauses. He had proven himself a valuable player, he was living at home with his parents, he had a good job in the government, and he certainly wasn't going to entertain the thought of being dropped from the team or of playing in any place but his home town. Clancy signed the contract, but with one amendment. Written in hand in the margin over the signature of T.P. Gorman and the initials "F.C." is the notation: "It is agreed that the Ottawa Hockey Association shall not sell, exchange or otherwise dispose of the said Frank Clancy." The cheerful young man from a humble Lowertown background had extracted a no-cut, no-trade contract from the savvy and sophisticated owners.

With that contract Frank Clancy was one year away from filling the position of the renowned Eddie Gerard, who retired following an injury in the 1923 Stanley Cup series in Vancouver. Though Gerard said little about the nature of the injury, it was later determined to be a growth in his throat, thought to have been a complication following a blow from a stick. Fortunately for the Senators, Gorman had signed New Edinburgh amateur Lionel Hitchman at the end of the 1923 season, and he filled the breach in 1923–24 before Clancy was ready to join George Boucher as a first-stringer on defence. Gorman's acquisition of Hitchman was itself controversial. The big Toronto native was an Ontario Provincial Police constable who had been assigned to Ottawa. The police had no objections to his playing amateur hockey while in the city, but after his first game as a pro, the police commissioner ordered him to leave the team, citing a regulation that prohibited members of the force from moonlighting. Criticized for putting the honourable career of a law-enforcement officer in jeopardy, Gorman, as he was skilled at doing, gave out a press statement defending the signing. "We want the championship and we feel that, in justice to our supporters and to the players themselves, who have battled desperately to the top of the league with the smallest squad and against great handicaps, that we ought to sign the big New Edinburgh star."

Aside from a keen sense of public relations, Gorman's greatest strength was in signing players and keeping them happy. Of all those he handled in his Ottawa years, Jack Darragh was the most difficult. "Jack had a strange disposition and at times it was almost impossible to humour him," Gorman recalled. Darragh was a respected individual on and off the ice. As a player he was talented and industrious. In his other life he was a dutiful family man and a highly regarded manager at the Ottawa Dairy, a job he continued to perform while playing hockey. But he could be erratic at critical moments. Gorman was put to the test on one such occasion. Following the Senators' loss to Seattle in the fourth game of the 1920 Stanley Cup finals in Toronto, Darragh threw down his skates and stormed out of the dressing room shouting, "I've had enough hockey for this season. You will have to get along without me in the final game." He returned to Ottawa on the midnight train. But Gorman was certain the Senators would have little chance without him. Employing his well-honed wiles, he sent Darragh a message saying Eddie Gerard and Frank Nighbour had taken ill and would not be in the lineup for the next game. "Don't throw us down," he wired, "we need you for the game tomorrow and the world's championship is at stake." The ruse worked. Darragh returned on the next train, joined the ever-healthy Gerard and Nighbor on the ice, and scored three goals to lead his team to victory.

But Darragh remained a headache for the Ottawa manager. After eleven years of annual contract signings, he decided before the start of the 1921–22 season that he was worth more than Gorman was willing to pay, and retired. Gorman coaxed him back the next year, but the longtime fan favourite was clearly in decline and retired again in 1924. In spite of their differences Gorman was stunned, as was all of Ottawa, by the sudden death from appendicitis of Jack Darragh a mere three months after his final game. "Jack Darragh was a genuinely good one," Gorman lamented.

When Gorman sold his interest in the Senators in January 1925 and left the organization, Frank Ahearn had no difficulty finding a new man to package a competitive team. He was Dave Gill, the most prominent figure in local amateur hockey and a business associate of Ahearn, both at the Ottawa Electric Railway and at the Auditorium, where he was acting secretary-treasurer. Gill was also secretary of the Ottawa and District Hockey Association and had long been associated with the New Edinburgh sports club, an important training ground for Senator players. He shared his predecessor's talent for storytelling and was known as a quiet-mannered diplomat. Gorman had left the club in good shape, with a balanced mixture of veterans and new blood. He had signed forward Frank Finnigan the previous February and only two months before Gill took over had added defenceman Ed Gorman (no relation) and goalkeeper Alex Connell. All three were local amateurs. There was no need for the new manager to make wholesale changes, and with a league-dictated salary cap of $25,000, Gill added only two new faces for his first full season, city-league graduates Hec Kilrea and Jack Duggan. He also addressed the coaching situation, which had been a factor in Gorman's departure. Pete Green had been the coach for many years and his energy was on the wane. That is likely why Gorman, as manager, had taken such an active interest in the on-ice affairs of the team in the first place. Gill's solution was to appoint Alex Currie as coach in September 1925. Favoured by the players, he had learned his hockey on city teams and had played briefly in professional ranks, including four games with the Senators in 1911.

Under Gill's management the Senators finished first in 1926 and won the Stanley Cup in 1927.

The Ones That Got Away: The Cook Brothers Contract Controversy

THE COOK BROTHERS' reputations had preceded them, but it wasn't until Ahearn saw the pair in action at his own Auditorium that he knew they would be perfect for the Senators. Bill and Fred "Bun" Cook had come east with the Saskatoon Crescents in the spring of 1926 for a series of exhibition games. The Crescents split two against the Senators, losing the first 4-3 and winning the second 7-5. In that second game Bill scored four times on the NHL's leading goalkeeper, Alex Connell.

The Cooks had grown up in Kingston, where they excelled in junior hockey. After a season in Sault Ste. Marie, Bill went west in 1922 to turn pro with the Saskatoon club, then known as the Sheiks. Bun followed two years later, having helped Sault. Ste. Marie win the Allan Cup. In the season just completed, Bill had tied Portland's Dick Irvin for the Western Hockey League scoring title with thirty-one goals in thirty games; and in a two-game playoff series, which the Crescents lost to Victoria, he had scored two more. Bill played right wing; his brother, who in two years as a pro had come into his own, was a left winger. Together on a line with a centre such as Frank Nighbor, the Senators would have a sure-fire gate attraction. But could the Cooks be persuaded? Both loved the West and had settled on the prairies as farmers. Ahearn had another question. Because they were under contract to a team in the Western Hockey League, would he be accused of tampering if he approached them? Ahearn was to have his answers after a tumultuous off-season of negotiations.

From the beginning Frank and Lester Patrick operated the Pacific Coast Hockey Association as a syndicate. They controlled the players and assigned them to member clubs as they saw fit. By 1923 the PCHA was in trouble, down to three teams: Vancouver, Victoria, and Seattle. When it became clear following the 1924 season that the Seattle franchise could no longer be sustained, the Patricks folded the PCHA. They then entered their Vancouver and Victoria teams in the Western Canada Hockey League, bringing the WCHL circuit to six clubs, including also Edmonton, Calgary, Saskatoon, and Regina. After one season the Regina club transferred to Portland and the league changed its name to the Western Hockey League (WHL).

With the NHL now making inroads into the American market, the Patricks and the other WHL owners realized they would no longer be able to compete for players, as the eastern owners were prepared to pay big salaries for the limited numbers of high-quality amateurs hoping to embark on pro careers. Thus, following the 1926 season, they decided to terminate WHL operations. The other owners, with the exception of Saskatoon, agreed to place their players in the Patricks' hands for disposal. In this way the owners' assets (the player contracts) could be sold to NHL operators by two of the most experienced hockey men in the business. The funds received would be divided among the owners proportionate to their contributions to the player pool. It was a brazen proposition because, in fact, the WHL standard player contract contained no reserve clause. In other words, in some cases the Patricks would be selling players that neither they nor the other owners for whom they were serving as agents actually still had the rights to. All they could point to in justifying such questionable dealings was an agreement between eastern and western operators that, in effect, disallowed tampering. In short order they sold individual players from the

Victoria, Vancouver, Edmonton, and Calgary clubs to Boston owner Charles Adams for a reported $50,000. They then disposed of the entire Portland team to the owners of the newly awarded Chicago entry in the NHL for $100,000, and then the Victoria team (with the exceptions of Frederickson and Halderson, who were part of the Adams deal) to the Detroit expansion entry for another $100,000.

In the meantime Calder interpreted a purported threat by the Patricks to form a rival league to the NHL as an abrogation of the East-West accord. He cancelled the agreement. To some NHL owners this was a green light to go after WHL players directly, and this they did. Some other owners viewed the players as property of the league's member clubs because these clubs were still legal entities even if they were no longer functioning. In any event the Patricks' arrangement with the other WHL owners to serve as their agents was a verbal one only. There was no substantiating documentation, which created a general sense of confusion among NHL clubs anxious to stock their teams with the now-available western players.

Ahearn chose to deal with Saskatoon management in his desire to bring the Cook brothers to Ottawa. There had been reports that Tom Duggan, managing director of the New York Americans, had taken out an option with Saskatoon owner Ben Hoeschen for the entire team, but either this had never actually happened or Duggan dropped the option. Whatever the case, Ahearn believed he had clearance to deal directly with Saskatoon. He paid $15,000 for the contracts of Bill and Bun Cook. Both the contracts and the $15,000 sat in escrow in a Saskatoon bank. Ahearn wrote to the Cooks advising them that the Ottawa Hockey Association had purchased their playing rights. In his courteous and even warm letter to Bill he said, "All the officials of the Ottawa Hockey Association and the members of the Ottawa team want to see you and your brother playing hockey with us. We all stand prepared to make things happy and pleasant for you both and we also are sure that you can count on a fine reception from the supporters of the Ottawa team." He enclosed a contract offering new terms. It was for three seasons at $5,000 per year, double what the Crescents had paid him. In stark contrast to Ahearn's communication, the registered letter from Crescents secretary Hubert Bishop to Bill Cook was terse: "Dear Bill: We have disposed of your services to the Ottawa Hockey Association in the National Hockey League. We trust that your crop is turning out as well as could be expected. With kind regards to yourself and Mrs. Cook. Yours very truly, The Saskatoon Hockey Club."

Meanwhile up-and-coming hockey manager Conn Smythe of Toronto entered the picture. Based on his growing reputation in senior amateur ranks Smythe was hired by the New York Rangers to assemble a team for the franchise's first season in the NHL. Smythe wanted the Cooks. In his memoir he recalled intercepting them in Winnipeg as they headed to Montreal to meet with the Maroons' James Strachan. Presumably they had not yet received Bishop's registered and Smythe persuaded the Cooks to sign with the Rangers. Bill's three-year agreement — officially with the Madison Square Garden Corporation, which owned the team — called for a $3,000 signing bonus and an annual salary of $8,000.

Clearly contractual matters throughout the league were out of control. To resolve the problems, NHL president Frank Calder decreed that all players whose contracts were in dispute would be put into a pool and then awarded to the various teams according to need. The committee formed to carry out this task assigned the Cooks to the Rangers and the league governors ordered the Rangers to pay Saskatoon a $15,000 transfer fee. Saskatoon's position was that the Rangers should be dealing with Ahearn, because he had already bought the contracts. Ahearn, of course, shared that view, but he had earlier offered an alternative proposal to the Rangers. He would keep the Cooks but would give up three other players of equal calibre for the $15,000. The Rangers did not bite and a stalemate followed. Soon coming to the realization that the Cooks were set on New York and would never agree to play for Ottawa, Ahearn reluctantly returned their contracts to Saskatoon management so that the league's edict could be met.

Courting the Public

IN THE OTTAWA ENVIRONMENT, fascination with hockey was a given. Nevertheless, because the public had a discerning eye for all matters connected with the game, its devotion to a particular team or league could not be taken for granted. The Senators were the only professional hockey club in the city, but many people, especially French Canadians in Ottawa and Hull, were avid followers of the Montreal Canadiens. And though the NHL was the premier league, many hockey followers were attracted to the amateur fare presented by the city league. Senators management understood the market and always worked hard at courting the public, especially through the press. The club succeeded in this, and, outside of one isolated dispute with the *Ottawa Citizen* in 1925, enjoyed comprehensive coverage in the three local dailies: pre-game lead-ups, game accounts, scoring summaries, player gossip, and management and league issues.

Dey, Gorman, and Ahearn, of course, relished the amount of ink bestowed on the club, but they must have silently envied the even greater coverage the papers extended baseball's World Series. The October classic produced more daily front-page copy than even the Senators' Stanley Cup achievements. Typical was the *Journal's* banner front-page headline in its "Sporting Extra" edition of October 5, 1921: "Yanks Win First Game: Score 3-0." Throughout the series the paper published these extras, featuring photos and inning-by-inning accounts, supplemented by copious stories in the sports section. Aside from column inches, however, there was a significant difference in how the World Series and the Senators' Stanley Cup contests were presented. While all of the baseball copy emanated from American wire services, the *Journal* and the *Citizen* had their own reporters on the scene for the Senators' championship games, even for series as far away as Vancouver. Their reports had the immediacy and hometown feel the public demanded and couldn't be matched by a dispassionate and remote news-gathering agency.

Through the winter the diet of hockey news was sufficiently steady to satisfy the appetite of the most ardent fan. So much so that Canadiens owner George Kendall once joked to Tommy Gorman and his publicist counterpart of Toronto, "If you fellows ever lose your typewriters, you will be out shovelling snow." Though a successful sports entrepreneur, Gorman was a newspaperman at heart and it was through his industry in creating timely, and often provocative, press releases that the Senators were constantly before the public. Ottawa's French-language daily, *Le Droit*, did its part, but its interest would have been even greater had there been a French connection. Club management was entirely English and there were no French players at all. Consequently *Le Droit*, with a large readership in Hull, paid almost the same attention to *Les Canadiens* as to *Le club de hoquet Ottawa*. This was especially so when French Quebec's beloved Canadiens encountered the Senators. But the paper, as with its English-language counterparts, pulled out all the stops for the 1927 Stanley Cup final, running numerous prominently placed stories and player photographs throughout the series.

A dispute with the *Ottawa Citizen* in the late winter of 1925 interrupted an otherwise-successful relationship with the capital's press. Up until the time he sold his interest in the Senators to Ahearn, Gorman had been supplying the bulk of the club's publicity to the newspaper. This included roster changes, player signings, injuries, preparations for forthcoming games — everything an avid fan would want to know about the team. The paper routinely ran these stories, virtually untouched. It was part of an advertising arrangement whereby the club paid the *Citizen* $1,000 per season for display advertising and write-ups on the sports page. When Gorman left the club, the flow of copy to the paper dried up. The paper's sports editor, Ed Baker, did nothing to fill the gap. Unlike the *Journal* and *Le Droit,* whose reporters kept in regular touch with manager Dave Gill and wrote their own stories, Baker was indifferent. Upset by the curtailment of coverage and following heated exchanges with Baker, Ahearn informed the *Citizen* that the club would not be renewing its advertising contract. The *Citizen's* advertising manager, F.W. Crabbe, replied that in his opinion coverage was adequate and the best way of handling the situation in future would be to charge the club the regular rate of twenty-five cents per line for all display ads and publicity material, a proposal that Ahearn could not accept.

Matters came to a head shortly after. A *Citizen* editorial seemed to leave the impression that the paper was accusing NHL teams of fixing games:

> Thousands of spectators pay good money every winter to cheer on the champions (sometimes to jeer at the other side) in what they believe to be genuine contests between Ottawa and "Boston" or some other club which carries on the business of hockey. They must be disturbed when the captain of the Hamilton team [Wilfred Green], speaking on behalf of the players ... gives the public a little peep behind the scenes....

Wilfred Green's comments had been fuelled by the refusal of club management to pay the players for the playoff games they were scheduled to engage in. "Commercial hockey is described as somewhat like vaudeville," the editorial sniped, attributing the remarks to Green. "The players put on shows at the different arenas, much as acrobats do at the variety halls...." The writer then quotes the Hamilton captain as observing: "Even the youngsters are remarking that it is the western league's turn to have the cup this year...."

Ahearn was furious. In his opinion the editorial was libellous and was clearly intended to do harm to the Senators. He connected it to his dispute with Baker and Crabbe. The Ottawa Hockey Association sued the *Citizen* for $45,000, alleging the editorial was published with malice and intent to injure. Appearing before the Supreme Court of Ontario in November, Ahearn said the editorial gave the impression that professional hockey games were not genuine contests but that the winner was known before-hand. "If the public were made to entertain the opinion that there was agreement as to the winning of games the club would lose revenue," he told the court. "If all people believed it there would be no revenue." The newspaper denied that the editorial was in any way influenced by the advertising dispute and insisted the writer had not been in communication with either the sports editor or the advertising manager before composing the piece. In any event, the *Citizen* maintained, the editorial did not make any accusation of game-fixing. What it meant by "genuine contests" was contests between cities where the players were hometown products who genuinely represented the community whose colours they wore. In actual fact, the paper argued, this was not usually so. The players, especially on a team such as Boston, were likely to hail from elsewhere. The judge agreed with Ahearn. He concluded that the *Citizen* had libelled the Ottawa Hockey Association but had not done so intentionally. He attributed the harmful statements to poor wording but said, "I do not think this is a case for any very considerable amount of damages." He awarded Ahearn's club $100 plus costs as a public vindication of the association so far as the *Citizen* charges were concerned. In one sense the matter ended amicably. Ahearn remained on friendly terms with his brother-in-law Harry Southam, of the Southam family that owned the *Citizen*. In another sense the matter continued to smoulder, at least so far as the Senators were concerned.

As the next hockey season approached it became evident to Ahearn that the *Citizen* was going to stick with the view that its coverage of the Senators was adequate and fair, and that all news should be as brief as pos-sible. The *Citizen*, in Ahearn's estimation, was suppressing Senators infor-mation, not merely condensing it. His response was to create the Ottawa Hockey Association's own biweekly publication, *Ottawa Hockey News*, which he distributed free of charge from racks on his Ottawa Electric Railway streetcars. The paper castigated the *Citizen* for dwelling on rival teams while ignoring the city's own. "The Citizen sports editor is evidently permitted to write of all the teams in the NHL — EXCEPT ONE." More than 18,000 copies of the first issue disappeared into passengers' hands.

The printed word was one thing, the spoken quite another, especially when sent forth instantaneously to thousands over great distances. Even as the inky invective of the Senators' anti-*Citizen* campaign was reaching the streets, a new medium of communication was coming into its own, and Fred Anderson was capitalizing on it. He was the "radio burglar," a residential break-in artist who specialized in the removal of the prized item and its associated speakers and batteries. By the time he was sentenced to six months in the Ontario Reformatory in December 1926, the magical instrument had become all the rage among more affluent households. But many Ottawans simply could not afford the Northern Electric Victor selling for $110 or the Atwater Kent (including receiver and speaker) at $128. For those whose parlour centrepiece was a radio set, however, stations from Chicago to Schenectady fed them a nightly fare of chamber music, popular ballads of the day, lectures, religious services, and sporting events.

Hockey's exposure over the airwaves began modestly enough on February 8, 1923. Shortly before ten o'clock, electromagnetic waves carried the voice of *Toronto Star* reporter Norman Albert through the night air. Penetrating brick walls as if they did not exist, the signal reached nearby listeners direct and bounced off the ionosphere to get into faraway meeting halls, veterans' hospitals, and affluent private residences — wherever there was a receiving apparatus. As the Northern Electric advertisement declared, "Distance means nothing to radio." Albert enthralled listeners with an eyewitness account of third-period action as it happened at Toronto's Mutual Arena, where Midland was engaging North Toronto in an Ontario Hockey Association intermediate match. He sat in a glass-enclosed booth beside the penalty timekeeper and spoke his words through a telephone connection to the newspaper's broadcast studio, CFCA.

The station's next hockey broadcast, on February 14 from the Mutual Arena, was a milestone event for the professional game. For the first time the NHL was on the air, as the Senators met the St. Patricks. As before, the announcer (again Albert, some historians suspect) picked up the action in the third period. Families such as the Hainsworths in Kitchener, Ontario, listened in. Their son George, who would go on to an illustrious career as a goaltender with the Canadiens and Toronto, had assembled a receiving set for his family. There were also receivers on the remote island of Anticosti in the Gulf of St. Lawrence, where inhabitants servicing the six lighthouses tuned in nightly. The CFCA signal, they said, was as clear as any from the powerful American stations. And so it was that curious listeners from near and far and parts unknown "watched" as Andrews eluded Boucher, outguessed Benedict, and put the puck past him for the first of six goals scored in a rousing final period.

246

By the mid-1920s there were two radio stations in Ottawa, the privately owned CKCO and the government-owned CNRO (or CKCH) operated by Canadian National Railways. They shared the same wavelength and broadcast their programs on different days. Service was intermittent and there was no advertising. The public's reaction to the two outlets was mixed. Some listeners praised the concerts aired by local performers; others grumbled about the frequent unexplained interruptions between programs. The loudest complaint was that the stations blocked the reception of popular American shows.

It was against this backdrop that Gorman and Ahearn gave their blessing to an experiment in 1924, when the Senators met the Canadiens in a two-game series for the NHL championship. Both matches were broadcast through CNR's radio department. The first was from Montreal on Saturday, March 8; the second from Ottawa on Tuesday, March 11. At rinkside in Ahearn's Auditorium for the first-ever airing of a hockey game from the nation's capital was CKCH station director George Wright, who, the *Citizen* said, "relayed a very clear and descriptive account of the game."

Alas, for local hockey fans, it was the first of few. As far as Senators management was concerned, the power of the press mattered most in generating publicity. This was especially so, they could see, because of the underdeveloped state of local radio. Ahearn was also uncertain about the effects of broadcasting on his gates. Would it encourage greater interest in the Senators and bring more fans through the turnstiles? Or would people stay home and listen? Though the airing of sports events had become a mainstay of many American stations, Ahearn remained skeptical of the possible benefits of such exposure for his Senators. So much so that even for the 1927 Stanley Cup finals between Ottawa and Boston, when sellouts were assured at the Auditorium and a captivated public was clamouring for all the information it could get, Ahearn turned his back on the medium. Thus at 8:30 p.m. on Monday, April 11, when the Senators and the Bruins were taking to the ice for the third game (and the first in Ottawa), CNRO began its broadcast of C.R. Twinn's lecture titled "Mosquitoes: Their Control in Canada." No hockey over the airwaves, but entomology and plenty of baseball. The *Journal's* radio listings informed Ottawans that WON Chicago would be carrying play-by-play of all home games of both the Cubs and the White Sox. "Baseball and the ethereal turnstiles spin merrily as each invisible spectator takes his place afront a loudspeaker," the paper enthused.

A Case of Bad PR

THE 1924 SEASON had not ended well for Ottawa. After a first-place finish on the heels of the previous year's Stanley Cup victory, the Senators lost both games of the league final to the Canadiens. Goalkeeper Clint Benedict had, for the most part, performed well through the season; but club officials had developed some serious concerns about his behaviour off the ice, behaviour that left coach Pete Green uncertain about the player's fitness to put on the pads on any particular night. On top of that Benedict had been giving Gorman a hard time on contractual matters. Ahearn and Gorman decided to end the relationship with the twelve-year veteran, and they wished to do so discreetly because Benedict was popular with the fans. With league expansion coming, perhaps a spot on another club would open and the whole affair could be transacted without public outcry. But Benedict had no intention of going quietly. He sued the club for $800 in salary he said was owing to him. The Senators counter-claimed for $300.

To Ahearn's chagrin county-court documents containing all the nasty details found their way onto the pages of the *Citizen* and the *Journal*. Readers would learn of Benedict's claim that the Ottawa Hockey Association had reneged on a renegotiated contract for the 1923–24 season. They would learn of the association's allegation that Benedict had a serious drinking problem that interfered with his performance on the ice and of a $300 fine the club had deducted from his pay for breaking training rules. The club's accusations were pointed: Benedict had shown up intoxicated for an overnight road trip to Toronto and had to be helped to his berth; club directors had confronted him on another train journey and had extracted a tearful promise from him to reform; he had disobeyed the coach's orders to the players to retire to their rooms at the Windsor Hotel after a playoff loss to the Canadiens and had, instead, spent the night drinking beer with non-hockey-playing friends. Benedict filed a response denying that he at any time had rendered himself unfit to carry out his contract.

It was an uncomfortable episode for Ahearn and Benedict. Both realized damage control was in order. Before the issue reached trial and could escalate further in the public imagination, their lawyers negotiated a settlement in which Benedict dropped his claim for the $800 and the Ottawa Hockey Association agreed to pay him $350. Needless to say, it was the end of the line for Benedict in Ottawa. Within weeks he had signed with the new expansion team in Montreal.

Economics and Expansion

IN THE SHORT SPAN OF NINE YEARS, 1919 to 1927, the NHL transformed itself from a struggling three-team, interprovincial circuit to an international enterprise of ten teams, six of them American. In fact, by the end of the 1919 season, the league was down to a paltry two, the Toronto Arenas having collapsed shortly before the schedule's conclusion. Only Montreal and Ottawa remained. In spite of the league's desperate shape, by 1920 the Senators were in a relatively healthy financial situation. Postwar euphoria meant good attendance in 1919 and the Stanley Cup championship season of 1920 kept the crowds coming. After an absence of two years, Quebec entered the 1919–20 schedule and the Toronto club resurrected itself as the St. Patricks. Ottawa's population had surpassed 100,000 and local business was booming. The nine-storey Jackson Building opened downtown, a new civic hospital was to be built in the suburbs, and the success of the American Banknote Company, a major employer, was being applauded. "Canadians have much to be thankful for on this Thanksgiving Day," the *Journal* declared on October 18, 1920. "Our soldiers have nearly all found their places in civil life. There has been no post-war depression yet; industry, commerce and business have been prosperous. There is little unemployment. One of the greatest harvests in the country's history has been reaped."

As evidenced by Ottawa's comfortable situation, the league realized that with adjustments, professional hockey had the potential not only to survive but to boom. At its meeting in the fall of 1920, league governors approved the transfer of the failing Quebec club to Hamilton, where a new artificial-ice rink had been constructed. Canadiens president George Kennedy had other changes in mind, which he pursued vigorously. He thought it made no sense that ticket prices should vary from city to city within the same league, which offered the same product in all its markets. Why should it be cheaper to get into a game in Ottawa, or possibly Hamilton, once play began, than in Montreal and Toronto? Gorman and Dey objected to the idea of uniform ticket prices. They had already determined that a price increase was necessary, but if it had to be hiked even further to meet Kennedy's demand, patronage would fall off. Kennedy's other idea was that visiting teams should share in the gates, a practice, he noted, that was applied in professional baseball. Again Ottawa management objected (though later they would reverse their position). Sharing their revenue from lucrative home gates and smaller away gates would result in a net loss of.revenue and would necessitate an even steeper ticket price. After considerable debate, governors rejected both of Kennedy's proposals; but they did decide that where a club found itself in a financial squeeze, league president Calder would be authorized to levy a special assessment on the other clubs.

Another thought was beginning to percolate in the back of the governors' minds. Resurrecting a defunct franchise, or shifting a team from one city to another, might be wise as a matter of practical necessity, but perhaps the time had come to be more ambitious, to exploit the game's appeal by adding new teams. Tom Duggan, managing director of Montreal's Mount Royal Arena, sought an option on new franchises and put a cheque for $1,000 on the table at the 1920 league meeting. Though the governors stalled on that occasion, Duggan was not deterred. When, in 1923, he was thought to be behind the creation of a rival league that would have American teams, Calder cobbled together a memorandum of agreement and had it signed by representatives of the league's four clubs: the St. Patricks Professional Hockey Club, the Hamilton Professional Hockey Club, the Ottawa Hockey Association, and the Canadien Hockey Club. The document said: "We agree for a period of five years from this date [November 10, 1923] to conduct a competition known as National Hockey League, for the purpose of determining and deciding the champion professional hockey club." Signing the agreement was one of Gorman's early official acts as a partner with Ahearn in the ownership of the Ottawa club. In effect the document was meant to give reassurance that none of the owners would jump ship and link up with Duggan's enterprise. It also exhibited the resolve of the owners to meet any potential competition head-to-head.

But the rivalry did not come to pass. Instead Duggan, with his expansionary ambitions, joined forces with the NHL. The league granted Duggan options for two franchises to be placed in the United States. It also granted a franchise for a second Montreal team to James Strachan and Donat Raymond. This team's home would be the new Montreal Forum, with play to begin in the fall of 1924. Meanwhile Duggan sold one of his options to Boston grocery magnate Charles Adams, whose Bruins would also enter in 1924. The league was now up to six teams. With all teams playing in arenas having ice-making plants, a longer season became possible and the schedule was increased to twnety-four games per team.

By the end of the 1924–25 season Duggan still had the option for a second American franchise in his pocket. Just at this time the legendary George Lewis "Tex" Rickard came on the scene. Rickard was a sports promoter whose specialty was prize fighting. He had put together a syndicate to construct a new Madison Square Garden in New York. It was scheduled to open in December 1925. Duggan wanted to place a franchise in New York and, because Rickard was receptive to the idea of installing an ice-making plant, even though he knew nothing about hockey, here was an opportunity. If Duggan could find a purchaser for the franchise, a perfect match would be made. He approached a New York wheeler and dealer by the name of Bill Dwyer, who, Duggan hoped, might take the franchise off his hands. "Big Bill" was a notorious bootlegger during those days of prohibition, but at least he had cash. By a remarkable coincidence the Hamilton franchise was about to come on the market. The entire Hamilton Tigers team had gone on strike because management refused to pay them for their playoff games. The series was cancelled and Calder suspended the players. Dwyer took the Duggan option and immediately hired Ottawa's Gorman as his manager, after the latter's falling out with Ahearn. Through Gorman, Dwyer bought the Hamilton franchise and New York had its first professional hockey team, dubbed the Americans because of their stars-and-stripes uniforms. Though it is widely assumed that Rickard footed the bill for the Garden's ice-making plant, Gorman says otherwise in his memoir: "The American owners installed the ice plant at a cost of $80,000." He also writes that the team owners paid the Garden 50 per cent of net receipts as rent, as well as 50 per cent of their take from exhibition games at the Garden and on the road. Clearly the economics of professional hockey was being elevated to a rarefied plane. Not only that, a small Canadian city had been cast aside and yet another American franchise, the Pittsburgh Pirates, joined Boston and New York.

Canadians were becoming uneasy. Was big-time hockey being taken over by the Americans? Ahearn went on the record. He had not been enthusiastic about the original expansion to Boston, and now, with New York and Pittsburgh entering, he was wary. "It is fair to assume," he told the *Montreal Gazette* in April 1925, "that the establishing of hockey in the large American cities will be very much of an experiment, and that nobody can say definitely what the result will be." He said that baseball history is well established in the United States. Even people who do not follow the game know Babe Ruth. Hockey, on the other hand, is practically unknown, and even

Canadians who have emigrated to Boston and were expected to be the backbone of support there have not shown up for the games in appreciable numbers. Ahearn got the results of the "experiment" in short order, at least so far as New York was concerned. The game was a hit in the metropolis, thanks in part to the deft publicity machine his ex-partner, Gorman, put in place. He hyped the players as exotic creatures from the far north. He made hockey a fashionable event for the society set to be seen at. Even hometown Ottawa caught the excitement. For the Americans' first appearance in the capital, before opening the new Madison Square Garden, a "shrieking, clamorous mob of 9,000" packed the Auditorium to its standing-room capacity. For the Senators' first game at the Garden, a full house of 17,000 spectators were, in the words of the *New York Times*, "kept in a state of nervous excitement as the two teams battled at even terms." Was this good news or bad news? No promoter of hockey could possibly be upset by this sudden surge of popularity the game was enjoying. But compare what a sellout meant in New York as against Ottawa. Was the writing on the wall? How on earth was Ahearn going to compete with such an economic imbalance looming? By this time, Big Bill Dwyer was behind bars and Tex Rickard was enjoying half the proceeds of the Americans' huge gates. Still, as an aggressive entrepreneur, Rickard was not about to rest on his Garden success. With his arena open only a month, he purchased a licence to erect a radio station at the top of the building. From it would emanate broadcasts of all the great sporting events below. He saw the coming power of radio as a promotional tool that would draw people to his venue. Ahearn could have taken note from a master promoter but chose to downplay the new medium's possibilities.

Ahearn's motives were not Rickard's. Rickard was all about moneymaking and bigger profits, a perfectly acceptable way of looking at the world. Ahearn was wealthy from his numerous business activities and was content to be a major business figure in his home town. As far as hockey was concerned, it was the love of the game that excited him. That and a genuine desire to give his fellow citizens the pleasure of having a fine team in hockey's major league. If the Senators did no better than break even, he would be satisfied. And even losing a little was acceptable.

With only a few games played in the 1925–26 season, and the New York Americans already giving signs they were going to be a financial success, Ahearn was at pains to explain his philosophy of team ownership. New Jersey interests, eyeing what was happening across the Hudson River at

Madison Square Garden, contacted the Ottawa owner. They were prepared to pay Ahearn $100,000 for his club and move it to a new rink planned for Jersey City. "I have talked with different members of the Ottawa team and they all feel the same as I do," Ahearn said. "None of us wants to leave Ottawa. This is our home and all of our interests are here." The cost of running the team the previous year was $59,000, leaving a net loss of $1,100. But for the current season, Ahearn estimated, operating costs were expected to be about $74,000. This, he thought, would result in a deficit of $3,000 to $4,000. Increased travel and a new salary cap of $35,000 would explain these higher costs. While insisting he was prepared to accept minor losses for the sake of keeping the Senators in Ottawa, Ahearn did allow that if the deficit became too great he would contemplate a move. Any such transfer, however, would be done only with Auditorium Ltd. taking an ownership interest. American investors had assured him that if he accepted that plan, profits would be such that the Auditorium's income would be even greater than with the team still in Ottawa.

If Canadians had been anxious about the first American expansion to Boston and then the addition a year later of New York and Pittsburgh, what would they think about a further shift in balance south, with new teams in Chicago and Detroit and a second club in New York approved for the 1926–27 season? Ahearn, for one, seemed resigned to the Americanization of the game. American owners assured him, for what it was worth, that they would do everything in their power to protect the Senators, operating in the league's smallest market. The Senators, after all, were a powerhouse team that attracted big crowds wherever they appeared. In voting for expansion Ahearn reasoned that he would be best served by aligning himself with owners who controlled their own rinks, as he did in Ottawa.

Whether regular citizens were assuaged by the soothing words soon to emanate from Tex Rickard and Charles Adams is not known, but from the tone of these remarks, people could be excused for any skepticism they might harbour. "For my part," Rickard said at one of the expansion meetings in Montreal, "I want to see Canada in hockey always. That gives the international flavour, and it is Canada's national game, so for every reason, Canada must be kept in." It was Rickard's Madison Square Garden that had been granted the second New York franchise. After seeing the success of the tenant Americans in his building, he concluded it would be even more profitable for the Garden to have its own team, one that would not have to pay rent and would create a natural rivalry with the Americans. Another of his comments might have given pause. "Some of your owners are narrow and small. They talk like children. They are against every suggestion to widen the game, particularly as concerns the United States." If not humiliating, it must have been at least grating for Ahearn, a professional hockey pioneer, to suffer patronizing remarks such as these.

Boston owner Charles Adams was soon to enter the debate. The *Montreal Daily Star* had reported on a "well-known" hockey director's observation that because professional hockey was drifting from "its national home" to larger American cities, there was sure to be a resurgence of interest in the amateur game in Canada. In a lengthy letter to the sporting editor, Adams took issue with the article's assumption that professional hockey would be lost to Canada and the implication that owners were indifferent to that possibility. "From the time of my entry into NHL affairs," he wrote, "I have never once, I hope, wavered in my loyalty to that body which was entirely Canadian in its traditions and its development." Then he promised: "Every substantial Canadian city within a territory that can be successfully travelled by the balance of the league, should always be represented, and as far as I am concerned, they always will."

As the 1926–27 season approached, it had to be obvious to any close observer of the pro-hockey scene that a power shift to the south was well under way — four Canadian franchises in three cities, six American franchises in five.

If the addition of big U.S. cities lent glamour to the NHL, that buzz was completely lost on Ottawa's hockey aficionados. Detroit, Boston, Pittsburgh, and Chicago drew poorly in Ottawa in 1927, averaging only about 3,500 per game. The Rangers and Americans did better at about 5,600, but even the flashily attired Americans attracted only 4,000 spectators in their final appearance of the season. When the Rangers played at the Auditorium before 5,600 two days before Christmas, their general manager, Lester Patrick, allowed that on the previous Sunday his team had attracted a gate of $19,000 at Madison Square Garden. Both New York teams were doing well. In four games over an eleven-day period in January, some 53,000 fans filed through the Garden turnstiles, a rate of 13,250 per game. In Ottawa the overall average attendance was about 5,000. The Montreal Forum saw regular crowds of 12,000, and Toronto owner Charlie Querrie said, "If we had the Ottawa team in Toronto with their record we would sell out on season tickets alone."

Senators management could never have anticipated that Ottawa fans would turn sour. It was not because of high ticket prices. Senators seats were the cheapest in the league. In a desperate move to bring in customers, in fact, management reduced prices even further mid-way through the season. Nor was the problem the Senators' record. By early January they were leading the league with fourteen wins, two losses, and two ties. At season's end they were still on top, with a record of thirty wins, ten losses, and four ties. Neither was the problem a sudden loss of appetite for hockey. The amateur city league attracted crowds of seven, eight, and nine thousand for playoff games featuring such teams as New Edinburgh and La Salle. For some puzzling reason the city had abruptly turned its back on the pro game. Some said it was the Senators' defensive style that turned the fans off. They still remembered the days of Jack Darragh and Eddie Gerard. But the Senators had exciting players: Frank Clancy, George Boucher, Frank Nighbor. What more could fans want? A Toronto newspaper blamed the bad attendance on the popularity of skiing in Ottawa.

Financially the Senators were struggling; but since a fixed percentage of their gates went to Auditorium Ltd., it too was feeling the pinch. Ahearn had always said he was not in hockey for the money. As sole owner he had never taken a dime from its operations. But he did have minority partners in the Auditorium and he was concerned about them getting a fair return on their investment. His financial priority was the rink, and to this end he voluntarily increased the rent paid by the hockey team in the 1925–26 and 1926–27 seasons. And even though the Senators advanced through the playoffs and won the Stanley Cup in 1927, the big crowds these games attracted did not greatly help his cause. After expenses and league fees, the Ottawa Hockey Association explained in a statement to the press in mid-season, the remainder of playoff gates would be distributed equally among all the teams in the league. Le Droit, nevertheless, said that if it had understood Ahearn correctly, the Senators showed a $1,000 surplus on the season and received an additional $4,000 or $5,000 from their share of playoff revenues.

It was not a death knell, but two ominous notes in 1927 did reverberate: one in February, a second in the midst of Stanley Cup euphoria. In mid-season when management was wrestling with the attendance crisis, the club let it be known that for a city of Ottawa's size, twenty-two home games posed too great a burden on the public. The answer was to seek league approval to schedule fewer games in Ottawa the following season and play the remaining "home games" in other cities. That could only mean American cities. Then, at the city-sponsored banquet in celebration of

Ottawa's fourth Stanley Cup in eight years, Mayor John P. Balharrie read a telegram from the absent Ahearn announcing the latter's intention to retire from hockey. The statement said Ahearn would sell or lease his interests in the club to other participants and that he anticipated they would continue to operate the team in Ottawa, if possible.

14 · The Super Six, Part II
The Game on the Ice, 1920–1927

But if plays were denied me, there was ice hockey,
and woe betide any member of the staff who tried to make
engagements for a Saturday night during the hockey season,
when I went regularly to 'root' for the Senators.
VISCOUNTESS BYNG OF VIMY
recollections, circa 1920s

A BAG OF FLOUR! It was the first of many gifts, honours, and accolades to be bestowed upon Frank Nighbor over the next eight years. A four-year veteran with Ottawa, the playmaking centre from Pembroke would lead his team in scoring in 1919–20 and would be voted the league's most valuable player in 1924 and the most gentlemanly player in 1925 and 1926. During the course of those eight seasons he would guide his team to six first-place finishes and four Stanley Cup victories. The trophies were certainly nice to receive, but what was a twenty-six-year-old single hockey player going to do with the flour? Albert Forde, local representative of the Peterborough Cereal Company, made the presentation in front of a home crowd on opening night, December 23, 1919, after Nighbor had scored the Senators' first goal of the season. The Senators defeated the St. Patricks 3-2 in the first of nineteen victories over the two halves of the schedule, a season in which they lost only five times.

Only two players, Cy Denneny and George Boucher, remained Nighbor's teammates over the full eight seasons. New stars, mainly from Ottawa's feeder system, would eventually be joining the team. Among them, but still in amateur ranks in 1920, were city-league standouts Frank Clancy of St. Brigids, Ed Gorman of the Munitions, and Alex Connell of Cliffsides.

The Birth of the Super Six

ANCHORING THE DEFENCE in 1919–20 were Sprague Cleghorn and Eddie Gerard. In an unexpected development, George Boucher became the third member of the defensive corps. Just before a late-January home game against the St. Patricks, Cleghorn came down with the flu. Club doctor Lorne Graham would not let him out of bed. In the dressing room, coach Pete Green made a surprise decision — left-wing substitute Boucher would be Sprague's replacement, not the versatile Jack Darragh, who would have been a logical choice. Boucher distinguished himself, playing a solid defensive role but also scoring a goal. "Saints Ducked in Whitewash Bucket," read the *Journal*'s breezy headline for the Senators' 7-0 victory. So impressed was Green that he converted "Buck" permanently to defence, naming him a starter eight more times. He was a heady player who excelled at the transition game — retrieving the puck, rushing, and finding the open man.

With Harry Cameron, Eddie Lowrey, and Skene Ronan gone from the previous season, and Boucher moved back to defence, there was room for the addition of two forwards, Morley Bruce, who had been with the team briefly two years earlier, and rookie Jack MacKell, up from the Munitions of the city league. As well New Edinburgh amateur Horace Merrill was called up for spot duty during the middle part of the season. Otherwise the team was blessed with established veterans. Joining Gerard, Cleghorn, Nighbor, Darragh, and Boucher for another go at the Stanley Cup were goal-keeper Clint Benedict and forwards Harry Broadbent and Cy Denneny. Hopes were high among players and fans alike.

As capable substitutes Bruce and MacKell played a robust style of game — an important consideration when starters were shaken up and needed a breather. And Darragh, who was known for his ability to adjust to any situation, got another chance to demonstrate this talent. In a mid-winter game against the St. Patricks before a sellout audience at Toronto's Mutual Arena, goalkeeper Benedict was ruled off with a penalty. With one punch he had dropped Gerry Heffenan, who had roared in on him. From the Ottawa bench coach Green ordered Darragh to take over in nets. Happy to oblige, Darragh assumed his new position between the pipes. Without goal pads and with only a forward's regulation gauntlets, he blocked successive hot shots from Reg Noble, Corb Denneny, and Babe Dye. Frustrated, Noble moved in and let a hard drive go at Darragh's head. With the coolness of Benedict at his best, Darragh caught the puck and casually tossed it aside. "That's where I broke in," he laughed after the game.

By finishing first in both halves of the schedule, the Senators won the NHL championship without the necessity of a playoff. They were now poised to meet the Pacific Coast champions for the 1920 Stanley Cup. When they completed their final regular-season game, a 10-4 drubbing at the hands of the last-place Quebec Bulldogs in a contest that meant nothing, the Senators knew there would be an eleven-day wait before the start of the series, scheduled for Ottawa. But they did not yet know who their opponents would be, and they did not know for sure whether they would have good practice ice in the interim, not to mention any ice at all for the series itself. The curse of mild weather had struck and there was deep concern that Dey's natural-ice rink would not hold up. But the players did manage to get in some workouts, concentrating on how they would adjust to the PCHA's seven-man rule, abolished in the East in 1912 but to be applied in alternating matches in this series. With the Seattle Metropolitans taking the coast title, PCHA boss Frank Patrick let it be known that the western representatives would refuse to play on soft ice. This sparked action from NHL president Calder, who immediately made contingency plans for Toronto's Mutual Arena should Ottawa's weather not co-operate.

Senators fans had not savoured a home-ice Stanley Cup series since 1911, and so geared up were they that the Seattle players, upon arriving at Central Station, had trouble making their way to waiting taxis through the thick crowds of clamorous Ottawans craning their necks to catch a glimpse of the western champs.

There was no doubt in anyone's mind that the Metropolitans had a formidable team of skilled and experienced players. Goalkeeper Harry Holmes had eight years of pro experience under his belt and had won three cups, two in the East with Toronto and one with Seattle. Centre Frank Foyston was also completing his eighth pro season and had won cups with Toronto and Seattle. In twenty-two league games in 1919–20 he scored a league-leading twenty-six goals. The Senators were also aware of Jack Walker. Though not a prolific scorer, he was adept at the key position of rover. Walker, too, had been a Stanley Cup champion, with Toronto and Seattle.

If fans had not been paying attention to press reports, they would have been startled to see the Senators file onto the ice for the first game in solid-white jerseys with a large red "O" on the chest. Management had agreed to switch from the customary red, white, and black barber-pole uniform because of its similarity to the Seattle jersey of red, white, and green horizontal stripes. If the Mets' jerseys looked good, the ice did not. It was soft and covered with water. The players could not effect any kind of combination play and had to be content with nudging the puck forward and chasing after it. As expected, Frank Foyston gave the Senators plenty of trouble.

By the midway point in the game he had scored both Seattle goals for a 2-0 lead. Finally Nighbor replied, and in the third period both Nighbor and Darragh scored to give Ottawa the victory. Now leading in the best-of-five series, the Senators and their supporters were confident. The main question was whether ice conditions would permit the series to be completed in Ottawa or force a conclusion in, of all places, Toronto.

Though the temperature remained mild, Calder decreed that the second game would go ahead as scheduled at Dey's Arena, and again the ice was slushy. With seven-man hockey in play, all eyes were on the two rovers. Jack Walker was as tenacious as scouting reports had said. He was all over the ice harassing his opponents and using his poke-check to break up numerous combination plays by Senators forwards. His counterpart, Boucher, also excelled, but in an offensive rather than defensive capacity. Ignoring the deteriorating state of the surface, he somehow managed to keep control of the puck and weave his way down the ice repeatedly to give his teammates a territorial advantage. His efforts paid off and the Senators took a two-game lead with a 3-0 win, on goals by Darragh, Gerard, and Nighbor.

As far as Senators management was concerned, the series was all but over. They began preparations for a victory banquet at the Château Laurier, to be held after the third, and presumably final, game. The Stanley Cup would be there for presentation, guest speakers were being lined up, and the Mets were invited. By Friday the ice was in such bad condition that the match could not be played that night. If the series was to be moved to Toronto, the game would have to wait until the following Tuesday because of previous bookings at the Mutual Arena. Anxious to get back in action, the players themselves insisted on continuing in Ottawa on Saturday. Arena maintenance staff were desperate to protect what remained of the surface. They had heard that to preserve the ice at another rink, workmen had covered it with a thick layer of snow and then shovelled it off just before the game. It sounded like a good idea to Ted Dey, but by this time there was no snow left to cart into his rink. Instead he brought in a mechanical scraping device that shaved off the top two inches of the soft ice, leaving a slightly harder surface for the players to put to the test.

Though still not good, the ice was a little better. The Mets were finally able to show their speed and passing ability, and after an early goal by Boucher, they began taking the play away from the home team. Foyston tied the game in the first period and scored again in the second. In the third Mets defenceman Roy Rickey worked a nice give and go with Jim Riley and, taking the return pass, whipped it past Benedict for the third and final goal. It was now time for the Château Laurier party, but it was the Seattle Metropolitans who had the broadest smiles when the throng gathered and the muted and slightly revised speeches were given.

Buoyed by their come-from-behind win on Saturday night, the Mets were even more confident the next day because Calder did what had to be done and switched the remaining games to Toronto. Finally the West Coasters would be guaranteed what they were convinced would give them an edge — the refrigerated hard ice of the Mutual Arena.

Cheered on by a crowd that recognized Foyston, Holmes, and Walker from their former days in Toronto, the Mets came out strong and by the halfway mark of the first period had a 2-0 lead. The Senators pressed in the second period, and at the start of the third trailed 3-2. Both the Mets' offensive and defensive games were clicking. Rickey and Foyston scored early, while Holmes thwarted several dangerous forays by Boucher, Darragh, and Denneny. On the strength of their 5-2 victory, the Mets had tied the series and the Stanley Cup seemed theirs for the taking. It was a disheartening loss for the Senators, and no one seemed to take it worse than Darragh. He abruptly left his team and returned to Ottawa on the overnight train. Though Gorman maintained Darragh had abandoned the team and had to be coaxed back — with the help of the confected tale of Nighbor's and Gerard's illnesses — the official story for press consumption was that Darragh's employer, Ottawa Dairy, had called him home on urgent business. Whatever the case, the brilliant-but-petulant forward returned in time for the deciding game.

The crowd of about 5,000 wasn't as large as for the first Toronto game; and with a noisy contingent of Senators supporters down for the contest, it seemed to have more divided loyalties than the strongly pro-Seattle throng two nights earlier. Lifted by the presence of their fans, the Senators stormed the Seattle goal right from the start of play. Mets goalkeeper Harry Holmes stopped Darragh cold and moments later it was Benedict's turn, as he went to his knees to rob Jack Walker. Halfway through the period, Mets defenceman Bobby Rowe, who had mastered stickhandling earlier in his career as a forward, captured the puck in his own end, weaved his way through the Ottawa defenders, and, stumbling as Benedict came out to meet him, knocked the puck in for the first goal. Boucher took note. As Ottawa's most gifted puckhandler, he recovered from a stiff check and duplicated Rowe's performance to tie the game.

There was no more scoring until the third period, when the Senators treated the fans to an astonishing display of offensive power. The Mets wilted under the ferocity of an attack that saw Darragh score three times and Gerard and Nighbor once each. With the final score reading 6-1, the Senators trooped to their dressing room, changed quickly, climbed into waiting cabs, and headed for the train station as Stanley Cup champions once again. Settled in their private coach, they calculated their shares of the $4,000 prize-winning cheque that Calder had obligingly written out after the game. It was at this point that master promoter Gorman dubbed his men the "Super Six."

Western Redemption

MANAGEMENT HAD NO INTEREST in tinkering with the lineup of such a successful combination. And this was fine with the players, who enjoyed their championship status and liked living in Ottawa. To start the 1920–21 season there was only one change in the lineup. Substitute Leth Graham, up from the Stewartons of the city league, replaced another substitute, Horace Merrill. But in a move to restore competitive balance following the transfer of the weak Quebec franchise to Hamilton, the league ordered Punch Broadbent to the Tigers and Sprague Cleghorn to Toronto after only three games. They had both been starters the previous year and represented a serious loss to the club. Nevertheless the Senators kept winning. Boucher replaced Cleghorn as Gerard's first-string defence partner, and Denneny joined Nighbor and Darragh as a starting forward.

The Senators dominated the first half of the season, winning eight and losing two. Denneny scored twelve goals in those ten games, Nighbor fourteen. Nighbor's second-last game in the first half, on January 19, was a memorable one for fans at Dey's Arena. Facing the lacklustre Hamilton Tigers, Nighbor took the puck from the opening faceoff, raced in, and beat goalkeeper Howard Lockhart after only ten seconds. It was the quickest goal ever scored in an NHL game. Nighbor ended the contest the way he started it, scoring in overtime to break a 3-3 tie.

The second half was an entirely different story. Why the Senators should experience the reversal they did was anybody's guess. Some chalked it up to complacency, saying that by winning the first half the Senators were assured of a playoff berth for the league championship anyway. Their decline began with the opening game against the Canadiens at the Mount Royal Arena on January 26.

In the first half of the season Ottawa had won two and lost one against their old rivals. Even before the teams took to the ice, the Ottawas were in a testy frame of mind. It had to do with the playing status of Punch Broadbent. Following his league-ordered temporary transfer to Hamilton for the first half of the season, Calder awarded Broadbent to Montreal. But preferring to return to his original team in Ottawa, he refused to report to the Canadiens, resulting in his suspension. The Senators had come to Montreal with only one substitute, Jack MacKell, and wanted to insert Broadbent into the lineup. Canadiens manager George Kennedy refused to sanction this addition, which, to the Senators, was just another example of his poor sportsmanship.

With Ottawa ahead 3-1 in the third period, Gerard shot and thought he had scored, but the goal umpire ruled he had not. Presently Didier Pitre scored to put the Canadiens within challenging distance. What happened next precipitated the game's forfeiture, the referee's resignation, and a hefty fine to Senators management.

Desperately trying to help his team tie the game, Harry Mummery sped down the ice far ahead of Newsy Lalonde, who had the puck. Spotting Mummery, Lalonde took a long shot toward the net. If goalkeeper Benedict or any other Senator were to touch the puck first, Mummery would not be ruled offside and might have a chance to get it. He did and scored. Captain Gerard and his teammates stormed referee Cooper Smeaton, yelling that it was an offside play. Smeaton ruled that the goal counted but did not explain his decision until after the game, when he said the puck had hit Denneny's stick and then bounced off Benedict before Mummery retrieved it.

With the Ottawa players milling about, Smeaton waved off Gerard's objections and abruptly faced the puck. Lalonde took it from a startled Nighbor and flew down the ice. Still protesting, Benedict stood aside and watched him score. Both the Senators and the fans were now in an uproar. Only the Canadiens, pleased that they had taken the lead, remained calm. They quietly took their positions while Gerard, his men, and coach Green continued their furious argument. Again Smeaton faced the puck, with the Senators paying no attention, and again Lalonde took it. This time he passed to Amos Arbour, who easily dumped it into the still-vacant net.

In a state of bewilderment and turmoil the Senator players skated to their bench, seeking instruction from Green. The next sequence of actions remained in dispute. Did Smeaton ring his bell to forfeit the game in favour of the Canadiens before or after the Senators left the ice and headed for their dressing room? The players and management were adamant they hadn't quit but had only abandoned the ice after Smeaton's game-ending bell had rung. Smeaton, the Canadiens, and 5,000 howling fans thought otherwise. Elmer Ferguson wrote in the next day's *Montreal Herald*, "Ottawa should change uniforms with Hamilton. The Hamilton uniform is yellow." The *Ottawa Journal* demurred, "Fergie knows better than that." Still upset the morning after the game, Smeaton issued a statement saying, "after last night's demonstration against me on the part of the Ottawa team and offcials, I have come to the conclusion that it is due to my self-respect to step out, much as I regret to cut the ties that have bound me to many fine fellows through my connection with professional hockey."

Despite their fury at the man, Ottawa players and officers voiced their regret at Smeaton's resignation and hoped that the veteran referee would reconsider. He did; but as for the Senators, Calder was not in a forgiving mood. He fined them $500, to be paid in $250 instalments. Even this was not satisfactory retribution for Kennedy. Making the dubious claim that Ottawa's action had caused a dropping-off of hockey interest in Montreal, he argued to no avail that the Canadiens should be given a percentage of Ottawa's gate receipts for the return match at Dey's.

The Senators recovered their poise, winning the next four games. But then it began — the dreaded losing streak that even the best teams sometimes endure. The slide started with the Canadiens' return match on February 12 and continued through March 2, for a total of seven-straight defeats. Even the return of Broadbent following the resolution of his dispute with the Canadiens did not help. He was in the lineup for the final four games. For Denneny, enough was enough. He broke the streak in the second-last match of the season, scoring the only goal in the Senators' victory over the Canadiens. He followed that with a stunning six in an 11-5 rout of Hamilton. The Senators had plummeted to a third-place finish, with a record of six wins and eight losses. But with the playoffs at hand the veteran team seemed rejuvenated.

And indeed it was. Continuing his torrid pace, Denneny scored three goals in Ottawa's 5-0 win over the St. Patricks at Dey's in the first game of the NHL championship series. Sprague Cleghorn, still with the St. Patricks after his transfer from Ottawa, was in the lineup but did not distinguish himself. Following the game, management released him. He was reported to have said he could not play his best against his old team. As far fetched as that sentiment seemed, he nevertheless reverted to Ottawa because of the Toronto action and would be eligible for the Stanley Cup against the West in the event of Ottawa advancing. In the return match at the Mutual Arena, it looked for a while that the Senators would not even have to play the game to be declared NHL champions. They were on the ice and ready to go at 8:20, but the St. Patricks were nowhere to be seen. They refused to come out because they were not going to be paid for the game. Finally, after owner Charlie Querrie agreed to give them a half-week's salary, they made their appearance. But even that incentive did them no good. The Senators blanked them again, 2-0. The Vancouver Millionaires and the Stanley Cup would be the next challenge.

In 1903 Ruby Westwick's honeymoon trip was to Montreal with her husband, Harry. The "Rat" and his Ottawa teammates were playing the Victorias in the first game of the Stanley Cup series. Eighteen years later another bride boarded the transcontinental with her husband, bound for Vancouver and another Stanley Cup series. To Ottawa Hockey Club players and officers, the demur young woman was "Mrs. Broadbent." Her proud husband would have it no other way, even in the relaxed surroundings of the team's private coach where singing, gramophone-playing, and poker games occupied the long days as the scenery of a seemingly endless country flashed past the windows.

With Cleghorn re-joining the Senators, Green decided to pair him with Gerard on defence and move Boucher to a forward position. On the Millionaires the players to watch were the high-scoring trio of Alf Skinner, Jack Adams, and Fred Harris. The once-prolific Cyclone Taylor, it was understood, would be in the lineup, but his career was all but over. He had appeared in only seven league games that year.

As in past East-West encounters, the series would be played under a combination of PCHA and NHL rules. In addition to the seven-man game, the western game differed from the eastern in three other ways: a larger forward-passing zone in the middle portion of the rink (seventy feet between the blue lines instead of forty feet in the East); forward passing by the goalkeeper allowed anywhere within the defensive zone; and no substitution for penalized players. Basically the western and eastern rules alternated game to game, but for one concession to each team. The first game was under the western rules except that there was no rover. The fourth game was under eastern rules except that no substitution was permitted.

It didn't seem to matter which rules or combination thereof were in effect. Vancouver won two games playing the six-man version, and Ottawa won two playing the seven-man game. Both teams scored twelve goals in the five-game series. Benedict took some time to adjust to the forward pass he was permitted and Ottawa lost the first game 3-1. The Senators recovered in game two with a come-from-behind 4-3 win. By game three, under western rules, Benedict had figured out how to turn the goalkeeper's forward pass to advantage and fed numerous long ones to his fast-breaking wingers. The Senators won 3-2. The Millionaires bounced back in game four with a 3-2 victory.

The stage was thus set for the fifth and final game with the western rules in force. Mickey MacKay was at rover for Vancouver, Frank Nighbor for Ottawa. The Denman Arena had never seen such a vast crowd. Eleven thousand fans got in, another two thousand were turned away. Clearly Gerard had a long memory and it wasn't a pleasant one of the final game in the previous series between the two rivals six years earlier when his team endured a 12-3 pasting. He started the game in a bad mood and within minutes had picked up the first of what would turn out to be a string of penalties by game's end. Now thoroughly comfortable with the forward-passing rule, Benedict took to lobbing the puck ahead by hand, a manoeuvre that caught the disapproving eye of referee Mickey Ion. With Alf Skinner scoring on a rebound, the Millionaires led 1-0 at the end of the first period. Jack Darragh also remembered the 1915 humiliation. He scored twice in the second period, while Gerard collected two more penalties. Leading 2-1 at the start of the third period the Senators were uncharacteristically adventurous. Their normal pattern was to fall back into a defensive style when ahead late in a game. Not this time. They rushed in on Lehman, who was forced to make several acrobatic saves off the sticks of Nighbor and Darragh. With Gerard still running around looking for trouble, the explosion everyone was waiting for finally erupted with three minutes remaining. Gerard took a run at Lloyd Cook, who responded with a swing of his stick that nearly connected with his attacker's head. Gerard immediately went after Cook, ably assisted by the ever-pugnacious Cleghorn. Within seconds a dozen men were hammering at each other. Somehow Ion restored order and threw Cook, Cleghorn, and Gerard out of the game. With no substitution allowed, the Senators were shorthanded and forced into their kitty-bar-the-door style. They withstood a furious onslaught and won the game.

Darragh was the individual star of the series with five goals. In the dressing room after that final game, he released the announcement of his retirement. "The time has come," the document said, "when I cannot longer jeopardize the things for which I have worked. There is a dual duty to my family and my employers which I cannot overlook." Though unexpressed, it was an equally poignant moment for Fred Taylor and for observant fans of the game's most dazzling player. The Cyclone could no longer keep up with the younger skaters, seeing only occasional duty as a spare in the series. His playing days were over. As for the jubilant Senators, they were now getting used to carving up the cash after a Stanley Cup championship. This year the take would be $630 per man, less $120 in British Columbia provincial tax.

Wednesday, January 11, 1922: Another Hockey Day in the Capital

BY MID-MORNING biting arctic air was whipping across the Ottawa River from the northeast. As if sensing what the weather office had barely bothered to forecast, Abraham Sauvé, a ByWard vagrant, had pilfered a coat from a Wellington Street second-hand shop and was now a little warmer, but in a jail cell across the Rideau Canal from Dey's Arena. At ten o'clock the rink's box office opened. Already a line was forming. The entrance was reached by a wooden gangway that traversed the gap between the raised roadway approach to the Laurier Avenue Bridge and the rink's upper level, where the main doors were located. The platform was angled east so that the natural formation of the growing queue was across the windswept bridge. Under grey skies office workers, youths, and the obliging wives of men who could not get time off stamped their feet in futile efforts to shake the cold from their bones.

Meanwhile the St. Patricks players, having arrived on an overnight train from Toronto, were at breakfast in their hotel. There was no such gathering for the Senators. Most had day jobs, which they were doing their best to concentrate on under the circumstances. Press hand George Boucher and clerk Frank Clancy were at their places in the government's giant printing plant opposite Major's Hill Park, where former Silver Seven forward Harry Westwick was also employed. Across town Eddie Gerard and Cy Denneny, immensely popular with their co-workers, were going about their business in the Geodetic Survey offices at the Experimental Farm.

Season-ticket subscribers held most of the best seats, but there were still several hundred spots higher up in the stands and in the south end. At eighty cents, $1.10, and $1.50, these tickets were going as fast as Ted Dey's staff could issue them from behind their tiny wickets. Standing room in the north end would not be available until 7:00 p.m., but at forty cents (twenty-five cents for "boys") a packed "millionaires" gallery was assured. While the ever-vigilant Ted Dey kept an eagle eye on the morning's business proceedings, a lawyer was preparing for the probate of brother Billy's will. Billy had been Ted's longtime rink partner — the other half of the duo known to all as "Dey Bros."

As for the match, it would be the Senators' first home appearance of the new year. They had played consecutive road games in Montreal, Hamilton, Toronto, and again in Montreal. Their record so far was five wins and two losses, the same as the St. Patricks'; but the Toronto squad had already beaten Ottawa twice. The encounter would be a showdown for first place. Among the visiting players the main attraction was goalkeeper John Ross Roach. Still a rookie, he had earned a reputation as a colourful performer whose jittery mannerisms in constantly sweeping the ice in front of him amused crowds. On the Senators' side newspapers were reporting that management had re-acquired journeyman Billy Bell. He had last worn the red, white, and black in 1915 and since then had seen spot duty with the Wanderers and the Canadiens. Though a marginal player, Bell was nevertheless the subject of controversy. The Canadiens, whose policy was to give preference to French players, had just released him; but when Ottawa claimed the veteran, Canadiens manager Leo Dandurand reneged and protested the league-sanctioned transfer. The matter was still in dispute, but Ottawa manager Tommy Gorman was not about to be cowed. Bell, he announced, would be in the lineup. In the stands would be the recently appointed governor general, Baron Lord Byng, who had accepted the Senators' invitation to serve as the team's honorary president. Lady Byng was also expected, along with the famed Governor General's Foot Guard Band, resplendent in their scarlet uniforms.

Early in the afternoon, snow began to fall, driven by winds of increasing strength. Workmen nevertheless continued construction of the toboggan slide at the Château Laurier in preparation for the great winter carnival later in the month. Tommy Gorman, it was announced that day, would oversee the festival's amateur hockey tournament. At the market, vendors lamented the slow sales of vegetables and poultry, as shoppers decided to stay indoors. Lady Byng, however, fulfilled her engagement to officially open the new Protestant Infants Home on Bronson Avenue. By that time, the soot-blackened and already-frayed flag nailed to the mast atop city hall on Elgin Street was in complete tatters from the wind's pounding. As the supper hour came and went, the drifting snow began to pack, making it difficult for outdoor-rink supervisors to clear off the ice for the evening's public-school matches. Somehow the games went ahead: Hopewell at Borden, Percy Street at Elgin Street, and Lady Evelyn at Cartier Street. At Dey's the employee in charge of the back door girded for an onslaught. The door, which gave direct access to the rush end, was the routine gathering point for gangs of boys, who choreographed mass assaults on it at every game. The attendant and his reinforcements were usually able to collar some of the slow-footed ones, but on most nights a few of the more nimble lads, much to the continuing annoyance of Dey, managed to slip through and disappear among the swelling masses inside.

Shortly before seven o'clock the players began arriving — Gerard from his home in suburban Rockcliffe Park, Clancy from Lowertown, Benedict from Ottawa East, others from Centretown and the west end. Striding in off Laurier Avenue, they could have been mistaken for successful business executives. Their double-breasted overcoats were tweed or melton, worn over custom-tailored three-piece suits. They sported the best in fashionable homburgs and derbys and trendy woollen caps. Eschewing the Dey taste in footwear, none wore protective spats over their polished black boots. Knots of youngsters who had gathered in the hope of catching the attention of their idols drew only glancing nods on this night as the players leaned into the slanting snow and made for the arena door.

Though sweeper cars were out on the tracks whisking aside the mounting snow, streetcars bound for downtown from points east, west, and south were running late as game time approached. Nevertheless when the players made their appearance on the ice through a narrow entrance at the middle of the east side shortly before 8:30, the rink was nearly filled. The Foot Guards Band was playing and the governor general's party were about to take their seats in the vice-regal box. The Senators were in their customary red, white, and black horizontally striped jerseys, but with the addition this year of a large crest sewn on the front proclaiming them to be "Champions of the World, 1920–1921." The visitors wore green sweaters bearing the identification "Toronto St. Pats" on a broad white band across the chest. Deafening cheers and howls of derision greeted the men as they circled their respective portions of the ice, Toronto at the Laurier end, the

Senators in front of the "millionaires," who stood on concrete tiers in a fenced-off section behind goalkeeper Benedict. There were fourteen rows of bench seating around the rest of the rink. In front of the stands were iron posts supporting the roof. Advertising billboards spanned the posts above the crowd. Electric globes suspended from the rafters illuminated the playing surface. The haze of cigarette smoke that would eventually shorten the players' breath had yet to form.

Veteran referee Cooper Smeaton from Montreal dropped the puck just after 8:30. Instantly Frank Nighbor took it and sped toward the St. Pats net. Roach was ready, but the Ottawa forward's rising shot whistled over the protective screen behind the goalkeeper and into the crowd, where it struck a young woman, cutting her nose and breaking a tooth. Smeaton stopped the game while Senators physician Dr. Graham rushed to her assistance. Before the period was out, Roach himself took a shot on the nose, causing another delay. There were no other incidents in a cleanly played period that ended with Ottawa ahead on two goals by Denneny, his tenth and eleventh of the young season.

Two rules introduced in 1921–22 opened hockey to a more offensive style of play. For the first time in the NHL, the goalkeeper was allowed to pass the puck forward to another player anywhere inside the defensive zone. Otherwise forward passes within the zone remained against the rules. The rink was marked into three areas — the two defensive zones and a centre zone. The areas were separated by lines painted across the ice. These zones of play dictated the other rule change. It resulted from the "kitty-bar-the-door" tactic perfected and long practised by the Senators. Whenever they got the lead in a close game and were trying to hang on, all five skaters would line up in front of Benedict to keep the attacking players at bay. Opposing teams became frustrated and spectators bored. The new rule said that when the opposing team is attacking, no more than two of the defending team's skaters (excluding the goalkeeper) are allowed to retreat behind the line until the puck crosses it.

In the second period the Senators proved to the big crowd that they could play the wide-open game the new rule encouraged. Rather than hang back, the Ottawa forwards forechecked relentlessly, led by the tireless Frank Nighbor, who time and again hooked the puck away from the St. Pats attackers. Midway through the period he followed up behind the play, took a drop pass, and fired the puck past Roach. Three minutes later Frank Clancy raced in from the wing, let fly with a shot, recovered the rebound, and pushed the puck through for Ottawa's fourth goal. Near the end of the period Corbett Denneny (Cy's brother) shook loose from his cover, burst in on Benedict, and put a sharp angled shot in the corner of the net for Toronto's first.

From the start of the third period, the St. Pats had no choice but to press the attack at the expense of their defensive responsibilities. This left the dangerous Punch Broadbent free. Reacting instinctively to Broadbent's piercing whistle, Boucher whipped the puck laterally to him. Broadbent, who had scored in each of the last five games, was aware of Roach's weakness — the high shot. Leaving opposing forward Reg Noble behind, he moved in, drew the puck back to get maximum leverage, and laced it up and over the crouching Roach's shoulder into the net. As the crowd roared its appreciation, many began wondering how long Broadbent's consecutive-game scoring streak might last. With the Senators ahead 5-1, Corbett Denneny added his second on a scrambled play to put him in a tie with his brother for the league's scoring lead. Continuing his strong offensive play, Boucher scored the game's final two goals. With their 7-2 victory, the Senators were now alone in first place. As he rose from his box seat, well satisfied with his first exposure to Canada's winter game, Baron Lord Byng made a mental note to telephone his congratulations to Ottawa captain Eddie Gerard.

Toronto players complained that snow had drifted in on them during the game through an opening in the roof that had been partially covered with canvass. Outside, the blizzard was still in full force as the spirited crowds pushed onto the streets. Work crews had done their best to clear the way for incoming trams to receive the throng, but heavy drifting snow along the more exposed portions of the suburban tracks was delaying the cars' return to downtown.

The Care and Feeding of Little Mervich

HOW HE EVER GOT THE MONIKER may remain an eternal puzzle, but it seemed to bother Frank Clancy not one whit that he should be dubbed "Little Mervich" at the start of his pro career in 1921–22. He was just happy to be in the big time. In fact he was a happy person, period. Why shouldn't he have been? Here he was, nineteen years old, discovered and signed by Tommy Gorman, playing in his home town for the team he idolized. As of 11:00 p.m., January 11, 1922, his team was in first place, and though he was not yet a starter, at least he was in the lineup and was

As a raw twenty-year-old, Frank Clancy negotiated a no-cut, no-trade contract with the Senators in 1923, proving he was as tough a customer at the bargaining table as he was on the ice. MCAULEY COLLECTION

making the most of his chances. In his first game, the opening of the schedule in Hamilton, he had watched from the bench through three periods as his teammates struggled in a 3-3 tie with the Tigers. To Clancy's astonishment, Green ordered him onto the ice in overtime. Shaking his initial nervousness, he asserted himself well with his speedy skating and deft stickhandling before veteran Broadbent scored the Senators' winning goal. In only his third game, replacing Boucher who had broken a lace, he delighted a crowd at Dey's by scoring his first professional goal in a 10-0 rout of the Canadiens. He did so with what was to become his trademark spunk. Driving the puck at Georges Vezina, no less, he skirted the feared defence combination of Bert Corbeau and Sprague Cleghorn, retrieved the rebound, and punched the puck between Vezina's pads. Coach Green and manager Gorman, it was no secret, had their differences when it came to player evaluation, but one thing they could agree on was that in Clancy they had a diamond in the rough. Break him in easily, allow him to observe the pros in action, put him in the game at the right moments, nurture his development. This they could easily afford to do. Veterans Boucher and Gerard, after all, were still two of the game's finest defencemen. Green and Gorman were content to be patient with Clancy.

A rare opportunity in the spotlight came in an early February home game against Hamilton. Two nights before at Dey's, Cleghorn had run amok. The volatile defenceman, who for some reason seemed to have it in for his former teammates, took his stick to Gerard, Denneny, and Nighbor in succession. Only the intervention of Ottawa players dissuaded police from arresting him on the spot. Nighbor came away with a bruised bone in his elbow, Denneny with a split under his eye, and Gerard with a nasty four-stitch gash under his. Against the Tigers, Clancy was to get his first starting assignment, as would two other spares, Frank Boucher (George's brother) and Morley Bruce. Even with three veterans on the sidelines, the Senators skated to a 10-6 victory. Replacing Gerard, Clancy put on a spirited performance, scoring two goals, the first on a mad dash through the whole Tigers team. But, as he was about to find out, playing pro hockey is no cake-walk. Still fuming from their loss to a weakened team, the Tigers exacted revenge in the return match, with Clancy again starting on defence. Scoring three goals, the venerable Joe Malone led the way as his team pummelled the Senators 9-1. A hastened return by Gerard put Little Mervich back on the bench for the next match. But he did see at least limited action in all twenty-four league games, even being let loose on the forward line from time to time.

Whether on the ice or from his spot on the bench in his first professional year, Clancy learned a great deal about hockey and what it takes to win. He witnessed the stunning combination work of the game's premier forward line: Nighbor at centre, Broadbent and Denneny at the wings. He observed Broadbent's raw determinaton and marvelled at the veteran's hand-to-eye co-ordination as he scored in sixteen consecutive games — a feat never before and never since attained. Broadbent would finish the sea son with thirty goals in twenty-four games, while his wing mate Denneny nearly matched him with twenty-eight goals in twenty-two games. Clancy was also exposed to something that he could use a little further tutoring in: discipline. The Senators, from times past, had acquired a well-earned reputation for rough play. A "saturnalia of butchery" is how a reporter once described an Ottawa match. But now, as defending Stanley Cup champions for two years in a row, the Senators were a poised outfit. At one point in the season they had gone an unheard-of six-straight games without incurring a penalty. The Senators were truly a well-oiled machine entering the playoffs, with a first-place standing of fourteen wins, eight losses, and two ties. Gone in 1921–22 was the split-season schedule. Instead, after the full twenty-four games, the top two teams would play off in a two-game, total-goals series for the league championship. The Toronto St. Patricks, who finished second, would be a formidable opponent. Cecil Dye had equalled Broadbent's scoring output, and Cy Denneny's brother Corbett had scored a highly respectable twenty goals. Moreover, Harry Cameron had added eighteen. On the season the St. Pats had won four, lost three, and tied one against the champions.

Here was Clancy in his first season thrust into a league championship, but mostly as a bench observer. Green had no intention of inserting a rookie into the starting lineup on defence when the great stars Gerard and Boucher were healthy. In the first game at Toronto's Arena Gardens, Corbett Denneny scored with five minutes remaining in the third period to give the St. Pats a 5-4 win. Back in Ottawa, in what was becoming a wearisome tradition, the teams skated out onto late-season slushy ice. Puck-carrying was impossible. The St. Pats resorted to an old Ottawa trick and set up a five-man defence. Ahead in the series by one goal, they only had to prevent the Senators from putting the puck in the net. As the bell sounded to end the third period, neither team had scored. The Toronto St. Patricks were the new NHL champions and would be competing for the Stanley Cup.

Slumped on his seat in the dressing room, Senators captain Eddie Gerard had been denied his ambition of equalling the great Silver Seven feat of three consecutive cup championships. Or so he thought. As it turned out, Vancouver came east to face the St. Patricks in a best-of-five series. In the third game, Toronto defenceman Harry Cameron suffered a shoulder injury. Surprisingly Vancouver manager Lester Patrick acceded to the Toronto request to insert Gerard, one of the game's greatest defencemen ever, into the lineup. Toronto won the game 6-0 to tie the series. Gerard played so well that Patrick had second thoughts and refused to allow him to continue. But Toronto won again and claimed the Stanley Cup. Though Gerard played in only one of the five games, his name went into the record books.

Again to the Coast

Partners Ted Dey and Tommy Gorman were, of course, disappointed that their team had not advanced to the Stanley Cup final. Just appearing in it, not to mention winning, would have strengthened even more the already-firm grip the Senators had on the adoring attention of the sporting public.

But the owners had no intention of shaking up the team. And, as partners, they were respectful of each other's domain in the management of the enterprise. Dey looked after the business side of the arena, content that large crowds brought him good revenues. Gorman presided over team management, confident that the roster needed little change for the coming campaign. Both were keenly aware that the 1922–23 season would bring to an end their five-year partnership agreement. And both very much wanted to complete their business relationship with a championship. To do so Gorman stuck with the aging Green as coach, re-appointed Gerard as captain, coaxed Jack Darragh out of retirement, and waited out Nighbor's threat to retire. Basically the team was set. The ever-reliable Benedict would return as goalkeeper, Boucher and Gerard would again be the starting defencemen. Nighbor, Denneny, and Broadbent would continue as the starting forward line. And Clancy was ready for a more prominent back-up role, substituting for Gerard and Boucher as a starter on defence when needed.

In his eleventh season as a professional, and his eighth as a Senator, Nighbor remained the team's anchor. This was never more evident than in the first seven games, when he played every minute of every match, three of which went into overtime, and in the course of which he scored six times. Darragh, it was clear, was slowing down in his twelfth season with the Senators. His retirement for one year had left him rusty, but his tenacious style and disciplined attitude made him a worthy substitute for Broadbent. Gorman's roster worked. The Senators again finished first, edging out Montreal by one point in the twenty-four game schedule. That rivalry remained as keen as ever over the season. So intent were the Canadiens in getting the upper hand in matches against Ottawa that they devised a new defensive tactic when ahead. While Ottawa's time-honoured technique was to fall into a five-man defensive style when leading late in a game, the Canadiens adopted a completely different approach — puck control. As long as they had the disk, the Senators couldn't score. Ahead 2-1 nearing the end of sixty minutes in a mid-season game at the Mount Royal Arena, the Canadiens captured the puck. Back and forth behind their net they skated, making no effort to advance down the ice. As the frustrated Senators forwards chased after the puck, the Canadiens nonchalantly lobbed it to and fro. Impatient with this blatant time-waster, referee Cooper Smeaton finally blew his whistle and ordered the players to centre ice for a new faceoff. Even *Montreal Herald* sportswriter Elmer Ferguson (a

Canadiens partisan if ever there was one) could not conceal his dissatisfaction with the play of his beloved team. "Glorified ragging," he scoffed in his column. As "unbeautiful," in Ferguson's judgment, as it was, the trick worked and Les Glorieux hung on for their first win of the season over their old rivals from the capital.

Meeting again in the playoffs, the Senators squeaked out a 3-2 win in a two-game, total-goal series to advance to the Stanley Cup final in the West. For the first time, however, the NHL champion team would have to dispose of two contenders to win the cup. A year earlier, the Western Canada Hockey League had come into existence and its champion played off with the PCHA winner to decide western opposition to the East. This year the eastern contender would play against the PCHA champion and the winner of that series would meet the WCHL survivor.

As in past western jaunts, it was nothing but the best for the Senators. They had their own private coach, the Neptune, under the supervision of CPR porter Sammy Webber. Attentive and congenial as he was, the team anointed him with what they considered to be an honorific title: club mascot. Prominent Ottawa piano manufacturer Frank Orme, whose firm had provided music lessons to past vice-regal families, arranged for one of his upright models to be placed on the car. Seizing the opportunity, Gerard happily displayed his keyboard talents, accompanying the dubious vocal offerings of Lionel Hitchman and trainer Cosey Dolan. Harry Helman had the foresight to bring along a drum. The absence, however, of two key members of the club tempered the group's jocularity as the CPR transcontinental pulled out of Central Station and began its long journey west. Green could not get away from the post office, so Gorman would be behind the bench. Then, at the last minute, Darragh notified Gorman that his managerial duties at Ottawa Dairy would prevent him from joining the team. The club and local employers had usually been able to reach accommodations when hockey games and regular jobs conflicted, but in this case absence from work for the anticipated four weeks it would take to go to the coast, play in possibly two separate series, and return would be too much for the post office and the dairy to accept. In a panic Gorman called Canadiens manager Leo Dandurand and obtained his permission to add Billy Boucher to the lineup. He then wired Frank Patrick for permission, but the PCHA president gave no definite answer. Gambling that Patrick would eventually consent, Gorman ordered Boucher onto the next train. The plan was that he would meet the team at a stopover in Calgary. Added to Gorman's headaches were the poor conditions of Denneny and Hitchman. In the first game of the Canadiens series, Billy Couture had clubbed Denneny, and Sprague Cleghorn had done the same to Hitchman. Both had their heads swathed in bandages as they climbed onto the Neptune. The vicious attacks had been so publicly condemned that Dandurand voluntarily suspended Couture and Cleghorn, a decision that contributed to the Canadiens' loss of the series. And it was his players' behaviour that undoubtedly kept Dandurand in a conciliatory frame of mind when Gorman approached him about Boucher.

Upon reaching Vancouver Gorman took Denneny and Hitchman to Patrick's office. He wanted Patrick to see for himself the condition of his players. He was also armed with the permission of Stanley Cup trustee William Foran to use Boucher so long as Patrick agreed. Gorman argued that the Senators would not stand a chance with two banged-up players and no substitute for Darragh. The consequence, he reasoned, would be a short series and smaller gate receipts. Patrick was unsympathetic; Boucher would not be in uniform.

With no substitute for Darragh, and Hitchman capable of only limited ice time, the Senators nevertheless prevailed in the opening game 1-0 on a goal by Broadbent, himself just recovered from the grippe. In spite of a suspected fractured skull, Denneny played a strong game, seeking relief only when overcome by spells of dizziness. Led by former Ottawa centre Frank Boucher, who scored two goals, the Maroons rebounded in the second game 4-1. More trouble followed for the Senators. Helman fell in practice, gashing his nose and cheek on Nighbor's skate. He had to be taken to hospital for surgery and was to remain there for several days. The Senators were down to two spares. Thirty-seven year old Tommy Gorman, who had never played a game of professional hockey in his life, appeared at practice the next day in full uniform. But Gorman stayed behind the bench for the remaining two games, which on the strength of an established starting lineup of seasoned veterans and the industrious backup play of the remaining two spares, Clancy and Hitchman, the Senators won 3-2 and 5-1. Their final test would be the WCHL-champion Edmonton Eskimos, who had been quietly waiting in the wings and studying the Maroons' and Senators' strengths and weaknesses. This series, too, would be played entirely in Vancouver; but now the Senators, admired for their grit, would be the local favourites.

Following a collision with Corbett Denneny late in the final game against the Maroons, Gerard had been forced to leave the ice with a painful shoulder. Doctors determined it was separated and wanted to put it in a cast, but Gerard refused. Unable to play in the opening game in the best-of-three series against the Eskimos, Gerard, with his arm in a sling, watched as Clancy replaced him, leaving Hitchman as the only spare. The Eskimos had five extras on the bench. Doing their best to conserve energy and wait for opportunities, the Senators trailed 1-0 in the third period. Midway through it, Hitchman, who had relieved Boucher on defence, took the puck from Eskimos winger Bob Trapp, rushed the length of the ice, and beat Hal Winkler to tie the game. Near exhaustion, the Senators hung on for over-time. Intercepting a misguided pass from Duke Keats, Denneny raced in and scored after two minutes and eight seconds of extra time.

Helman had by now recovered from nasal surgery and declared him-self ready for the second game. Gerard, against the advice of his teammates, also insisted on dressing. He had trainer Dolan and a medical specialist secure his shoulder with plaster and adhesive tape and started the game. Midway through the first period, Broadbent scored. In the third period, with no further scoring, Gerard crashed into the boards and again threw out his shoulder. Hitchman replaced him, but as fate would have it, he too had to leave the ice. Meanwhile Dolan was frantically working on Gerard's shoulder and fixed him up sufficiently to allow him to return to action. The Senators hung on and were again Stanley Cup champions.

A New Ice Age

THEY CALLED IT ARTIFICIAL ICE: that is, ice produced by human skill and not occurring naturally. Specifically, ice frozen by mechanical refrigeration whereby a brine solution is run through rows of cooling pipes under a con-crete floor covered with a layer of water. But ice is frozen water no matter whether formed outdoors by Mother Nature or indoors through engineer-ing genius. The ice is not artificial, only the means of forming it is. NHL play-ers had been skating on "artificial" ice in Toronto since the league was formed, and since 1920 in Hamilton. If they were lucky enough to reach a Stanley Cup series out west, there too would they experience the hardness of the man-made surface.

Installing an ice-making plant was a costly investment. In his book *The Physics of Hockey*, Alain Haché calculates that for a typical rink of two-centimetre thickness, the energy required just to bring the temperature of the water down to zero degrees is 2.7 billion joules, enough to look after the needs of an average house for two weeks. Another 11 billion joules must be generated to freeze the water, the "latent heat of fusion," the professor calls the process. More energy is needed to maintain the ice, especially in a vast arena such as Madison Square Garden, where owner Tex Rickard liked to keep his audiences in comfort at sixty degrees Fahrenheit. After a Senators game in New York against the expansion Americans, team captain Buck Boucher complained directly to the great impresario. "It is so hot out there that a player is bound to lose a lot of weight." He claimed that he had put his equipment on the scales before and after the game and found that from his own perspiration, it was three pounds heavier when he took it off.

By the mid-1920s the transition from natural to artificial ice in big-league rinks was complete. Ironically, hockey's first city, Montreal, was the last of the game's major centres in Canada to modernize. Frank Ahearn's Ottawa Auditorium was equipped with an ice-making plant when it opened in November 1923. But the Mount Royal Arena in Montreal still depended on winter's cold temperatures, unreliable as they proved to be. In fact, the Canadiens were forced to postpone the first three home dates of the 1923–24 season because of unco-operative weather. Smug Ottawans took to calling Les Canadiens the "slush kings." Finally, in November 1924, Montreal went artificial with the opening of the Forum. League expansion followed: a second Montreal team and Boston in 1924; Pittsburgh (along with the transfer of the Hamilton franchise to New York) in 1925; and Detroit, Chicago, and a second New York team in 1926. With the addition of new teams came longer schedules. From a twenty-four game season in 1923–24, the NHL went to thirty games in 1924–25; to thirty-six in 1925–26; and to forty-four games in 1926–27.

More teams and longer seasons meant greater travel to more distant points. Take, for example, the Senators' six games over a fifteen-day period from November 30 to December 14, 1926. On Tuesday afternoon, November 29, the players boarded a private rail coach for Montreal. At Windsor Station they were hooked up to the CPR express for the run south in the dead of night through Vermont's Adirondack Mountains, into Massachusetts, and east toward Boston. With a blinding beam of light piercing the blackness and signalling the approach of the mighty engine, it would have been a soul-stirring moment indeed for any small-town New Englander out in those pre-dawn hours to witness the *Red Wing* thunder through the main thorough-fare's level crossing at seventy miles per hour. Oblivious to the roar outside Connell, Clancy, Denneny, Nighbor, and their mates slept on between the crisp, white CPR-issue linen sheets folded into their berths, not stirring until the iron monster eased into Boston's North Station at 7:15 a.m. Then it was to their hotel and, finally, to the arena for the 8:30 p.m. game against the Bruins. On Thursday they returned to Ottawa by the same route — a 1,000-mile round trip. They played at home on Saturday. On Monday, missing Frank Finnigan (who had crashed his Nash sedan into a tree while driving Denneny home after Saturday's game and was laid up with head injuries), the Senators departed for Chicago. This route took them to Toronto, where their car was hooked to the train bound for Windsor, by way of Hamilton and London, then to Detroit, across southern Michigan through Ann Arbor, Battle Creek and Kalamazoo, and south to Michigan City, Indiana, around the southern tip of Lake Michigan and up through Cicero, Illinois, to Chicago for Tuesday-night's game. The next day, it was back to Windsor (where the Detroit Cougars were based for their inaugural NHL season) and a Thursday-night game. On Friday coach Dave Gill and his men headed east to Toronto and connected for the Ottawa run and completed another 1,500 miles. They played at home on Saturday, took Sunday off, and on Monday climbed onto their special coach yet again. Once more they connected at Montreal for the journey straight south. Down the west shoreline of Lake Champlain, on to Albany, and then down the Hudson River Valley and into New York City. There, on Tuesday, the Senators engaged the New York Americans. The next day, December 15, they returned to Ottawa. With that 1,000-mile junket complete, the Senators had followed some 3,500 miles of steel rail in sixteen days, just 350 miles short of their entire regular-schedule travel for the 1923–24 pre-expansion season.

Travelling much of the time on a Pullman-style private coach, with an obliging porter in full-time attendance, may have been easy to take, but life on the road was not without its share of unwelcome adventure. On one occasion in the dead of winter 1924, the Canadian National Railway passenger train carrying the Senators (this time by regular coach) to Montreal for a crucial game got stuck in a snowdrift east of Hawkesbury, Ontario. A CNR snowplow dispatched to the scene could not set the train free as a blizzard raged all around. Manager Gorman, with ex-Senators president Ted Dey along for the ride, could not get word to Montreal because lines were down and the nearest telephone was miles away. The Senators and an eclectic band of travellers, including a Dominion cabinet minister, a bridal party, and a young mother taking her sick infant to Montreal for an operation, were stranded. In a manly effort to free the great locomotive, Darragh,

Denneny, Dolan, and crew members took to the shovels but soon realized the futility of it all. With the slim provisions on board soon consumed, Clancy and Denneny set out with the conductor to find food, especially milk for the ailing child. They found it at a farmhouse a mile away; but in the course of their trek Denneny fell down a well and had to be hauled out by his companions. The train eventually shunted back to Hawkesbury and hours later made a fresh start for its destination. The Senators tumbled into their beds at the Windsor Hotel at 8:30 on the morning following the scheduled match, having left some 6,000 spectators completely in the dark as to why there was no game.

One year later a CPR express, on which the Senators were returning home from Toronto, hurtled through an open switch onto a siding at Glen Tay Station near Perth, Ontario, and crashed head on into a standing freight train. The players and officials were in the dining car at the time. Cutlery, dishes, food, tables, and chairs flew in every direction, taking passengers with them. Ahearn landed under a table, later discovering he had suffered broken ribs. Green lay pinned under smashed furniture, choking on a piece of food. Only the quick action of Boucher, who put his finger down Green's throat to dislodge the obstruction, saved his life. Glass from broken windows was everywhere and coaches were wrecked. Amazingly, though many of the passengers, including most of the hockey players, suffered cuts and bruises, no lives were lost. Only goalkeeper Alex Connell, the team's resident comedian, found humour in the chaos: "We wouldn't have minded so much if we had almost finished but there were a good many dishes on the table that we hadn't sampled."

The mid-1920s, then, signalled the beginning of a new era in professional hockey. Several of the Ottawa players, such as Nighbor, Broadbent, Benedict, Denneny, and Boucher, had been in the game long enough to be impacted by the dramatic changes occurring between 1923 and 1927: the end of natural ice rinks, bigger and more up-to-date arenas, longer seasons, more-distant travel, glamorous American cities on the itinerary. Not so for Eddie Gerard. Weeks before the start of the 1923–24 season, as the Senators eagerly anticipated their move to Ahearn's gem of an arena, the Ottawa Auditorium, Dr. Graham declared the captain unfit for play. Graham had consulted with a specialist in Philadelphia, who advised that a growth in Gerard's throat, benign though it was, would interfere with his respiratory efficiency under the severe physical stress of hockey. After ten stellar seasons with Ottawa the revered Gerard hung up his skates.

Darragh, too, was at the end of the line. He made the 1923–24 team, but only as a spare. Suffering a split knee in late December, he was out of the lineup for five games, replaced by Rod Smylie, who had been cut by Toronto. Following his return Jack was used sparingly and finished the season with only two goals in eighteen appearances. That season was also the last as Senators for Benedict and Broadbent, both of whom were sent to the new Montreal expansion team, later to be known as the Maroons. Remaining from the old guard were Boucher, Denneny, and Nighbor. In Nighbor's latter years it was his defensive qualities more than his offensive that made him the club's stalwart player. In the early part of his career the number of goals he scored in a season often exceeded the number of games he played — forty-one goals in nineteen games in 1917, and even as late as 1920 it was twenty-five goals in twenty-three games. Throughout his career Nighbor had excelled equally in offensive and defensive play, his sweep-check being renowned and emulated throughout the league. Now, in the mid-1920s, with his goal production on the wane, Nighbor's intellectual mastery of the game of hockey sustained his extraordinary value to the team as a defensive contributor. Denneny, always a prolific scorer, was now Ottawa's dominant offensive threat. He led the league in scoring in 1923–24 and was the team's leading scorer in every season from 1923–24 to 1926–27. Curly haired and stocky of build, he went down the left-wing side with a vengeance, unleashing a hard and sure shot. Denneny attributed its speed and accuracy to his unique stick. By straining and bending the blade he produced a curve in it. So hard was the resulting shot that on one occasion at practice in the old Dey's Arena, he split two of the boards behind the net. "You know, Cy," Denneny recalled Dey admonishing him, "that's going to cost you twenty dollars; lumber costs money today."

Veterans and Rookies

FOLLOWING THEIR STANLEY CUP victory in 1923 the Senators finished first in three of the next four seasons, culminating in a fourth Stanley Cup in eight years. Between 1924–25 and 1926–27 the club enjoyed the stability of a hard core of talented players, who were surrounded by emerging new stars gaining experience in supporting roles. Alex Connell, the promising goaltender of the amateur Ottawa Shamrocks, proved his mettle in succeeding Benedict. Clancy had met and even exceeded management expectations and was now established as a starting defenceman, paired with

Boucher. With the departure of longtime favourite Punch Broadbent, the Senators signed amateur Reginald "Hooley" Smith from the Olympic-champion Toronto Granites in 1924, and he immediately won a starting position on right wing. At centre was Nighbor, as usual; at left was Denneny, of course. Frank Finnigan, the Ottawa Montagnard amateur who signed with four games remaining in 1924, slowly came into his own and, well established by his third season (1926–27), frequently started at right wing. Yet another graduate of the local amateur ranks, Rideaus star Hector Kilrea, joined the Senators in 1925. A versatile player, he filled in capably at all three forward positions while earning a reputation as a first-rate professional.

With the addition of the New York Rangers, Chicago Black Hawks, and Detroit Cougars in 1926–27, the NHL was now up to ten teams structured into two divisions with a forty-four-game interlocking schedule. The New York Rangers, Boston, Chicago, Pittsburgh, and Detroit made up the American division; the Senators, the Canadiens, the Maroons, the St. Patricks, and the New York Americans comprised the Canadian. In each division the second- and third-place teams would play off to see who would meet the first-place team. The divisional winners would then contest the league championship and the O'Brien Trophy. Since the other major professional league, the WHL, had folded the previous season, no challenge series for the Stanley Cup was anticipated, in which case the esteemed prize would go by default to the NHL champion.

The 1927 season went well for Ottawa. With the steady Alex Connell in goal, Boucher and Clancy on defence, and Nighbor, Smith, and Denneny leading the attack, the Senators won thirty games, tied four, and lost only ten. They finished first in their division, ahead of the Canadiens, whom, as it turned out, they would meet in a two-game, total goals divisional final. In six regular-season contests between the two teams, the Senators won five and lost one. Key to their success was their ability to hold the electrifying Howie Morenz, the Canadiens' leading scorer, to two goals in the six games. Moreover, he was the only Montrealer to score more than once in those games. By contrast Ottawa's Boucher, Finnigan, and Denneny each counted three times.

Like Benedict before him, Connell chose to wear a black, peaked cap on the ice. It may have fallen off or been knocked off on occasion, but likely not deliberately because goaltenders were not usually the object of physical confrontation. It was a rare sight indeed, however, for a forward to adorn himself with such apparel, though old-time fans might have remembered the pink handkerchief Quebec's Herbie Scott wrapped around his head in the 1890s. It was therefore a doubly colourful treat when the Canadiens and Senators met, for Aurel Joliat, the Canadiens' wiry little bundle of energy, sported the same signature headgear as his adversary in the Ottawa net. Time after time in the playoff series Black Cap One weaved and twisted his way into shooting position, and time after time Black Cap Two thwarted the assault. In the first game, at the Forum, neither Black Cap One nor any of his red-shirted friends scored any goals at all. It was Ottawa 4, Canadiens 0 as the teams headed to the capital for the second of the two games. In the less stressful course of the long regular season, Senators players liked to see who among them might be the one to separate the cap from the head of the "Mighty Atom," as Joliat was fondly known. In the playoffs, however, such amusements had to be forgone in the interests of objectives rated at a higher plane. The cap stayed attached and Joliat stayed scoreless, as did his centreman, Morenz. Only Sylvio Mantha scored for the Canadiens and Ottawa won the series five goals to one.

Meanwhile in the American division the New York Rangers, in their inaugural season, finished first, thanks in large part to the work of Bill and Bun Cook, both of whom Ahearn had tried but failed to sign for the Senators. In the divisional final, however, the Boston Bruins, now in their third year, defeated the Rangers and were set to meet the Senators for the league championship. In four encounters over the season the Senators won three, but none by more than one goal. Coach Gill's men understood it would be a tough series. One reason was the Bruins' defence combination of Lionel Hitchman and Eddie Shore, with Sprague Cleghorn in reserve, just in case. Hitchman, of course, had started his pro career with the Senators in 1923 and went to the Bruins midway through their first season. Shore, from Fort Qu'Appelle, Saskatchewan, was completing his first season with Boston, having broken into pro hockey two years earlier in the western league. Wasting no time establishing himself as one of the NHL's roughest customers, he clocked 130 minutes in penalties over the regular schedule, second only to the Maroons' Nels Stewart, who spent 133 minutes on the sidelines. Cleghorn, a veteran of sixteen seasons in the NHA and NHL, was coming to the end of his career; but his style of play had not mellowed and he remained one of the most feared men in the league — 84 penalty minutes in only a substitute role. Up front, Frank Fredrickson, a Canadian Olympic champion, centred Harry Oliver on right wing and Percy Galbraith on left. Fredrickson and Oliver had come to the Bruins from the defunct

WHL, Galbraith from the central league. Goaltender Hal Winkler was another western refugee, whom the Senators still remembered from the 1923 Edmonton series. Winkler joined the Bruins in mid-season from the Rangers and proved a reliable addition.

Despite the hype in Boston (this was the first appearance of a team from the eastern United States in a Stanley Cup final) the opening game there was a disappointment. In a cautious display of conservative hockey, neither team scored, even after a twenty-minute overtime period. There had been more than 30,000 applications for tickets and the 9,500 fans fortunate enough to enter the arena went home frustrated, both because their favourites had not won and because there was no decisive conclusion to the evening's fare. Most present wanted the game to go on, but the two teams agreed with the referees' judgment that the condition of the ice had deteriorated too much for play to continue. The series was to be a best of five, but now there was a possibility that after the five games the clubs could be deadlocked and a sixth would be required. League president Calder, however, decreed that there would be no sixth game. Evidently he was concerned that the public would think the league was milking the series for the sake of an extra gate. Instead of a sixth game, the team with the most wins in the five matches would be declared the champion. If the teams were even, there would be no champion at all and the players would split their playoff share equally. Meanwhile Stanley Cup trustee William Foran had received word that the Duluth Hornets, champions of the American Hockey Association, were contemplating a challenge. If an Ottawa-Boston deadlock were to occur, and if Foran were to recognize a challenge from what many regarded as a minor-league club, Duluth would have no opponent. Would Foran then award the trophy to the American Hockey Association champion by default?

These considerations were far from the minds of the Senators and Bruins players. All that mattered was the next game. Again it was a tightly contested affair, but it was also entertaining. With opening-night jitters out of the way, both teams ventured an offensive style. Early in the first period, with the Bruins shorthanded, Clancy got hold of the puck at their blue line and unleashed a high, hard shot. The black puck on the dark ice, so the explanation went, rendered the disk difficult to pick out when it began its journey and it ended up, to Winkler's surprise, in his net. Five minutes later Kilrea spotted Finnigan alone on the right side and fed him a long pass. Taking it at full speed he bore down on the goal and, waiting until Winkler

Team captain George Boucher, bottom centre, led the 1926–27 Senators to their last Stanley Cup. MCAULEY COLLECTION

made the first move, tucked the puck into the corner of the net. There was no further scoring until late in the third period when Oliver replied for the Bruins. With seconds remaining and the Bruins pressing furiously, Denneny broke away and scored the clinching third goal.

The series shifted to Ottawa for games three and four, but Calder was still undecided about the venue for a fifth game, should it be required. If the Ottawa public had been indifferent to the Super Six through the long winter and had failed to fill the seats in a modern arena, even for a first-place hometown team, they were now on the bandwagon. The lineup at the Auditorium box office began forming at 3:00 a.m. on game day. Hopefuls lit bonfires to keep warm. By ten o'clock a line of several thousand snaked south on O'Connor Street and east on Catherine Street. The enthusiasm heartened the Senators players as they arrived for a late-morning practice. Ever attuned to the relationship between gates and player shares, the always-cheery Clancy eyed the throng. "Tell the crowd it's our game tonight and we want them to be on hand," he quipped.

The match the packed house took in was more robust than the series opener in Boston, but no more conclusive. Every player seemed intent on bashing an opponent. First it was Hooley Smith and Hitchman jousting at centre ice, then Smith clashing with Shore. Clancy also got in his licks with the Bruins' tough guy. Connell was not to be outdone. Black cap firmly pulled down over his forehead, he raced out of his net to flatten a startled Hitchman as the husky Bostonian prepared to let a shot go. Jimmy Herberts scored for Boston in the first period, Denneny tied it in the second, and after twenty minutes of overtime the game ended in a draw. A win for the Senators in the fourth game would give them the championship. Only if the Bruins were victorious would a fifth be played.

Senators coach Dave Gill was one of hockey's early strategists. He was a shrewd observer of the game's nuances and liked to throw opposing teams off guard through unexpected on-ice player combinations. He had begun every game in both playoff series with Nighbor at centre, Smith on right wing, and Denneny on left. Again facing the formidable line of Fredrickson, Galbraith, and Oliver, Gill made a change. Finnigan replaced Smith, and Kilrea took Denneny's opening spot. The move served two purposes. Finnigan and Smith were superb and tireless skaters. They would hold the starting Bruins trio in check. What Gill had primarily in mind, though, was to save the offensive power of Denneny and Smith until second-string players replaced the Bruins' starting line. The move was partially successful. The Bruins were held off the scoreboard in the first period, but so were the Senators. In the second Finnigan scored, and less than three minutes later, so did Denneny.

By the third period the Bruins were a desperate team, frustrated by Ottawa's traditional tight checking, especially by Finnigan and Kilrea. Denneny scored, Oliver replied. Now late in the period, and the Bruins trailing 3-1, matters came to a boil. The Hitchman-Smith feud from the previous game resumed, each slamming the other hard into the boards. This drew the attention of Boucher, who came to his teammate's aid, resulting in Boucher and Hitchman being ejected from the game. Smith then knocked the mild-mannered Oliver senseless in the mistaken belief, Smith later contended, that his opponent was Shore. If that was his wish, he got it; Shore then went after Smith and they were both tossed. The game, in short, ended in a shambles; but the rhubarb did not stop there, even as the Senators' on-ice celebration of a Stanley Cup victory continued. From his seat near the boards Boston owner Charles Adams, along with manager Art

Ross from behind the bench, had pilloried referee Dr. Jerry Laflamme throughout the game. They were particularly incensed by the ejection of Jimmy Herberts, who had made threatening gestures toward Laflamme after an altercation with Kilrea. As the players left the ice, Adams and Ross followed Laflamme down the corridor to the referees' dressing room and confronted him at the door. Soon the whole Bruins team was milling about and Laflamme ended up being knocked to the floor. Calder, who was about to leave the rink, rushed to the scene to restore order.

It was a disgraceful way for the NHL to conclude its first season as exclusive keepers of the Stanley Cup. There was no challenge from the Duluth Hornets after all, and even if there had been, it is doubtful that any such series would come off, late in the season as it was and uninterested as the Senators and the league would be in engaging what they saw as an inferior minor-league team. Calder was quick in taking action to restore some credibility to the league. He identified Bruins relief defenceman Billy Couture as the one who had assaulted Laflamme and expelled him from the NHL. And for his attack on Oliver, Calder suspended Smith for one month, starting at the beginning of the next season.

The Super Six had won a fourth Stanley Cup in eight years. They had reached the pinnacle of success. They were mostly a hometown lot and would have a full summer to bask in glory amidst a doting public. Not far from the minds of the players and their supporters, however, was the uneasy thought that all good things come to an end.

15 · The Collapse of the Ahearn Dream

my father hasn't come home
he is in Chicago playing the Black Hawks
who are very big and black
he is in Boston playing the Boston Bruins
who are very big and brown
JOAN FINNIGAN
"Ottawa and the Valley"

THERE WAS A DISTINGUISHED yet approachable air about Frank Ahearn as he reached middle age in the late 1920s — strong chin, neatly trimmed moustache, and wavy dark air combed to the side. But it was those large round eyes. They were the kind you would expect to widen in delight or bulge in anger depending on whether he was greeting a good friend or staring down a contrary business adversary. He was, after all, accustomed to having his own way even if, on some issues, it might take a little persuasion. But Ahearn was, above all, a gentleman, widely respected and liked in both the world of business and the community at large. He was fair and principled in his business dealings and generous in support of local charities, especially his beloved Ottawa Boys Club. He was particularly good to his hockey players, for whom he had a genuine fondness, often having them to his spectacular country home on Thirty-One-Mile Lake in the Gatineau Hills. "Frank Ahearn was a perfect gentleman to us all, all the time," recalled Frank Finnigan. To King Clancy, Ahearn was "the salt of the earth."

From its opening in 1926, the Ottawa Electric Building was where Frank Ahearn could be found most days, overseeing his Rowatt-Ahearn insurance agency and assisting in the business ventures of his father, Thomas Ahearn, a member of the Privy Council and a renowned entrepreneur. The nine-storey structure on the south side of Sparks Street near Elgin was a hive of business enterprise dominated, of course, by the Ottawa Electric Railway Company (OER), Ottawa Light, Heat and Power, and Ottawa Gas — all controlled by the senior Ahearn. The elder

289

In the twenties and thirties, Senators owner Frank Ahearn could often be found a few doors down from his Sparks Street office at Bowles Lunch, a laid-back diner that buzzed with chatter about business, politics, and hockey, of course. MCAULEY COLLECTION/DETAIL

Ahearn's office on the seventh floor was just above the OER executive suite in room 614, where the Ottawa Hockey Association board of directors frequently met. The Ottawa Electric Building was the perfect place for Frank to orchestrate his numerous business activities. Conveniently, it was a three-minute walk to the exclusive Rideau Club (where years before, P.D. Ross and an aide to Lord Stanley of Preston tossed around ideas for a championship hockey trophy). There Ahearn would meet associates over lunch, and, in the summer months, could sometimes be spotted at a table on the second-floor balcony, which offered a splendid view of the verdant lawns of Parliament Hill and a Wellington Street becalmed by stately elms.

But Frank was equally at ease over soup and a sandwich at Bowles Lunch, a few doors down Sparks from his office. The cafeteria-style serving area was in the middle of the room. Single seats with attached trays ran along the east and west walls. From his place he would absorb what the street was saying about local politics and global concerns, and certainly what diners offered up on his hockey team. The street would have had plenty to say about the Senators, and if the comments reverberating around the eatery amidst the clatter of dishes and cutlery could have been captured and condensed over the seven years form 1927 to 1934, they would come down to three words: decline, depression, and demise.

Decline, 1927–1929

EVEN AS A CONFUSING emotional mix of joy and dismay overtook the capital at the beginning of July 1927, hockey was not far from Frank Ahearn's thoughts. Celebrating the Diamond Jubilee of Confederation and the dedication of the new Peace Tower on Parliament Hill, crowds thrilled to the spectacle of Charles Lindbergh circling the downtown in his *Spirit of St. Louis*, fresh from a triumphant solo dash across the Atlantic. Landing at the Uplands airfield, one of his U.S. Air Corps escort planes crashed, killing the pilot, Thad Johnson. As word spread, a heavy gloom befell the city.

Ahearn himself was in a state of conflicting emotions. On the one hand he was buoyed by the challenge of an even greater role in his father's business affairs. Frank was already a director of the Ottawa Electric Railway, which was about to add twenty more double-truck, treadle type cars to its growing fleet. Now with Ahearn Sr. preoccupied with his recent appointment as head of the new Federal District Commission, Frank would be taking the lead on several other successful enterprises. On the other hand, his hockey business was not going at all well. Though Stanley Cup champions, the club had lost thousands on the past season's operations. Attendance had dipped to 80,000 — far less than half the numbers for big-city franchises in New York, Montreal, and Boston. Moreover, league governors were about to abolish the $35,000 salary cap and increase the waiver price from $2,500 to $5,000. Making a profit had become impossible for the Senators. The best Ahearn could hope for was to keep losses affordable. This might be made possible with a more generous gate-sharing formula. Ahearn had long argued that the 3½ per cent figure worked to the disadvantage of his club because the Senators drew far bigger crowds on the road than at home. Hockey fans in larger cities flocked to Senators games, filling the pockets of the owners. The Senators should, in fairness, be entitled to a bigger cut of those gates, he repeatedly told league president Frank Calder. He pointed to major-league baseball as the model to follow. Calder was unsympathetic and urged owners not to listen to Ahearn. He was of the view that gate-sharing would lead to complacency among weaker clubs, which would lose the incentive to improve their situations and instead rely on cash flowing from more successful operations. Just days after the abrupt termination of the Jubilee festivities, a clearly frustrated Frank Ahearn repeated his threat of two months earlier that he was going to step down as president of the Ottawa Hockey Association. It became increasingly evident in the weeks and months following, however, that the owner just could not let go of his executive position.

Ahearn returned to the gate-distribution issue in September, sending club director and legal counsel Redmond Quain to the league governors' meeting in Chicago. Quain presented the case for increasing the share to weaker clubs from 3½ per cent to up to 15 per cent, if that was necessary to meet a team's expenses. The governors provisionally agreed to only 10 per cent, subject to review by an ad hoc committee. Reporting at the December meeting, the committee rejected any increase at all. A disheartened Ahearn wrote to Calder to complain about the governors' intransigence but added, "I propose to keep plugging along and to trust that the league will recognize that they are not acting fairly after this season's operations are over."

Meanwhile plans were afoot to make going to Senators games a more attractive proposition. The Ottawa Hockey Association restored the lower ticket prices of two years earlier and offered an incentive to non-season-ticket holders. Those attending twelve or more games were advised to save their ticket stubs to qualify for the purchase of coveted playoff tickets, should the Senators enter post-season play. The Auditorium did its part, too, for the fans if not the bottom line. It put a fresh coat of paint on the seats, all bench-style, and increased their width from the seventeen inches introduced the previous year to the original twenty-two inches. Effectively, this reduced capacity by about 1,135 seats, but the reasoning behind the decision was that if all those more comfortable pews could be filled all the time, there would be a net increase in attendance by as much as 20,000. Further, reacting to the impression that a twenty-two home-game schedule was too great a burden for the average fan, the Senators transferred two games to the spacious new Olympia rink in Detroit.

Even with these progressive moves, local fans had good reason to be nervous about the future of their team: Ahearn's periodic announcements that he was stepping down; reported financial losses in the tens of thousands of dollars; rumours that the team was up for sale and that American investors were interested. Then came the unsettling news that Hooley Smith had been sold to the Montreal Maroons for a reported $22,500. Smith was a popular player, who had established himself with Ottawa supporters through his robust play and diligent defensive work. The only black mark on his record was the fight he had in the final game of the Stanley Cup series against Boston and the month-long suspension that followed. Punch Broadbent returned to Ottawa as part of the deal, for the $5,000 waiver fee, but the veteran was near the end of his career and would not be able to compensate for Smith's loss. The message was clear: the Ottawa Hockey Association was cash-strapped and desperately needed the record price received for Hooley. No sooner had that deal been done than Redmond Quain, on behalf of Ahearn, began fending off rumours that King Clancy would be the next to go.

To spark greater interest in the team, especially among French-speaking fans, management tried a long shot in the person of one Hozomer Godin. In hindsight, one might label him the French *disconnection*. For whatever reason, the Senators brain trust had never shown interest in recruiting from French-Canadian ranks. The fabulous Aurel Joliat, it will be recalled, was one who was allowed to escape local amateur rinks, only to become one of the game's greatest stars with Les Canadiens. This long-standing neglect was despite the urgings of board member Edgar Chevrier, an eclectic French-speaking lawyer who as a member of Parliament was fond of quoting Virgil in Latin. Chevrier thought there should be at least one representative of the segment of the city and area making up one third of the population.

Rockland, Ontario, a small, largely French-Canadian farming community forty kilometres east of Ottawa, was, at least in hockey sentiment, far closer to Montreal than to the Dominion Capital. It was there in the early 1920s that Hozomer Godin learned the game. Seeking employment, he moved to Ottawa as an eighteen-year-old and found a job at the Department of Public Works. He joined the departmental team in the civil-service league, which presented a decent brand of hockey a notch below that of the Ottawa City League, a senior loop. Of compact build, he had powerful legs, big hands, and broad shoulders. He could skate like the wind and had a hard, accurate shot. With these attributes, it was no surprise he dominated the league and was voted its most valuable player. At the same time, he played on the Frontenac team of the Hull league, where he enjoyed similar success and increasing attention.

Tipped off by former Senator coach Pete Green, manager Dave Gill took a look for himself and liked what he saw. Though lacking the tutoring expected of a player being considered for the pro game, thought Gill, Godin did have the raw talent and hustle required of the big time. Added to that, management was finally heeding Chevrier's advice and was on a quest for a French-Canadian star. With a so-so record of eight wins, seven losses and four ties in mid-January 1928, the Senators signed the prospect amidst a fanfare unprecedented for a player plucked from the second-tier of amateur hockey. The extra attention resulted, in part, from the Senators' publicity machine, which produced lengthy background copy, duly reported by the three local dailies. The *Journal* went further, turning Godin into a quaint habitant character, sure to become the object of public adoration. "Chee Pee," as the paper said he was familiarly known (to *Le Droit* he was "Ti-Bi") "is a fine personality of 20 years of age, and while he speaks in broken English he understands it perfectly." "I have always had ambition to be good hockey player," the *Journal* had him saying. "Right now me I am green, but I can skate like de wind if nuthing else." We may never know Frank Ahearn's reaction, but Edgar Chevrier must surely have winced at the *Journal's* next attempt to endear poor Godin to readers. Over the name Joe Latour, the doggerel began:

> It' H'Ottawa hooraw wit'me
> Since de big club sign up "Chee Pee."
> For long I do not wrote to you
> But mus' wrote now, and den I'm
>   throo.
> Dat's smartest boy, our Hozomer,
> And when he's play Rockland be
>   dere
> De Frontenac and Hull, Eastview
> And all Lower Town to help him
>   throo.
> Of all our boy he is de bes
> More better yet than Lajeunesse
> For sure dat boy can skate like
>   breeze
> More faster yet than Hurtubise.

Were the denizens of Hull, Eastview, and Lowertown, along with the broader community, impressed? Ahearn and company were about to find out. Following limited action against the Americans at Madison Square Garden, Godin was slated for his home debut against the Chicago Black Hawks. This would be a true test of the success of the Godin publicity because the Hawks, with a dismal record of four wins and eighteen losses, were not themselves a draw. If a bigger crowd than usual were to show up,

Senators goaltender Alex Connell, dubbed 'The Little Fireman,' set an NHL record with six consecutive shutouts in 1928.
MCAULEY COLLECTION

it could only be because of the "Rockland Rocket." Public Works employees would surely be there in large numbers. After all, the department's superintendent would be presenting Chee Pee with a gold watch. Alas, fewer than 2,000 souls occupied the Auditorium's recently widened seats. It was the smallest crowd of the season. Godin saw no action until the third period, when he came close to scoring on three occasions as the Senators won the game 9-6. Unfortunately for Senators management and Godin himself, things did not work out. He played in twenty remaining games, seeing little ice time, and did not figure in the scoring. He started the next season in the minors, was called up for the final twenty-four games, and then disappeared from the local hockey scene.

Perhaps Hozomer Godin would never have looked at it that way, but he was in some measure a part of hockey history, for it was only in his eighth game with the Ottawa Senators that his goaltending teammate Alex Connell began a remarkable streak of six consecutive games without allowing a goal, a feat never before or since equalled. It began on January 31 at the Auditorium when the Senators met the Toronto Maple Leafs. Ottawa had been playing mediocre hockey to that point in the season, but on this night they were impressive, raining in forty-nine shots on John Ross Roach and scoring four times while holding the Leafs to twenty-four shots, most of them from far out thanks to the stone wall thrown up by George Boucher and Frank Clancy. Two nights later, again on home ice, the Senators held off the Montreal Maroons with an overtime 1-0 victory. "It was a good win," commented Frank Ahearn as he left the rink with his father, a devoted Senators fan.

Connell and his teammates were then off to New York for an engagement with the Rangers at Madison Square Garden. Clancy was a favourite with Garden fans and did not disappoint the 10,000 on hand. "The brilliant Ottawa defense man," reported the *New York Times*, "drew wild plaudits from the crowd in the early minutes with some superb runs." It was a telling observation because, fan-pleasing though they were, these solo dashes were fruitless. The Senators had withdrawn into a defensive style of play and were showing little interest in any sort of coordinated attack. The burden was therefore on Connell and he came through, making several of his customary sprawling saves, only to be matched at the other end of the rink by the rangy Lorne Chabot. The game ended in a scoreless overtime draw. Back in Ottawa, the two teams went at it again, with the same result. And again, Connell drew gasps, diving to snare loose pucks, including one that glanced off the post on a surprise backhander from a frustrated Bill Cook.

Fans complained that games were becoming boring. They wanted more goals. In Ottawa, Clem Beauchamp, a House of Commons translator who was later known for his contributions to the annual National Hockey League guidebook, was one. With the diving, sprawling, puck-smothering antics of Alex Connell fixed in his mind, he thought the league should return to the former rule prohibiting goalkeepers from falling to the ice to make saves — a style cultivated years earlier by former Senators goalkeeper Clint Benedict. But it worked for Connell and he wasn't about to abandon it.

And so it continued. After a layoff of six days, during which Connell spent much of the time in bed with the flu (while also waiting out a broken finger), the Senators met the Pittsburgh Pirates at the Auditorium. Perhaps Clem Beauchamp had a point, for a mere 3,000 fans witnessed yet another scoreless draw — the third in a row and Connell's fifth consecutive shutout. The Senators' next contest, again at home, was against the league-leading Canadiens. It didn't matter whether any pucks at all would go in the net, hundreds of Habitants supporters from neighbouring Hull were determined to be on hand, thus ensuring a jam-packed house. Halfway through the third period in a scoreless game, Frank Finnigan started a rush and passed to Hec Kilrea, who dished the puck off to Len Grosvenor. The rookie from the city league's Rideaus moved in and beat George Hainsworth cleanly for his first professional goal. There was no further scoring and Connell had his sixth, stopping seven shots in each period.

In those six games the Senators won three and tied three, while scoring a paltry six goals. Yet that performance gave them nine points out of a possible twelve in the league standings. Most chroniclers view those six games in isolation, but that record should properly be looked at from a broader perspective. Preceding the Connell streak, the Senators had won three in a row (one by a shutout), and following it they won the next three (two by shutouts). In other words, Connell had recorded nine shutouts in twelve games and the Senators had won eight and tied four, giving them twenty out of a possible twenty-four league points. Had it not been for that February spurt, the Senators would not have made the playoffs, for they immediately reverted to early-season form and finished the schedule in third place with twenty wins, ten fewer than in the previous year. Maroons won both games of the playoff round and the Senators were finished for the season.

It was a discouraging, even humiliating, time for Frank Ahearn. The season's attendance had risen by nearly 20,000, thanks in part to the two home games transferred to the huge new Olympia in Detroit, but these gains were offset by lower ticket prices at the Auditorium. Net revenue for the season came to only $92,000, compared, for example, to Detroit's $211,000. In a letter to NHL president Frank Calder, Ahearn explained that the Senators were not able to pay the $2,000 league assessment and asked that the money be taken from the club's equity account. "If we had got better support here we would have been in a position to send you a cheque," he wrote.

Shortly after that contrite letter, and in the midst of his worries about the future of the Senators, Ahearn would have paused to reflect on times past for the hockey club. The nostalgia lay in the smoldering ruins of the Russell House hotel, a block east of his offices. On a Saturday night in the early spring of 1928, flames lit up the sky for miles around as fire gutted the grand old structure. The acrid stench from the blackened rubble lingered for days. Mackenzie King's government had expropriated the hotel, and for two and a half years it had sat in desuetude, only a few street-level shops remaining open as it awaited demolition. For years, in the bar off the lobby, in the candlelit café, and in the elegantly panelled dining room, the Russell had been the gathering place of the powerful, the wealthy, and the famous, before the society set gravitated to the modern and even more luxurious Château Laurier. In hockey terms, the Russell was to Ottawa what the Windsor Hotel was to Montreal — a natural haunt for owners, visiting teams, newspaper reporters, and sporting gamblers. It was where Lord Stanley's aide announced the governor general's intention to donate a trophy for the champion team of the Dominion; where Chauncey Kirby stood on a table responding to a banquet toast in honour of his Ontario champion Ottawas; where, in its busy rotunda, Dawson City Klondikers sponsor Joe Boyle met and cajoled cabinet ministers on his frequent trips to the capital; where Ottawa Hockey Club president Bob Shillington shook players' hands one final time before pulling up stakes and heading north to seek his fortune in silver-mining country. Another remnant of bygone glory days had, only a year earlier, met its fate when short yards away on Laurier Avenue the wrecking ball levelled the Senators' former home, Dey's Arena. The arena and the Russell were making way for the federal government's downtown beautification plan, under the supervision of Ahearn Sr.

Times were indeed changing, and Frank Ahearn must surely have pondered what future was in store for his Senators as the costs of pro hockey escalated beyond the capacity of his home town to bear. Ahearn wanted to sell the team, but this did not necessarily mean he was giving up on Ottawa as its home. That was because of his sense of responsibility to the many investors he had persuaded to back the Auditorium when it was no more than a vision in his mind's eye. Without a big-league hockey team as its main tenant, the Auditorium would be in a precarious position. Frank and his father were the major shareholders, but there were about 160 smaller investors who were patiently looking for returns. Ahearn, therefore, was prepared to sell the team and franchise for well below market value so long as the buyers, preferably local, were prepared to keep the club in Ottawa. His price was $125,000 under that condition; otherwise he would be forced to consider offers of $250,000 and more from sports entrepreneurs in Philadelphia, Boston, and Chicago seeking teams to fill existing or proposed new arenas in those cities.

Meanwhile, the Ottawa Hockey Association (the Senators' corporate name) had no choice but to gamely plug away at putting a team on the ice while struggling to keep costs under control. Cy Denneny, at age thirty-seven, had come to the end of the line after twelve years as a Senator, and the club graciously eased his departure to Boston, where he had been offered the position of playing coach. To replace him, manager Dave Gill purchased an industrious younger forward, Bill Touhey, from the Maroons for the relatively modest sum of $5,000. City league vice-president Raoul Mercier, it was well known, dearly wanted the Senators to sign up some French-Canadian players; but aside from the brief return of Hozomer Godin, nothing was done to accommodate the Lowertown fan base.

The Senators again transferred two home games to Detroit, but also relocated a third when Ahearn agreed to a request from the former American ambassador to Berlin to play a "home" game at Madison Square Garden in support of the Westside Neighbourhood Club, a social-service agency specializing in boys' work. The crowds at these games were better than at home, and with the team performing poorly (only five wins by the midpoint in the season), management tensions were evident.

The play of defenceman Milt Halliday had become an issue between manager Gill and Ahearn early in the season. Halliday was a member of the Senators' Stanley Cup team of 1927, but in 1928 spent most of his time in the minors. Gill had faith in the "Blonde Flash," seeing him as a useful substitute, but Ahearn thought otherwise and wanted to send him to the club's minor-league affiliate in London, where the famous Newsy Lalonde was coach. Here was a classic case of the owner involving himself in day-to-day affairs that ought to be the purview of the hired manager. In this case, perhaps Ahearn's interference was understandable, given anxieties in the boardroom over the team's struggle just to survive, let alone win. But, as was usually the case, Ahearn's will prevailed and immediately after Christmas celebrations Halliday got word to pack his bags for the minors.

The Senators were playing poorly and drawing poorly. The small crowds at pro games, however, did not mean Ottawans had lost interest in hockey. The senior amateur game was generating plenty of interest, and, as it turned out, notoriety. Following a city league game, promising Shamrocks player Harold Starr became entangled in a brawl at the Cavendish Café, a popular Chinese restaurant. Attempting to break up the fight, he was attacked by a waiter wielding a red-hot poker. Senior hockey had achieved such a high local profile that at Harry Woo's trial, sports fans packed the courtroom to hear Harold Starr's testimony, while hundreds more gathered outside. Ottawa Hockey Association management could not help but ruefully note the swelling interest in city-level teams. In fact, over the last half of the 1928–29 season, the amateur fare (usually twin bills) was outdrawing the Senators by two to one, culminating in playoff attendance of 31,000 for four games over an eight-day period.

In mid-January Frank Ahearn publicly admitted that he was going to have to move the franchise or sell it. The Senators had printed notices in four successive game programs warning that support would have to improve. Attendance at the following four home dates was even worse. It was a sign, he said, "to get out." The Senators' popularity was not helped weeks later when Ahearn announced that the club had traded George Boucher to the Maroons for Joe Lamb. Lamb was a good player who would help the floundering team, but Boucher was an icon — in his fourteenth season with the Senators. King Clancy, his defence partner, openly wept in the dressing room when Boucher said his goodbyes.

Three days after Ottawans had been jarred by the Boucher news, Major Fred Burpee, president of the Auditorium Company Limited, stood before a Rotary Club luncheon at the Château Laurier to announce that the Auditorium was buying the Senators. He told the assembly, augmented on this auspicious occasion by members of the famous old Silver Seven team, that the Senators would remain in Ottawa for at least another year. Not the most reassuring statement, but better than that the team would be moving at season's end. Punctuating the warning implicit in Burpee's choice of words, head-table guest Frank Calder rose. "The team cannot live on tradition and sentiment. In the last analysis it depends on the people of Ottawa whether the team remains or not."

In a meeting with shareholders at the Ottawa Electric Building to approve the purchase, Burpee explained the plan. The $125,000 price would be raised by the sale of 5,000 shares of preferred Auditorium stock at a par value of $25 each. In taking over the team, the Auditorium would have three options: operate the franchise in Ottawa, operate it in a large American city, or sell the asset to the highest bidder. He estimated that the club could be sold for $300,000 and that those funds would cover the Auditorium's $290,000 bond issue, thus ensuring the arena's success even without a big-time team. But he advised investors: "I feel sure you will agree with me that ... every effort should be made to operate it in Ottawa before considering the other alternatives." Shareholders did agree and the sale of stock commenced. While the takeover details were being ironed out, the object of the purchase was concluding a hapless season. In the five-team Canadian division the Senators finished fourth and out of the playoffs with only fourteen wins — six fewer than the previous season and sixteen behind their 1927 Stanley Cup year. Frank Finnigan and Hec Kilrea were the team's leading scorers, with twenty and nineteen goals respectively.

Depression, 1929–1931

AS EARLY AS DECEMBER 1928, there were signs of a looming economic downturn. Stock prices suffered a collapse on the New York Stock Exchange. Investors were becoming nervous. In Ottawa, Auditorium president Fred Burpee admitted he was having trouble selling the required number of preferred shares in Auditorium stock to complete the purchase of the hockey team. Finally, after getting a deadline extension from Ahearn, the acquisition proceeded.

At its usual meeting place in room 614 of the Ottawa Electric Building, Ottawa Hockey Association directors instructed the secretary-treasurer on September 9, 1929 "to see that the Stock Certificates of the Association were placed in the name the Auditorium Limited or its nominies [sic] pursuant to the Ahearn-Auditorium agreement." Meeting minutes record Burpee's announcement that the new owners had appointed a fresh slate of directors, himself one of them. Another was well-known sportsman and Civil Service Commission secretary William Foran, who also happened to be a Stanley Cup trustee. The meeting dutifully elected Foran president of the Ottawa Hockey Association. Observed an *Ottawa Citizen* editorial on the acquisition: "It was no easy task; but it has been successfully accomplished. For this action, the Auditorium directors deserve high praise." The *Ottawa Journal* portrayed Ahearn's divestment of the team as a clean break. "President Frank Ahearn turned over his interests to the new body and will devote his time to private interests. His retirement from hockey is being widely regretted."

During his tenure Ahearn had maintained a steady correspondence with league president Frank Calder on Senators affairs — a line of communication that would continue over the next few years, whether or not Ahearn had any formal relationship with the team. In his doctoral dissertation *The Development of Professional Hockey and the Making of the National Hockey League*, John Chi-Kit Wong cites sixteen letters between 1928 and 1933. There may have been more. Four of these were during the two-year presidency of William Foran, when Ahearn was not formally associated with the team; and four were written over the next two years after Redmond Quain succeeded Foran and Ahearn had returned as a director. Throughout this period Ahearn still had standing as a director of the parent company,

Auditorium Ltd., but even so, it was Fred Burpee, not Frank Ahearn, who was Auditorium president. Ahearn's letters on the financial affairs of the team and musings about moving to another city made it sound as if he personally still owned the franchise. In short, Ahearn was exerting his considerable leverage as a major shareholder in the Auditorium and as a dominant business figure to influence the direction of the hockey team. He was calling the shots. He had not retired from hockey.

Perhaps it could be chalked up to his love of the game and the enjoyment he derived from being around the team, but Ahearn could not let go, even to the extent of involving himself with individual player contracts. Within two months of his supposed departure and Foran's succession to the club's presidency, Foran advised the board that at the former owner's request, the Senators had claimed Harry Connor on waivers from the New York Americans. Connor was a fringe player, but Ahearn had apparently taken a liking to the Ottawa boy, who had previously played in the city league. So much so that Ahearn was paying the waiver price, which also made Connor his property and not the Senators'. Even if the club might subsequently wish to trade him, they would not be able to do so without Ahearn's consent.

At the same time, the Ottawa Hockey Association board was wrestling with the Frank Nighbor contract. The fourteen-year Senators veteran was holding out and had sent word from Pembroke, where he was in the insurance business, that he would not play for less than his previous year's salary. The Senators, in fact, had been trying to trade him because they judged his play to be on the wane. Their offer was $5,000 and they were holding firm. That is until Ahearn, a longtime admirer of the "Pembroke Peach," took an interest. He "volunteered" to mediate, with the result that the chairman of the players' committee, J. Ambrose O'Brien, reported to the board that Nighbor had accepted an offer of $7,000 and would be arriving that day to sign. Manager Dave Gill's reservations about Nighbor's usefulness proved correct. Relegated to a substitute centre's role behind Joe Lamb, Nighbor suited up for only nineteen games and saw little action before being traded to Toronto

Nudgings from Ahearn were not needed in the signing of Syd Howe, since the Senators prized the eighteen-year-old, who was an all-round athlete at Glebe Collegiate and a star with the Rideaus hockey team. Nevertheless, because of the former owner's ubiquitous presence, the contract cost the team a little more than anticipated. Management had decided

An all-round athlete in his high-school days at Ottawa's Glebe Collegiate, Syd Howe garnered a $450 contract with the Senators in 1929.
MCAULEY COLLECTION

to offer him $300 for the year but felt obliged to up the ante when Howe produced a letter that Ahearn had given him while still owner, promising $450.

Howe was a popular mid-season addition to the team, but fans became unhappy when new coach Newsy Lalonde gave him no ice time, even though he was in uniform. The Senators had sought a clarification from the league on the waiver status of rookies. Their understanding was that so long as a first-year player had not seen active action, he could be sent to the minor leagues without being subject to a claim on waivers by another team. If he had been put on the ice in Ottawa before being sent down, concluded management, he would have to be recalled by a February 15 deadline to avoid the very real threat of being grabbed by another team. Howe did go to London but was hastily returned when the league finally advised management that a player only had to be in the lineup and not necessarily on the ice to be eligible for a waiver claim. Howe scored his first National Hockey League goal in the last game of the season, and so began a brilliant fifteen-year career in the premier league.

Finishing in third place, the Senators fell to the New York Rangers in a two-game, total-goals playoff series. Attendance in the 1929–30 season had improved, as had revenues, but even with these positive signs, secretary-treasurer Clare Brunton advised the board in May that the operating loss was going to be about $25,000, adding, in what one can only imagine as a plaintive tone of voice, that the final amount depended on the salaries to be paid to the manager and himself. (Brunton and Gill withdrew from the meeting while the directors considered the question before passing the buck to the Auditorium board.)

By mid-1930 the worldwide economic spiral had become a full-blown depression. Excess capacity in factories and on farms, coupled with declining international trade, was hurting Canada badly, especially in the West where the bottom had dropped out of the wheat market and drought was robbing the land of its fertility. In Ontario and Quebec unemployment was rising rapidly, though a more diversified industrial base kept many men on the job. Ottawa, being the centre of government, was more fortunate than most cities and towns. Employment in the civil service remained steady, which in turn had a beneficial effect on local shops and services. In fact, in 1930 government employment actually rose locally from 6,933 permanent jobs the previous year to 7,658; and even though average salaries dropped by two dollars to $161 per month, the overall monthly government payroll for permanent and temporary civil-service employees increased from $1,515,000 to $1,587,000. Moreover, because the cost of living was declining faster than salaries, conditions became marginally better for those with secure jobs. Nevertheless, even in Ottawa joblessness had become a serious problem. Firms, and even homeowners looking for casual labour to do repair work, were invited to fill out newspaper coupons stating the nature of the work they were offering, its duration and pay, and submit these for follow-up by the Employment Service. The Ottawa Electric Railway, too, was feeling the pinch. The Ahearn streetcars were carrying fewer passengers, the city would not allow a fare increase, shareholders were going without dividends, and the company's ability to meet bond obligations was uncertain.

Likewise the depressed state of affairs was having its effects on the mood of the local sporting scene as investors showed little enthusiasm for propping up a wobbly professional hockey franchise. The sale of Auditorium stock to cover the cost of the Senators purchase was not going as quickly as hoped — only $50,000 of the $125,000 issue having been subscribed to — but since fewer than sixty prospects had been approached, Auditorium directors remained optimistic. Until such time as Ahearn received his final payment, however, he would have control of the disposal of player contracts, a point he made clear in a letter to Frank Calder, cited in the Wong thesis.

When Frank Ahearn announced his so-called retirement from hockey to pursue "private interests," perhaps he had given no thought whatsoever to actually embarking on an even more public life than he had experienced as a high-profile hockey club owner. But when Prime Minister Mackenzie King called a general election for the summer of 1930, Ahearn entered the race as a Liberal candidate for one of two Ottawa seats in the House of Commons. His running mate, Ottawa Hockey Association director Edgar Chevrier, was the incumbent of the other. At an Auditorium rally, Ahearn introduced King, telling the vast assembly that following the Senators' 1927 Stanley Cup victory the prime minister was one of the first to offer his congratulations. Both Ahearn and Chevrier were elected, but the King government fell to R.B. Bennett's Conservatives, who convinced the public that they were the ones to deal with the Depression. Within months Bennett brought in unemployment-relief legislation, which provided for the appropriation of up to $20 million for public-works construction projects.

Civil servants could still afford to go to hockey games, but would they, given uncertainties about job security? Many others who had bought tickets in the past could no longer do so because they were out of work. And Auditorium directors, who had been counting on the affluent business community to buy shares in the company, came to realize that their earlier optimism had been misplaced. The Senators were broke and hard decisions were required on the future of the team, in Ottawa or elsewhere. Basically, these decisions fell into two areas: solvency and putting a competitive team on the ice. When Auditorium took over the Ottawa Hockey Association, it had in mind delegating full responsibility for operating the team to the separate board of directors it had appointed in 1929.

Under the chairmanship of Ottawa Hockey Association president William Foran, the new board had started out enthusiastically, scheduling weekly meetings and setting up a players' committee and a gates-and-tickets committee. But the board was hamstrung. It had no money and had to rely on the parent Auditorium to fund a new season. Under the circumstances, the Auditorium retained a strong interest in the running of the team. The dominance of the parent company was soon reflected in the reduced frequency of Ottawa Hockey Association meetings. By the beginning of 1930 these had become irregular and infrequent, at the call of the chair. Through the summer and autumn of 1930, OHA directors held no meetings at all in preparation for the new season. In fact, following its meeting of May 7, the board would not gather again for sixteen months. Why should it if the real authority rested with Auditorium directors? Such was the dynamic as the 1930–31 hockey season approached — a critical period in the team's history.

There had been rumours that King Clancy was up for sale. The Montreal Maroons, newspapers reported, had made an offer. So had the Rangers. Foran, sounding out of the loop (and certainly circumspect given Clancy's popularity), said he had not heard of any negotiations. Auditorium president Fred Burpee issued denials. Then in early October, Toronto Maple Leafs manager and part owner Conn Smythe paid a visit to Ottawa. Toronto directors had agreed with Smythe that the club needed strengthening and that Clancy would be the way to do it. They authorized $25,000 for his purchase; but to land him, more than that would be needed. It so happened that Smythe, an inveterate gambler, had recently won more than $10,000 at the Woodbine racetrack when a long-shot horse he owned came in first. Foran and Burpee had no choice but to hear what Smythe had to say, but they were in a dilemma. To operate successfully the Senators would have to draw fans, and Clancy was the franchise player. On the other hand, without a supply of immediate cash, there could be no season. They opened negotiations with Smythe and gave him a one-week option on Clancy. Within two days the two sides came to terms in the biggest money transaction professional hockey had ever witnessed. Clancy went to Toronto for $35,000 and two journeymen, left-winger Eric Pettinger and defenceman Art Smith. In a farewell scene that was becoming all too familiar, Clancy, after nine years as a Senator, made his way around the dressing room after the club's first practice at the Auditorium to shake hands with his former teammates. In a gesture of thoughtfulness typical of the man, Clancy, as he was leaving the room, turned to trainer Eddie Gleason and presented him with a fountain pen in appreciation of his personal attentiveness over the years.

With no Clancy, the nineteen home games would be a hard sell. (Two "home" games were being transferred to Detroit and one to New York.) The scale — $0.75, $1.00, $1.35, $1.75, $2.20 — was already the lowest in the league, but the Senators were offering a further inducement of a 15 per cent discount to season-ticket holders paying cash in advance. Thus a pair of discounted, mid-price season tickets would cost $43.60, the equivalent of one month's supply of food for a family of five, or one and a half month's rent for a six-room house with modern conveniences. For some this outlay would pose no problem, but Ottawa was no New York, where there were sixty such prospective ticket buyers for every one in the northern capital. And no sooner had the public come to terms with Clancy's departure than the Senators sold three more popular players (all three born and raised locally) to Philadelphia for another $35,000 — Allan Shields, Wally Kilrea, and Syd Howe. Especially hard to take for Ottawa supporters was the loss of Howe, the youngest of the three at nineteen years of age. He was the team's future, if, fans began to worry, the Senators did indeed have one.

With barely one month gone in the season, another crack in the team's foundation appeared. After a loss to the Maroons in Montreal, Foran announced that on the recommendation of the club physician, coach Newsy Lalonde was taking a leave of absence for an indefinite period. Foran did not say why. The team's record of four wins, five losses, and a tie was not that good; but under the circumstances imposed on him, it was not that bad, either. Lalonde had been highly regarded by management, who had valued his previous role in preparing younger players for the big time while coaching the Senators' minor-league affiliate in London. Nevertheless manager Dave Gill would now do double duty by going behind the bench. Auditorium secretary Clare Brunton insisted to *Le Droit* that the popular Lalonde had not been let go, but within weeks his outright release was confirmed. No reasons were given to the public. As a matter of economics, however, the Senators had been cutting back on their playing roster (only twelve men in uniform for most games, while opponents were dressing up to fifteen). The departure of the coach left the distinct impression that Lalonde was just another casualty of payroll reductions. The Senators lost their next eight games.

At the end of December a desperate Burpee wrote to Calder, advising him that the Auditorium was putting the club up for sale. The price was $200,000. A new owner would have to enter a ten-year rental agreement with the Auditorium and play at least 25 per cent of the team's home games there. Additionally the buyer would have to pay the Auditorium $1,200 for every "home" game played elsewhere. The Auditorium was "at the end of the rope," confided Frank Ahearn to Calder in another of his letters.

No $200,000 bid materialized, but Auditorium director and legal adviser Redmond Quain let it be known that local offers, presumably for a lesser amount, would be considered. Expressions of interest came in, one, it was rumoured, from former Silver Sevens star Harvey Pulford, another from

Tommy Gorman in Mexico, where he was managing the Aqua Caliente Jockey Club. Neither followed through, but an unnamed local consortium approached the club with a takeover proposal of $100,000. This was not enough for Quain, who thought he could get more by selling players individually; and negotiations ended when the consortium made it clear it was not interested in absorbing the club's debt. Meanwhile NHL governors continued to turn their backs on Ottawa's pleas for league assistance.

Another possibility ended with an ironic twist. Of all the owners, the Black Hawks' Major Fred McLaughlin had consistently been the most supportive of having the league lend assistance to financially weak teams. To be assured of a successful alliance, he reasoned, the owners should look after one another in times of need. He had, for instance, supported the Senators' requests for a richer gate-sharing formula, in spite of Calder's advice to the contrary. A consortium of local investors, including James Norris, a wealthy grain broker of Canadian origin, had just completed building the cavernous Chicago Stadium, where McLaughlin's Black Hawks had taken up residence. The group wanted a second NHL franchise to ensure the arena's viability. They were ready to buy the Senators for $300,000 and move the team to Chicago. But McLaughlin's co-operative spirit had its limits when his own interests were at stake. As the exclusive NHL franchise holder for the city, he refused to allow a competing team in his territory; so the Senators' financial plight continued.

On the ice, the players were having as rough a time as the men in suits. In the midst of another winless skein (six-straight losses this time), the Senators met a strong Leafs team in the Auditorium at the end of January. Foster Hewitt had come to Ottawa to broadcast the game back to Toronto, and, in a rare hookup, the game was also being aired locally over radio station CNRO. Ahead 2-0 at the start of the third period, the Senators blew their chance to end the skid when the Leafs scored three unanswered goals. Fans were furious, targeting coach Gill for the poor performance; but Foran absolved him, choosing instead to publicly blame the players for not following the coach's instructions.

Tensions were rising and the Senators' organization was unravelling. The team finished the 1931 season in last place with ten wins in a forty-four-game schedule and a deficit of $70,000. Foran had had enough. Clearly the Auditorium board, which directly represented the owners of the franchise, was in control and intent on running the team. As far as Foran was concerned, the Ottawa Hockey Association board and his role as president had proved redundant. Besides that, it had become painfully obvious to him that the Senators' days were numbered. Either McLaughlin would relent and clear the way for the Senators' sale to the Norris group, or the team would cease to operate. In either event he would have no say. Why be the figurehead for a ghost organization? Foran handed in his resignation.

The public, of course, was in the dark about the details of the Senators' deteriorating state, but hockey fans had reason to believe that something was up because through the summer months newspapers noted the presence in town of Calder on several occasions, as well as a visit by Col. John Hammond of the Madison Square Garden Corporation. Hammond in Ottawa in August? A few days later Conn Smythe arrived, but he was a familiar figure in the capital anyway, always looking for players. Nearing the end of September there was widespread conjecture that the Senators were finished. The NHL governors were meeting in Montreal and there likely would be an important announcement. Even though half-expected, the news stunned the city. Two troubled franchises, Philadelphia and Ottawa, were suspending operations for the 1931–32 season. "We might as well resign ourselves, then, to disappearing from the big league hockey map," a rueful *Ottawa Citizen* editorial said.

There were two aspects to the Senators' suspension: player relocation and financial considerations. The governors placed all the players from both clubs in a pool and conducted a dispersal draft to remaining clubs in reverse order of their finish in the standings. The two bottom teams (the Americans in the Canadian division and Detroit in the American division) were each given two initial selections. The following Senator players were selected:

Alex Connell	Detroit Falcons
Frank Finnigan	Toronto Maple Leafs
Len Grosvenor	New York Americans
Hec Kilrea	Detroit Falcons
Joe Lamb	New York Americans
Alex Smith	Detroit Falcons
Harold Starr	Montreal Maroons
Bill Touhey	Boston Bruins

At the October 26, 1931, meeting of a resuscitated Ottawa Hockey Association board, Redmond Quain read out the financial details to directors.

In consideration of the sum of $25,000 to be paid to us by the League, we agreed to lease all or players to the League for the playing season 1931–32, it was further agreed that,in the event of the Ottawa Hockey Club not being transferred en block by July 1st 1932, and again asking for suspension of playing operations, the NHL shall have the option of again leasing the players for the playing season 1932–33 for a consideration of $15,000 and similarly for the playing season 1933–34 for a consideration of $5,000. The National Hockey League agreed to endorse notes to the amount of $28,000 now endorsed by T.F. Ahearn M.P. and gave the Ottawa Hockey Association the privilege of selling players to realize an amount sufficient to liquidate said notes. In the event of these notes not being paid by July 1st 1932, the NHL may, if they see fit, sell a player or players in order to retire the notes which they have endorsed. The Ottawa Hockey Association will have the right, providing the notes endorsed by the NHL are paid off, of resuming operations in the NHL for the season of 1932–33 and thereafter. It is understood that the Ottawa Hockey Association retains its membership in the NHL with full rights and privileges.

Resolved and carried unanimously that the agreement as set out as above is ratified by the board.

The extract makes clear the depth of Ahearn's financial involvement with the hockey team, quite apart from his equity position in Auditorium Ltd. It is little wonder, then, that while staying a respectful distance at another hotel as the governors' meeting was going on in Montreal, Ahearn remained in constant communication with Quain during his negotiations with the other owners.

The Ottawa Hockey Association board meeting at which the financial details were discussed also ratified the board's new structure. Not only was it leaner under its new chairman, Quain (down to four from the nine under Foran), but all directors were also Auditorium directors. One of these was Ahearn, back in a formal decision-making capacity after a two-year hiatus (as if his absence, *officially*, had made any difference whatsoever). While having a separate corporate status it was, in effect, now a committee of the Auditorium board — a committee with nothing to do, at least for the forthcoming season. Starved hockey fans would be following the exploits of the erstwhile red, white, and black colour-bearers in the local press as they plied their trade for enemy teams, but it just wasn't going to be the same.

Demise, 1931–1934

IN SUSPENDING OPERATIONS Ahearn and his group were buying time. If the clouds of the Depression were soon to part; if the other owners would finally agree on a revenue-sharing formula to accommodate small-market clubs; and if they would also resolve to rein in operating expenses — then the Senators just might be able to return and make a go of it. But this scenario did not look promising and Ahearn was prepared to continue his search for a new home, preferably in Canada. "Damned if I want to see the team go across the border," he wrote in another of his letters to Calder, as recorded in the Wong thesis. Knowing that Conn Smythe, owner of the spanking-new Maple Leaf Gardens in Toronto, was looking for a second tenant for his rink, Ahearn approached him; but Smythe's terms were too stiff — a $100,000 guarantee for the season. Part of Ahearn's plan would have seen Smythe, Canadiens co-owner Joe Cattarinich, and Maroons president James Strachan buying half ownership of the Senators, with the Auditorium retaining the other half. "It would be a good gamble and would stop the menace of American control," he remarked in a letter to Calder.

Meanwhile Frank Finnigan was doing very well at Maple Leaf Gardens and at the Royal York Hotel, where he stayed during his leased season with the Leafs. He was a hockey celebrity, whose company was sought by the wealthy and influential. Years later Joan Finnigan captured the glamour in a poetic ode to her father:

and I remember the millionaires who courted him
whose money had not brought them youth
and the golden skates of fame;
one of them especially used to invite him
into his suite at the Royal York for an oyster feed,
then ordered up by phone,
crustaceans, wine, stove, pans, chef and all.

Reunited with his old Senators teammate King Clancy, Finnigan was in uniform for the grand opening of the Gardens, and throughout the 1931–32 season played a strong supportive role on a line backing up the future Hall of Fame trio of Harvey Jackson, Joe Primeau, and Charlie Conacher. Energized by the huge crowds that made the Gardens an immediate financial success, the Leafs defeated the Chicago Black Hawks and the New York Rangers in two playoff rounds to win the Stanley Cup for the first time in ten years. Still uncertain about whether he would be able to reassemble his scattered team for the next season, Ahearn would have noted with pleasure the steady performance of one of his favourite players. Finnigan, after all, was a business asset as well as a friend.

Crunch time for Ahearn and the Ottawa Hockey Association loomed at the end of June. The club was stuck with a Bank of Montreal loan of $28,000, which it could not pay and was due on July 1. By the club's agreement with the NHL for the suspended season, the league had relieved Ahearn of his original endorsement of the note. If the club were unable to pay off the loan, the league would have the right to sell the Senators players' contracts in order to satisfy the bank. Desperate to hold onto those assets the club tried to renew the loan, pledging the contracts as collateral, but the bank would have none of it. On behalf of the Ottawa Hockey Association Ahearn appealed to his father, who, accepting the contracts as security, anted up the necessary funds. Coming as it did in a time of economic depression when one of Ahearn Sr.'s main enterprises, the Ottawa Electric Railway, was struggling to meet its own bond obligations, the loan represented a remarkable faith in, and loyalty to, his son and business successor.

As autumn approached, the Senators' status remained unclear and a new season was soon to begin. The public was left to wonder whether the team would sit out another year, would re-enter, or be sold and moved to another city. In mid-September Tommy Gorman was back in the city with the announcement that he was buying the team. All that was needed was the approval of the league, which, he indicated, was a foregone conclusion because all the governors were in favour of the deal. He promised a shake-up on the ice and in the boardroom. "Control will remain in my hands," he told the press, "but the president and board of directors will be consulted at all times and in all matters pertaining to the club and the team." Notwithstanding these brave pronouncements, Gorman did what he had done in 1924 and backed out. Clauses having to do with the right to sell or relocate the team at some future date were, evidently, unacceptable to his financial backers.

At this point, having the agreement of the players to accept reduced salaries, the Auditorium decided it would, after all, operate the team for at least one more year. It would do so through a restructured Ottawa Hockey Association board, with Ahearn replacing Quain as president. Its first act was to thank Dave Gill for his services as manager and to hire Cy Denneny in the dual capacity of manager and coach. It was a popular choice, for Denneny had been a fan favourite over his twelve prolific goal-scoring years with the Senators before going to Boston for one final season in 1928. He explained his system, saying it was based on the one employed when Nighbor was at his peak. "We always concentrated on chasing the opposing puck carrier into the middle on a rush. Our chief aim on the wings was to never allow the puck carrier to get between us and the boards. If he succeeded in getting through he was always dangerous, but it was our job to prevent this and it worked out well."

Evocations of past glory from a coach who seemed to know what he was talking about would surely sell tickets, as would the lower prices management announced. But the Depression was still on, and for Ottawa matters were being made worse by Prime Minister Bennett's bill to reduce salaries in the public service by 10 per cent. Liberal Edgar Chevrier, the former Ottawa Hockey Association director, had fought against the bill in the House of Commons. "I am," he intoned "sorely disappointed, and must quote the words of Virgil, *una salus victis nullam sperare salutem* — that to the vanquished there is but one hope of salvation, to hope for no salvation." A more prosaic Ahearn followed. "Mr. Speaker.... Dismissals and reductions should come last of all and not in the middle of the government's efforts to retrench." Ironically Ahearn's Ottawa Electric Railway had just one year earlier reduced the wages of its car men by the same 10 per cent. Either that, Ahearn reasoned at the time, or employees would be laid off. On Saturday, November 12, 1932, while last-minute plans for a weeklong civic emergency relief campaign were being nailed down, some 8,500 fans turned out as if there were no depression at all for the Senators' season opener (a 2-1 loss to the Maroons). Then on Monday at lunchtime four Royal Canadian Air Force planes roared through the dreary skies, showering the downtown with leaflets calling on citizens to raise $50,000 in six days for jobless families.

By 1932 there were about 13,000 radio sets in the capital, reaching perhaps 40,000 listeners; the time had finally come for the Senators to take advantage of this medium and for the local broadcaster to exploit the popularity of hockey. The hockey club put Denneny and his players on the air in special broadcasts promoting the Senators and upcoming games. In a novel twist radio station CNRO had popular commentator Bill Sims doing "ghost" play-by-play reconstructions of famous games from a bygone era. In the first of these, enthralled listeners heard the Silver Seven struggling to overcome an eight-goal deficit in their 1906 Stanley Cup series against the Wanderers. Sims also engaged the public with telegraphic reconstructions of the current team's away games.

The promotions had little effect, and by the end of January the team was in dire financial straits. Hunched over the books in room 614, directors fretted over an $80 shortage in ticket-revenue deposits, along with $100 being missing from petty cash. What with all of their troubles, were the Senators now the victims of bad bookkeeping, or worse? Turning to travel expenses the directors decreed that no longer would players be treated to dinner after games in Montreal, and forthwith the club would not be picking up the check for breakfast, but would give the players a dollar each for their morning meal on Montreal trips.

Management's picayune belt-tightening was no help to player morale, but more dispiriting was the team's record as it took to the ice for a Saturday-night home game against the Rangers on January 28. After twenty-nine contests the Senators had won but eight. Ralph Weiland, with eleven goals, and Hec Kilrea, with ten, were leading the club in scoring. Management was warning of a shake-up unless the boys started winning; trade rumours were in the air. The board's players' committee had just given coach Denneny permission to levy $100 fines to under-performing players. Alex Connell was Ottawa's starting goalie, his fifth game back after missing seventeen as a result of severe facial lacerations suffered in early December. By the midway mark of the first period, the Rangers were ahead 2-0. Early in the second both Bun Cook and brother Bill scored for the Rangers, and the Ottawa team was looking more and more lethargic. At the next whistle the huge crowd gasped in astonishment and dismay as Denneny opened the gate and substitute goalie Bill Beveridge glided onto the ice. As he moved toward the Senators' net, Connell skated out to greet him. The veteran tipped his cap and shook hands with the rookie. As Connell left the ice and headed through the narrow exit to the dressing room, the audience erupted in cheers. It was as if, in some uncanny way, they intuitively understood that this was the end of the line for the "little fireman," as he was affectionately known. In essence they were right, for three nights later at the Montreal Forum, Connell played his last game with the Senators. Beveridge's replacement of Connell on the Saturday night did no good. The Rangers scored five more times against a demoralized Ottawa team and won the game 9-3.

The substitution of a goalie during the course of a period (except for an injury) was highly unusual, if not unprecedented, violating, as it seems to have done, one of the tenets of professional hockey's mystical code of conduct. To the audience it was a shocking insult to a proud and gifted hockey player. To coach Denneny it was no more than a tactical move to motivate his team. "A coach must use every effort to win games, and I thought that putting in Beveridge in the circumstances might be a help," he explained. The ensuing public controversy did not escape the attention of the board of directors, who, as secretary-treasurer Brunton recorded in the minutes, "supported Manager Denneny's decision to use Beveridge in goal against Boston [following Connell's last game] and to keep doing so as long as he continues to play well."

The Ottawa Hockey Association was not alone in facing financial hard times. In March 1933 a currency crisis swept the United States as depositors rushed to empty their accounts. Banks in forty states closed their doors. When the United States treasury authorized their re-opening it was for the issuance of clearinghouse certificates, or scrip, instead of real money. Sports promoters at New York's St. Nicholas Rink and Madison Square Garden were accepting canned goods, haberdashery, and soap for tickets to boxing and wrestling. Hockey teams did not adopt the barter system but were prepared to take personal cheques. The advance demand for the Black Hawks-Ottawa game at the Chicago Stadium on March 7 was practically non-existent. The Senator players, their curiosity sparked by newspaper headlines, skated onto the ice to be greeted by 2,700 fans, the smallest crowd of the season in the huge arena.

On March 6, as the Senators travelled from Detroit to Chicago for the Black Hawks game, the Ottawa Hockey Association was meeting at its customary room 614 location with a single purpose in mind. The directors desperately needed $3,000 to meet immediate travel and payroll costs, and the Bank of Montreal was refusing to co-operate. Only if Frank Ahearn personally guaranteed the loan would the bank advance the money. Ahearn did so on condition that the association pledge player contracts as collateral. The fact that the contracts had already been pledged to Ahearn Sr. was dealt with in a handwritten codicil to the enacting bylaw, "subject however to prior rights of T.A." One is left with the impression in poring over the association directors' minutes that they were recorded as a tiresome formality, and that real decisions and commitments remained in the heads of the key participants. No one, least of all Ahearn Sr. and Jr. (and apparently not the Bank of Montreal), seemed concerned about the simultaneous pledging of the same assets to two different parties. It was understood that the Ahearns would meet their obligations. The paperwork was a detail. At that meeting, in a belated act of conscientiousness, directors finally got around to approving the minutes of six previous meetings dating back some sixteen months. Then, two days after the team closed out its season with a win in Montreal against the Maroons, but finishing in last place, the directors met again. The club was "indebted to its players and others in the sum of $6,300," and papers needed to be signed formalizing a loan, this time from the elder Ahearn. Once more the seemingly bottomless well of player contracts served as the necessary guarantee.

Figures compiled by Wong in his doctoral dissertation reveal the effects of the Depression on NHL teams for the 1932–33 season. Average net gate receipts (after the deduction of arena rent) were just over $8,500, compared with $11,000 for the previous year. By comparison the gravity of the Ottawa situation is shown by a 1932–33 average of $3,700 (after visiting teams' share). It was little wonder that the Senators would show an operating loss of more than $17,000, even without paying any rent to the Auditorium. When approached by the press at the close of the season, Frank Ahearn said he had not heard of a report from Hamilton that investors were considering building a new rink there and that they wanted to purchase the Senators. "We have often thought that it would be a good arrangement to have a team representing both Hamilton and Ottawa," he commented. "We could sell the Hamilton interests half the stock and give them fifty per cent representation on the board." As an impromptu answer to an unexpected question, Ahearn's reaction was remarkably definitive. He sounded anxious to grasp immediately at any pie-in-the-sky solution to the team's financial woes.

Nothing came of the Hamilton rumour and by September Ahearn and his co-directors were planning a new season. Having earlier thanked Cy Denneny "for his untiring efforts and loyal service during the past season," the directors were on the lookout for a new manager/coach. Among the five applicants were two of the Ottawa Hockey Club's greatest former stars, Harvey Pulford and George Boucher. The directors gave Boucher the job at a $3,000 salary, plus a $250 bonus if the Senators made the playoffs, and a full share of the players' playoff pool. If Boucher dreamed about his bonuses, he did so in Technicolor. Weeks after he signed, the directors sold the team's biggest star, Hec Kilrea, to the Toronto Maple Leafs for $10,000. By the end of December that money, along with whatever amounts the club garnered from gate receipts, had run out. So what? All the directors had to do, it seemed, was take a broom handle and rap three time on the ceiling of room 614 and old Ahearn in the office directly above would come running downstairs with the needed cash: $3,500 two days before Christmas, and another $5,000 one week later. The magical player contracts again served as collateral. So routine had the paperwork become that the bylaw authorizing the second loan duplicated the wording of the first, even neglecting to change the amount from $3,500 to $5,000. Nobody noticed

Readers of the *Ottawa Citizen* edition of Saturday, December 30, 1933, would have learned that "Buck" Boucher and his Senators had just returned from Chicago, that they would be leaving for New York the next day, and that they would be back on Thursday for a game against Boston. Added the *Citizen* in a supportive tone, "it goes without saying that they will be accorded a rousing reception by local fans when they skate out against the Bruins." There was no such boosterism in the *Journal* that morning. In fact, there was nothing at all about the team. Since the season began, the *Journal* had printed thousands of lines of "complimentary, co-operative reading material" about the Senators. Ahearn was furious at the omission of any coverage on this occasion. Within hours of the *Journal's* appearance on the streets, Ahearn was on the phone to the paper's editor demanding to know why there was nothing about his team. Upset by the paper's response that in its opinion there was nothing newsworthy to report, Ahearn had Brunton call right back to say the Ottawa Hockey Association was cancelling its contract with the *Journal*. The agreement was for the paper to carry display ads, together with colour stories favourable to the team, all for the rate of $70 per game. Understandable though Ahearn's reactionary fit of pique may have been, coming on the very morning the hockey club was finalizing its $5,000 loan from Ahearn Sr., it went against Ahearn the younger's better sense of judgment and was bound to hurt the hockey operation. His anger reverberated through team management to the point where club representatives on the Senators' promotional radio broadcasts started warning listeners that news about the team appearing in the *Journal* should not be taken as authoritative.

Making a public issue out of a promotional disagreement revealed a mood of desperation in the Senators camp. Management's treatment of the players, too, was becoming strained. Unhappy with a penalty taken by Earl Roche, which to an overtime win for the Leafs, management dispatched the team's top scorer to the minors, subject to immediate recall. It seemed like excessive punishment and drew the wrath of the Senators' dwindling ranks of supporters. Days later it was Danny Cox's turn to feel the heat. There may have been justification for his release (he was a little-used substitute), but it was the manner of his dismissal, as revealed by the *Journal*, incidentally, that caused public resentment. The distressed Cox, a four-year veteran, showed a reporter the contents of an envelope handed to him by an Ottawa Hockey Association messenger. The terse note signed by secretary-treasurer Brunton said simply, "Please be advised you are granted your unconditional release pursuant to the terms of your contract."

The Senators were mired in last place when Cox left, and that is where they finished the season. Their final home game on March 15, 1934, was against the New York Americans and, because it was "bargain night" (50 cent admissions for everyone), an unusually large crowd of 6,000 showed up. But it was not a happy throng as throughout the match disgruntled fans pelted the players with carrots, parsnips, lemons, oranges, and "other unidentified objects." Struck in the eye by a wayward stick, the Americans' goalie, Roy Worters, was forced to retire at the end of the first period. Skating out to take his place at the start of the second was former Senator Alex Connell, wearing his old red, white, and black barber-pole jersey. Over the final two periods he stopped nineteen shots as the Americans defeated the Senators 3-2. It was the one and only appearance of Connell on Auditorium ice following his abrupt benching the year before.

Connell's farewell fillip gave the Senators castoff a few moments of quiet satisfaction; but for team supporters, players, and management that final Auditorium game marked a dismal conclusion to the season. Though there were as yet no formal announcements, it was becoming apparent to the public that an era had ended. Following a year of suspended play, the Senators had finished in last place two years in a row. Many of the better players had been dealt away, the club was losing money year after year, and it was no secret that Auditorium Ltd. wanted to dispose of the franchise. It was only a matter of time, people sensed, before the city would be informed that the Senators were no more.

Unknown to the public, Ottawa Hockey Association legal counsel Redmond Quain had been quietly negotiating with St. Louis interests to move the team to the Missouri city, but without a change of ownership. Auditorium would continue to be the franchise holder. When word leaked out that Quain had been in St. Louis, Auditorium president Fred Burpee admitted that the team would have to move, though he did not indicate a destination. Burpee told the *Citizen* that the club had had to borrow some $60,000 over the past two seasons and that it could not succeed in a city the size of Ottawa, even with a winning team. "It is therefore apparent that we must try to move the Ottawa Senators to some very large city which has a large rink, if we are to protect the Auditorium shareholders and pay off our debts. Selling players' contracts will no longer supply the needed relief."

On April 21 Quain completed negotiations with C.D.P. Hamilton Jr., receiver for the National Exhibition Company, the former owner of the St. Louis Arena. Under the terms of the agreement the Ottawa Hockey Association was granted exclusive rights to operate its hockey team in the arena for seven years, but with the privilege of an annual cancellation clause. The rink owner was to be granted the same privilege in the event rental revenues did not meet stated targets, starting at $15,000 after the second year. Of the total regular-season gate receipts, the rink would receive the first $10,000, 100 per cent of any amount between $120,000 and $150,000, 50 per cent of any amount between $150,000 and $200,000, 40 per cent of any amount between $200,000 and $250,000, and 35 per cent of anything exceeding $250,000. Thus, assuming a generous estimate of $200,000 in gate receipts, the St. Louis Arena's share would be $10,000 plus $30,000 plus $25,000: a total of $65,000. The Ottawa Hockey Association would retain all receipts between $10,000 and $120,000. The agreement also granted the rink owner an option to purchase the team for $250,000.

On paper the numbers sounded good; but were there solid reasons for being optimistic about the transfer? Would big-league hockey be an attraction in the American Midwest? The minor-professional St. Louis Flyers of the American Hockey Association had assured the rink of a season's worth of revenue-producing dates, yet the rink had gone into receivership. The Depression was still on. Unanswered questions faced Auditorium Ltd. and the Ottawa Hockey Association as their directors and shareholders looked south with equal measures of anticipation and apprehension.

Hockey fans in the capital had nowhere to look. Hockey had been introduced to Ottawa fifty-one years earlier when Jack Kerr and Halder Kirby brought the game to the city from Montreal in 1883. There had been, with the exception of the missed season of 1931–32, a representative team in hockey's highest circles from the earliest days of organized league competition. Players born and raised in Ottawa could be found on professional teams wherever the game was played. The Silver Seven was a household name. The Senators had been one of the biggest attractions in American arenas during the formative days of U.S. expansion. King Clancy's portrait, for heaven's sake, had hung in the Madison Square Garden foyer. Recovering from its adversarial relationship with the Senators, the *Ottawa Journal* pined in an editorial, "So Ottawa is to pass out of professional hockey! It will be as though England gave up cricket."

St. Louis' youthful Eagles will do battle ... at the Arena tonight
in the first major league contest ever played in this city.
ST. LOUIS POST-DISPATCH
November 8, 1934

WITH THE COMPLETION in April 1934 of negotiations for the use of the St. Louis Arena, the Ottawa Hockey Association was now committed to the midwest American city. But myriad financial, administrative, and personnel decisions still had to be made. Underlying all of this was the challenge of positioning big-league hockey in a market where the game had no tradition and little exposure.

Situated on the west bank of the Mississippi River just below the confluence of the Missouri, St. Louis was once known as the gateway to the West. In its early days it had been the biggest slave market in the state of Missouri, and by 1934 it was experiencing a rapid growth in its black population, some 100,000 blacks in a city of 820,000. The racial mix was a far cry from what Redmond Quain and his fellow directors had known in Ottawa, where differences were accentuated along language lines. Though hit by the Depression, as all cities were, St. Louis did enjoy the benefits of strong manufacturing and wholesale sectors; and, with the repeal of Prohibition in 1934, the city was seeing a revival of its once-formidable brewing industry. Encouraging, too, for Quain was the city's vibrant sporting life. Baseball's Cardinals, playing at the picturesque Sportsman's Park, held the citizenry in thrall. Through fall and early winter, the Washington University Bears and St. Louis University Billikens football teams dominated the sports pages. Though a peripheral attraction, the St. Louis Flyers minor professional team in the American Hockey Association had been on the scene for six years, most recently at the St. Louis Arena.

The arena was as powerful an inducement for Quain as the city itself. Erected in 1929 to accommodate the annual National Dairy Show, the structure was one of the largest indoor sports venues in America, on a par with the famous Madison Square Garden and Chicago Stadium. The immense domed roof and ornamental towers on either side of the entrance made the arena an immediate landmark that citizens pointed to with pride. With a seating capacity of up to 16,000 (depending on the configuration for different events), the arena had room for an additional 4,000 standees. When used by the Flyers, the skating surface measured 200 by 100 feet, but with the addition of ice-level seats the width would be reduced to the NHL regulation 85 feet. The steeply banked seating tiers afforded excellent sight lines for hockey. Years later Frank Finnigan recalled the rink: "There was a fence up in the stands; the black people sat on one side and the white people sat on the other side." Black or white, it was an open question whether the public, accustomed to warm weather and warm-weather sports, would take to the royal winter game in sufficient numbers to make big-league hockey a paying proposition. On the minds of other NHL governors was the geographical perspective. Two years before, they had turned down a proposal to locate a franchise there. The city, after all, was 300 miles southwest of Chicago and would be the league's outpost. With the new franchise being 1,200 miles from Boston and nearly the same distance from Montreal, travel would be expensive, not to mention the wear and tear on players (if that made any difference to the owners).

Meet Me in St. Louis

THERE HAD ALWAYS BEEN a strained relationship between the National Hockey League and the minor professional American Hockey Association, in which the St. Louis Flyers competed. The AHA clubs had viewed NHL teams as predators that raided them at will to pick off their best players. When the AHA decided to position itself as a major league (under the name American Hockey League for that period) it soon found it could not compete with the big money of the NHL owners and so reached an accord with the premier league to smooth things out. Under the arrangement, the AHA would serve as a feeder league, and the NHL would not encroach on AHA territory and would draft AHA players only in a controlled and limited manner. The agreement was for two years, ending in September 1934. When word got out that the Senators were relocating to St. Louis, the AHA threatened legal action. St. Louis Flyers owner Frank Wainwright was upset on two counts — he would be competing against a big-league team in his own territory, and that team was to have exclusive use of the arena where the Flyers had operated the year before. NHL president Frank Calder's defence of the Ottawa move to St. Louis was that the agreement would be expiring on September 24. The AHA's position was that the territorial clause did not have a time limit.

Anticipating just such trouble, the NHL governors, in agreeing to the Ottawa transfer, had insisted that the Ottawa Hockey Association protect the League and its member clubs from any action that might be taken against them over territorial rights. The Ottawa directors approved the wording of an indemnification agreement on June 8, 1934, and gave legal counsel Redmond Quain the authority to sign the document and use it as needs be. It stated that the Ottawa Hockey Association agreed "to hold such members of the National Hockey League forever free and blameless from any cost of any legal action which may be taken against said National Hockey League as a whole, or against any of its members separately." As it turned out, the AHA took no action, while Frank Wainwright, who had contemplated an injunction against the intruders, abandoned the idea and relocated his Flyers to the small Winter Garden rink, where they had originally played before moving to the arena.

Writing on House of Commons letterhead, August 23, 1934, Frank Ahearn tendered his resignation as president of the Ottawa Hockey Association. In typical fashion he permitted himself a recommendation: "I suggest Mr. Redmond Quain, who has had charge of all the dealings and negotiations at St. Louis, and who understands that situation better than any of the rest of us, should be elected to succeed me as President of the Hockey Association." That accepted, Quain took over for his second stint as president and within two weeks signed Eddie Gerard as manager and coach for a salary of $4,000, plus $500 if the team made the playoffs and another $500 if it won the Stanley Cup. The former Senators captain would be bringing a wealth of experience to the new club, having coached and managed both the Montreal Maroons and New York Americans since retiring as a player in 1923.

Next came the formation of the Hockey Association of St. Louis, a subsidiary company of the Ottawa Hockey Association (in turn a subsidiary of Auditorium Ltd.), with Quain as president and Clare Brunton as secretary. Taking note of the corporate shuffling and not wishing to lose the thread of the directors' obligations, Ahearn Sr. thought it advisable to remind Ottawa Hockey Association directors of the amounts he had advanced to the association over the previous few years, some $72,061.33 including interest. In addition to the players contracts that he had originally agreed to accept as collateral, he was now asking for "such additional security as was within the power of the Company." It amounted to an assignment of the NHL franchise itself, together with any and all other assets of the Ottawa association. Ahearn Sr. was not necessarily turning the screws, but he was tidying up the bookkeeping. In a formal resolution the directors acknowledged the debt and pledged the security. In another resolution they showed how far they were prepared to go in tapping into Ahearn Sr.'s goodwill while recognizing they were also trying his patience. In it they authorized the president and secretary-treasurer to borrow from their benefactor such additional funds as might be necessary to keep the subsidiary Hockey Association of St. Louis in operation, but further directed the appointed officers "to borrow the said amounts from any other person, firm or corporation, instead of from T. Ahearn who has requested the company to get funds elsewhere if possible."

In taking over the operations of the hockey club, the Hockey Association of St. Louis assumed all the assets and obligations of the old Senators, including the liability to pay the salaries of all players under contract. The total salary commitment of $65,750 is itemized in a schedule to the Ottawa Hockey Association board minutes of October 26, 1934:

W. Cowley, $3,500	C.C. Shannon, $4,000
D. Roche, $3,750	W. Kalbfleish, $4,000
F. Blake, $2,500	E. Roche, $3,750
R.B. Bowman, $4,000	A. Cook, $2,500
W. Beveridge, $4,250	Vern Ayres, $3,500
C. Voss, $4,000	Irvine Frew, $3,500
S.H. Howe, $4,000	B. Williams, $3,500
M. Kaminsky, $4,000	G. Brydson, $3,500
F. Finnigan, $4,250	N. Wasnie, $3,250

This was the roster handed to Quain and Gerard as the committee appointed "to handle all players and trades in preparation for the coming season."

With the home opener looming, decisions had to be taken on the scaling of the immense new rink and on a publicity strategy to sell tickets for those seats. After some discussion on the need for more accommodation in the lower price range, management settled on six categories: 1,450 seats at $0 .75, 4,750 at $1.00, 1,850 at $1.10, 1,640 at $1.50, 430 at $1.75, and general admission at $0.50. The club hired J. Van Pelt of St. Louis as publicity agent and arranged for the *Ottawa Citizen*'s assistant sports editor, Tommy Shields, to cover the team's training sessions in Ottawa and send dispatches to Van Pelt, along with player photos. Ottawa Hockey Association board minutes, however, do not reveal what the secretary had in mind when he "gave details of plans which he and [arena manager] Mr. Hamilton were making for special publicity designed to attract the better class of people in St. Louis." The team was to be known as the Eagles and the players would sport white jerseys with blue trim and the name "St. Louis" in red on the chest above a red eagle.

But the Eagles' publicity machine would have to wait a while yet for results, for the St. Louis Cardinals, as fate would have it, had just won the National League pennant in baseball and the October Classic was about to get under way. Manager Frankie Frisch and his "madcap Cardinals" dominated the front page, the sports page, and pages in between. Jerome "Dizzy" Dean, the press said, had won thirty games over the season and had struck out 195 batters. He and brother Paul (they called him "Daffy") were slated to be the starting pitchers in alternating games against the American League-champion Detroit Tigers. Tigers pitcher Lynwood "Schoolboy" Rowe asserted on the front page of the *St. Louis Post-Dispatch* that he wasn't "scared," but he did admit he was "glad the Deans aren't triplets." The Cards have left for Detroit, readers learned; they have arrived safely, they were assured. Dizzy and Daffy were having breakfast with "Pa" Dean. On and on it went, while back in Ottawa the new entrant on the St. Louis sporting scene was preparing in anonymity. Not since the 1904 World's Fair had such excitement and pride overcome St. Louisans as when their beloved Cardinals returned home victorious. When that fervour subsided the Billikens and Bears college football teams captured the public's attention. Soon, though, Tommy Shields's reports were getting through; and, lo and behold, only five days after the Cards' victory the *Post-Dispatch* ran a full-length portrait of Frank Finnigan in his old Senators uniform under the caption "He'll Soon Be Here."

A New Start on the Ice

SOME 3,000 NOSTALGIC Ottawans bid farewell to their Senators on October 22 as the old familiar names wrapped up training at the Auditorium with

EDDIE GERARD'S GANG

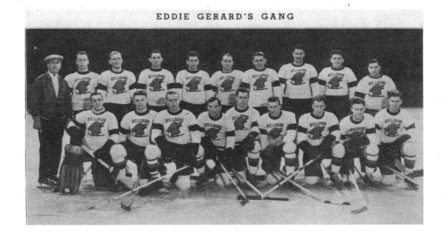

The St. Louis Eagles held their training camp at the Ottawa Auditorium before leaving for America's heartland in the autumn of 1934. The soon-to-be-replaced coach Eddie Gerard is shown standing beside his team at left.
LIBRARY AND ARCHIVES CANADA E008446854

an intra-squad game. Bill Cowley, well known locally from his days with Primrose and the Shamrocks, scored a goal in that scrimmage and seemed destined for a successful big-league career. In the months and years ahead Ottawa fans would be able to *read* all about it.

Shepherded by Eagles publicity man J. Van Pelt, press photographers gathered at St. Louis Union Station, Saturday, October 28, to capture the new team as it disembarked after the long haul from Ottawa. The next afternoon a curious public numbering in the thousands turned out at the arena for an open practice. The club was getting off to a good start in cultivating local attention, and newspapers were co-operating with positive stories about who these athletes were and where, exactly, they came from. The *Post-Dispatch*'s W.J. McGoogan, for one, did his part, filing daily stories profiling players and educating readers about the fundamentals of the game. As opening night approached, McGoogan turned his attention to the visiting team, the Stanley Cup-champion Chicago Black Hawks. Fans would be seeing one of hockey's biggest stars, Howie Morenz, in his first game as a Black Hawk after eleven years with the legendary Montreal Canadiens. A publicity shot shows him bursting through the defence in practice at the arena, his eyes fixed on the camera. Much as St. Louisans may have been persuaded that the "Stratford Streak" was a worthy attraction and that a hockey match between the Eagles and the Black Hawks would be interesting to watch, what really moved them was the visceral inter-city rivalry itself that had long existed between the two proud metropolises of America's heartland. In introducing big-time hockey to St. Louis, the NHL's schedule-maker in Montreal, Frank Calder, had got it right.

Caught up in the sense of occasion, the Eagles were skittish, especially rookie Mickey Blake. Rooming with veterans Bill Beveridge and Frank Finnigan at a hotel in the west end of town, he tossed a lighted cigarette into a curtain while getting ready to leave for the game. The fire department had to be called, but it was never reported whether Blake's cigarette was the Camel brand that manufacturer R.J Reynolds claimed all but two of the St. Louis Cardinals favoured. Blake needn't have been fidgety after all, for, as he found out on reaching the rink, Gerard had no intention of putting him in the lineup that night.

The game was scheduled to begin at 8:45 p.m., and though the lower sections were slow to fill, the cheaper upper levels were packed by eight o'clock. Fans scanned the arena for a glimpse of movie star Irene Castle, who was supposed to be attending with her husband, Black Hawks' owner Frederic McLaughlin. It was a festive occasion, with 12,622 spectators bringing the rink to near capacity. The mayor was there for the ceremonial face-off, as was Calder. The governor of Missouri came in from the state capital, Jefferson City. With Beveridge in goal, Ralph Bowman and American Burr Williams on defence, and Max Kaminsky, Gerry Shannon, and Frank Finnigan as the forward line, major-league hockey was under way in St. Louis.

The connection between the players on the ice and the fans in the stands was instantaneous. The big crowd had come for a good time, and if many were confused by the offside rule, it mattered not, for the hectic action and heavy hitting presented a novel and highly entertaining spectacle. The louder the crowd, the more furious the pace, and vice versa. It was music to Clare Brunton's ears, especially the eruption of partisan disapproval as the Eagles' Gerry Shannon was sent off for five minutes when all he had done was spill Marty Burke's blood on the ice with a high stick to the forehead. Johnny Gottselig dampened spirits midway through the second period when he took a pass from fellow substitute winger Howie Morenz to score the game's first goal. Minutes later Earl Roche tied the game, bringing a celebration from not only fans in the rink, but thousands more listening in to the Dixcel Gasoline Dealers' broadcast on radio station KMOX. Two more Black Hawks goals in the third period sent fans home disappointed by the outcome but not by the show.

Crowds of 6,000 greeted the Eagles for the second and third of their three-game home stand, in which they defeated the New York Rangers and lost to the Montreal Maroons. That defeat was the first of an eight-game losing streak, broken in early December when they shut out the New York Americans. Following two more losses, bringing the record to two victories in thirteen starts, a disheartened Gerard submitted his resignation and returned to his Ottawa home. Management handed the reins to Gerard's longtime Senators teammate and former Rockcliffe Park neighbour George Boucher. It made no difference. In their first game under their new coach, the Eagles dropped an 11-2 encounter with the Detroit Red Wings at home before a mere 3,500 fans — an attendance equalled by the minor-league Flyers on any of their occasional sellout nights.

The Sunday-Night Experiment and the Sell-Off

CONCERNED ABOUT DWINDLING attendance, Eagles business manager Clare Brunton thought his team would draw bigger crowds on Sunday nights than on the scheduled Saturdays. This notwithstanding the fact that the minor-league Flyers traditionally played their weekend home games at the Winter Garden on Sundays. The already-testy relationship between Brunton and Flyers owner Frank Wainwright became even more strained when Brunton went ahead and obtained league approval to switch a Saturday home date with the Canadiens (February 2) to the next evening. In response to Wainwright's objection, Brunton irritated him more by announcing he would try to reschedule additional games on Sundays.

The Sunday experiment turned out to be a watershed event. Up to that point management had retained hope of reaching the Stanley Cup playoffs, which would give the club a financial boost in light of ticket-revenue shortfalls. The Eagles were in last place and would have to jump over the fourth-place Americans and then overtake the third-place Canadiens, who, with twenty-five points in the standings, were ahead of the Eagles by eight. A big win before a big crowd would provide the team and its management with some needed encouragement. Brunton was right about Sunday night. The game drew 8,700 fans, the second-largest crowd of the season. But the Eagles had to settle for a 1-1 draw, thus failing to gain ground on their playoff rivals. Meanwhile, before a sellout crowd of 3,500, the Flyers defeated the league-leading Tulsa Oilers 3-1 and were now threatening for first place. Wainwright saw his team as challenging the big time Eagles for fan affection. With the increasing success of the Flyers and their enhanced popularity, he sought Brunton's permission to play the remainder of the Flyers' home games at the cavernous St. Louis Arena. Brunton flatly refused him, even though it proved impossible for the Eagles to change any further games to Sundays.

With only fifteen games remaining and potentially lucrative Sunday dates denied, it was now painfully obvious to Eagles owners back in Ottawa that there was no hope of reaching the playoffs and generating further ticket sales. There was red ink all over the ledger book. This was the point where they changed direction. No longer were the owners going to fight the good fight and try to build a team for the future. They were going to cut their losses and bail out. With Thomas Ahearn looking over their shoulder, what else could they do? Eight days after the Sunday experiment, the sell-off began. Club president Quain dealt defenceman Ralph Bowman and forward Syd Howe to Detroit. Bowman had scored the overtime winning goal against the Black Hawks four nights earlier. Howe was the team's leading scorer, and fourth in the league, with fourteen goals and thirteen assists in thirty-six games. Two days after that, Quain disposed of Finnigan to Toronto. The two transactions together netted $45,000, an unprecedented amount for the transfer of players by one team within such a short time. From that point on it was just a matter of going through the motions for the remaining twelve games in the season. In fact, before the Eagles final game (a 5-3 loss to Toronto at Maple Leaf Gardens) two players had already departed for home: Cliff Purpur to Grand Forks, North Dakota, and Frank Jerwa to Boston. It was an ignominious end to a disappointing season in which the Eagles won but eleven games, while tying six and losing thirty-one.

Franchise Termination

NO SOONER HAD THE PLAYERS begun fanning out to their summer abodes than rumours began to circulate about the fate of the club. Newspapers in several of the league's cities reported Quain as first suggesting the team was for sale and then denying any such thing. The minutes of the Ottawa Hockey Association directors' meeting of May 13, 1935, however, reveal that the involvement of the present Ottawa owners was on the verge of ending. The organization's indebtedness to Ahearn Sr. stood at $89,122.59, and that was after the $45,000 proceeds from the sale of Bowman, Howe, and Finnigan had been turned over to him. Appended to the minutes is the Hockey Association of St. Louis's statement of receipts and disbursements for the season. Net gate receipts of $61,158.41, together with $1,824.39 in program sales, $1,268.53 in programme advertising, and $1,300.00 in sundry revenue brought total receipts to $65,551.33. Against this were expenses of $127,154.40, excluding interest on borrowed money. Players' salaries of just over $56,000, team travel at $20,000, and arena rent of $10,000 were the major items, but a relatively hefty sum of $7,000 for publicity is also shown. The operating loss of $61,603.07 was a daunting figure for the directors to deal with, especially in light of the string of deficits from past years, the continuing economic depression, and the bleak (or non-existent) prospects for future success in St. Louis. Nevertheless, by securing an extension to August 1, 1935 of the deadline for the exercise of the option to cancel the St. Louis Arena lease, Quain was keeping his options open, including the possibility, after all, of finding a buyer who would take over the rental agreement.

Addressing a service-club dinner, Frank Ahearn held out a slim ray of hope that the team could be restored to Ottawa. "It was a terrible thing to see the team go and nobody felt worse than I did over the final defeat," he told the Kinsmen. The only way professional hockey could be brought back to the capital, he thought, was to make it a community affair. He said that Auditorium directors were prepared to sell the franchise and team to bond holders for two-thirds the price offered by any outside group, provided they keep the team in Ottawa for seven years. It was a familiar pitch that was to elicit the same response as in the past — no interest. In his speech Ahearn made a striking admission about his relationship with Gorman, with whom he had had a falling out years earlier when Gorman was his hockey partner. "I am awfully sorry it ever happened," he said. Referring to his buyout of Gorman after a dispute over club personnel, Ahearn continued, "If Tommy Gorman had stayed here it would have been the greatest thing ever happened for Ottawa in a hockey sense." Now the warmest of friends again with his former co-owner, he judged Gorman to be the best person to take over management of the club, if only he were available. But Gorman, as vice-president and general manager of the Montreal Maroons and general manager of the Canadian Arena Company, was simply not in a position to return to Ottawa. Ahearn's audience could not have gone home in an opti-mistic frame of mind about seeing the Senators again.

Through the summer Quain kept refusing to confirm or deny various despatches and rumours about the status of the club — that it was going to suspend for one year, that it was about to fold, that it would soon be sold to a St. Louis buyer. Finally, at the league governors meeting in Toronto on September 28, he was forced to confront the situation. He sought permis-sion to suspend play for 1935–36, in which case he would grant free use of his players to the other clubs for the season. The other owners had been through this before and were in no mood to repeat. They rejected the pro-posal and stated flatly that either the Eagles continue to operate or forfeit the franchise. In the latter case the league would pay Quain's group $35,000 for the player contracts. The *Ottawa Citizen* quoted an unnamed St. Louis official (likely Quain because he was the Eagles' representative) as assert-ing, "this proposition was so shabby that we left the meeting." Shabby because Quain reckoned his team was worth up to $100,000.

Quain was given a few days to consider his options, but time quickly ran out as the playing schedule had to be decided. At an emergency meet-ing of the governors in New York on October 15, the league purchased outright the St. Louis franchise, players, and rights for an undisclosed amount, reported to be $40,000. (Purchase-price figures for individual players, as reported by Charles Coleman in *The Trail of the Stanley Cup*, add up to $34,250.) Though nowhere near what Quain had demanded, the proceeds would make a substantial dent in the Ottawa Hockey Association's debt obligation to Ahearn Sr. Of the twenty-three players purchased, eighteen were taken by other NHL teams and five were left to be placed with minor-league clubs. Clubs drafted as follows: New York Americans: Pete Kelly, Eddie Finnigan; Montreal Canadiens: Bill Beveridge, Irvine Frew, Henri Lauzon, Paul Drouin; Detroit Red Wings: Carl Voss, W. Peterkin; New York Rangers: Glen Brydson, Vernon Ayres; Montreal Maroons: Joe Lamb, Bill Taugher; Boston Bruins: Bill Cowley, Teddy Graham; Toronto Maple Leafs: Gerry Shannon, Cliff Purpur, J. Dewey, Mickey Blake. The Chicago Black Hawks did not participate. Only six of these players would have resonated in any way with the Ottawa sporting public — an indication of just how distant the team had become from its former home in one short year. Beveridge, Voss, and Lamb had worn the barber-pole stripes. Finnigan, Drouin, and Cowley were known for their days in local amateur ranks.

That was it. In one coldly calculated boardroom meeting, the Ottawa Hockey Association franchise in professional hockey, a mainstay since the beginning of the pro game in Canada in 1907, had come to an abrupt end. As the passing of the club was sinking in, some of its former greats were preparing for another season, in off-ice positions. Frank Nighbor was going to Buffalo to coach the Bisons of the International League; George Boucher was leaving for Springfield, Massachusetts, to take over as general manager of the Indians in the Canadian-American League; and Clint Benedict was sailing for England to coach the Wembley Canadians. Many others of the old guard, such as Alf Smith, Harry Westwick, Punch Broadbent, and Horace Merrill, remained lifelong residents of the city. Dave Gill, whom both Frank Ahearn and Tommy Gorman judged to be the finest talent scout the Senators ever had, continued with the Ottawa Electric Railway until his retirement as general manager in 1956.

In July 1936, only nine months after the demise of the franchise, Auditorium bondholders foreclosed on the debt-ridden arena, which then continued under the control of the Royal Securities Corporation until 1945, when a group headed by Gorman took over. The colourful promoter passed away in Ottawa in 1961. Ahearn served one more term as a member of Parliament and following the death of his father in 1938 succeeded him as president of the Ottawa Electric Railway. So distraught was he when the City of Ottawa bought the company in 1948, shortly after he had retired, he could not bring himself to attend the deed-exchange ceremony to which he had been invited. Ahearn died at his Ottawa home in 1962.

Afterword

A spinning whisper, a sibilant twang,
As the stroke of the steel on the tense ice rang.
CHARLES G.D. ROBERTS
"The Skater," 1901

THE STORY OF THE Ottawa Hockey Club opens yet another window on the history of Canada's capital. It says something about urban geography, the city's physical and social infrastructure, athletes and athletic perform-ance, sportsteam officials, supporters (both ordinary folk and the exalted), the economics of the game, and the financial capacity of the community and its citizens to support hockey at the professional level. One might not have expected to see much, if anything, about street-rail passenger service in a hockey book; but in the case of Ottawa, especially, streetcars and the hockey team were intertwined. Ahearn money controlled the Senators and the Ottawa Electric Railway Company. The cars brought fans to the games and took them back home again. It was a cosy relationship.

The original Senators and winter were also inextricably linked. Today hockey is without season. Ice surfaces produced by mechanical refrigera-tion see to that. More teams and escalating costs prolong the schedule. The trophy put up by Lord Stanley of Preston while posted in Ottawa is com-peted for in June. Hockey schools and recreational leagues run through the summer. Many people today say they do not like winter. Come January they yearn for the balmy breezes and sandy beaches of the south. But in Ottawa before and after the turn of the last century, winter was a season to be looked forward to, not to escape. To be sure, it had its harsh realities. The observation in chapter one that people did not know what to do with the snow that piled up everywhere was not a throwaway line. They really didn't, for snow removal on residential streets was virtually non-existent and there was plenty of the white stuff. Sleighs rode over top, and into the

Sir Sandford Mr Barker
Charlie Fleming Lil   Noel Exshaw
On the Winterholme private Rink.

White-bearded hockey enthusiast Sandford Fleming shown entertaining family
and friends on his Winterholme rink in Sandy Hill, just days before the Senators
1908 home opener. LIBRARY AND ARCHIVES CANADA PA203559

first years of the twentieth century giant horse-drawn rollers packed it
down. Seasonal layoffs caused hardships for many working-class families.
Late fall inevitably brought grief, too, when heedless youths and young
adults ventured prematurely onto the thin ice of the Rideau and the
Ottawa. The first drowning of the season in November 1895 prompted lurid
details in the press. The young victim, finally found after unsuccessful
attempts with grappling hooks, had in his pocket the house key he had
begged his older brother to give him.

On balance, though, the inconveniences and the occasional tragedy
brought on by the cold were more than made up for by the vigour of the
bracing air and the exhilaration of winter recreation. There was also a sense
of satisfaction and assurance in being prepared for winter. The coal to feed
furnaces and stoves was ordered, delivered, and paid for. Storm windows
to replace summer screens were washed and up. Moths had not eaten

through the long johns, woolen sweaters, and breaches that had been carefully folded and stored in steamer trunks the previous spring. For children, youths, and adults alike there was the joy of skiing, sledding, snowshoeing, and, oh, the skating and the hockey. Skating carnivals drew hundreds of costumed citizens to indoor and outdoor rinks, including the surface set among pines and maples on Rideau Hall's rolling grounds. That rink, still seasonally in operation, is often confused with the old Rideau Rink, a covered structure in Sandy Hill patronized by the likes of Sandford Fleming and that served as the home of the Rideau Rebels vice-regal team.

Above all it was the hockey that caught the public's fancy. From school- and church-league teams to city and industrial leagues for older boys and young men, the game abounded. The legendary King Clancy once reminisced on CBC radio about the bare-bones instructions he had received from his teacher-coach at St. Joseph's school: you shoot the puck into the goal at that end, and keep it out of the goal at the other end. Though an exceptional case, the story about the lad, who, unbeknownst to his parents, switched from a Catholic to a public school to play on a better team, exemplified the place of the game in the mind of one small boy and the overzealous teacher who recruited him.

Ottawa's first players had received no training in the sport. They had not been brought up with hockey and had no models to learn from or emulate. The game itself was new to everyone. A few, like Albert Peter Low and Thomas Green, had had no more than rudimentary exposure to hockey at McGill University before coming to Ottawa, while others in the city just picked up the game as they went along. For original Ottawa Hockey Club players, such as Frank Jenkins, hockey was simply an amusing diversion, but, nevertheless, one they wished to become proficient in. One has to wonder at the seeming incongruity of Jenkins the hockey player and Jenkins the church organist. On Saturday afternoons his hands gripped a heavy rock-elm stick as he hurled himself into intense physical confrontation. On Sunday mornings those same hands moved deftly over the keys, inspiring piety, peace, and goodwill to man among the St. Andrews congregation.

The plight of Tom Green gives pause, for it was hockey, not government policy, that brought him a measure of relief from the racial discrimination he suffered. The Mohawk Indian from Brantford, Ontario, was a qualified land surveyor and a graduate in applied sciences from the esteemed McGill University. Yet highly placed officials in the Dominion government thwarted his goal of permanent employment in the civil service, in spite of the urging of Sir John A. Macdonald. The hockey fraternity saw Green for what he was — a good man. He played the game so well and his judgment was so trusted that his peers elected him the first president of the world's first hockey league. This little-known fact has never been exploited by native leaders.

By Frank McGee's time, hockey had become a structured sporting discipline and its best practitioners were enjoying wide recognition. Never has there been a more riveting description of a hockey player than that of McGee penned by the *Calgary News Telegram*'s Billy Grant, as quoted in part in chapter six: "His hair was as perfectly parted as though he had just stepped out of a tonsorial parlor; his spotless white pants were creased to a knife-like edge; his boots had been polished; his skates glistened under the glare of the arc lamps and his complexion — that was what magnetized my attention — seemed as pink as a child's." It is worth recording what a captivated Grant then went on to say: "For a minute or so, I stood spellbound. Someone formally introduced us and McGee quickly pulled off his gauntlet and held out a soft, though muscular hand. Then he jumped over the rail amidst another wild whoop of delight and I decided to watch him." What he saw was a dazzling display of skating and stickhandling dexterity. "Then," Grant concluded, "I ceased to wonder why this boyish, doll-like hockey star was the idol of that crowd. I, too, joined in the hysterical shouting for Frank McGee — the world's greatest hockey player." Tommy Gorman, the former part owner of the Senators, was clearly as enchanted with Grant's prose as Grant was with McGee himself. In his memoirs, published in the *Weekend* supplement of the *Ottawa Citizen* fifty years after the Calgary newsman's account, Gorman borrowed liberally from Grant's phrasing in his own recollections of the great Ottawa athlete: "His white pants had been pressed to a knife-like edge. His blond hair combed to perfection, his boots shined...."

On a more human than god-like scale, one can picture the Senators' home-grown star Jack Darragh parading down Sparks Street one fine day in 1915, cradling his newborn daughter in one hand while passing out cigars with the other. The occasion remains a matter of family lore, but one that Darragh's daughter Aileen thought, out of modesty, would be of no interest to readers. Darragh, the devoted family man and a highly regarded manager at Ottawa Dairy, is just one example of the typically close connections existing in days gone by between Ottawa Hockey Club players and their hometown fans — ties that are far less frequent in today's professional sporting environment. Another was Eddie Gerard, senior clerk of the Geodetic Survey and Senators captain. The story has been told in different versions of how Senators business manager Frank Shaughnessy enticed the New Edinburgh star into signing a professional contract halfway through the 1914 season by laying out several hundred dollars in bonus money on a table. Did it happen? Imagine your author's delight when poring over the Senators' ledger book to find a $400 cash withdrawal by Frank Shaugnessy the day before the signing. Gerard's total pay, including the bonus, for the eleven games he played was an even $1,000.

Though when Gerard agreed to terms there were still some purists around who thought that professionalism sullied the ideals of sportsmanship, most hockey fans didn't mind at all. At least it was out in the open. The previous hypocrisy of players being paid secretly while purporting to be amateurs, in it for nothing but the love of the game, had ended by 1906. Fans wanted to see the best players, and they were, of course, the professionals. In the early years of the pro game, most players would not, unlike today, have been able to live year round on their hockey pay, but that coupled with earnings from day jobs (sometimes obligingly arranged by Senators management) made for a relatively comfortable life.

For owners, financial gains were rare. Before the game turned professional, monetary risks were minor. Senators executive officers, such as John Dickson and Bob Shillington, gave selflessly in keeping the Senators going, and with limited travel, short schedules, and no salary contracts (albeit some cash rewards under the table), they were able to do so without running into red ink. They were involved strictly for the love of the game. For E.P. Dey, seeking profit was the motivation for involving himself with hockey. As an arena owner he needed attractions and when, during the Great War, the Senators were in danger of folding, he had no choice but to take over the team. If there were no profits to be made from the club itself, at least there would be rink rental fees. Tommy Gorman was a sports entrepreneur with a flare for salesmanship. When his partnership with Dey ended he struck a new one with Frank Ahearn, and in selling his 50-percent share to him for $35,000 became the only Senators owner ever to make money out of the club.

Frank Ahearn was an entirely different story. Scion of the industrial titan Thomas Ahearn, he was an eminently successful businessman in his own right, one who loved hockey and his community in equal measure. It was this dual passion that led him to buy the Senators, spearhead the building of the Auditorium, and accept losses on the hockey operation year after year with little complaint. Ottawa, he believed, should have a big-league hockey team. It helped that Ahearn Sr. could be counted on, sometimes a little reluctantly, to bankroll the team, especially during the Depression's darkest days. In the end, however, reality caught up with the Ahearns. A small-market team in an expanded league dominated by owners in very big American cities simply could not survive. Ahearn felt as badly, probably worse, than anyone when the Ottawa Hockey Association finally threw in the towel in 1935. It would be well for sports-minded Ottawans of today to give a nod in recognition of one of the city's most notable hockey boosters of the past.

AND FINALLY A WORD about storytelling and legend. In several books, American writer and editor George Plimpton explored the mindset of professional athletes. Of all he was most fascinated by hockey players. He delighted in their camaraderie and described the fraternity in almost-tribal terms. To him they were "mainly an aural society; they soaked up the great hockey stories so they could pass them on." In the course of research for this book, I came across many that unfortunately just could not be fitted into the main text. Here's one recounted by Cyclone Taylor while lounging around a newspaper office shortly after joining the Senators in 1907. One night while sitting on a train in northern Michigan and waiting to leave on a road trip, Cyclone and a teammate thought they would have time to get off and have a sandwich and coffee in a diner across from the tracks. The train was behind some sheds but from the diner they could see the last car. Their plan was to sprint for the platform as soon as the car began to move. It didn't, and the players enjoyed a leisurely snack. When they got to the platform to board the train they were startled to see it heading down the tracks. The car they had been keeping an eye on had been uncoupled from the rest of the train. Their teammates were all in the sleeper disappearing down the line.

Frank McGee's record of fourteen goals against the Klondikers in the second game of the 1905 Stanley Cup series is no legend. It is recorded fact. But what may have been behind that performance makes for a good story, as told by Ahearn many years later. Ahearn said he had been acquainted with Klondikers manager Joe Boyle, who took him aside before the series. Boyle asked him to have a word with the Ottawa players and suggest they go easy on his team. Boyle was not expecting the Klondikers to do very well, but he had a lengthy tour lined up and didn't want his boys to look completely outclassed. Ahearn spoke to the Ottawas and, as he recalled, McGee simply stared at him, giving no response. Then he went out and scored his fourteen goals. Some time later Ahearn found out that McGee had had a terrible row with Boyle back in their Ottawa Rowing Club days and was in no mood to forgive and forget that night at Dey's Rink.

The Stanley Cup has certainly been treated casually by its Ottawa holders. It once spent a summer in the attic of Eddie Gerard's Rockcliffe Park home. At least one neighbourhood kid was invited up to see it. But was it ever really kicked or tossed into the Rideau Canal? The story, in varying versions, is one of hockey's greatest legends. Some say the incident occurred in 1903, others in 1905. The venerable trophy hit the frozen surface downtown near the Laurier Avenue Bridge, according to one account; but according to another it was at the Bank Street Bridge near the Aberdeen Pavilion, a former Silver Seven home. Call it an admission of research failure if you wish, but I found no primary evidence that it ever happened. But it's just the sort of thing that might have.

Appendices

1 · OTTAWA HOCKEY CLUB ROSTERS BY SEASON, 1884–1934

All games: tournament, scheduled, playoff, exhibition

	# of games
1884	
Thomas Gallagher	4
Thomas Green	4
Frank Jenkins	4
Jack Kerr	4
Halder Kirby	4
Albert Low	4
Nelson Porter	3
George Young	1
1885	
G. Currier	3
Thomas Gallagher	3
Thomas Green	3
Frank Jenkins	3
Jack Kerr	3
Halder Kirby	3
William O'Dell	3

1886	
no external matches	
1887	
G. Currier	1
Edwin Dey	1
Thomas Green	1
Jack Kerr	1
S. Howe	1
Halder Kirby	1
Albert Low	1
F. McVeity	1
Percy Myles	1
1888	
no external matches	
1889	
Edwin Dey	1
Frank Jenkins	1
Jack Kerr	1
Halder Kirby	1
Nelson Porter	1
George Young	1
Weldon Young	1
1890	
Reginald Bradley	1

Edwin Dey	2
Thomas Green	2
Frank Jenkins	1
Jack Kerr	2
Chauncey Kirby	1
Halder Kirby	2
George Young	1
Weldon Young	2

1890–91

Reginald Bradley	6
Clark	1
E.C. Grant	9
Thomas Green	2
Kavanagh	2
Jack Kerr	11
Halder Kirby	10
Chauncey Kirby	14
Albert Morel	7
Philip Ross	13
C. Smith	5
George Young	4
Weldon Young	14

1892

Reginald Bradley	10
Frank Jenkins	3
Jack Kerr	9
Chauncey Kirby	9
Halder Kirby	9
Albert Morel	10
Bert Russell	10
Weldon Young	10

1893

Reginald Bradley	10
William Dey	1
Frank Jenkins	1
Jack Kerr	7
E.C. Grant	3
Chauncey Kirby	10

Halder Kirby	10
Albert Morel	10
Herbert Russell	10
Weldon Young	10

1893–94

Reginald Bradley	2
E.C. Grant	3
Chauncey Kirby	11
Halder Kirby	2
Joe McDougal	8
Sam McDougall	9
Albert Morel	11
Harvey Pulford	8
Herbert Russell	11
D.C. Watters	1
Weldon Young	11

1894–95

Fred Chittick	9
Chauncey Kirby	9
Joe McDougal	8
Sam McDougall	5
Harvey Pulford	13
Herbert Russell	14
Jim Smellie	5
Alf Smith	15
H. Taylor	1
D.C. Watters	4
Harry Westwick	7
Weldon Young	13

1896

Fred Chittick	9
Chauncey Kirby	9
Harvey Pulford	9
Herbert Russell	7
Alf Smith	9
Harry Westwick	9
Fred White	2
Weldon Young	9

1897

Fred Chittick	10
William Dey	1
H. Hutchison	1
Alf Living	2
Harvey Pulford	10
Alf Smith	10
Dan Smith	1
Moxie Smith	7
Charles Spittal	9
Harry Westwick	10
Weldon Young	9

1898

Paddy Baskerville	2
Fred Chittick	6
Alf Cope	4
Dave Gilmour	1
H. Hutchison	10
Alf Living	6
Myers	1
Harvey Pulford	8
Harry Rosenthal	2
Charles Spittal	9
Harry Westwick	6
J. White	6
E. Woolsey	1
Weldon Young	10

1899

Fred Chittick	5
Harold Henry	4
Bouse Hutton	3
Chauncey Kirby	7
Bert Macdonald	8
Henry Nolan	6
Henry O'Connor	1
John "Mac" Roger	6
Charles Spittal	1
Bruce Stuart	2

Hod Stewart	4
Fred White	4
Weldon Young	7

1900

W. Duval	8
Harold Henry	10
Bouse Hutton	10
Henry Nolan	4
Henry O'Connor	1
Harvey Pulford	8
John "Mac" Roger	10
Arthur Sixsmith	1
Bruce Stuart	8
Hod Stuart	10

1901

Fred Chittick	1
W. Duval	9
Harold Henry	10
Bouse Hutton	9
Harvey Pulford	6
Jim McGee	1
John "Mac" Roger	8
Arthur Sixsmith	9
Jack Smith	4
Charles Spittal	3
Harry Westwick	9

1902

Aumond	2
Butterworth	1
Chambers	1
W. Duval	5
Fraser	5
Dave Gilmour	2
Harold Henry	8
Bouse Hutton	10
Art Moore	1
Harvey Pulford	5
Charles Spittal	7

Bruce Stuart	10
C. Watts	3
Harry Westwick	10

1903

Arthur Fraser	1
Billy Gilmour	12
Dave Gilmour	8
Sutherland Gilmour	11
Bouse Hutton	13
Frank McGee	10
Art Moore	12
Harvey Pulford	12
Percy Sims	2
Charles Spittal	2
Harry Westwick	7
Fred Wood	1

1903–04

Billy Gilmour	2
Sutherland Gilmour	12
Bouse Hutton	13
Frank McGee	13
Jim McGee	5
Art Moore	10
Harvey Pulford	10
Scott	2
Alf Smith	12
Harry Westwick	13

1905

Angus Allen	6
Dave Finnie	13
Horace Gaul	2
Billy Gilmour	3
Frank McGee	10
Art Moore	13
Harvey Pulford	10
Hamby Shore	4
Alf Smith	13
Harry Westwick	13

Fred White	4

1905–06

Nick Bawlf	2*
Chamberlain	2*
Dion	2
Jack Ebbs	1
Sutherland Gilmour	1
Billy Hague	19
Percy LeSueur	1
Frank McGee	13
Art Moore	20
Harvey Pulford	20
Hamby Shore	1*
Alf Smith	20
Harry Smith	17
Tommy Smith	4
Harry Westwick	18

1906–07

Billy Baird	6
Billy Hague	2*
Percy LeSueur	12
Art Moore	3
Harvey Pulford	12
Charlie Ross	1*
Jack Ryan	1
Hamby Shore	14
Alf Smith	13
Harry Smith	13
Snelling	1
Charles Spittal	5
Harry Westwick	13
Tommy Westwick	1
Jack Williams	1

1908

Bobbie Harrison	3
Percy LeSueur	13
Art Moore	3
Neate	1*

Tom Phillips	13		Marty Walsh	21
Harvey Pulford	11		**1912**	
Alf Smith	10		Jack Darragh	19
Fred Taylor	13		Joe Dennison	3
Marty Walsh	11		Albert "Dubbie" Kerr	21
Harry Westwick	13		Eddie King	4
1909			Fred Lake	21
Edgar Dey	10		Percy LeSueur	21
Billy Gilmour	13		Skene Ronan	20
Albert "Dubbie" Kerr	11		Hamby Shore	21
Fred Lake	15		Fred Taylor	1
Percy LeSueur	15		Marty Walsh	15
Hamby Shore	1*		**1912-13**	
Bruce Stuart	11		Clint Benedict	8
Fred Taylor	14		Harry Broadbent	21
Marty Walsh	15		Jack Darragh	20
1910			Joe Dennison	12
Albert "Dubbie" Kerr	8		Fred Lake	13
Fred Lake	19		Percy LeSueur	19
Percy LeSueur	20		Eddie Lowrey	15
Ken Mallen	3		Horace Merrill	12
Bruce Ridpath	20		Skene Ronan	22
Gordon Roberts	13		Hamby Shore	22
Hamby Shore	19		Tommy Westwick	12
Walter Smail	7		**1913-14**	
Bruce Stuart	13		Clint Benedict	10
Marty Walsh	19		Harry Broadbent	18
1910-11			Alex Currie	1
Alex Currie	4		Jack Darragh	21
Jack Darragh	22		Angus Duford	13
Horace Gaul	2		Greg George	2
Albert "Dubbie" Kerr	22		Eddie Gerard	12
Fred Lake	22		Leth Graham	14
Percy LeSueur	22		Percy LeSueur	16
Bruce Ridpath	22		Horace Merrill	19
Hamby Shore	22		Miller	2
Bruce Stuart	4		Skene Ronan	18
Fred Taylor	2*		Hamby Shore	16

Harry Smith	3
Allen Wilson	13

1914-15

Billy Bell	12
Clint Benedict	25
Harry Broadbent	25
Jack Darragh	22
Angus Duford	18
Eddie Gerard	24
Leth Graham	23
Sammy Hebert	8
Fred Lake	2
Eddie Lowrey	6
Horace Merrill	25
Art Ross	21
Hamby Shore	25
Arthur Sullivan	2

1915-16

Clint Benedict	25
George Boucher	21
Morley Bruce	1
Jack Darragh	22
Angus Duford	21
Eddie Gerard	25
Billy Gilmour	2
Sammy Hebert	7
Gordon Meeking	5
Horace Merrill	25
Frank Nighbor	24
Art Ross	20
Hamby Shore	21
Hank Staveneau	20
Harry Westwick	2

1916-17

Clint Benedict	20
George Boucher	20
Jack Darragh	21
Corbett Denneny	8

Cy Denneny	10
Jack Fournier	4
Eddie Gerard	21
Sammy Hebert	2
Carroll Kendall	10
Ossie Laing	1
Eddie Lowrey	18
Horace Merrill	20
Frank Nighbor	21
Hamby Shore	21
Hank Staveneau	2

1917-18

Clint Benedict	22
George Boucher	22
Morley Bruce	6
Russell Crawford	13
Jack Darragh	18
Cy Denneny	22
Eddie Gerard	21
Sammy Hebert	1
Harry Hyland	12
Eddie Lowrey	12
Horace Merrill	4
Frank Nighbor	9
Dave Ritchie	14
Hamby Shore	19

1918-19

Clint Benedict	28
Billy Boucher	2
George Boucher	26
Harry Broadbent	23
Harry Cameron	16
Sprague Cleghorn	28
Jack Darragh	20
Cy Denneny	28
Eddie Gerard	27
Eddie Lowrey	10
Frank Nighbor	25

Skene Ronan 10

1919–20

Clint Benedict 29
George Boucher 28
Harry Broadbent 23
Morley Bruce 28
Sprague Cleghorn 26
Jack Darragh 28
Cy Denneny 29
Eddie Gerard 25
Jack MacKell 29
Horace Merrill 7
Frank Nighbor 28

1920–21

Clint Benedict 33
George Boucher 32
Harry Broadbent 17
Morley Bruce 31
Sprague Cleghorn 9
Jack Darragh 32
Cy Denneny 33
Eddie Gerard 33
Leth Graham 16
Jack MacKell 31
Frank Nighbor 33

1921–22

Billy Bell 18
Clint Benedict 26
Frank Boucher 26
George Boucher 25
Harry Broadbent 26
Morley Bruce 25
Frank Clancy 26
Cy Denneny 24
Eddie Gerard 23
Leth Graham 1
Frank Nighbor 22

1922–23

Clint Benedict 33
George Boucher 29
Harry Broadbent 33
Frank Clancy 33
Jack Darragh 26
Cy Denneny 33
Eddie Gerard 31
Harry Helman 30
Lionel Hitchman 11
Frank Nighbor 31

1923–24

Clint Benedict 28
George Boucher 27
Harry Broadbent 28
Earl Campbell 18
Frank Clancy 30
Jack Darragh 24
Cy Denneny 28
Frank Finnigan 6
Leth Graham 1
Sammy Hebert 2
Harry Helman 23
Lionel Hitchman 30
Frank Nighbor 26
Rod Smylie 14

1924–25

George Boucher 30
Earl Campbell 33
Frank Clancy 34
Alex Connell 34
Cy Denneny 30
Frank Finnigan 33
Ed Gorman 34
Leth Graham 3
Harry Helman 1
Lionel Hitchman 14
Frank Nighbor 30
Alex Smith 10

Reginald Smith 32

1925–26

George Boucher 42

Frank Clancy 41

Alex Connell 42

Cy Denneny 42

Jack Duggan 33

Frank Finnigan 42

Ed Gorman 25

Leth Graham 2

Hec Kilrea 41

Frank Nighbor 41

Alex Smith 41

Reginald Smith 35

1926–27

Jack Adams 48

George Boucher 46

Frank Clancy 49

Alex Connell 50

Cy Denneny 48

Frank Finnigan 42

Ed Gorman 47

Milt Halliday 44

Stan Jackson 8

Hec Kilrea 48

Frank Nighbor 45

Alex Smith 48

Reginald Smith 48

1927–28

George Boucher 46

Harry Broadbent 45

Gene Chouinard 8

Frank Clancy 42

Alex Connell 46

Cy Denneny 46

Frank Finnigan 41

Hozomer Godin 23

Len Grosvenor 44

Milt Halliday 12

Hec Kilrea 45

Frank Nighbor 44

Allen Shields 9

Alex Smith 45

1928–29

George Boucher 30

Harry Broadbent 1

Frank Clancy 44

Alex Connell 44

Cy Denneny 1

Fred Elliott 42

Frank Finnigan 44

Hozomer Godin 24

Len Grosvenor 41

Milt Halliday 16

Hec Kilrea 40

Joe Lamb 4

Frank Nighbor 31

Allen Shields 40

Alex Smith 44

Bill Touhey 43

1929–30

Frank Boucher 2*

Frank Clancy 47

Alex Connell 49

Harry Connor 25

Dan Cox 27

Frank Finnigan 48

Art Gagne 32

Len Grosvenor 18

Syd Howe 17

Bill Hutton 16

Hec Kilrea 47

Wally Kilrea 42

Joe Lamb 49

Gerry Lowrey 2*

Frank Nighbor 19

Allen Shields	48		Syd Howe	49
Alex Smith	48		Hec Kilrea	49
Harold Starr	33		Wally Kilrea	32
Bill Touhey	49		Gerry Lowrey	7
1930–31			Bert McInenly	30
Bill Beveridge	18		Hib Milks	16
George Boucher	4*		Desse Roche	16
Leo Bourgeault	28		Earl Roche	20
Glen Brydson	1*		Harvey Rockburn	18
Alex Connell	38		Allen Shields	49
Harry Connor	10		Alex Smith	33
Dan Cox	45		Harold Starr	32
Frank Finnigan	48		Bill Touhey	48
Art Gagne	47		Ralph Weiland	48
Len Grosvenor	39		**1933–34**	
Syd Howe	1*		Bill Beveridge	49
Hec Kilrea	45		Ralph Bowman	47
Wally Kilrea	1*		Alex "Bud" Cook	21
Ray Kinsella	15		Dan Cox	30
Joe Lamb	49		Frank Finnigan	49
Eric Pettinger	13		Percy Galbraith	3
Allen Shields	4*		Bill Hollett	27
Alex Smith	37		Syd Howe	42
Art Smith	45		Walter Kalbfleisch	22
Harold Starr	39		Max Kaminsky	38
Bill Touhey	47		Albert Leduc	37
1931–32			Bert McInenly	4
Senators suspended for season			Desse Roche	48
1932–33			Earl Roche	46
Bill Beveridge	37		Ted Saunders	18
Leo Bourgeault	36		Jerry Shannon	49
Marty Burke	12		Allen Shields	48
Bert Burry	4		Bill Touhey	47
Alex Connell	17		Carl Voss	39
Dan Cox	49		Nick Wasnie	36
Frank Finnigan	45		Ralph Weiland	9
Gus Forslund	49			
Norm Gainor	1		*Played exhibition game(s) only*	

2 · St. Louis Eagles Roster, 1934–35

All games are regular schedule

	# of games
Oscar Asmundson	11
Vernon Ayres	47
Bill Beveridge	48
Mickey Blake	8
Ralph Bowman	31
Glenn Brydson	48
Gene Carrigan	4
Alex "Bud" Cook	4
Bill Cowley	41
Eddie Finnigan	12
Frank Finnigan	34
Irvine Frew	48
Ted Graham	13
Syd Howe	36
Frank Jerwa	16
Walter Kalbfleisch	3
Max Kaminsky	12
Pete Kelly	25
Joe Lamb	31
George Patterson	11
Clifford Purpur	25
Vic Ripley	31
Dessie Roche	7
Earl Roche	19
Jerry Shannon	25
Carl Voss	48
Nick Wasnie	13
Archie Wilcox	8
Burr Williams	9

3 · Most Appearances in a Senators Uniform

All games: tournament, scheduled, playoff, exhibition

player	seasons or parts thereof	career span with Ottawa
Frank Nighbor	429	1915/16–1929/30
George Boucher	424	1915/16–1928/29
Frank Finnigan	397	1923/24–1930/31, 1932/33–1933/34
Cy Denneny	374	1916/17–1928/29
Frank Clancy	346	1921/22–1929/30
Alex Connell	320	1924/25–1930/31, 1932/33
Alex Smith	306	1924/25–1930/31, 1932/33
Jack Darragh	295	1910/11–1920/21, 1922/23–1923/24
Clint Benedict	287	1912/13–1923/24
Punch Broadbent	253	1912/13–1914/15, 1918/19–1923/24, 1927/28
Eddie Gerard	242	1913/14–1922/23
Bill Touhey	233	1928/29–1930/31, 1932/33–1933/34
Punch Broadbent	214	1912/13–1914/15, 1918/19–1923/24
Hamby Shore	206	1905–1906/07, 1909–1917/18
Allen Shields	197	1927/28–1930/31, 1932/33–1933/34
Dan Cox	150	1929/30–1930/31, 1932/33–1933/34
Harvey Pulford	142	1893/94–1898, 1900–1908
Len Grosvenor	142	1927/28–1930/31
Percy LeSueur	139	1905/06–1913/14
Reginald Smith	115	1924/25–1926/27
Horace Merrill	112	1912/13–1917/18, 1919/20
Syd Howe	108	1929/30–1930/31, 1932/33–1933/34

4 · LEAGUE STANDINGS, 1893–1935

Amateur Hockey Association of Canada

1893	W	L	D	GF	GA
Montreal	7	1		38	18
Ottawa	6	2		49	22
Crystals	3	5		25	34
Quebec	2	5	1	23	46
Victorias	1	6	1	20	35

1894	W	L	D	GF	GA
Montreal	5	3		25	15
Ottawa	5	3		25	16
Victorias	5	3		36	20
Quebec	5	3		26	27
Crystals	0	8		10	43

1895	W	L	D	GF	GA
Victorias	6	2		35	20
Montreal	4	4		33	22
Ottawa	4	4		25	24
Crystals	3	4		21	39
Quebec	2	5		18	27

1896	W	L	D	GF	GA
Victorias	7	1		41	24
Ottawa	6	2		22	16
Quebec	4	2		23	23
Montreal	2	6		24	33
Shamrocks	1	7		16	30

1897	W	L	D	GF	GA
Victorias	7	1		48	26
Ottawa	5	3		25	18
Montreal	5	3		31	26
Quebec	2	6		22	46
Shamrocks	1	7		27	37

1898	W	L	D	GF	GA
Victorias	8	0		53	33
Montreal	5	3		34	21
Shamrocks	3	5		29	35
Quebec	2	6		29	35
Ottawa	2	6		28	44

Canadian Amateur Hockey League

1899	W	L	D	GF	GA
Shamrocks	7	1		40	21
Victorias	6	2		44	23
Ottawa	4	4		21	43
Montreal	3	5		30	29
Quebec	0	8		12	31

1900	W	L	D	GF	GA
Shamrocks	7	1		49	26
Montreal	5	3		34	36
Ottawa	4	4		28	19
Victorias	2	6		44	55
Quebec	2	6		33	52

1901	W	L	D	GF	GA
Ottawa	7	0	1	33	20
Victorias	4	3	1	45	32
Shamrocks	4	4		30	25
Montreal	3	5.		28	37
Quebec	1	7		21	43

1902	W	L	D	GF	GA
Montreal	6	2		39	15
Ottawa	5	3		35	15
Victorias	4	4		36	25
Quebec	4	4		26	34
Shamrocks	1	7		15	62

1903	W	L	D	GF	GA
Ottawa	6	2		47	26

Victorias	6	2		48	33
Montreal	4	3		34	19
Quebec	3	4		30	46
Shamrocks	0	8		21	56

1904	W	L	D	GF	GA
Quebec	7	1		50	37
Victorias	5	3		75	48
Montreal	3	5		34	49
Shamrocks	1	7		32	74
Ottawa*	4	4		32	15

Quits league over game dispute

Federal Amateur Hockey League

1905	W	L	D	GF	GA
Ottawa	7	1		60	19
Wanderers	6	2		44	27
Brockville	4	4		34	30
Cornwall	3	5		18	37
Montagnards	0	8		19	62

Eastern Canada Amateur Hockey Association

1906	W	L	D	GF	GA
Ottawa	9	1		90	42
Wanderers	9	1		74	38
Victorias	6	4		76	73
Quebec	3	7		57	70
Montreal	3	7		49	63
Shamrocks	0	10		30	90

1907	W	L	D	GF	GA
Wanderers	10	0		105	39
Ottawa	7	3		76	54
Victorias	6	4		101	70
Montreal	3	7		58	83
Quebec	2	8		62	88
Shamrocks	2	8		52	120

1908	W	L	D	GF	GA
Wanderers	8	2		63	52
Ottawa	7	3		86	51
Quebec	5	5		81	74
Shamrocks	5	5		53	49
Victorias	4	6		73	78
Montreal	1	9		53	103

Eastern Canada Hockey Association

1909	W	L	D	GF	GA
Ottawa	10	2		117	63
Wanderers	9	3		82	61
Quebec	3	9		78	106
Shamrocks	2	10		56	103

Canadian Hockey Association

1910

League folds January 15; Ottawa has played two games

National Hockey Association

1910	W	L	D	GF	GA
Wanderers	11	1		91	41
Ottawa	9	3		89	66
Renfrew	8	3	1	96	54
Cobalt	4	8		79	104
Haileybury	4	8		77	83
Shamrocks	3	8	1	52	95
Canadiens	2	10		59	100

1911	W	L	D	GF	GA
Ottawa	13	3		122	69
Canadiens	8	8		66	62
Renfrew	8	8		91	101
Wanderers	7	9		73	88
Quebec	4	12		65	97

1912	W	L	D	GF	GA
Quebec	10	8		81	79

Ottawa	9	9		99	93
Wanderers	9	9		95	96
Canadiens	8	10		59	66

1913	W	L	D	GF	GA
Quebec	16	4		112	75
Wanderers	10	10		93	90
Ottawa	9	11		87	81
Toronto	9	11		86	95
Canadiens	9	11		83	81
Tecumsehs	7	13		59	98

1914	W	L	D	GF	GA
Canadiens	13	7		85	65
Toronto	13	7		93	65
Quebec	12	8		111	73
Ottawa	11	9		65	71
Wanderers	7	13		102	125
Ontarios	4	16		61	118

1915	W	L	D	GF	GA
Ottawa	14	6		74	85
Wanderers	14	6		127	82
Quebec	11	9		85	85
Ont. Shamrocks	7	13		76	96
Canadiens	6	14		65	81

1916	W	L	D	GF	GA
Canadiens	16	7	1	104	76
Ottawa	13	11		78	72
Quebec	10	12	2	91	98
Wanderers	10	14		90	116
Toronto	9	14	1	97	98

1917 · *1st half*	W	L	D	GF	GA
Canadiens	7	3		58	38
Ottawa	7	3		56	41
228th Battalion	6	4		70	57

Toronto	5	5		50	45	
Wanderers	3	7		56	72	
Quebec	2	8		43	80	
1917 · *2d half* *						
Ottawa	8	2		63	22	
Quebec	8	2		54	46	
Canadiens	3	7		31	42	
Wanderers	2	8		38	65	

228th Battalion ships overseas; Toronto withdraws

National Hockey League

1918 · *1st half*	W	L	D	GF	GA	PTS
Canadiens	10	4		81	47	20
Toronto	8	6		71	75	16
Ottawa	5	9		67	79	10
Wanderers	1	5		17	35	2
1918 · *2d half* *						
Toronto	5	3		37	34	10
Ottawa	4	4		35	35	8
Canadiens	3	5		34	37	6

Wanderers withdraw

1919 · *1st half*	W	L	D	GF	GA	PTS
Canadiens	7	3		57	50	14
Ottawa	5	5		39	39	10
Toronto	3	7		42	49	6
1919 · *2d half*						
Ottawa	7	7		32	14	14
Canadiens	3	5		31	28	6
Toronto	2	6		22	43	4

1920 · *1st half*	W	L	D	GF	GA	PTS
Ottawa	9	3		59	23	18
Canadiens	8	4		62	51	16
Toronto	5	7		52	62	10
Quebec	2	10		44	81	4
1920 · *2d half*						
Ottawa	10	2		62	41	20

Toronto	7	5		67	44	14
Canadiens	5	7		67	62	10
Quebec	2	10		47	96	4

1921 · 1st half	W	L	D	GF	GA	PTS
Ottawa	8	2		49	23	16
Toronto	5	5		39	47	10
Canadiens	4	6		37	51	8
Hamilton	3	7		34	38	6

1921 · 2d half						
Toronto	10	4		66	53	20
Canadiens	9	5		75	48	18
Ottawa	6	8		48	52	12
Hamilton	3	11		58	94	6

1922 · 1st half	W	L	D	GF	GA	PTS
Ottawa	14	8	2	106	84	30
Toronto	13	10	1	98	97	27
Canadiens	12	11	1	88	94	25
Hamilton	7	17		88	105	14

1922 · 2d half						
Ottawa	14	9	1	77	54	29
Canadiens	13	9	2	73	61	28
Toronto	13	10	1	82	88	27
Hamilton	6	18		8	110	12

1924	W	L	D	GF	GA	PTS
Ottawa	16	8		74	54	32
Canadiens	13	11		59	48	26
Toronto	10	14		59	85	20
Hamilton	9	15		63	68	18

1925	W	L	D	GF	GA	PTS
Hamilton	19	10	1	90	60	39
Toronto	19	11		90	84	38
Canadiens	17	11	2	93	56	36
Ottawa	17	12	1	83	66	35
Montreal	9	19	2	45	65	20

Boston	6	24		49	119	12

1926	W	L	D	GF	GA	PTS
Ottawa	24	8	4	77	42	52
Montreal	20	11	5	91	73	45
Pittsburgh	19	16	1	82	70	39
Boston	17	15	4	92	85	38
Americans	12	20	4	68	89	28
Toronto	12	21	3	92	114	27
Canadiens	11	24	1	79	108	23

1927 · Cdn. div.	W	L	D	GF	GA	PTS
Ottawa	30	10	4	86	69	64
Canadiens	28	14	2	99	67	58
Montreal	20	20	4	71	68	44
Americans	17	25	2	62	91	36
Toronto	15	24	5	79	94	35
1927 · U.S. div.						
Rangers	25	13	6	95	72	56
Boston	21	20	3	97	89	45
Chicago	19	22	3	115	116	41
Pittsburgh	15	26	3	79	108	33
Detroit	12	28	4	76	105	28

1928 · Cdn. div.	W	L	D	GF	GA	PTS
Canadiens	26	11	7	116	48	59
Montreal	24	14	6	96	77	54
Ottawa	20	14	0	78	57	50
Toronto	18	18	8	89	88	44
Americans	11	27	6	63	128	28
1928 · U.S. div.						
Boston	20	13	11	77	70	51
Rangers	19	16	9	94	79	47
Pittsburgh	19	17	8	67	76	46
Detroit	19	19	6	88	79	44
Chicago	7	34	3	68	134	17

1929 · Cdn. div.	W	L	D	GF	GA	PTS
Canadiens	22	7	15	71	43	59
Americans	19	13	12	53	53	50
Toronto	21	18	5	85	69	47
Ottawa	14	17	13	54	67	41
Montreal	15	20	9	67	65	39
1929 · U.S. div.						
Boston	26	13	5	89	52	57
Rangers	21	13	10	72	65	52
Detroit	19	16	9	72	63	47
Pittsburgh	9	27	8	46	80	26
Chicago	7	29	8	33	85	22

1930 · Cdn. div.	W	L	D	GF	GA	PTS
Montreal	23	16	5	141	114	51
Canadiens	21	14	9	142	114	51
Ottawa	21	15	8	138	118	50
Toronto	17	21	6	116	124	40
Americans	14	25	5	113	161	33
1930 · U.S. div						
Boston	38	5	1	179	98	77
Chicago	21	18	5	117	111	47
Rangers	17	17	10	136	143	44
Detroit	14	24	6	117	133	34
Pittsburgh	5	36	3	102	185	13

1931 · Cdn. div.	W	L	D	GF	GA	PTS
Canadiens	26	10	8	129	89	60
Toronto	22	13	9	118	99	53
Montreal	20	18	6	105	106	46
Americans	18	16	10	76	74	46
Ottawa	10	30	4	91	142	24
1931 · U.S. div.						
Boston	28	10	6	143	90	62
Chicago	24	17	3	108	78	51
Rangers	19	16	9	106	87	47

Detroit	16	21	7	102	105	39
Philadelphia	4	36	4	76	184	12

1932 · Cdn. div.*	W	L	D	GF	GA	PTS
Canadiens	25	16	7	128	111	57
Toronto	23	18	7	155	127	53
Montreal	19	22	7	142	139	45
Americans	16	24	8	95	142	40
1932 · U.S. div.						
Rangers	23	17	8	134	112	54
Chicago	18	19	11	86	101	47
Detroit	18	20	10	95	108	46
Boston	15	21	12	122	117	42

*Ottawa suspends for season

1933 · Cdn. div.	W	L	D	GF	GA	PTS
Toronto	24	18	6	119	111	54
Montreal	22	20	6	135	119	50
Canadiens	18	25	5	92	115	41
Americans	15	22	11	91	118	41
Ottawa	11	27	10	88	131	32
1933 · Cdn. div.						
Boston	25	15	8	124	88	58
Detroit	25	15	8	111	93	58
Rangers	23	17	8	135	107	54
Chicago	16	20	12	88	101	44

1934 · Cdn. div.	W	L	D	GF	GA	PTS
Toronto	26	13	9	174	119	61
Canadiens	22	20	6	99	101	50
Montreal	19	18	11	117	122	49
Americans	15	23	10	104	132	40
Ottawa	13	29	6	115	143	32
1934 · U.S. div.						
Detroit	24	14	10	113	98	58
Chicago	20	17	11	88	83	51
Rangers	21	19	8	120	113	50
Boston	18	25	5	111	130	41

Metcalfe, *Canada Learns.*
Roxborough, *One Hundred.*

p. 1 "If I was a horse": *Citizen.* Mar. 11, 1875.
p. 3 "nothing but a small villa": Hubbard, *Rideau Hall,* 21.
p. 4 "Parliamentary Pills," "wind and indigestion": *Citizen.* Feb. 20, 1875; "cash up": *Citizen.* Feb. 20, 1875; "in full blast": *Citizen.* Mar. 9, 1875.
p. 7 "with a number of friends": *Citizen.* Jan. 2, 1877.

Chapter 2

General

Ottawa Citizen, Dec.–Mar. 1880–1884.
Ottawa Free Press, Feb. 1–Mar. 6, 1883; Jan. 24–Feb. 20, 1884.
Census of Canada. 1880–81.
Ottawa Directory. 1880–1884.

Early hockey

Cox, *History of Sports.*
Fitsell, *Hockey's Captains.*
Lindsay thesis.
Roxborough, *One Hundred.*
Vaughan, *Puck Starts.*

Montreal Winter Carnival

Don Morrow. "Frozen festivals: Ceremony and the *Carnaval* in the Montreal Winter Carnivals, 1883-1889". *Sport History review.* vol. 27, no. 2, 1996, 173–90.
Souvenir of the Montreal Winter Carnival.
Montreal Gazette. Jan. 23–27, 1883; Feb. 4–11, 1884.
Montreal Herald. Feb. 4–12, 1884.
Montreal Star. Feb. 4–11, 1884

Biographical information

Ottawa Hockey Club, 1884
   Ottawa Citizen. Jan. 19, 1935.
Gallagher, Green, Jenkins, Kirby, Low, Taylor, Young
   Ottawa Directory. Ottawa: 1884–1901.

Census of Canada. 1901. (LAC. Microfilm T6487, T6488.)
Green
    LAC. RG15 D-II-1, microfilm T12558, file 57629.
Jenkins
    Ottawa Citizen. Dec. 9, 1930.
    Ottawa Journal. Dec. 6, 1930.
    Frank and Annie Jenkins Collection. LAC. MG30 D183, vol. 1, 2.
    LAC. McCurry Family Papers. Music Division. MUS27. Mr. and Mrs.
    Jenkins Personal Papers. Boxes 1, 2.
Kerr
    Beechwood Cemetery registry, Ottawa.
    Ottawa Citizen. Feb. 17, 1933.
Kirby
    Ottawa Journal. July 14, 1924.
Porter
    Ottawa Citizen. Feb. 14, 1961.
Low
    Canadian Men and Women of the Times.
    Geological Survey of Canada. *Report on Explorations.*
    Hall, *Early Canada.*
    Montreal Gazette. Oct. 10, 1942.
    LAC. RG15, Interior, series D-II-1, vol. 452, microfilm T13141, file 119931.
    Ottawa Journal. Oct. 10, 1942.
    Zaslow, *Reading the Rocks.*

p. 11 "When a player hits the ball": *Montreal Gazette.* Feb. 27, 1877.
p. 14 "From the hour when Jacques Cartier": *Montreal Gazette.* Jan. 23, 1883.
p. 16 "an active and energetic officer": LAC. Interior. D-II-1, vol. 452,
    microfilm T3141, file 119931.
p. 17 "Tragically": Zaslow, *Reading the Rocks,* 263; "the honour to humbly
    request" and following: LAC. RG15 D-II 1, vol. 291, microfilm T12558,
    file 57629.
p. 21 "to adjourn for two or three days": *Debates.* Jan. 31, 1884. p. 83; "The
    weather is fine": *Ottawa Citizen.* Feb. 5, 1884.
p. 22 "Trains run by standard time": *Ottawa Citizen.* Feb. 4, 1884.
p. 23 "The correct position of a bark canoe": *Ottawa Citizen.* Jan. 29, 1884.
p. 25 "Go it Ottawa": *Montreal Star.* Feb. 8, 1884; "an indescribable
    struggle": *Montreal Herald.* Feb. 9, 1884.

p. 26 "splendidly directed shot": *Montreal Herald.* Feb. 12, 1884; "team returned home": *Ottawa Citizen.* Feb. 12, 1884.

Chapter 3

General
Ottawa Citizen, Ottawa Free Press, Ottawa Journal. 1884–90.
Ottawa Directory. 1884-1890.

Montreal Winter Carnival
Montreal Gazette. Jan. 24–Feb. 2, 1885.
Montreal Herald. Jan. 26–Feb. 2, 1885.

Hockey in Montreal
Montreal Gazette daily issues 1884–90.

Ottawa Hockey Club meetings
Ottawa Amateur Athletic Club. *Annual Report.* "Ottawa Hockey Club."
Ottawa Citizen. Nov. 19, 1884; Dec. 5, 1885; Dec. 8, 1886.
Ottawa Free Press. Dec. 5, 1885.
Ottawa Journal. Jan. 26, 1889.

Ottawa Hockey Club game-related activities
Ottawa Citizen, Ottawa Free Press, Ottawa Journal. 1884–90.

Biographical information
Green
    LAC. RG15 D-II-1, microfilm T12558, file 57629.
Ross
    LAC. Ross Collection.
    Smith, *Journal Men.*

p. 28 "beautifully lighted": *Ottawa Citizen.* Nov. 24, 1884; "In roystering fun": *Montreal Gazette.* Jan. 24, 1885.
p. 30 "a dangerous experiment": *Ottawa Free Press.* Dec. 16, 1885.
p. 31 "The puck must be": *Montreal Gazette.* Jan. 8, 1886; "Do away with the offside rule": *Montreal Gazette.* Jan. 25, 1886.
p. 32 "challenge," "championship trophy": *Montreal Gazette.* Dec. 23, 1886.

p. 35 "to improve, foster and perpetuate": *Montreal Gazette*. Dec. 23, 1886; "kindly feeling": *Montreal Gazette*. Dec. 23, 1886.

p. 40 "A Humble Votary": *Ottawa Journal*. Feb. 4, 1889.

p. 42 "practice on the horizontal bar," "to have a few rounds": *Ottawa Citizen*. Nov. 21, 1889.

p. 42 "The qualification for membership": *Ottawa Citizen*. Nov. 21, 1889.

p. 44 "The new members": *Ottawa Journal*. Oct. 29, 1889; "Article III. Colors, Uniform and Badge": *Constitution and By-laws of the Ottawa Amateur Athletic Association*; "a greater number would": Ottawa Amateur Athletic Club. *Annual Report*. 1890.

p. 45 "If it is seen fit": *Ottawa Free Press*. Feb. 4, 1890; "joined in the game," "whether it was at": *Ottawa Journal*. Feb. 10, 1890; "recent illness": *Ottawa Journal*. Feb. 17, 1890.

Chapter 4

General
Ottawa Citizen, Ottawa Journal daily issues 1890–92.
Ottawa Directory. 1890–92.

Refrigeration
Ottawa Citizen. Nov. 24, 1884.
Canadian Patent Office Record. 1883–88.
Donald M. Clark. "Early Artificial Ice". *Total Hockey*. 1st ed., 564–65

Hockey in Montreal
Montreal Gazette daily issues 1890–92.

Ottawa Hockey Club meetings
Montreal Gazette. Nov. 20, 1890.
Ottawa Amateur Athletic Club. *Annual Report*. "Ottawa Hockey Club". 1890–99.
Ottawa Journal. Nov. 20, 1890; Nov. 13, 1891.
Toronto Empire. Nov. 20, 1890.

Ottawa Hockey Club game-related activities
Ottawa Citizen, Ottawa Journal, Montreal Gazette daily issues 1890-1892.

p. 48 "That it is desirable": *Ottawa Journal*. Nov. 20, 1890.

p. 50 "Practice was almost": Ottawa Amateur Athletic Club. *Annual Report*. 1891; "dozens of shots": *Ottawa Journal*. Jan. 15, 1891; "large proportion of the fair sex": *Ottawa Journal*. Feb. 12, 1891.

p. 52 "The Montreal passing," "The Ottawas played," "A very enjoyable": *Ottawa Journal*. Feb. 23, 1891.

p. 53 "Engaged in changing": LAC. Ross Collection. Diary entry, Feb. 28, 1891.

p. 54 "professed themselves": Ottawa Amateur Athletic Club. *Annual Report*. "Ottawa Hockey Club." 1891; "Got hack": LAC. Ross Collection. Diary entry, Mar. 13, 1891.

p. 55 "Championship of": *Ottawa Journal*. Mar. 16, 1891.

p. 64 "From a hockey": *Montreal Gazette*. Jan. 6, 1892; "to give immigrants": *Ottawa Journal*. Feb. 19, 1892.

p. 65 "legality rushers": *Toronto Empire*, quoted in *Ottawa Journal*. Mar. 3, 1892.

p. 66 "Grand Championship Match": *Ottawa Citizen*. Mar. 7, 1892; "sporting men": *Montreal Gazette*. Mar. 8, 1892.

p. 67 *Montreal Gazette*, *Ottawa Journal*. Mar. 8–10, 1892.

Chapter 5

General

LAC. Ross Collection.
Ottawa Citizen, *Ottawa Journal*. 1893 1903.
Ottawa Directory. 1892–1903.
Taylor, *Ottawa*.

Bessie Blair, Henry Harper drowning

Gwyn, *Private Capital*.
Ottawa Citizen. Dec. 7, 10, 1901.
Ottawa Journal. Dec. 7, 9, 1901; Apr. 25, 1903.

Hockey associations and management

Index to Incorporated Bodies. [Includes all letters patent for Canada and Ontario to Jan. 1, 1901; no reference to any Ottawa hockey organization.]
Montreal Gazette, *Ottawa Citizen*, *Ottawa Journal* daily issues 1892–93.

LAC. RG95, vol. 1765, file: Ottawa Hockey Association Limited. [application to Secretary of State of Canada for incorporation (and revisions), associated correspondence, and letters patent, Oct. 20–Dec. 1, 1911]

Ontario Gazette. 1900–18. [Includes all letters patent for Ontario; no reference to any Ottawa hockey organization]

Ottawa Amateur Athletic Club. *Annual Report*. "Ottawa Hockey Club." 1890–99.

p. 69 "I would urge": *Montreal Gazette*. Dec. 15, 1892.

p. 70 "the centre of government": Taylor, *Ottawa*, 81; "the suburbs of civilization": *Ottawa Journal*. Feb. 11, 1899.

p. 71 "the shantyman is passing": *Ottawa Journal*. Sept. 17, 1898; "ill fortune" and following: *Ottawa Journal*. Feb. 11, 1899.

p. 72 "drawing room": *Ottawa Journal*. Jan. 30, 1893; "There was little": *Ottawa Journal*. Mar. 18, 1893; "Socialites as we know them" and following: *Ottawa Journal*. Mar. 6, 1894; "Erminie" and following: *Ottawa Free Press*. Feb. 18, 1893; "the first of": *Ottawa Journal*. Nov. 28, 1895.

p. 73 "The skating": *Ottawa Journal*. Nov. 29, 1895; "For god's sake Harper": Gwyn, *Private Capital*, 324.

p. 75 "Toronto Hoggy": *Ottawa Journal*. Dec. 9, 1893.

p. 76 "Brilliancy" and following: *Ottawa Citizen*. Dec. 12, 1898.

p. 77 "unanimous vote": *Montreal Gazette*. Dec. 15, 1898.

p. 78 "win, tie or wrangle": *Montreal Gazette*. Mar. 13, 1893; "Rickety, rickety": *Ottawa Journal*. Jan. 28, 1895.

p. 79 "A radical change" and following: *Ottawa Journal*. Jan. 24, 1901.

p. 81 "great exodus": *Ottawa Citizen*. Feb. 11, 1899.

p. 86 "who had always": *Ottawa Journal*. Dec. 15, 1896.

p. 87 "Hockey in Canada": *Ottawa Journal*. Dec. 18, 1896.

p. 89 "The Ottawa Hockey Club": *Ottawa Journal*. Nov. 20, 1900; "which should be held": *Ottawa Citizen*. Mar. 19, 1892.

Chapter 6

Player profiles
General

Ottawa Citizen, Ottawa Journal various issues 1892–1962.

Ottawa Directory. 1890–1904.

Chittick, Henry, Hutton, McGee, Morel, Smith
  Census of Canada. 1901. LAC. Microfilm T6487, T6488.
Chittick
  Civil Service List of Canada. 1891–1903.
Hutton
  Ottawa Journal. Oct. 29, 1962.
McGee
  Dictionary of Canadian Biography, vol. 14, 701–02.
  Ottawa Citizen. Sept. 25, 1916.
  Don Reddick. "The Death of Frank McGee." In *Total Hockey*, 2d ed.,
  48–50.
  N.B. The *Dictionary of Canadian Biography* gives McGee's birth date as
  Nov. 4, 1882. The *Civil Service List* states his date of birth as Nov. 4, 1880.
  The 1901 census does not give a year of birth but states McGee's age
  as 21. The *Ottawa Citizen* says McGee was 35 at the time of his death,
  Sept. 16, 1916. I have concluded McGee was born November 4, 1880.
Pulford
  Ottawa Journal. Nov. 1, 2, 4, 1940.
Smith
  Ottawa Journal. Aug. 22, 24, 1953.
Westwick
  Ottawa Journal. Apr. 4, 1957.

p. 90 "Not quite certain": *Ottawa Citizen*. Mar. 19, 1892.
p. 91 "His Excellency's Conditions": *Montreal Gazette*. Feb. 23, 1894.
p. 94 "club": *Ottawa Citizen*. Feb. 14, 1899.
p. 95 "I have returned" and following: *Ottawa Citizen*. Feb. 20, 1899.
p. 98 "ambitious": *Ottawa Journal*. Feb. 17, 1896; "splendid": *Ottawa Journal*.
  Feb. 26, 1894.
p. 99 "cool, steady": *Ottawa Journal*. Jan. 29, 1894; "reliable": *Ottawa Journal*.
  Feb. 18, 1903.
p. 100 "He was always": *Ottawa Journal*. Nov. 1, 1940; "the four white
  jerseys": *Ottawa Journal*. Jan. 29, 1894.
p. 101 "quite proper": *Ottawa Citizen*. Jan. 30, 1899; "big rough brute":
  Ottawa Journal. Feb. 25, 1895.
p. 102 "Time and time again": *Ottawa Journal*. Jan. 25, 1903; "miserable
  insignificant rat": *Ottawa Journal*. Jan. 26, 1957.
p. 103 "glided down the ice": *Ottawa Citizen*. Jan. 16, 1899; "Smith mostly

played": *Ottawa Journal*. Jan. 11, 1897; "Smith took it easy": *Ottawa Journal*. Jan. 18, 1897.

p. 106 "almost recovered": *Ottawa Citizen*. May 5, 1900; "I asked which was McGee": *Ottawa Citizen*. Sept. 25, 1916.

p. 107 "he generally decorates": *Ottawa Journal*. March 7, 1902; "Too bad old man": *Ottawa Citizen*. Feb. 18, 1899; "the grandest and gamest": *Ottawa Citizen*. Sept. 25, 1916.

Chapter 7

New York excursions
New York Times. Mar. 24, 25, 1900; Mar. 23, 24, 1901; Mar. 22, 23, 1902.
Ottawa Journal. Mar. 21, 24, 26, 28, 29, 1900; Mar. 20, 22, 23, 25, 1901; Mar. 17, 22, 24, 1902.

Game-related activities
Coleman, *Trail*. vol. 1.
Ottawa Citizen, Ottawa Journal various issues 1903.

p. 111 "almost an entirely": *Ottawa Journal*. Feb. 21, 1898.

p. 112 "round corners," "It seems like": *Ottawa Citizen*. Jan. 30, 1899.

p. 113 "barber poles": *Ottawa Journal*. Feb. 23, 1903; "rough riders": *Ottawa Citizen*. Oct. 19, 1898.

p. 114 "Who let you in" and following: *Ottawa Journal*. Mar. 10, 1903.

p. 117 "Bob Shillington": *Ottawa Journal*. Jan. 26, 1957.

Chapter 8

Silver Seven name
For three of Ottawa's Stanley Cup series (Winnipeg, 1904; Dawson, 1905; and Wanderers, 1906) accounts in the following newspapers were examined: *Halifax Herald, Halifax Morning Chronicle, Fredericton Daily Gleaner, Montreal Gazette, Ottawa Citizen, Ottawa Journal, Kingston Daily Whig, Belleville Intelligencer, Toronto Globe, Hamilton Spectator, Fort William Daily Times Journal, Manitoba Free Press, Calgary Herald, Vancouver Province.* In addition, *Ottawa Citizen* and *Ottawa Journal* reports of all Ottawa Hockey Club regular-season and playoff games (1904–06) not included in the above search were reviewed.

Management profiles
Shillington
> *Canadian Parliamentary Guide.* 1909, 1914.
> *Ottawa Citizen, Ottawa Journal.* Jan. 11, 1934 and various issues 1900–06.
> *Toronto Mail and Empire.* Jan. 12, 1934.

Dickson
> *Ottawa Journal.* Feb. 27, 1904; and various issues 1900–06.

National notice
See Silver Seven sources
Manitoba Free Press. Oct. 4, 1907.
Kesterton, *History of Journalism.*

Professionalism
Cosentino thesis
Ernie Fitzsimmons. "Early Pro Leagues." In *Total Hockey.* 2d ed.
LAC MG28 I 150, microfilm M-3209, 3210, 3211. Minutes. Board of
> Governors. Canadian Amateur Athletic Union.
Don Morrow. "A Case Study in Amateur Conflict: The Athletic War in
> Canada, 1906–1908." In Mott, *Sports in Canada.*

p. 120 "so crude": *Manitoba Free Press.* Oct. 4, 1907; "the rate charged":
> Kesterton, *History of Journalism,* 159; "so necessary": *Manitoba Free Press.*
> Oct. 4, 1907.
p. 121 "Ottawa, Ont. Jan. 1, 1904 — 8 p.m.": *Manitoba Free Press.* Jan. 2, 1904.
p. 123 "close corporation": *Ottawa Journal.* Dec. 1, 1903.
p. 125 "Section 3 of the Laws of Hockey," "That in view": LAC. MG128 I 351.
> Canadian Amateur Hockey League. Secretary's Book, microfilm H-
> 1871, Executive Council, Feb. 6, 1904.
p. 127 "instructed to acknowledge": quoted in *Ottawa Journal.* Dec. 12, 1904.
p. 133 "to tell the plain truth" and following: *Ottawa Journal.* Dec. 15, 1905.
p. 134 "amateurs competing against professionals": LAC. MG28 I 150, Canadian
> Amateur Athletic Union, June 26, 1905, microfilm M-3209, 151–2.

Chapter 9

Ottawa Hockey Club game-related activities
Coleman, *Trail.* vol. 1.

Manitoba Free Press. 1903, 1904.
Ottawa Citizen, Ottawa Journal. 1903-1906.
Taylor, *Sourdough*.

McGee in civil service
Civil Service List. 1906, 1907.
LAC. RG15, Interior Series. D-II-1, vol. 990, microfilm T-14568

p. 136 "was as pleasant": *Smith's Falls Rideau Record*. Jan. 7, 1904.
p. 137 "hospital list": quoted in *Ottawa Journal*. Jan. 6, 1904.
p. 139 "post-prandial proceedings": *Ottawa Citizen*. Jan. 6, 1904; "nothing good": *Ottawa Journal*. Feb. 24, 1904.
p. 141 "I might just add": *Ottawa Journal*. Sept. 10, 1904.
p. 142 "It was only": quoted in Taylor, *Sourdough*, 85.
p. 143 "1,060 pounds": *Ottawa Journal*. Mar. 6, 1905.
p. 144 "Frank McGee was": *Ottawa Journal*. Mar. 10, 1905; "racing condition": *Ottawa Journal*. Mar. 13, 1905.
p. 145 "though our fellows": *Ottawa Journal*. Mar. 14, 1905.
p. 147 "a complete failure": *Ottawa Journal*. Mar. 15, 1906.
p. 149 "The team": *Ottawa Journal*. Mar. 23, 1906; "I always felt sorry": *Ottawa Citizen*. Jan. 9, 2000.

Chapter 10

Ottawa Hockey Club game-related activities
Coleman, *Trail*. vol. 1.
Ottawa Citizen, Ottawa Journal. 1906–13.
Ottawa Free Press. 1907–08.

Ottawa Hockey Club business-related activities
IHM. A.E. Smith contract with Ottawa Hockey Club, Dec. 4, 1907.
Kitchen, *Dey Brothers' Rinks*.
LAC. RG95, vol. 1765, file: Ottawa Hockey Association Limited. [application to Secretary of State for Canada for incorporation (and revisions), associated correspondence, and letters patent, Oct. 20–Dec. 1, 1911]
LAC. MG30 C129. Gorman Collection, vol. 1, file 7: Ottawa Hockey Club ledger.
Thomas D. Picard. "The Pacific Coast Hockey Association." In *Total Hockey*. 1st ed., 35–41.

Economic conditions
Historical Statistics of Canada.
Labour Gazette. Various issues 1906–1914.

Biographical data
Civil Service List of Canada. 1906–14.
Ottawa Directory. 1906–14.
Cosentino, *Renfrew Millionaires.*
Whitehead, *Cyclone Taylor.*
Young, *O'Brien.*

p. 151 "Hockey and football": quoted in *Ottawa Journal.* Oct. 9, 1906; "ten years ago": *Ottawa Citizen.* Dec. 10, 1909.

p. 152 "do away with": *Ottawa Journal.* Oct. 29, 1906; "scum": *Ottawa Journal.* Oct. 29, 1906; "to all intents and purposes": *Ottawa Journal.* Nov. 9, 1906; "The league is strong enough": *Ottawa Journal.* Nov. 12, 1906.

p. 153 "At least one professional": *Montreal Gazette.* Nov. 12, 1906.

p. 159 "I had in view": *Ottawa Journal.* Dec. 18, 1907; "Prompt attention": *Ottawa Journal.* Dec. 17, 1907.

p. 160 "Taylor came here": *Ottawa Free Press.* Jan. 13, 1908; "Cyclone": Whitehead, *Cyclone Taylor,* 70; "the Listowel Cyclone": *Ottawa Citizen, Ottawa Journal.* Feb. 10, 1908.

p. 161 "Senators": *Ottawa Citizen.* Dec. 24, 1908.

p. 164 "to all interested in hockey": *Montreal Gazette.* Nov. 26, 1909; "the storm centre": *Montreal Gazette.* Dec. 4, 1909.

p. 165 "he would not take": *Renfrew Mercury.* Dec. 10, 1909.

p. 166 "We did not have to": *Montreal Gazette.* Dec. 4, 1909; "I have just written": *Ottawa Citizen.* Dec. 4, 1909.

p. 167 "les suisses": *Ottawa Journal.* Jan. 11, 1910; "I would rather": *Ottawa Journal.* Nov. 18, 1910; "I would gladly give back" and following: Coleman, *Trail,* vol. 1, 202.

Chapter 11

Great War
Brown, *Canada.*
Debates. House of Commons. Dec. 5, 1912; May 15, 1913.
Herridge, *Call of War.*

Morton, *Years of Conflict*.
Don Reddick. "The Death of Frank McGee." In *Total Hockey*. 2d ed.
Whitehead, *Patricks*.
Wilson, *Ontario and the First World War*.
Peter Wilton. "Hockey in World War I." In *Total Hockey*. 1st ed.

Ottawa Hockey Club game-related activities
Coleman, *Trail*. vol. 1.
Montreal Gazette, Ottawa Citizen, Ottawa Journal. 1913–17.

Ottawa Hockey Club and National Hockey Association business-related activities
Holzman, *Deceptions*.
Len Kotylo. "Hockey and the Courts." Paper delivered at Putting it on Ice conference sponsored by Gorsebrook Research Insitute, St. Mary's University, Halifax, Nova Scotia, Oct. 2001.
LAC. MG30 C129. Gorman Collection, vol. 1, file 7: Ottawa Hockey Club ledger.

p. 175 "We are not worrying": *Ottawa Journal*. Oct. 29, 1913; "the big Pembroke boy": *Ottawa Journal*. Jan. 5, 1914.

p. 176 "Carrie Nation rooter": *Ottawa Journal*. Feb. 7, 1914.

p. 177 "Do not listen": LeSueur, *How to Play Hockey*, 14; "A small pad" and following: ibid., 89.

p. 179 "Very grave events" and following: *Ottawa Journal*. Aug. 18, 1914; "Comfortable and complacent": Brown, *Canada*, 227.

p. 180 "Any employee of The Journal": *Ottawa Journal*. Aug. 6, 1914; "Admiral Alf Smith" and following: *Ottawa Journal*. Jan. 4, 1915.

p. 182 "Well, if you have had enough": *Ottawa Journal*. Feb. 18, 1915; "There were three hundred women" and following: *Ottawa Journal*. Feb. 18, 1915; "Remember fellows," "What time does the train": *Ottawa Journal*. Mar. 11, 1915.

p. 183 "low altitude": *Ottawa Journal*. Mar. 23, 1915.

p. 184 "I have got to": *Ottawa Journal*. Mar. 27, 1915.

p. 185 "Because others do their duty": Wilson, *Ontario and the First World War*, xxxiv; "Exchange the stick and puck": Peter Wilton. "Hockey in World war I." In *Total Hockey*. 1st ed; "We have some 750 players": *Ottawa Journal*. Ap 1, 1916; "He that hath no sword": Herridge, *The Call of the War*.

p. 186 "The two brothers": Whitehead, *Patricks*, 125; "Does the clerical gentleman" and following: *Ottawa Journal*. Jan. 9, 1917.

p. 188 "Lieut. Frank McGee": *Ottawa Citizen*. Sept. 25, 1916; "Body unrecovered for burial": Don Reddick. "The Death of Frank McGee." In *Total Hockey*. 2d ed.; "good": LAC. RG150, acc. no. 1992-93/166, box 6829-29. Frank Clarence McGee.

p. 190 "The Patricks declared": *Ottawa Journal*. Nov. 10, 1915.

p. 192 "I have received" and following: *Ottawa Citizen*. Oct. 28, 1916; "Advertising": LAC. MG30 C129 Gorman Collection, vol. 1, file 7: Ottawa Hockey Club ledger.

p. 195 "We are not bluffing": *Ottawa Citizen*. Feb. 13, 1917.

p. 197 "loafing around": *Ottawa Journal*. Mar. 12, 1917.

p. 199 "not likely to become": LAC. RG150, acc. no. 1992-93/166, box 7396-39. Discharge Documents; "The season for professional hockey" and following: *Ottawa Journal*. Mar. 12, 1917.

Chapter 12

Great War
Brown, *Canada*.
"World War I"; "Passchendaele, Battle of." *Canadian Encyclopedia*.
Morton, *Years of Conflict*.

Ottawa Hockey Club game-related activities
Coleman, *Trail*. vol. 1.
Montreal Gazette, *Ottawa Citizen*, *Ottawa Journal*. 1917–19.

Ottawa Hockey Club and the court
A.O. Quinn v. Dey. Supreme Court of Ontario, 1918, 1919. [writ, statement of claim, affidavits, statement of defence, examinations, associated documents]
AO Toronto Hockey Club Limited v. Ottawa Hockey Association et al. Supreme Court of Ontario, 1917–19. [affidavits, statement of claim, examinations, associated documents]
Holzman, *Deceptions*.
Lenard Kotylo. "Hockey and the Courts: Legal Action off the Ice." *The Hockey Research Journal*. Fall 2001, 23–28.
Lenard Kotylo. "Hockey and the Courts." Paper delivered at Putting it on

Ice conference sponsored by Gorsebrook Research Institute, St. Mary's University, Halifax, Nova Scotia, Oct. 2001.

Ottawa Hockey Club business-related activities

Jim Coleman. "The Great Gorman." *Maclean's Magazine.* Mar. 1, 1946, 16, 55–57.

Tommy Gorman. "Financial History of Pro Hockey in Ottawa." *Ottawa Citizen.* Jan. 25, 1927.

Tommy Gorman. "Tommy Gorman Remembers." *Weekend Magazine.* (*Ottawa Citizen*) May 4 (p. 2–4, 51); May 11 (p. 58–62); May 18 (p. 22–25, 62)

LAC. RG95, vol. 1756, file: Ottawa Hockey Association Limited. [application to Secretary of State for Canada for incorporation, associated correspondence, and letters patent, Oct. 20–Dec. 1, 1911]

LAC MG30 C129. Gorman Collection, vol. 1, file 8: First annual report of the Ottawa Hockey Club, Oct. 23, 1918; annual meeting of the Ottawa Hockey Club, Nov. 4, 1918; first annual meeting of the Ottawa Arena Club, Nov. 14, 1918.

Ottawa Citizen, Ottawa Journal. May 15, 16, 1961. [T.P. Gorman obituaries]

Jack Darragh

Ottawa Directory. Various editions 1910–1919.

Total Hockey. 2d ed.

Aileen Wills (daughter of Jack Darragh). Interview Sept. 22, 2003.

p. 200 "the firing line": *Ottawa Citizen.* Oct. 30, 1917; "fuelless Fridays": Morton, *Years of Conflict,* 75; "in view of": *Ottawa Citizen.* Sept. 5, 1917.

p. 201 "The Ottawa Hockey Club Limited": LAC. RG95 vol. 1765, file: Ottawa Hockey Association Limited. Letter, Oct. 20, 1911; "to conduct and carry on" and following: LAC. RG95, vol. 1765, file: Ottawa Hockey Association Limited. Application and correspondence.

p 203 "Few people who see": LAC. MG30 C129. Gorman Collection, vol. 4. Clipping dated House of Commons, May 16, 1904.

p. 204 "I was an owner": AO *Quinn v. Dey.* Supreme Court of Ontario. Examination of E.P. Dey, Dec. 23, 1918. p. 4; "In the fall of 1917": *Ottawa Citizen.* Jan. 25, 1917; "Our receipts were": LAC. MG30 C129. Gorman Collection, vol. 1, file 8: First annual report of the Ottawa Hockey Club, Oct. 23, 1918.

p. 206 "Inquirer.... How comes it": *Ottawa Citizen*. Nov 30, 1917.

p. 207 "night and day": *Ottawa Journal*. Feb. 16, 1905.

p. 208 "That was a fine" and following: *Ottawa Journal*. Feb. 11, 1916; "After last night's game": *Ottawa Journal*. Feb. 24, 1916.

p. 209 "acting honestly": Lenard Kotylo. "Hockey and the Courts: Legal Action off the Ice." *Hockey Research Journal*. Fall 2001. p. 23.

p. 212 "Toronto, Oct. 2/18. I hereby agree" AO *Quin v. Dey*. Supreme Court of Ontario. Statement of Claim, Dec. 30, 1918. p. 15.

p. 213 "Dey is working": *Ottawa Citizen*. Oct. 5, 1918.

p. 215 "Mr. Dey was part owner": *Ottawa Citizen*. Oct. 19, 1918; "Mr. Dey was a part owner": *Ottawa Journal*. Oct. 19, 1918; "Mr. Dey announced": LAC. MG30 C129. Gorman Collection, vol. 1, file 8: Annual meeting of the Ottawa Hockey Club, Nov. 4, 1918; "In 1918, Mr. Rosenthal": *Ottawa Citizen*. Jan. 25, 1927.

p. 216 "this day" and following: LAC. MG30 C129. Gorman Collection, vol. 1, file 8: Annual meeting of the Ottawa Hockey Club, Nov. 4, 1918.

p. 217 "conveying the assurances" and following. LAC. MG30 C129. Gorman Collection, vol. 1, file 8: First annual meeting of Ottawa Arena Club, Nov. 14, 1918.

p. 218 "had heard stories"; *Ottawa Citizen*. Nov. 11, 1918; "outside of discussing them": AO *Quinn v. Dey*. Supreme Court of Ontario. Examination of Percy J. Quinn, Jan. 14, 1919. p. 6; "of a good professional": ibid. p. 12.

p. 219 "Ottawa is known as": AO *Quinn v. Dey*. Supreme Court of Ontario. Jan. 14, 1919. p. 13; "grim" and following: Morton, *Years of Conflict*, 90–91; "Particularly is it desirable": *Ottawa Journal*. Dec. 7, 1918.

p. 220 "Dear Santy": *Ottawa Journal*. Nov. 23, 1918; "phenomenal success" and following: *Ottawa Journal*. Dec. 19, 1918.

p. 222 "My sister is dead": *Ottawa Journal*. Feb. 24, 1919.

p. 223 "I am really sorry": *Ottawa Journal*. Apr. 7, 1919.

Chapter 13

Frank Ahearn

Finnigan, *Old Scores*.

Who's Who in Canada. 1925–26.

Ottawa Citizen, Ottawa Journal. Nov. 7, 8, 1962, [obituaries]

The Cook Brothers
Letters and contract, courtesy of W.T. Cook, Kingston, Ontario

Ottawa Hockey Association and Auditorium Limited
Bugyra, *Match Penalty.*
Wong thesis.
Notice of letters patent for The Auditorium Ltd. *Canada Gazette.*
    Dec. 9,1922.
Ottawa Citizen, Ottawa Journal. 1922–27.

Pacific Coast Hockey
Thomas D. Picard. "The Pacific Coast hockey Association." In *Total Hockey.*
    1st ed, 35–41.
Whitehead, *Patricks.*

U.S. expansion
Coleman, *Trail.* vol. 1.
Fischler, *Metro Ice.*
Montreal Gazette, Ottawa Citizen, Ottawa Journal. 1924-1927.

Dey's Arena
Land Registry Office, Ottawa. CR80572, microfilm 5-554. Lease dated
    February 13, 1907.

p. 226 "exclusive and unrestricted services" LAC. MG30 C129. Gorman
    Collection, vol. 1, file 10: Memo of Agreement; "to construct, erect,
    lease" and following: *Canada Gazette.* Dec. 9, 1922. p. 2504.
p. 229 *"Dorothy Vernon of Haddon Hall," "The Ten Commandments"*: *Ottawa
    Journal.* Sept. 12, 1924; "What'll I do?": *Ottawa Journal.* Sept. 29, 1924;
    "Frank Ahearn may sell": *Ottawa Journal.* February 12, 1924.
p. 230 "We wanted to put an end": *Ottawa Journal.* Feb. 13, 1924.
p. 231 "I am anxious": *Ottawa Citizen.* Dec. 26, 1924; "give up the
    management": *Ottawa Journal.* Dec. 17, 1924; "an unedifying public
    squabble" and following: *Ottawa Journal.* Jan. 9, 1925.
p. 232 "I sold out to Ahearn": *Weekend Magazine* (supplement in *Ottawa
    Citizen*). May 4, 1957. p. 51.
p. 234 "We do not believe": *Ottawa Journal.* Jan. 1, 1921; "the Boucher who
    is" and following: *Ottawa Journal.* Nov. 29, 1921.

p. 236 "Hunting big game": *Montreal Standard*. Mar. 7, 1925.

p. 237 "reasonable fines": LAC. MG30 C129. Gorman Collection, vol. 1, file 12: Clancy contract; "It is agreed that": LAC. MG30 C129. Gorman Collection, vol. 1, file 12: Clancy contract.

p. 238 "We want the championship": *Ottawa Journal*. Mar. 2, 1923; "Jack had a strange": *Montreal Standard*. Feb. 28, 1925; "I've had enough hockey": *Montreal Standard*. Feb. 28, 1925; "Don't throw us down": *Montreal Standard*. Feb. 28, 1925; "Jack Darragh was": *Montreal Standard*. Feb. 28, 1925.

p. 241 "All the officials": Letter from T.F. Ahearn to W.O Cook, Sept. 6, 1926 courtesy of W.T. Cook, Kingston, Ontario; "Dear Bill: We have disposed": Letter from Hubert Bishop to W.O. Cook, Sept. 13, 1926 courtesy of W.T. Cook, Kingston, Ontario.

p. 243 "If you fellows ever lose": *Montreal Standard*. Feb. 28, 1925.

p. 244 "thousands of spectators" and following: Quoted in *Ottawa Journal*. Nov. 23, 1925.

p. 245 "If the public": *Ottawa Journal*. Nov. 23, 1925; "I do not think" *Ottawa Journal*. Nov. 24, 1925; "The Citizen sports editor": *Ottawa Hockey News*. vol. 1, no. 2, Oct. 31, 1925.

p. 246 "radio burglar": *Ottawa Journal*. Dec. 30, 1926; "Distance means nothing": *Ottawa Journal*. Feb. 15, 1923.

p. 247 "relayed a very clear" *Ottawa Citizen*. Mar. 12, 1924; "Mosquitoes: Their Control": *Ottawa Journal*. Ap 11, 1927; "Baseball and the ethereal": *Ottawa Journal*. Apr. 12, 1927.

p. 250 "We agree for a period": LAC. MG30 C129. Gorman Collection, vol. 1, file 10.

p. 251 "The American owners": LAC. MG30 C129. Gorman Collection, vol. 1, file 10; "it is fair to assume": reprinted in *Ottawa Journal*. Apr. 30, 1925.

p. 252 "shrieking, clamorous mob": *Ottawa Journal*. Dec. 11, 1925; "kept in a state of": *New York Times*. Jan. 12, 1926.

p. 253 "I have talked": *Ottawa Citizen*. Feb. 22, 1926; "For my part": *Ottawa Journal*. May 3, 1926.

p. 254 "well known," "its national home": *Montreal Star*. May 12, 1926; "From the time of my entry" and following: *Montreal Star*. May 12, 1926; "If we had the Ottawa team": *Ottawa Journal*. Jan. 12, 1927.

Chapter 14

General

Coleman, *Trail*. vols. 1, 2.
Diamond, *Hockey Hall of Fame*.
Duplacey, *Rules of Hockey*.
Haché, *Physics of Hockey*.

p. 258 "Saints Ducked": *Ottawa Journal.* Jan. 29, 1920; "That's where I": *Ottawa Journal.* Jan. 29, 1920.
p. 264 "Ottawa should change": quoted in *Ottawa Journal.* Jan. 28, 1921; "Fergie knows better": *Ottawa Journal* . Jan. 28, 1921; "after last night's": *Montreal Star.* Jan. 27, 1921.
p. 267 "The time has come": *Ottawa Journal.* Apr. 4, 1921.
p. 271 "Little Mervich": *Ottawa Journal.* Feb. 2, 1922;
p. 273 "a saturnalia of butchery": Coleman, *Trail*, vol. 1, 108.
p. 276 "Glorified ragging ... unbeautiful": *Montreal Herald* quoted in *Ottawa Journal.* Jan. 19, 1923.
p. 279 "It is so hot": *Ottawa Journal.* Feb. 2, 1926; "slush kings": *Ottawa Journal.* Jan. 18, 1924.
p. 281 "We wouldn't have minded": *Ottawa Journal.* Feb. 27, 1925.
p. 282 "You know, Cy": LAC. Video VI 2004-01-0003. *Hockey Night in Canada* interview with Cy Denneny, 1967.
p. 286 "Tell the crowd": *Ottawa Journal.* Apr. 11, 1927.

Chapter 15

General

Federal Heritage Buidings Review Office. *Nineteen Federally Owned Properties*.
Heritage Ottawa. www.heritageottawa.org
Sparks Street Mall Walk Tour. www.sparksstreetmall.com/walkingtour

Ottawa Hockey Club

Bugyra, *Match Penalty*.
Bliss, *Northern Enterprise*.
Neatby, *Politics of Chaos*.
Statistics of the Civil Service of Canada.

Debates. House of Commons. Apr. 4, 1934. [Public Service — Salary Deduction]

Labour Gazette. July, Aug., Sept. 1931; Jan. (supplement), Dec. 1934. [retail prices, employment, wage rates, unemployment, cost of living]

Frank Ahearn

LAC. PA91057. Photographic portrait.
Canadian Parliamentary Guide. 1931.
Who's Who in Canada. 1928–29.
Finnigan, *Old Scores.*
McFarlane, *Clancy.*
Ottawa Citizen, Ottawa Journal. Nov. 7, 8, 1962 [obituaries]

p. 289 "Frank Ahearn was": Finnigan, *Old Scores,* 125; "the salt of the earth": McFarlane, *Clancy,* 219.

p. 292 "I propose to keep": Wong thesis, 306.

p. 294 "Chee Pee": *Ottawa Journal.* Jan. 16, 1928; "Ti-Bi": *Le Droit.* Jan. 27, 1928; "is a fine personality" and following: *Ottawa Journal.* Jan. 16, 1928; "It H'Ottawa": *Ottawa Journal.* Jan. 18, 1928.

p. 295 "Rockland Rocket": *Ottawa Journal.* Jan. 16, 1928.

p. 296 "It was a good win": *Ottawa Citizen.* Feb. 3, 1928; "The brilliant Ottawa": *New York Times.* Feb. 8, 1928.

p. 297 "If we had got better": Wong thesis, 308.

p. 300 "to get out": *Ottawa Journal.* Jan. 24, 1929; "The team cannot live": *Ottawa Journal.* Feb. 18, 1929; "I feel sure": *Ottawa Journal.* Mar. 2, 1929.

p. 301 "It was no easy task": *Ottawa Citizen.* Oct. 1, 1929.

p. 307 "at the end of the rope": Wong thesis, 318.

p. 309 "We might as well": *Ottawa Citizen.* Sept. 28, 1931.

p. 311 "Damned if I want to see": Wong thesis, 327; "It would be a good": ibid., 325; "and I remember the millionaires": "Grey is the Forelock of the Irishman." In Kennedy, *Going Top Shelf,* 88.

p. 312 "Control will remain": *Ottawa Journal.* Sept. 15, 1932.

p. 313 "We always concentrated": *Ottawa Journal.* Nov. 3, 1932; "I am sorely disappointed": *Debates.* House of Commons. Apr. 4, 1932. p. 1680; "Mr. Speaker.… Dismissals": *Debates.* House of Commons. Apr. 4, 1932. p. 1689.

p. 315 "A coach must": *Ottawa Journal.* Jan. 30, 1933; "supported Manager Denneny's decision": IHM Ottawa Hockey Association. Board of Directors. Minutes. Feb. 3, 1933.

p. 316 "subject however to": ibid. Mar. 6, 1933; "indebted to its players": ibid. Mar. 23, 1933; "We have often thought" and following: *Ottawa Journal*. Mar. 29, 1933; "for his untiring efforts": IHM Ottawa Hockey Association. Board of Directors. Minutes. Mar. 23, 1933.

p. 317 "it goes without saying": *Ottawa Citizen*. Dec. 30, 1933; "complimentary, co-operative": *Ottawa Journal*. Apr. 6, 1934.

p. 318 "Please be advised": *Ottawa Journal*. Feb. 1, 1934; "bargain night" *Ottawa Journal*. Mar. 16, 1934; "other unidentified objects": *Ottawa Citizen*. Mar. 16, 1934.

p. 319 "It is therefore apparent": *Ottawa Citizen*. Apr. 7, 1934.

p. 320 "So Ottawa is to pass": *Ottawa Journal*. Apr. 10, 1934.

Chapter 16

Ottawa Hockey Association and St. Louis Eagles

IHM Ottawa Hockey Association. Board of Directors. Minutes. Sept. 9, 1929–May 13, 1935.

IHM newspaper scrapbook, Jan. 1935–Oct. 1947.

p. 322 "There was a fence": Finnigan, *Old Scores*, 123.

p. 323 "to hold such members": IHM Ottawa Hockey Association. Board of Directors. Minutes. June 8, 1934; "I suggest": ibid. Aug. 23, 1934.

p. 324 "such additional security": ibid. Oct. 26, 1934; "to borrow the said amounts": ibid; "to handle all players": ibid.

p. 325 "gave details of plans": ibid. Oct. 4, 1934; "madcap Cardinals": *St. Louis Post-Dispatch*. Oct. 1, 1934; "scared": ibid. Oct. 2, 1934; "glad the Deans": ibid. Oct. 5, 1934; "He'll Soon Be Here": ibid. Oct. 14, 1934.

p. 330 "It was a terrible thing": *Ottawa Citizen*. May 31, 1935.

p. 331 "This proposition was so shabby": *Montreal Gazette*. Sept. 30, 1935.

Afterword

p. 336 "His white pants": *Weekend Magazine*. May 4, 1957. p. 4.

p. 338 "mainly an aural society": Plimpton, *Open Net*, 66.

Bibliography

Monographs

Albinson, John G. and Richard S. Grunau. *Canadian Sport: Sociological Perspectives*. Don Mills: Addison-Wesley, 1976.

Berton, Pierre. *Depression, 1929–1939*. Toronto: McClelland and Stewart, 1990.

Bliss, Michael. *Northern Enterprise: Five Centuries of Canadian Business*. Toronto: McClelland and Stewart, 1987

Brown, John James. *Ideas in Exile*. Toronto: McClelland & Stewart, 1967.

Brown, Robert Craig and Ramsay Cook. *Canada, 1896–1921: A Nation Transformed*. Toronto: McClelland & Stewart, 1974.

Bugyra, Shaun. *Match Penalty: The Demise of the Ottawa Senators*. Ottawa: Historical Society of Ottawa, 2001. (Bytown Pamphlet Series, no. 66)

Canadian Encyclopedia. Toronto: McClelland & Stewart, 1999.

Canadian Men and Women of the Times. Toronto: William Briggs, 1898.

Census of Canada, 1880–1881. Ottawa: MacLean, Roger, 1882.

Coleman, Charles. *The Trail of the Stanley Cup*. 3 vols. Montreal: National Hockey League, 1966–1977.

Constitution and By-laws of the Ottawa Amateur Athletic Club. Ottawa: A.S. Woodburn, 1889.

Cosentino, Frank. *The Renfrew Millionaires: The Valley Boys of Winter*. Burnstown, Ont.: General Store, 1990.

Cummings, C.C. *Canada's Sports Heritage: A Selection (1807-1914)*. Ottawa: Information Canada, 1975.

Diamond, Dan, ed. *Hockey Hall of Fame: The Official History of the Game's Honour Roll.* Toronto: Doubleday, 1996.

——— *Total Hockey: The Official Encyclopedia of the National Hockey League.* 1st and 2d editions. New York: Total Sports, 1998 and 2000.

Dictionary of Canadian Biography. vol. 14, 1911–20. Toronto: University of Toronto Press, 1998.

Duplacey, James. *The Rules of Hockey.* Toronto: Dan Diamond & Associates, 1996.

Federal Heritage Buildings Review Office. *Nineteen Federally Owned Properties, Sparks Street, Ottawa.* Building Reports. vol. 14 [1985?].

Finnigan, Joan. *Old Scores, New Goals: The Story of the Ottawa Senators.* Kingston: Quarry Press, 1992.

Fischler, Stan, with Tom Sarro. *Metro Ice: A Century of Hockey in New York.* New York: H&M Productions, 1999.

Fitsell, J.W. *Hockey's Captains, Colonels and Kings.* Erin, Ont.: Boston Mills Press, 1987.

Gard, Anson. *The Hub and the Spokes: Or, the Capital and its Environment.* Ottawa: Emerson, 1904.

Geological Survey of Canada. *Report on Explorations in the Labrador Peninsula Along the East Main, Koksoak, Hamilton, Manicuagan and Portions of Other Rivers in 1892-93-94-95.* Ottawa: NP, 1896.

Glazebrook, G.P. de T. *Life in Ontario: A Social History.* Toronto: University of Toronto Press, 1968.

Gwyn, Sandra. *The Private Capital: Ambition and Love in the Age of Macdonald and Laurier.* Toronto: McClelland & Stewart, 1984.

Haché, Alain. *The Physics of Hockey.* Vancouver: Raincoast, 2002.

Haig, Robert. *Ottawa: City of the Big Ears.* Ottawa: Haig & Haig, 1969.

Hall, E. *Early Canada: A Collection of Historical Photographs by Officers of the Geological Survey of Canada.* Ottawa: Department of Energy, Mines and Resources, 1967.

Herridge, W.T. *The Call of War: Recruiting Sermon.* Ottawa: Minister of Militia and Defence, 1915.

Historical Statistics of Canada. 2d ed. Ottawa: Statistics Canada, 1983.

Holzman, Morey and Joseph Nieforth. *Deceptions and Doublecross: How the NHL Conquered Hockey.* Toronto: Dundurn, 2002.

Hubbard, R. H. *Rideau Hall: An Illustrated History of Government House, Ottawa, from Victorian Times to the Present Day.* Montreal: McGill-Queen's UP, 1977.

Index to Incorporated Bodies and to Private and Local Law Under Dominion, and

Manitoba, Ontario and Quebec Statutes, Proclamations and Letters Patent, 1777 to Jan. 1, 1896; and *Supplement, Jan. 1, 1896–Jan 1, 1901.*

Kesterton, Wilfred. *A History of Journalism in Canada.* Toronto: McClelland & Stewart, 1967.

Kennedy, Michael P.J. ed. *Going Top Shelf: An Anthology of Canadian Hockey Poetry.* Surrey: Heritage House, 2005.

Kitchen, Paul. *Dey Brothers' Rinks Were Home to the Senators.* Ottawa: Historical Society of Ottawa, 1993.

LeSueur, Percy. *How to Play Hockey.* NP: 1909.

McFarlane, Brian. *Clancy: The King's Story.* Toronto: ECW Press, 1997.

McKeown, Bill. *Ottawa's Streetcars: The Story of Electric Railway Transit in Canada's Capital City.* Pickering: Railfare DC Books, 2006.

Metcalfe, Alan. *Canada Learns to Play: The Emergence of Organized Sport, 1807–1914.* Toronto: Oxford UP, 1987.

Morton, Desmond. *Years of Conflict, 1911–1921.* Toronto: Grolier, 1983.

Mott, Morris, ed. *Sports in Canada: Historical Readings.* Toronto: Copp, Clark, Pitman, 1989.

Neatby, H. Blair. *The Politics of Chaos: Canada in the Thirties.* Toronto: Gage, 1972.

Plimpton, George. *Open Net.* New York: Lyons & Burford, 1993.

Regan, John W. [John Quinpool]. *First Things in Acadia.* Halifax: First Things Publishers, 1936.

Rowan, John J. *The Emigrant and Sportsman in Ottawa.* London: Stanford, 1876.

Roxborough, Henry. *One Hundred — Not Out: The Story of Nineteenth Century Canadian Sport.* Toronto: Ryerson, 1966.

Smith, I. Norman. *The Journal Men: P. D. Ross, E. Norman Smith and Grattan O'Leary of the Ottawa Journal.* Toronto: McClelland & Stewart, 1974.

Souvenir of the Montreal Winter Carnival. Montreal: Canadian Railway News, 1884.

Taylor, John. *Ottawa: An Illustrated History.* Toronto: Lorimer, 1986.

Taylor, Leonard. *The Sourdough and the Queen: The Many Lives of Klondyke Joe Boyle.* Toronto: Methuen, 1983.

Vaughan, Garth. *The Puck Starts Here: The Origin of Canada's Great Winter Game.* Fredericton: Goose Lane Editions, 1996.

Walker, Kathleen. *Ottawa's Repast: 150 Years of Food and Drink.* Ottawa: Ottawa Citizen, 1995.

Whitehead, Eric. *Cyclone Taylor: A Hockey Legend.* Toronto: Doubleday, 1977.

Whitehead, Eric. *The Patricks: Hockey's Royal Family*. Toronto: Doubleday, 1980.

Wilson, Barbara. Ed. *Ontario and the First World War, 1914–1918: A Collection of Documents*. Toronto: University of Toronto Press, 1977.

Woods, Shirley E. *Ottawa: The Capital of Canada*. Toronto: Doubleday, 1980.

Young, Scott and Astrid Young. *O'Brien*. Toronto: Ryerson, 1967.

Zaslow, Morris. *Reading the Rocks: The Story of the Geological Survey of Canada*. Toronto: Macmillan, 1975.

Newspapers, Periodicals, Directories

Belleville Intelligencer

Calgary Herald

Canada Gazette

Canadian Parliamentary Guide

Canadian Patent Office Record Montreal: Desbarats, 1883–88 [microfilm edition, Canadian Institute for Historical Microreproduction]

Civil Service List of Canada. Sessional Paper no. 30. 1891–1916.

Debates. House of Commons.

Fort William Daily Times Journal

Fredericton Daily Gleaner

Halifax Herald

Halifax Morning Chronicle

Hamilton Spectator

Hockey Research Journal

Kingston Daily Whig

Labour Gazette

Le Droit, Ottawa

Maclean's

Manitoba Free Press

Montreal Gazette

Montreal Herald

Montreal Standard

Montreal Star

New York Times

Ontario Gazette, 1900–18

Ottawa Amateur Athletic Club. *Annual Report*. 1890–99.

Ottawa Citizen

Ottawa Directory. Ottawa: Woodburn, 1874–80.

Ottawa Directory. Ottawa: 1884–1919.

Ottawa Free Press

Ottawa Hockey News

Ottawa Journal

Renfrew Mercury

Smith's Falls Rideau Record

Sport History Review

Toronto Empire

Statistics of the Civil Service of Canada. Ottawa: Dominion Bureau of Statistics. 1927–34.

St. Louis Post-Dispatch

Toronto Globe

Toronto Mail and Empire

VancouverProvince

Weekend Magazine (Ottawa Citizen)

Who's Who in Canada

Theses

Cosentino, Frank. "A History of the Concept of Professionalism in Canadian Sport." Ph.D. Alberta, 1973.

Cox, Alan Elton. "A History of Sports in Canada, 1868–1900." Ph.D. Alberta, 1969.

Lindsay, Peter Leslie. "A History of Sport in Canada, 1807–1967." Ph.D. Alberta, 1969.

Wong, John Chi-Kit. "The Development of Professional Hockey and the Making of the National Hockey League." Ph.D. Maryland, 2001.

Manuscript Collections

Archives of Ontario (AO)
    Supreme Court of Ontario

Land Registry Office, Ottawa

Library and Archives Canada, Ottawa (LAC)
    Canadian Amateur Athletic Union, MG28 I 150.
    Canadian Amateur Hockey League, MG28 I 351.
    Census of Canada, 1901, microfilm
    Military Records, RG150.
    Frank and Annie Jenkins Collection, MG30 D183.
    Interior Department, RG15 D-II-1.
    McCurry Family Papers, Music Division, MUS27.
    Philip Dansken Ross Collection, MG30 D98, vols. 1–9.
    Secretary of State of Canada, RG95.
    Thomas Patrick Gorman Collection, MG30 C129.
    Video V1 2004-01-0003.

International Hockey Museum, Kingston (IHM)
    A.E. Smith contract with Ottawa Hockey Club
    Ottawa Hockey Association scrapbook
    Ottawa Hockey Association minutes

Index

A

Aberdeen, Lord 85

Aberdeen Pavilion 124, 126, 130–1, 136–7, 142, 148, 191, 213, 215

Acme skates 6–7. *See also* skates and skating

Adams, Charles 241, 250, 253–4, 287–8

Ahearn, T. Franklin 190, 217, 225–32, 237, 238–9, 240–2, 243–5, 247, 248, 250–6, 279, 281, 284, 289–300, 301–5, 307, 310, 311–17, 323, 330–2

Ahearn, Thomas 41, 60–1, 64, 67, 225, 289, 291, 296, 298, 312, 315–17, 324, 329–32

Albert, Norman 246

Allan Cup 239

Amateur Athletic Association of Canada (AAAC) 88

Amateur Athletic Federation of Canada (AAFC) 154

Amateur Hockey Association of Canada (AHAC) 19, 32, 35, 36, 38, 43–4, 47, 49, 51, 68, 76, 83–4, 104, 109, 123: championships 49, 62–5, 69, 91–3, 110; executive 19, 32, 50, 74, 75, 98, 110; founding 32; rules 32–5, 48, 74; scheduling 49, 50, 69, 74, 75, 77, 110, 127; travel 49, 74, 76–7

amateurism 20, 27, 89, 132–5, 151–4, 160–1, 167: gentlemen amateurs 9–11, 74. *See also* sports — attitudes toward

American Hockey Association (AHA) 319, 321, 322–3: accord with NHL 322

American Hockey League. See American Hockey Association

Ami, Henry 14, 20, 27, 39

Anderson, Fred 246

Arena Gardens (Toronto) 274

Ashbury College 81, 83

Auditorium Ltd. 226–9, 235, 239, 247, 252–5, 279, 281, 292, 295–8, 300, 301–11, 313, 316, 318–19, 323, 330, 332

Ayres, Vern 324, 331

B

Baird, Billy 153–4

Baker, Ed 244

Balharrie, John P. 256

Barber Poles 113. See Ottawa Senators — uniforms

Barron, John 48–9, 185

Bate, Llewellyn N. 86, 122, 158, 160, 166, 168, 190, 195, 201–2, 203, 214, 217

Beauchamp, Clem 296

Bell, Billy 268

Benedict, Clint 170–1, 178–80, 181–2, 184, 193, 194, 197, 206, 208, 210, 214, 221,

223, 246, 248, 258, 261, 263, 266, 269–71, 275, 281–2, 283, 296, 332

Bennett, R.B. 305, 313

Beveridge, Bill 314–15, 324, 327, 331

Birkett, Thomas 18

Bishop, Hubert 241–2

Blair, Bessie 73

Blake, Mickey 327, 331

Boland, John F. 201, 205

Borden, Robert 173

Boston Bruins 247, 250, 284–8, 309, 331

Boucher, Billy 234

Boucher, Frank 234, 273, 277

Boucher, George 192, 207, 223, 234, 237, 246, 255, 257–8, 260, 262, 265, 267, 271, 272, 274, 275–8, 279, 281–2, 283, 287, 300, 316 17, 328, 332

Bowles Lunch 290

Bowman, Ralph 324, 327, 329–30

Boyle, Joe 141–2

Bradley, Reg 67, 84

Brandon, Manitoba 140

Brice, Malcolm 155, 188

Broadbent, Harry "Punch" 170, 176, 179 80, 182, 184, 199, 200, 206, 220 3, 230, 233, 258, 262–5, 271, 272–4, 275, 277–8, 281–2, 283, 292–3, 332

Bruce, Morley 208, 258, 273

Brunton, Clare 304, 307, 315, 317 18, 323, 327, 328 9

Brydson, Glen 331

Buena Vista Hockey Club 225

Burch (Professor) 6

Burpee, Frederick 227, 229, 231, 300, 301–2, 306, 319

Buttler, Percy 114, 123, 130, 162, 169, 190, 203

Byng, Lord and family 268–9, 271

Bytown and New Edinburgh Shintie Club 9

Bytown Museum 9

C

Calder, Frank 194–5, 198, 216–7, 225,

230–1, 235, 241–2, 250–1, 259–62, 263–4, 285–6, 288, 291, 297, 300, 301, 305, 307–9, 311, 323, 327

Calgary News Telegram 106

Cameron, Harry 221, 258

Canadian Amateur Athletic Union (CAAU) 88, 105, 123, 132–5, 152–4

Canadian Amateur Hockey Association (CAHA) 185

Canadian Amateur Hockey League (CAHL) 109, 119, 123, 125–9, 137, 139: championship 103–4, 111, 113; equipment 79; founding 77; membership 80; rules 79–80, 125; schedules 77, 125

Canadian Hockey Association (CHA) 164 6, 214 6

Canadian Railway Hockey League 96, 100, 106

Capital Athletic Association (CAA) 76, 83, 98. *See also* Ottawa Capitals

Capital Lacrosse Club 87–8, 95, 98, 102, 104, 118

Carrie Nation rooter 176. *See also* hockey, ice fans

Cattarinich, Joe 311

Central Canada Exhibition Association 130, 213

Central Canada Hockey Association (CCHA) 83, 92

challenge system 32, 34, 47, 49–50, 51, 54, 55, 62, 65, 68, 83, 91–2, 109, 115, 141, 156, 161, 163, 166, 283

Château Laurier 260–1, 268, 298, 300

Chevrier, Edgar 293–4, 305, 313

Chicago Black Hawks 241, 283, 294, 308, 312, 315, 326–9, 331

Chicago Stadium 308, 315, 322

Chittick, Fred 84, 93–6, 111

Citizen, the Ottawa 2, 5, 7, 14, 21, 23, 26, 42, 81, 95, 99, 101, 103, 106–7, 112, 116, 162, 166, 188, 192, 195, 203, 206, 212–3, 214–5, 217–8, 242–5, 247, 248, 301, 309, 317, 319, 325, 331

Civil Service Amateur Athletic Association 152
Civil Service League 293
Clancy, Frank "King" 233, 236–7, 255, 257, 267, 269–70, 271–4, 275, 277–8, 279, 281, 282–3, 285–7, 289, 293, 296, 300, 306–7, 320
Cleghorn, Sprague 220–1, 223, 230, 233–4, 257–8, 262, 264–6, 272–3, 284
Coleman, Charles 331
Conacher, Charlie 312
Connaught, Duke of 179
Connell, Alex 233, 239, 257, 279, 281, 282–3, 287, 295–7, 309, 314–15, 318
Connor, Harry 302
Cook, Bill and Fred "Bun" 239–42, 284, 314
Cosby, A. Morgan 49, 54, 76. *See also* Ontario Hockey Association — championships (Cosby Cup)
Cosentino, Frank 166
Cowley, Bill 324, 331
Cox, Danny 318
Crabbe, E.W. 244
Crawford, Rusty 206, 207–8
Cruise of the Neptune (Low) 16
Crystal Skating Rink (Montreal) 11, 13, 29, 51, 62, 64
Currie, Alex 239

D
Daly, T. Mayne 85
Dandurand, Leo 230, 234, 268, 276–7
Darragh, Harold 233
Darragh, Jack 170, 175–6, 180, 182–3, 192–3, 197, 207–8, 210, 220–3, 238, 255, 258, 260–2, 266–7, 275–7, 280, 282
Dartmouth, Nova Scotia 8
Davidson, James 80, 98, 124
Dawson City, Yukon 99, 141–3
Dawson Daily News 142
Dawson Klondikers 141–3, 183, 298
Denman Arena (Vancouver) 183, 266

Denneney, Corbett and Cy 192, 194–5, 197, 207, 214, 221, 223, 230, 257–8, 261, 262–4, 267, 279–82, 283, 286–7, 270–1, 273–4, 275, 277–8, 298–9, 313–16
Dennison, Joe 175
Depression (1929–) 290, 301, 304, 311, 313, 315–16, 319, 321
Detroit Cougars 241, 280, 283
Detroit Falcons 309
Detroit Red Wings 328, 331
Dey, Edgar 160, 191
Dey, Edwin P., Frank, and William 35, 47, 51, 62, 92, 110, 112, 130–1, 143–5, 155, 189–93, 203–5, 209, 210–18, 219–20, 223, 224–8, 243, 249, 260, 268–9, 274–5, 280, 282
Dey's Arena 155, 161, 171–2, 176, 182, 189, 192, 194–5, 204, 207–8, 212, 215–6, 218, 220–1, 228, 232, 259–60, 262, 264, 267–9, 274, 282, 298
Dey's Rink 28, 35, 38, 47, 48, 51, 62, 95, 106, 110–12, 115, 124, 130–1, 142, 145, 155, 189–91, 207: Pirates 50, 191
Dickson, John P. 86, 116, 122–3, 125–9, 133–4, 157, 159
Dolan, Cosey 276, 278, 281
Drouin, Paul 331
Dufferin, Lord and family 3, 5, 7, 9–10
Dufferins (snowshoe club) 5. *See also* sports — snowshoeing
Duford, Angus 175, 179–80, 182, 192, 199, 206
Duggan, Jack 233, 239
Duggan, Tom 241, 250–1
Duval, William "Peg" 96, 100, 102, 105, 107, 112, 132
Dwyer, Bill "Big" 251–2

E
Eastern Canada Amateur Hockey Association (ECAHA) 129, 135, 152–3, 160
Eastern Canada Hockey Association (ECHA) 146, 160–1, 162–4

Ebbs, Jack 145–6
Edmonton Eskimos 277–8
Edmonton Hockey Club 167

F
Federal Amateur Hockey League (FAHL)
    119, 122, 124, 126–9, 132, 139–41, 143,
    145, 146, 149, 152, 156, 161
Ferguson, Elmer 264, 275–6
Findlay, J.A. 69
Finnie, Dave 81, 83, 122, 145
Finnigan, Eddie 331
Finnigan, Frank 239, 280, 285, 287, 289,
    296, 300, 309, 311–12, 322, 324–5, 327,
    329–30
Finnigan, Joan 311
Fleming, Sandford 7, 62; Winterholme
    8, 72
Fooks, Fred 4, 7, 14
Foran, William 153, 277, 285, 301–2,
    305–10
Forbes, John 6–7
Foster, Philip 14
Free Press (Ottawa) 14, 19, 45, 62, 63, 72,
    155, 160, 188
Frew, Irvine 324, 331
Frieman, A.J. (department store) 216

G
Gallagher, Tom 18, 22, 24–6, 39
Gard, Anson 8
Gaul, Horace 143, 179
Gault, Matthew 21
gentlemen amateurs. See amateurism
Geological Survey of Canada 14, 16, 20,
    101
Gerard, Eddie 175–6, 179–80, 182–3, 190,
    193, 195–7, 201, 207–10, 214, 221–2,
    237–8, 255, 257–8, 260–2, 263,
    265–6, 267, 269, 271, 272–4, 275–8,
    281–2, 323–4, 327–8
Gill, David 232, 235–6, 239, 244, 280, 284,
    287, 293, 299, 302, 304, 307–8, 313,
    332

Gilmour, "Billy", Dave and Sutherland
    "Suddy" 81, 83, 105, 112–6, 122, 137,
    139, 143–4, 160
Gleason, Eddie 306
Godin, Hozomer 293–5, 299
Gorman, Ed 233, 239, 257
Gorman, Thomas Patrick "Tommy" 188,
    192, 203–5, 206, 209–10, 211–8, 221,
    224–32, 233–9, 243–4, 247, 248,
    249–52, 261–2, 268, 271–2, 274–7,
    280, 308, 312, 330, 332
Governors general 3, 5, 7, 25, 39, 41, 45,
    53, 71–3, 85, 90, 268–9: prize for
    curling 9–10
Graham, Leth 175, 179–80, 199, 206, 262
Graham, Lorne 258, 270, 281
Grand Union Hotel 39–40, 45
Grant, Ed 49–50
Green, Pete 231, 233, 239, 248, 258, 263,
    272, 274, 275–6, 281, 293
Green, Thomas D. 14–15, 17, 20, 22–5,
    31–2, 35, 39
Green, Wilfred 244
Grey, Lord 159–60
Grierson, Frank 152–3
Grosvenor, Len 297, 300

H
Haché, Alain 278–9
Hague, Billy 145–7, 149, 152–3, 155, 178
Hainsworth, George 246
Halifax 8
Halifax Crescents 92
Halifax Rules 8
Hall, Joe "Bad" 223
Halliday, Milt 299
Hamilton, C.D.P. Jr. 319
Hamilton Tigers 233–5, 244, 249–50, 251,
    262–4, 272–3
Hammond, John 309
Hanlan, Ned 6, 10
Harper, Henry 73
Hearn, William (chemist) 4
Helman, Harry 276–8

Henry, Harold "Chic" 88, 103, 105, 111, 112, 132
Herridge, William T. 185–6, 189
Hewitt, William 155
History of Journalism in Canada (Kesterton) 120
Hitchman, Lionel 237, 276–8, 284
hockey, field 11–12, 120: Hockey Association rules 11
hockey, ice: business 150, 174; equipment 12, 30, 79, 177–8; fans 176–7, 187, 198; Hall of Fame 96, 312; player drafts 174–5; press coverage 31, 120–1, 132, 142, 158, 177, 180, 186–8, 198–9; puck 2–3, 12–13, 18, 31; referees and refereeing 51, 65, 68, 79, 94–5, 98, 121, 140, 144, 181–2, 209–10, 263–4, 270, 288; rules 8, 11–12, 13, 30–1, 74, 210, 220; salaries 174, 180; schedules 47, 78, 90, 201; uniforms 12, 46
Hockey Association of St. Louis 323–4, 330
Hoeschen, Ben 241
Holzman, Morey 197–8
How to Play Hockey (LeSueur) 177
Howe, Syd 302–3, 307, 324, 329–30
Hub and the Spokes, The (Gard) 8
Hutton, John Bowser "Bouse" 84, 96, 100, 111, 112, 136, 161
Hyland, Harry "Hibernian" 209–10

I

ice, artificial 46–7, 108–9, 132, 169, 225, 227–9, 249–51, 261, 278–9
ice, natural 7–8, 13–14, 20, 23, 37–8, 46–7, 67, 72–3, 108–9, 144, 197, 219, 225, 259–60, 274, 279, 281
Irvin, Dick 240

J

Jackson, Harvey 312
Jenkins, Frank Maurice Stinson 18, 20–4, 26, 30, 35, 39, 44–5, 47–8, 54–5, 59, 62, 71, 73, 84
Jerwa, Frank 329
Joliat, Aurel 233, 235, 284, 293
Jubilee Rink (Montreal) 164, 209, 211, 216, 222

K

Kaminsky, Max 324, 327
Kelly, Pete 331
Kendall, Carroll 175
Kennedy, George (aka Kendall) 170, 189, 198, 204–5, 209, 213, 223, 243, 249–50, 263–4
Kenora Thistles 159
Kerr, Allen "Dubbie" 155, 160, 162, 165–7
Kerr, Jack 13–14, 18, 20–1, 22, 24, 26, 28, 35, 37, 39, 44, 51, 54, 64, 66–7, 92, 319
Kesterton, Wilfred 120
Ketchum skates 177. *See also* hockey, ice – equipment
Ketchum's sporting goods store 220
Kilcoursie, Lord 61, 89, 90, 290, 298
Kilrea, Hec 239, 283, 278–8, 285, 297, 301, 309, 314
Kilrea, Wally 307
King, Mackenzie 73, 297, 305
Kirby, Chauncey 51, 54, 67–8, 79, 84, 86–7, 99, 101, 110, 298
Kirby, Halder and family 13–14, 18, 20–1, 22, 24–5, 35, 37, 39, 44, 51, 54, 59, 66–7, 69, 101, 102, 122, 126, 319

L

Laflamme, Jerry 288
Lake, Freddie 155, 160–1, 165–6, 170, 175
Lalonde, "Newsy" 165–6, 169, 175, 189, 196, 235, 263, 299, 303, 307
Lamb, Joe 300, 309, 331
Lampman, Archibald 19, 71
Lansdowne, Marquis of and family 22
Latour, Joe 294, 302
Laurier, Wilfrid 69, 73, 85, 107, 203
Lauzon, Henri 331

Le Droit 243–4, 255, 294, 307
LeSueur, Percy "Peerless" 136, 147–8, 149, 153, 159–60, 170–1, 175, 177–8, 179
Lichtenhein, Sammy 195, 197–8, 204–5
Livingstone, Eddie 189, 193, 195, 197–8, 201, 205, 209, 211–3, 216–7
London Restaurant 4, 7
Lorne, Marquis and family 6–7
Low, Albert Peter 13–17, 22, 24–6, 28, 35, 39
Lowertown 4, 6, 8, 107, 269, 294, 299
Lowrey, Eddie 180, 208, 258
lumbering and lumber mills 1, 3, 70: Booth, J.R. 1, 22, 41, 66; Gilmour 1; MacLaren 1; shantymen 70–1
Lumsden, John 14
Lunn skates 177. *See also* hockey, ice — equipment

M

Macdonald, John A. 17, 21, 42
MacKell, Jack 258, 263
Madison Square Garden (New York) 46, 242, 251–4, 279, 294, 296, 299, 309, 315, 320, 322
Mail (Toronto) 3,7
Manitoba Free Press 120–1, 137
Maple Leaf Gardens (Toronto) 311–12, 329
Masquerade balls 7, 14, 26, 226
Masson, Hugh and family 8–9
McConnell, Richard 14
McDougal, Joe 84
McDowell, Thain 231
McGee, Frank 83, 92, 97, 105–7, 112–13, 115–16, 120–2, 136–7, 139–41, 142–6, 148, 149, 152, 179, 188–9, 199, 230
McGee, Jim 92, 140–1
McGee, Thomas D'Arcy 152, 168–9, 190, 201
McGiffin, Minnie "Wild Man" 182
McGill University 8, 10, 11, 13–18, 23–7, 29, 31–2, 35, 36, 50, 51, 160

McGoogan, W.J. 326
McGrath, Eddie 207
McIntyre, William 227
McKay, Thomas 3, 9
McKinnon, John 9
McLaughlin, Fred 308–9, 327
McMartin, Jack 22, 24, 26
Mercier, Raoul 299
Mercury (Northampton, England) 6
Merrill, Horace 170–1, 179–80, 182, 210, 258, 262, 332
Metropolitan Club (Montreal) 11
Minto, Lord and family 73, 85, 115, 121
Montreal All-Montreals 164, 166
Montreal Amateur Athletic Association (MAAA) 13, 29–30, 32, 39–40, 42, 50, 51, 62–5, 66–8, 76–7, 99, 113, 123–4, 132, 152, 160: championships 49, 52, 67–8, 91–2, 93, 110, 112
Montreal Arena 112, 124–5, 128–30, 146, 196, 205, 207, 209, 211, 218
Montreal Canadiens 164, 168, 169–70, 175, 180, 189, 193, 194, 196–8, 201, 204, 207–10, 211, 213, 217, 220–3, 230, 233–5, 242–3, 246–7, 248, 249–50, 262–4, 268, 275–7, 279, 283–4, 293, 296, 311, 326, 328, 331
Montreal city championship 30–1
Montreal Crescents 50, 51
Montreal Crystals 26, 30, 32, 35
Montreal Daily Witness 3
Montreal Forum 250, 254, 279, 315
Montreal Gazette, The 2, 14, 21, 28, 31, 64, 67–8, 129, 164, 251
Montreal Herald 26, 167, 264, 275–6
Montreal Hockey Club 127–9, 132, 153–4. *See also* Montreal Amateur Athletic Association
Montreal Maroons 242, 283–4, 297, 299–300, 306–7, 309, 311, 313, 316, 323, 328, 331
Montreal Nationals 124, 128, 163–6
Montreal Shamrocks 50, 51, 64, 70, 76–7, 100, 106, 111, 113, 127–9, 146, 153–4,

160–1, 164–7, 180
Montreal Star 37–8, 254
Montreal Sunday Sun 133
Montreal Victorias 14, 24–7, 29–30, 32,
    35, 45, 50, 51, 72, 76–7, 84, 94, 98,
    101, 102, 106, 110, 113–5, 124–9, 145,
    153–4, 160
Montreal Wanderers 27, 124, 127–9, 132,
    140, 146–9, 153–4, 156, 159–62,
    163–5, 167–70, 175–7, 180, 181–3, 192,
    195, 197–8, 201, 204–6, 207–9, 211,
    268
Montreal Winter Carnivals 13–14, 20–7,
    28, 30, 32, 37: Carnival Cup 14
Moore, Art 115, 120, 122, 140, 152–3, 155,
    160–1
Morel, Albert 50, 51, 52, 67, 93, 96, 107
Morenz, Howie 283–4, 326–7
Mount Royal Arena (Montreal) 250, 262,
    275, 279
Mulligan, Dave 162–4
Murphy, George P. 86, 95, 128–9
Mutual Arena (Toronto) 54, 246, 258–61
Myles, Percy 30

N
National Club (Toronto) 212
National Hockey Association (NHA)
    162–71, 174, 178, 180, 181, 187,
    189–90, 192, 193, 197–8, 200–2, 204,
    208–9, 211, 236, 284: accord with
    PCHA 174–5, 181, 241, 265; Battalions
    deployment crisis 195–8; dispute
    with PCHA 189–90; Livingstone
    lawsuit 197–8, 201, 209, 217;
    schedules 193, 201; suspension of
    operations 205, 211
National Hockey League (NHL) 32, 205,
    209, 211–2, 214–8, 220, 227–8, 230,
    233–5, 239, 242, 245–6, 250, 255,
    291–2, 303, 308, 323: accord with
    AHA 322; accord with PCHA 235, 241;
    championships 206, 247, 258,
    264–5, 273–7, 283–8; dispersal draft

309–10; expansion 240, 249–55, 279,
    322; founding 205; guidebook 296;
    parity 233–5, 291–2, 308; players 236,
    240, 284; rules 220, 265, 270, 296;
    schedules 206, 250, 255, 279, 327, 331
National Lacrosse Association 10
New Edinburgh Hockey Club 8–9,
    174–6, 232, 235, 237, 239, 255, 258
New York, NY 108–9, 168
New York Americans 241, 251–4, 279–80,
    283, 294, 302, 309, 318, 323, 328, 331
New York Athletics 109
New York Herald 5
New York Rangers 234, 242, 254, 283–4,
    303, 306, 312, 314–15, 328, 331
New York Times 252, 296
Nieforth, Joseph 197–8
Nighbor, Frank 175, 183–4, 190, 192–3,
    194, 196–7, 206, 221–3, 230, 238, 240,
    255, 257–8, 260–2, 263, 266, 270, 275,
    277, 279, 281–2, 283, 287, 302, 313, 332
Norris, James 308
Northey, Bill 129–30

O
Oatman, Eddie 198–9
O'Brien (Young and Young) 166
O'Brien, Michael John and J. Ambrose
    158, 164, 165–6, 170, 302
O'Brien Trophy 283
O'Dell, William 28, 39
Olympia (Detroit) 292, 297
Ontario Hockey Association (OHA) 47,
    62, 83, 185, 246: ban on Cyclone
    Taylor 155; championships (Cosby
    Cup) 53, 54–5, 65, 75–6; executive
    49, 54, 73, 74–5; founding 48–9;
    resignation of Ottawa Hockey Club
    75, 108; rules 74; schedules 70;
    travel 74
Ontario Professional Hockey League
    (OPHL) 165–6
Ottawa, city of: churches 3, 19, 45, 185;
    city hall 3; council 19, 30, 131, 213,

256; growth of infrastructure 4, 41

Ottawa Aberdeens 81–4, 94, 106, 112, 123, 136, 140, 174

Ottawa Amateur Athletic Association (OAAA) 41, 89

Ottawa Amateur Athletic Club (OAAC) 42–4, 47, 56, 68, 76, 89, 119, 134: membership 42–3, 47; rules 42, 44

Ottawa Amateur Orchestral Society 19, 71

Ottawa and District Hockey Association 239

Ottawa Arena Club 216–7, 224, 227

Ottawa Boys Club 289

Ottawa Capitals 76–8, 80, 81, 83–4, 92, 102, 104, 110, 123–4, 128, 139

Ottawa Car Manufacturing Co. 227

Ottawa city championships 50–2

Ottawa City League 56, 232–3, 293, 297, 299, 302

Ottawa Cliffsides 174, 207, 232, 257

Ottawa College 39, 45, 48, 50, 52–3, 84, 93, 104, 105, 107. *See also* University of Ottawa

Ottawa Curling Club 5. *See also* sports and leisure — curling

Ottawa Dairy 261, 276

Ottawa Electrics 81–4, 104

Ottawa Emmetts 143, 145, 174

Ottawa Football Club 16, 93, 97, 99, 106, 113, 118

Ottawa Gladstones 48, 54–5

Ottawa Hockey Association Ltd. 202, 203–4, 211, 214–5, 226–9, 231, 236–7, 241, 245, 248, 250, 255, 290–3, 298, 301–2, 305–6, 308–10, 312–15, 321, 323–5, 329, 331–2

Ottawa Hockey Club (Ottawas). *See* Ottawa Senators

Ottawa Hockey News 245

Ottawa Journal 20, 38, 40, 45, 50, 52, 55, 63–4, 67–8, 70–2, 75, 79–80, 81, 86, 89, 102, 103, 107, 111, 116–17, 126, 133, 141, 142, 144, 147, 152, 155, 168, 175,

178, 179–80, 186–8, 199, 207–8, 214–15, 219–20, 231–2, 243–4, 247, 248, 249, 258, 264, 294, 301, 317–18, 320

Ottawa Munitions 232, 257–8

Ottawa Rough Riders 96, 113, 116, 140, 175. *See also* Ottawa Football Club

Ottawa Senators 14, 16, 17, 20, 23–27, 35–6, 42, 44, 45, 47–50, 76, 81: arena lockouts 191, 212–3; baseball team 179; championships 50–1, 53–5, 62–5, 111, 115–17, 119, 122, 127, 139, 141–5, 146, 151, 155, 163, 166, 168, 177, 191, 210, 229, 233, 237–9, 243, 247, 249, 255–6, 257, 262, 267, 278, 282, 287–8, 291, 298, 305, 314; Chittick affair 94–5; coaching 82, 104, 110–11, 112, 116, 145, 231, 233, 239, 275, 287, 307, 313, 315; dispute with CAHL 139; dispute with *Citizen* 243–5; dispute with NHA 195, 199; dispute with OHA 75–6, 108; executive 19, 36, 39, 47, 84–9, 90, 98, 101, 110, 114, 119, 122–31, 162, 168, 175, 188, 190–1, 195, 200–2, 206, 224, 249, 260, 262–3, 312, 318, 323; fans 61, 64, 74, 81, 147–8, 187, 235, 242, 247, 252, 259–61, 263–4, 293–6, 318, 325–6; finance 20, 35, 48, 55, 59, 64, 84, 122, 170, 187, 189–93, 202, 204, 249, 253, 291–3, 297, 299–300, 304–10, 312–17, 319; juniors 84, 93; Kirby affair 86–7; legal issues 43–4, 89, 169, 177, 197–8, 201–2, 212, 217–19, 243–5, 248, 323; membership 28, 43–4, 92; ownership 203–4, 211–16, 224–32, 253, 274–5, 298, 300, 301–10, 319, 329, 331; players 17–20, 174, 190, 202, 214, 227, 232–7; press coverage 67–8, 120–1, 158, 177, 187–8, 214–15, 242–7, 294, 317–18, 326; professionalism 87–8, 89, 95, 102, 132–5, 150, 153, 154–5, 161; salaries 151, 165–72, 175–6, 190–3, 200, 207–8, 233–4,

236–7, 248, 253, 291, 302, 304, 324;
schedules 47–8, 56–8, 84, 114, 199;
suspension of operations 309–12,
331; ticket sales 85, 116, 130–1, 142,
150, 159, 161, 187, 189, 191, 196, 235,
247, 249–50, 254–5, 267–8, 291–2,
297, 303–7, 318, 324–5, 328–9; travel
49–50, 53, 75, 84, 85, 128, 146, 183,
201, 205, 233, 253, 265, 276, 278–81,
314; uniforms 24, 28, 44, 50, 113, 167,
237, 259, 269, 318; Young affair 86–7
Ottawa Shamrocks 282, 299
Ottawa Stadium 225, 227
Ottawa Victorias 156–8, 232

P

Pacific Coast Hockey Association (PCHA)
165, 169–71, 181, 183, 189, 196, 198,
206, 214, 235, 240, 258–9: accord
with NHA 174–5, 181; accord with
NHL 235, 241, 265; dispute with NHA
189–90
Parliament 38, 45, 173, 179, 183, 203:
buildings 3, 70, 178, 290–1; House of
Commons 2, 4, 21, 41, 48, 49, 203,
293, 296, 305, 313, 323, 332;
Parliamentary Press Gallery 38, 41
Patrick, Frank, Joseph, Lester and family
140, 148, 166, 168–70, 174–5, 184,
186, 189–90, 198, 214, 228, 235,
240–1, 254, 259, 274, 276–7
Peacock, James 9
percentage system 193–7
Pettinger, Eric 306
Phillips, Tommy 155, 159–60, 169
photographers and photography 8, 191:
Notman, William 8, 13; Pittaway
Studio 122; Sandham, Henry 8;
Topley, William J. 8, 55
Physics of Hockey, The (Haché) 278–9
Pittsburgh, PA. 88, 100, 103–5, 112, 132,
154, 160–1
Pittsburgh Pirates 233, 251, 296
Pittsburgh Sun 153

Porter, Nelson 18–19, 22, 24–5, 39, 172
post office 3, 18–19, 30, 139, 276
Primeau, Joe 312
puck. *See* hockey, ice — puck
Pulford, Harvey "Slugger" 84, 86–7,
96–100, 103, 110–1, 112, 114–15, 120,
122, 136–9, 141, 146, 149, 151–3, 155,
159–60, 307, 316
Purpur, Cliff 329, 331

Q

Quain, Redmond 292–3, 301, 307–10, 313,
319, 321–2, 323, 329–31
Quebec Chronicle 102
Quebec Hockey Club 14, 32, 64–5, 76–7,
78, 110, 113, 125, 128–9, 153–4, 160–2,
164, 166, 170, 176, 189, 194–6, 201,
204–5, 211, 218, 249, 259, 262
Queen's University, Kingston 48–9,
52–3, 65, 74–5, 92, 146, 159
Querrie, Charles 201, 254, 265
Quinn, Emmett 174–5, 189
Quinn, Mike 204–6
Quinn, Percy J. 211–19

R

Radio 246–7, 252, 308, 313–14, 317–18,
328: CFCA 246; CKCH 247; CKCO 247;
CNRO 247, 308, 314; KMOX 328
Railroads: Canada Atlantic Railway (CAR)
22, 41, 51, 67, 81, 96, 100, 103;
Canadian National Railway (CNR)
247, 280; Canadian Pacific Railway
(CPR) 7, 21, 51, 61, 65, 106, 276, 280–1;
Grand Trunk Line 22, 30, 123, 190;
Ottawa City Passenger Railway 4,
61; Ottawa Electric Railway (OER)
60, 81, 225, 227, 239, 245, 289, 291,
304, 312–13, 332
Rat Portage (Ontario) Thistles 114–6,
143–5
Ratte, Antoine 7
Raymond, Donat 250
Red Cross Association 187

regional elimination (tie) system 62
Renfrew Millionaires 157–8, 164–70
Renfrew Millionaires (Cosentino) 166
Rickard, George Lewis "Tex" 251–3
Rideau Canal 7–8, 13, 28, 38, 208, 219, 267
Rideau Club 40, 90, 290
Rideau Colts 101
Rideau Hall 3, 5–6, 7, 9, 38–9, 45, 53, 61, 90
Rideau Hockey Club 48, 50, 84, 283, 297, 302
Rideau Rebels 41, 45, 48–9, 65, 81, 84, 185
Rideau Rink 39–40, 45, 50, 53, 55, 61–2, 64, 65, 67–8, 72, 75, 78, 90, 94, 98, 101, 110, 112, 130, 167, 232
Rideau River 72
Rideau Skating and Curling Club 39–40
Rink Music Hall 5, 7
Ritchie, Dave 206, 209–10
Roberts, Jack 132
Robinette, T.C. 182
Robinson, Frank 195, 197
Roche, Earl 318, 324
Roger, John McLean "Mac" 103, 100, 111, 112
Rogers, S. Maynard and family 86–7, 93, 110
Roman Catholic Separate School Board 4: Christian Brothers School 4
Ronan, Skene 165, 170, 175–6, 179, 220, 258
Rosenthal, Martin 168–9, 189–92, 198, 201, 203–5, 209, 211–17
Rosenthal, Sam (jeweller) 131, 143, 149
Ross, Art 167, 177, 180, 182–3, 190, 192, 287–8
Ross, Philip Dansken "P.D." 36–45, 47–9, 51, 52, 53–5, 61, 64, 70–3, 79, 84, 86, 90–2, 110, 122, 124–7, 131, 133, 135, 141–2, 147, 152–3, 167, 179, 199, 219, 231, 290
Rowan, John 6
Roxborough, Henry 10

Royal Rink 14, 20, 35
Royal York (Toronto) 311
Russell, Herbert "Bert" 67, 69, 86, 101
Russell House 3–4, 47, 66–8, 139, 142, 148, 159, 196, 297–8
Russell Theatre 71, 146

S
St. Brigid's Hockey Club 221, 232, 236, 257
St. James Club (Montreal) 11
St. Louis Arena 319, 321–2, 329–30
St. Louis Eagles 325–29, 331
St. Louis Flyers 319, 321–3, 328–9
St. Louis Post–Dispatch 325–6
St. Nicholas Rink (New York) 108–9, 162, 315
St. Vincent de Paul Society 5
Saskatoon Crescents 239–42
Saskatoon Sheiks 235, 239
Scott, D'Arcy 50
Seattle Metropolitans 197, 223, 225, 259–61
Senators. *See* Ottawa Senators
series system 34, 49, 90, 109: NHA/NHL-PCHA "East-West" series 174, 181, 225, 265, 276–8
Shannon, Gerry 327, 331
Shaughnessy, Frank 175–6, 182, 184, 189–90
Sheppard, Ed 129
Sherwood, Esther 224
Shields, Allan 307
Shields, Tommy 325
Shillington, Bob 116–17, 118–19, 122–4, 126, 129, 134–5, 142, 145, 149–50, 298
shintie 3, 8. *See also* hockey, ice
Shore, Hamby 143, 153, 170–1, 175, 179–80, 192, 195, 200, 207–8, 210, 219
Silver Seven 117, 118, 276, 274, 300, 308, 314, 320. *See also* Ottawa Senators
Sims, Bill 314
Sims, Percy 115–6, 227
Sixsmith, Art 88, 111

skates and skating 2–3, 6–8, 39, 72–3, 177, 220, 226: accidents 72–3; Canadian skating championships 45

Smeaton, Cooper 181–2, 263–4, 270, 275

Smith, Alex 309

Smith, Alf 82–4, 88, 97, 100, 103, 110–11, 112, 120, 122, 132, 136–9, 142, 145–9, 152–4, 155, 158–61, 180, 183, 193, 230, 332

Smith, Art 306

Smith, Harry 145–8, 152–3, 165, 175, 179

Smith, J.W. 89

Smith, Reginald "Hooley" 283, 287–8, 292–3

Smith, Tommy 146, 152, 165, 189, 196–7

Smiths Falls, Ontario 146–7

Smylie, Rod 282

Smythe, Conn 242, 306, 309, 311

Soper, Warren 41, 60–1, 64, 67, 225

Southam, Harry 245

Spittal, Charlie 84, 88, 104–5, 112, 132, 153, 179

sports and leisure 2: attitudes toward 9, 20, 27, 87, 151–4, 186, 230, 274; baseball 10, 20, 87, 89, 107, 171, 179, 203, 223, 243, 247, 249, 251, 321, 325; boxing 5, 37, 99; canoeing 20, 23, 98, 175–6; cricket 10, 320; curling 2, 5, 9, 14, 23, 216; cycling 10, 223; ice trotting 5, 14, 23; lacrosse 9–10, 18, 20, 31, 37, 66, 87, 96, 99, 102, 104, 107, 118, 133–4, 155, 203; professionalism in 10, 35, 102, 104, 110–11, 132–5, 150, 151–4, 167; rowing 10, 37, 87, 99, 120, 223; rugby/football 10, 18, 99, 107, 118, 133, 151, 175, 321; skiing 255; snowshoeing 5, 11, 23; tobogganing 5–6, 39

Stadium of Ottawa Ltd. See Ottawa Stadium

Stanley, Arthur 49

Stanley, Lord and family 39, 41, 45, 48–50, 70, 72, 89, 90, 290, 298

Stanley Cup 70, 74, 83, 89, 90–2, 93, 96, 98, 99, 102, 105, 110–13, 115–16, 119, 123, 127, 136, 137, 139–40, 141–3, 146–8, 149, 151, 156–7, 161–2, 166, 168, 175, 181, 184, 193, 196–7, 199, 206, 209–10, 223, 225, 229, 233, 237, 239, 243, 247, 255–6, 258–62, 265, 267, 274, 276–8, 282–3, 285, 287–8, 290, 298, 305, 312, 314, 323, 326, 328; rules 90–1, 147, 153, 194, 196; trustees 71, 90, 110–11, 115, 122, 124, 126, 140, 141, 147, 153, 157, 175, 277, 285, 301

Starr, Harold 299, 309

Starr Manufacturing Co. (Dartmouth, N.S.) 7. See also skates and skating

Stewarton Hockey Club 207, 262

Strachan, James 242, 250, 311

Stuart, Bruce 84, 88, 100, 105, 112, 132, 160–1, 167

Sutherland, James T. 185

Sweetland, John 71, 90–2, 110, 122, 124, 126, 141, 147, 153

T

Tackaberry, Wilson 188

Taylor, Ernest and family 18, 22, 24

Taylor, Frederick Wellington "Cyclone" 154–62, 165–6, 168–70, 183–4, 265, 267

Taylor, John H. 4

Toronto 228th Battalion 193–5, 198–9

Toronto Arena 181, 201, 205, 209, 216–17, 221

Toronto Arenas 249

Toronto Blueshirts 193, 195

Toronto Granites 48–9, 53, 75, 283

Toronto Hockey Club 181, 190, 197, 205, 209–10, 221

Toronto Maple Leafs 295, 306, 308–9, 311–12, 317, 329, 331

Toronto Marlboros 139, 155

Toronto St. George's 48–9, 53–5, 62

Toronto St. Patricks 233–5, 246, 249–50,

258, 264–5, 267–71, 274, 283
Toronto Shamrocks 180
Toronto Star 246
Toronto Telegram 151
Toronto Victorias 54
Toronto Wellingtons 92, 114–15
Touhey, Bill 299, 309
Trail of the Stanley Cup, The (Coleman) 331

U
University of Ottawa 4–5. *See also* Ottawa
    College
Upper Ottawa Valley Hockey League 156

V
Van Pelt, J. 325–6
Vancouver Hockey Club 210
Vancouver Maroons 234, 277
Vancouver Millionaires 183–4, 265–6,
    274
Vankoughnet, Lawrence 31
Vezina, George 207–8, 221, 272
Victoria, Queen 3: death of 69–70
Victoria Museum 227
Victoria Skating Club (Montreal) 2–3, 8, 11
Victoria Skating Rink (Montreal) 11, 14,
    23, 26–7, 32, 35
Victoria Skating Rink (Toronto) 53–4
Voss, Carl 324, 331

W
Wainwright, Frank 323, 328–9
Walsh, Marty 155, 159–62, 165–6
Ward, Henry 49
Webber, Sammy 276
Weiland, Ralph 314
Western Canada Hockey League (WCHL)
    235, 240–1, 276–8
Western Hockey League (WHL) 240–1,
    283, 285
Western Pennsylvania Hockey League
    88, 132, 160
Westmount Arena (Montreal) 183, 218
Westwick, Harry "Rat" 83–4, 87–8,

102–3, 111–15, 120, 122, 137, 142,
    145–6, 148, 152–3, 155, 159–61, 171,
    179, 265, 267, 332
Westwick, Tommy 170
Whitehead, Eric 155, 160, 166, 186
Williams, Burr 324, 327
Wilson, Allen 175, 206
Wilson, F. Howard 129
Windsor, Nova Scotia 8
Windsor Hotel (Montreal) 14, 21, 23, 31,
    77, 95, 125, 134, 163–4, 189, 205, 248,
    281, 298
Winnipeg Rowing Club 120–1, 137–40
Winnipeg Victorias 70, 92, 98, 111, 113,
    116
Winter 3, 46, 60, 66, 72, 259, 267–71,
    280–1
Wong, John Chi–Kit 301, 304–5, 311, 316
Woo, Harry 299
World War I 173, 179, 184–90, 193, 200–1,
    206–7, 211, 219, 225
Wright, George 247

Y
Young, Astrid 166
Young, George and family 18, 22, 24–5,
    39, 51, 54, 86–7, 97
Young, Scott 166
Young, Weldy "Chalk" 18, 39, 44, 51, 54,
    67, 69, 86–7, 96–100, 110, 141–3

Win, Tie, or Wrangle was designed and typeset by Dennis Choquette in the fall of 2008. It was printed, Smyth-sewn, and cased in at Tri-Graphic, Ottawa. The text face is Cartier, 10.5/13; captions and tabular matter are set in Neutra. The paper is Rolland Opaque Natural, 70 lb.